LIFE OF

ANDREW HULL FOOTE,

REAR-ADMIRAL UNITED STATES NAVY.

BY

JAMES MASON HOPPIN,

PROFESSOR IN YALE COLLEGE.

WITH A PORTRAIT AND ILLUSTRATIONS.

NEW YORK:

HARPER & BROTHERS, PUBLISHERS,

FRANKLIN SQUARE.

1874.

TO THE

HON. GIDEON WELLES,

EX-SECRETARY OF THE NAVY,

THIS VOLUME

IS RESPECTFULLY INSCRIBED

BY

THE AUTHOR.

PREFACE.

The life which has been imperfectly set forth in these pages deserves to be remembered as that of one who labored and accomplished much for his country; and as a life in itself pure, manly, and heroic. It followed the law of right even when leading to sharp sacrifices and death. It was one of those lives that by the simple force of character raises the spirit of its times to a higher moral level of manhood.

Though encountering great disappointments and trials, and not permitted to realize what would appear to be his just anticipations, the career of Admiral Foote may be still regarded in many respects as a brilliant one. He did many notable and noble things. He was, in fact, a great naval commander, of the same stamp—though perhaps, from the lack of opportunities, not so famous—as Decatur, Hull, Lawrence, McDonough, and Perry.

In this biography I have not indulged in highly wrought descriptions of military scenes and events, but with great pains have endeavored to keep on the exact level of truth, carefully verifying every fact and statement by all the authorities at my command, so that (though the hope may be a vain one) this volume might form a slight contribution to the material of future history, especially the history of the late war in one of its most peculiar and important phases.

I have desired, above all, to make a book that would be read with interest by officers and seamen in the Navy; in order that young men in that service might be led to emulate his example, who died for his country as truly as if he had fallen in battle on the deck of his gun-boat. I would wish them to see that what the hero of Fort Henry and the Mississippi accomplished was no accident of fortune, but was prepared for in the earlier stages of a life devoted to the highest aims. His example, as well as his reputation, belong especially to the Navy. He was a genuine American sailor; and we can not do thorough justice to him unless we view him in this light. His qualities of mind and temperament have the smack of the salt sea—the free play and rough force of old ocean. He was a true child of the sea—of a fluent spirit, moved by powerful impulses, loving honor, bold and affectionate.

Yet he was more than this. To the simple sailor-spirit of indomitable loyalty to duty was added a religious enthusiasm that fitted him to contend with foes more formidable than winds or waves. Here lay the real strength of his character.

I acknowledge with gratitude the good offices of the Hon. Gideon Welles, for valuable letters placed at my disposal; and also the kindness of the venerable Rear-Admiral Joseph Smith, in the aid rendered by him in obtaining for me access to the files and records of the Navy Department at Washington.

The spirited sketches of actions on the Tennessee, Cumberland, and Mississippi rivers, from which the engravings in this work were made, were drawn expressly for the book by the gallant Rear-Admiral H. Walke, and lend the authority of an eye-witness and of a principal actor in those scenes to the excellent drawings themselves. To other members of the Navy, and to the Hon. John A. Foote and George A. Jarvis, Esq., who have given me their kind counsel and assistance, I would also return thanks.

J. M. H.

NEW HAVEN, *July*, 1874.

CONTENTS.

CHAPTER XIX.

CHAPTER XX.

CHAPTER XXI.

CHAPTER XXII.

CHAPTER XXIII.

CHAPTER XXIV.

CHAPTER XXV.

CHAPTER XXVI.

ILLUSTRATIONS.

THE LIFE OF

REAR-ADMIRAL

ANDREW HULL FOOTE, U.S.N.

CHAPTER I.

BIRTH, FAMILY, AND EARLY DAYS.

ANDREW HULL FOOTE was born in what is known as the "Buddington House," on the corner of Union and Cherry Streets, in New Haven, Connecticut, Sept. 12, 1806. Though the blood of the "De Veres, the Bohuns, and the Bigods" did not run in his veins, he was descended from good New England stock of God-fearing Puritans, whose first American ancestor, from whom he was removed about eight generations, was Nathaniel Foote, who came from England to Watertown, Mass., in 1630, and in 1635 was one of the company of emigrants of whom Trumbull, in his history of Connecticut, says they were fourteen days in the wilderness on their journey from Watertown and vicinity to begin settlements on the Connecticut River, at Hartford, Wethersfield, and Windsor. Nathaniel Foote settled at Wethersfield, and belonged to the original proprietors of that town, where he died in 1644. His son Robert, from whom Admiral Foote is directly descended, emigrated to Branford, Connecticut, and was among the early settlers of that town. Wethersfield, Hadley, Branford, and Cheshire numbered among their earliest and best citizens the descendants of Nathaniel Foote; and in all the trials and marked events of New England history—in pioneer labors, the witchcraft delusion, Indian conflicts and captivities, the colonial wars and the war of the Revolution—this well-known and widely spread family bore its full share, some of its members having shed their blood and given their lives on the battle-field for their country. They were chiefly agriculturists; but filled every responsible position in social and civil life, and by their sturdy worth and intelligence helped to build up the good old commonwealth of Connecticut.

The grandfather of Andrew was John Foote, a native of North Branford, who was a graduate of Yale College in 1765, and for about fifty years was pastor of the church in Cheshire, Connecticut, where he died in 1813. He was one of the old-fashioned New England ministers, who were settled over their parishes for life, and whose life formed an integral part of the history of the town itself. For nearly a hundred years the grandfather and great-grandfather of the Admiral were the pastors of the village church, the one succeeding the other.*

* The following incident respecting Lucinda Foote, daughter of Rev. John Foote, which has been recently revived in the public prints, shows that that reverend gentleman was not of the opinion of Aaron Burr, who thought that one tongue was enough for a woman. At the age of twelve years Lucinda Foote was fitted to enter Yale College, as appears from the following copy of a translation of a certificate in Latin, written upon parchment, given to her by President Stiles, and also inserted by him in his diary on the same date:

"The President of Yale College to all to whom these presents shall come.—Greeting: Be it known to you that I have examined Miss Lucinda Foote, twelve years old, and have found that in the learned languages—the Latin and the Greek—she has made commendable progress, giving the true meaning of passages in the Æneid of Virgil, the Select Orations of Cicero, and in the Greek Testament; and that she is fully qualified, except in regard to sex, to be received as a pupil in the Freshman Class in Yale University. Given in the College Library, the 22d of December, 1783.
Ezra Stiles, President."

Though kept out of college, Miss Foote pursued a full course of college studies, and also studied Hebrew with President Stiles. She married at eighteen, and died at the age of sixty-two, having been the mother of ten children.

His parents were Samuel Augustus Foote and Eudocia Hull, daughter of General Andrew Hull (militia general), of Cheshire. His father, Samuel Augustus, was Governor of Connecticut in 1834–5, and United States Senator from 1827 to 1833. He was known in the political history of the country as the mover of "Foote's Resolutions," which gave occasion to the famous passage of arms between Webster and Hayne. In his political sentiments Governor Foote was originally a Jeffersonian Democrat, but afterward became a member of the National Republican party, which in 1832 was reorganized as the Whig party under the leadership of Clay and Webster.

In the winter of 1829–30 it was determined by the leaders of the Republican party to provoke the Southern members who held nullification principles to an open discussion which should compel them to show their colors. Senator Foote assumed the task of moving the resolutions, which bore mainly on the question of the final disposal of the public lands and the proceeds of their sales; but he consented to do this on the condition that he should not make a speech upon his own resolutions. This was characteristic of the man. While in Congress, and, in fact, during a long and successful political life, he rarely was known to make a speech, although, whenever he did speak, it was to the point. His success was owing to his stanchness and sagacity of character. He was a man of positive opinions, often standing quite alone, as on the Missouri Compromise question; but he was known to friend and foe as a politician of inflexible honesty, and one who despised intrigue. He led men by his force of will and independence of character. If not an orator, it is an interesting fact that the father of Admiral Foote was a prominent actor in the first great public strife of opinion between the North and the South, and between those principles which go to strengthen and uphold the authority of the national government, and those which tend to its dissolution. The father may thus be said, in some sense, to have begun the contest which ended in the war of the Rebellion, and the triumph of the principles of republican government—a war in which his son bore so distinguished a part.

The childhood and youth of Admiral Foote were those of a boy brought up in strict Puritan principles, modified perhaps by the gentler influence of his mother, who, by her womanly tact in ordinary matters, was the true executrix of the household, although the father, as in the old Hebrew household, held the supreme authority, which was never relaxed in a real difference of opinion.

Unquestioning obedience was the rule of the family life. This held good not only in respect of domestic authority, but extended also to teachers and all superiors in age and rank. The schoolmaster stood *in loco parentis*, and the most rigorous discipline administered at school was taken at home as good evidence that it was well deserved, and admitted of no appeal.

It was held that talents were given to be used, and idleness was looked upon as the great sin. The day began with the song of the birds. The son was expected to give his spare hours to the service of his parents at home or in the field, and the most deferential respect was enjoined in their presence. Plain diet, simple apparel, hard work, and, above all, profound reverence for the Sabbath, and unfailing attendance upon public worship and all religious ordinances, characterized this and other sober Puritan households, even down to the beginning of the present century, in Connecticut, "the land of steady habits."

Andrew was a lively boy, indisposed to study or routine of any kind; and though he had no bad traits, he loved freedom and fun. The family consisted of robust boys, with no sister's softening influence; and many were the pranks of these youngsters, in which Andrew was the leader. One story is told of him, which, considering the austere setting of circumstances in which it appears, must have been at the time ludicrous enough. His oldest brother John, who shared his fun-loving temper, had played some successful prank, which, by all principles of boy-law, it was incumbent upon Andrew to return with interest. He armed himself with a no less effectual and no more destructive missile than a rotten apple, and, standing behind a door, patiently awaited his opportunity. At length hearing some one approaching whom he supposed to be his brother, he darted from his concealment, and threw the apple with all his force, when, to his horror, he saw that it had taken effect in the bosom of his father's ruffled shirt, who had just come out of his chamber, having carefully arrayed himself for the occasion of delivering a public address on the return of peace. The indignant sire, supposing that the jest was intended for himself, rushed to seize the offender, but fright lent wings to his feet; and as the church-bell was already tolling for the public service, the pursuit was necessarily abandoned to allow time for a speedy change of dress; so that an opportunity was gained by Andrew to send in an explanation and apology; and, to his infinite satisfaction, the young rogue was released with a severe reprimand.

Other anecdotes are told, quite as trivial in themselves, which, however, are characteristic of the spirit of the boy, and show that his resolute nature manifested itself early. While but a wee bit of a lad, he was one day leading his younger brother Augustus, who was dressed in a red frock, across a meadow where there was a large merino ram. The buck, excited by the red dress, charged furiously upon the little fellow. Andrew bravely threw himself in the way, and received the shock; and this he did several times, until they had reached the fence in safety. His brother (Hon. John A. Foote, of Cleveland, Ohio, who tells this story) says of the occurrence, that it was undoubtedly the admiral's *first ram fight.*

Another story of Andrew's youthful days might have been told of hundreds and thousands of plucky boys, but which, at all events, shows that the spirit of *fight* was born in him, and was ready to manifest itself on any real provocation of insult or injustice. When he had grown to be a bigger lad, he went one winter's day into a shoemaker's shop, and left the shop door open behind him. One of the workmen thereupon ordered him in a peremptory way to shut the door. Andrew thought the tone was too authoritative, and refused to shut the door unless asked civilly. The workman, thereupon growing wrathful, told him that if he did not close the door he would thrash him; and at once the ire of our young hero was kindled, and Crispin was laid helpless across his own bench, while the old master, who had watched the affair over his spectacles, instead of interfering, cried out, "Bravo! bravo! well done, lad!"

His brother John says of his early years: "He was a stuttering, stammering, left-handed little boy. A cot was fitted tightly over his left hand, and he was required to use only his right. When he commenced speaking, he was admonished to speak slowly, and to beat time with his right hand.

"When we were boys together, it was a rule in our family to commence the Sabbath early on Saturday evening, and play was to be suspended until we could see three stars on Sunday evening. Herschel and other distinguished men have had great credit for discovering new stars, but I have sometimes queried whether the future admiral did not in those days discover some stars never seen by any of them. Very certain I am that the play sometimes commenced before I could see any stars; and I am equally certain that he never, in after-life, watched for them in a storm at sea, or on a lee shore, more anxiously than when a boy, on a Sunday evening, he watched for them as a license to begin his sports.

"As a boy, he was full of fun and frolic—*a real boy*—but

he was genial, kind, and popular, and I do not remember of his ever being quarrelsome."

Such incidents of his youthful days might be multiplied; it would, however, be interesting to inquire what it was that gave the first turn to his life, and led him to seek the sea. It is said Hugh Miller remembered that when a child not three years old he went into the garden one day, and saw there "a minute duckling, covered with soft, yellow hair, growing out of the soil by its feet, and beside it a plant that bore as its flowers a crop of little mussel-shells of a deep red color." This really belonged to the vegetable kingdom; and the discriminating observation of a new fact in nature by one so young seemed prophetic of the future man of science.

Nothing remarkable of this kind is recorded of Admiral Foote's childhood. The sea is a magnet that draws its own to it wherever they may be. The plowboy on the hill-side or on the prairie far away hears in his mind's inner sense the perpetual undertone of ocean, and drops the plow, and makes his way to the coast to embark upon the adventurous life of the sailor. The love of the sea is one of those instincts that are original in the nature of some. This only is to be said of our hero's youth, that his earliest recollections were of ships. His father, when he lived in New Haven, was engaged in the West India trade, and his place of business was upon the well-known quay called "Long Wharf." For the first ten years of his married life his father was, as he himself supposed, subject to an affection of the lungs, and occasionally made a voyage to the West Indies, in the capacity of supercargo of one of his own vessels. As these absences were infrequent, the going and coming produced a strong impression upon the imagination of his children, as they watched the departing or returning sail, and probably awoke in one of them at least the vague and wild desires after a sailor's life.

It is also not altogether improbable that the war of 1812,

which was almost altogether a naval war, and the brilliant victories of our sea-captains at that time, kindled unconsciously in the ardent mind of the boy the first faint fires of military glory connected with the sea. When those stories of combats on the ocean and on the great lakes were related with enthusiasm at the family fireside or table, it is quite impossible that a mind so susceptible even as a child to honor, should not have caught the spirit and the glow of such stirring events.

The war of 1812, and the severe illness of his father, brought about a change of scene; and the family removed from New Haven to Cheshire, a beautiful inland village in the same state and county, in the spring of the year 1813. There they continued to reside, in a fine old family mansion, until the death of Governor Foote in 1846.

A word more should here be said of the father of the Admiral, for from him the son inherited some of his strongest traits of character.

Samuel A. Foote was born November 8, 1780. Though of a delicate constitution in childhood and youth, he prepared for and graduated at Yale College before he was seventeen years of age. He subsequently pursued the study of the law with Judge Reeve, of Litchfield, Connecticut, until impaired health compelled him to give it up; and he began business in New Haven, in the West India trade, in 1803. From 1817 to 1835 he was in public life, filling all the chief political offices in the state. While governor of the state he received the degree of LL.D. from Yale College. He was a notable example of an intelligent and practical American statesman, or, perhaps, the better word would be politician, of the old school, with the marked conservatism of the shrewd men of his state, and with the still higher qualities of independence and firmness.

These sterner traits, enforced often by a severe countenance and piercing look, were mingled with a vein of kindly humor, which made him popular with all classes, and even with his

THE GOVERNOR FOOTE HOUSE. Cheshire, Conn.

political opponents; so that, through his known inflexibility of purpose, that could not be turned by any amount of outside pressure or party drill, and his courteous manners, he truly, as a man, wielded a great influence. His mode of speaking was simple, and as in conversation. He never attempted a methodized discourse; but aiming directly at what he considered the essential thing, and developing but one idea at a time, he soon exhausted what he had to say, though it was generally found that he struck at the heart of the matter, and said the true and weighty word. It is related of him, however, that he fully appreciated the value of the ability to speak well in a free country, and encouraged his sons to train themselves in the art of public address.

Undoubtedly Andrew learned his first lesson of obedience —the prime word in a sailor's creed—at home; yet father and son were so much alike in stubbornness of will that Governor Foote once said that he thought he "had succeeded pretty well in *controlling* all his boys with the exception of Andrew—him alone he had only attempted to *guide*." Yet in both father and son there was, as has been said, a kindly, genial vein; and they were both what might be truly called popular men with all classes. Courtesy, indeed, was inculcated as a prime principle in the family life; and the example of Washington—the American gentleman as well as hero—was not as yet forgotten. This gentler side of the Puritan character and education is sometimes lost sight of. Doubtless there was too little of the spirit of indulgent sympathy with innocent enjoyment, and too intense a stress laid on obligation and not enough on love; but the Puritan family was by no means like a planet journeying on in perpetual eclipse. It rolled out sometimes into broad and pleasant sunshine upon Thanksgiving days, election days, and the holiday sports of childhood and youth, and whenever original Anglo-Saxon humor, good-nature, and cheerful piety fairly asserted themselves. We have but to add, what has already been hinted, that Governor Foote, being himself a high-toned Christian man, reared his family in the strict principles of New England morality; religion, as the foundation of character, was laid at the bottom. Though it was not in Andrew's case the immediate cause of a religious life, who can tell what a profound influence this home piety, leading the mind constantly to view the practical earnestness, and even solemnity of life—its obligations to God—had upon his whole future career?

In regard to the schoolmasters and school-days of Andrew Foote, a word might be said—and but a word—for his was a nature that did not easily take mould from without, but rather developed itself by a native force from within. He was not a man of thought so much as of action. The strength of his nature was on its moral side. What he purposed he thought; what he willed he did. His life is in his deeds. Silent in preparation, issuing from deep sources, his acts, like the acts of men of his kind, were rapid; their results are open to every eye, and the world does not care very much to know about the early shaping influences of a power which is noiselessly generated like electricity in the hidden springs of nature. In fact, his schools and schoolmasters did not probably have much to do in making the man. He drew his sagacity to plan, his courage to dare, his power to act, from his parents, and from the nature God gave him. His first school—upon entering which, it is said, he made a desperate but, in this sole instance, unsuccessful fight for freedom—was in New Haven, and was kept by Miss Betsey Bromham, afterward Mrs. Austen, who was permitted to visit the Admiral in his last sickness in New York, and then and there to express the life-long interest which she felt for her former child-pupil.

When the family removed to Cheshire, Andrew was sent first to the common or district school kept in that village, and afterward was placed at the Episcopal Academy of Cheshire, then in charge of an able and noted instructor, Dr. Tillotson Bronson.

It is not probable that young Foote distinguished himself as a scholar, for that was not his bent; but in these schools in Cheshire he became fitted to pass the examination then required to become a member of West Point Military Academy, the entering of which institution was a kind of compromise with his parents, since he had already declared his intention of going into the Navy, to which his mother was particularly opposed. We may, however, suppose that his school-years were not wholly lost time, as his literary attainments and productions in after-years gave good proof. He mastered the common English branches, and always wrote in a clear and flowing style. He said to a friend in the latter part of his life that he had never read a book through consecutively, but was accustomed to glean its contents by a rapid glancing over it, and that he had found this to be the method of some distinguished men. One of his schoolmates at the Episcopal Academy in Cheshire was Gideon Welles, recently Secretary of the Navy, who proved to be one of his warmest friends, and who, in the trying scenes of the war, gave the Admiral his generous and unfailing support. From the testimony of another schoolmate,* young Foote was noted while at the academy for his amiability and tact in getting out of the difficulties which his frolicsome disposition plunged him into; and even the stern old doctor, a stickler for discipline, was not able to resist his winningly frank, gentle, and affectionate manners.

This healthy, bold, adventurous boy, we may imagine, was learning a great deal of human nature and of the world that God made in those school-days in the picturesque country vil-

* George A. Jarvis, Esq., of Brooklyn, N. Y.

lage among the green Connecticut hills. He knew where the tallest hickory-trees grew, and the biggest chestnuts ripened:

> "Knowledge never learned of schools,
> Of the wild bee's morning chase,
> Of the wild flower's time and place,
> Flight of fowl and habitude
> Of the tenants of the wood;
> How the tortoise bears his shell,
> How the woodchuck digs his cell,
> And the ground-mole sinks his well;
> How the robin feeds her young;
> How the oriole's nest is hung."

He fished in the trout-brooks, swam in every stream, and explored every cave; and, more than all, he explored his own heart, and found out what he was made for; for early in his Cheshire boyhood-life he stoutly declared his intention of going to sea, and said that if prevented, he should do so the moment he was twenty-one years old.

West Point proved a stepping-stone to his darling plan. He remained at the Military Academy of West Point but a few months—say from June to December—and in the latter part of the year 1822, at the age of sixteen, he was transferred to the Navy.

CHAPTER II.

FIRST CRUISES AND SEA-LIFE.

THE active temperament of young Foote, ready for any thing but still life on shore, had found its right direction. On the 4th of December, 1822, he was appointed acting midshipman, and was stationed on board the schooner *Grampus*, under Commander Gregory, in whose fleet, upon the coast of Africa, he afterward held his first separate command. The *Grampus* belonged to the elder Commodore David Porter's squadron, which was sent out in 1823 to break up the piratical nests among the West India Islands. He thus entered at once upon the arduous duties of his profession. He was thrust into the "rough and ready" school of the older naval service; not passing through a preparatory academic training on shore, which is a comparatively modern invention. His habits of promptness and discipline were learned in the schoolroom of old ocean, among hard-handed tars and the stern realities of sea-life. From the testimony of his commander, he was an eager learner in the duties belonging to his profession; and at whatever hour of the day or night Lieutenant Gregory was called on deck, there would be found Midshipman Foote—in Gregory's own words—"dogging his heels:" ready to aid in taking an observation, active in running aloft, and with his eye and hand always on the right rope. He was equally devoted to the study of books then used in the science of navigation; in fact, as he often said, his life's ambition was to make himself a perfect naval officer—it ran in the line of his profession. The following is an extract from a boyish letter, dated on board the United States schooner *Grampus*,

March 6, 1823, and addressed to an early friend and schoolmate:*

"I hope you will excuse my negligence in not writing before this time, for I assure you that it did not proceed from want of affection, but on account of the inconvenience in writing while at sea on board of a vessel of this tonnage. To my great astonishment and satisfaction I received a midshipman's appointment, which you probably recollect I applied for a short time before going to West Point. We left the port of New York on the 1st of January, 1823, and filled away for Tampico; and we have made the ports of Matanzas, Havana, Tampico, and New Orleans. When we left Havana for Tampico, and had made the land, the wind commenced blowing a heavy gale from the northeast, so that it carried away our topmast studding-sail boom, and sprung our mainmast. She took in hogsheads of water in the wardroom and steerage; life-ropes were rove on the windward side of the vessel, and one of the officers observed that 'we were going to —— with studding-sails set.' This gale was much more severe than it was in September, about sixteen months since. I am very well pleased with the service. I had a desire to visit foreign nations. The duty of the officers is nearly as hard as that of the men, as we have to be on the watch one third of the time day and night, four hours on and eight off."

He was, above all, in this first cruise, introduced to the most severe perils and hardships of the naval service in the pursuit of pirates among the reefs of the Gulf. These pirates were the lineal descendants of the freebooters who at the end of the seventeenth century established themselves in the West India seas to prey upon Spanish commerce. The unquiet spirits of all countries resorted to them. Issuing from their strongholds—the island of Tortuga, on the west coast of St. Domingo, and Port Royal, in Jamaica—they committed such audacious and successful robberies on the Spanish-American cities as to win almost the honors of legitimate heroes.† The original buccaneers, however, who had some show of legaliza-

* William A. Browne, of Cheshire, Connecticut.

† Hildreth's History of the United States, vol. ii., p. 38.

tion, degenerated into regular pirates, who, later in the eighteenth century, in Captain Kidd's time, were the terror of the seas, and who with waning power continued their depredations until their final extinction by the American Navy. With picked crews in open boats the officers cruised among the innumerable islands of the Cuban archipelago, where many a bloody sea-fight had taken place:

> " The scream of rage, the groan, the strife,
> The blow, the gasp, the horrid cry,
> The panting, throttled prayer for life,
> The dying's heaving sigh,
> The murderer's curse, the dead man's fixed, still glare,
> And fear's and death's cold sweat—they all were there!"

Our poet Dana's sombre fancy did not overdraw those horrid scenes when the reign of these desperadoes was at its height. The phantom of the "long, low, black-hulled" craft lingers in these seas even to this day. The American Navy has prided itself on the thoroughness of the work it did in abolishing the whole thing. It swept this curse from the seas. Not unfrequently the wily foe, who eluded pursuit in a thousand ways, turned and challenged the avengers of blood to hand-to-hand conflict. For six months of the time officers were out boating on these stormy waters, and it is said that young Foote personally distinguished himself in this service. He certainly acquired those habits of discipline, skill, and daring which afterward were so useful to him, and which could not have been learned under the best masters on shore.

On the 6th of December, 1823, he was transferred from the *Grampus* to the *Peacock*, commanded by William Carter, master commandant; and on the 11th of the same month he was warranted as midshipman. The *Peacock* belonged to the Pacific squadron, under Commodore Hull. Before sailing, in a letter, dated January 29, 1824, he gives vent to a thoughtless, ambitious wish for action:

"We are ready for sea, and only waiting for sailing orders from the Department; but we hear little from Washington except the next Presidential election, the Greek cause, and the Holy Alliance, which I sincerely hope may produce a war. Then the prospect of the naval officer would brighten, and in the space of a few years would elevate us who are now in service to the highest rank, which will take some time if the country remain at peace with all nations much longer."

The *Peacock* sailed from Norfolk for the Pacific on the 29th of March, 1824. During the period of this South American cruise, which covered three years of service, our Navy was compelled to observe a strict neutrality in the wars of liberation of the South American republics with old Spain, which was a difficult and certainly not an enviable position for Americans, although there seemed to be lacking the elements of that high morality and that capacity for self-government which dignified our own struggle for independence. Foote was detached from the *Peacock* and transferred to the frigate *United States*, Commodore Isaac Hull commanding, September 8, 1824. A letter written during this period to his Cheshire friend and schoolmate is worth transcribing, not as containing any thing brilliant, but as being the letter of a manly youth:

"U. S. Frigate 'United States,'
Callao, Peru, *Sept.* 15, 1824.

"Dear Friend,—I have so much to communicate that this small sheet will admit of giving no more than a concise detail of circumstances which have fallen to my observation.

"Until our arrival at Callao we experienced in our little ship every pleasure and hardship incident to a mariner's life. A few days after our departure from the United States we had a very heavy thunder-storm, and one flash of lightning struck the ship, killing four men instantly and wounding several others dangerously, who, however, have recovered partially; yet the greater part of them will never perfectly be restored. From that time to our arrival at Rio Janeiro nothing worthy of mention took place. For a description of that city, I refer you to John's letters. After spending ten pleasant days at Rio, we weighed anchor and stood to the southward and westward, shaping our course round Cape Horn. The weather as we made southing grew cold very sensibly, owing to the winter having already set in. We were as far south as 60° 15′; and, in the winter month of January, it is useless to add we suffered from the inclemency of the weather. You know by experience the cold weather which prevails in the mild climate of 41°; then judge its severity in that of 60°, adding to this the constant heavy gales prevalent off the Cape. However, our time would have been rather more pleasant had the small-pox not have paid us a long and exterminating visit. We lost twelve valuable men by this disease, and at a time when the ship appeared to be at the mercy of the waves. Their loss was severely felt, owing to the fact that the vessel was then too short-manned. But after an unpleasant run of fifty-six days, we arrived at Valparaiso, as light-hearted and in rather better spirits than when we left Rio. Owing to Commodore Hull being at Callao, our stay at Valparaiso was short. We left with a convoy for Callao, first, however, landing the American consul at Coquimbo; we then made the harbor of Callao on the 15th of August, and here saw the broad pendant of Commodore Isaac Hull. We saluted him with the usual number of guns that his rank was entitled to. Our time was now pretty actively employed, the revolutionary state of the country rendering it necessary for us to keep on the alert, owing to the advantage the privateers took of seizing and condemning our merchant ships, under pretense of their being engaged in smuggling arms to the Patriots. A few days after our arrival the Peruvian admiral entered the harbor with a frigate and two brigs, and blockaded the harbor, the Spaniards having at the time one frigate, two brigs, and ten gun-boats. No signs of an attack were made by the Spaniards until Sunday, the 5th of this month, when the gun-boats pulled for the brig, which unfortunately came out of gun-shot of the frigate. The attack commenced with every prospect of crowning the Royalists victors; but their want of courage enabled the brig to haul under cover of the frigate before she received any serious injury. After a spirited engagement of one hour, the Spaniards retreated with the loss of about thirty men killed, and nearly the same number wounded; two boats sunk, and seven others badly injured. The loss of the Patriots was one killed on board the brig, and two in the frigate. The Spaniards, since their unsuccessful attack, seem to be little disposed to hazard another engagement. The Royalists at the time were in constant expectation of a heavy naval reinforcement from Spain. The 12th of this month the *Asia* and *Constantia* arrived, the former a 74-gun ship, the latter a

22-gun brig. The Patriots' force at this time consisted of a 36-gun frigate, and one small 10-gun brig. The Spanish force, you will perceive, was greatly superior. Notwithstanding, Admiral Grey slipped his cable, stood out of the harbor, hove to, and fired three 44's at the Spaniards; hauled up his courses, and waited for the Spanish frigate; but she most cowardly made sail, and declined an engagement. As she passed, we were at quarters, and it would have taken little provocation from her to have been complimented with a broadside from Uncle Isaac. I will now pass over the strife between the two hostile parties, and mention my object in becoming attached to the flag-ship. On the arrival of the *Peacock*, some difficulty took place in regard to Captain Carter, which terminated in his return to the United States. Several of the officers left the *Peacock*, and joined other ships; and I was induced to send to Commodore Hull an application for his ship, it being larger than the *Peacock*, and the accommodation better. I came on board on the 8th. The commodore has his wife and Miss Hart with him. We get a glance at them occasionally. Excuse haste and deficiencies, and believe me your friend,

"Andrew H. Foote."

In another letter to the same friend, dated Chorilos, August 12, 1825, he further speaks of his Pacific coast experiences:

"We are now lying in an open roadstead unprotected from the sea, consequently the motion is very troublesome, and the surf at times so heavy as to render landing dangerous. It is necessary to make this the port of entry, as Callao is blockaded by a squadron consisting of seven sail, two of which are frigates. As soon as Callao falls we shall return to that port; but when she will capitulate is uncertain, as the city expends from two to three hundred shot daily, and is well provisioned.

"We have less opportunity for enjoying ourselves on shore than we had in Chili, as Lima is nine miles distant, and Chorilos a small place containing but a few huts. A party of us visited Lima a short time since, where we spent four days very pleasantly. The city may still be styled one of the richest cities in the world, although poor to what it was before the revolution. During the struggle it has alternately been in possession of Royalists and Patriots, who have robbed the churches of vast quantities of plate. From a single altar was coined one hundred thousand dollars. We saw the grand palace where Pizarro resided; also the apartment in which he was assassinated. I forgot to mention the walking-dress of the ladies, which is admirably calculated to carry on an intrigue. The part from the waist down contains thirty yards of silk, plaited in such a manner as to set perfectly smooth, in order to show a fine shape. The robe covering the head is also silk, and large enough to conceal the face excepting one eye. Equipped in this manner, I have seen ladies watch the movements of their husbands by following them through the city, the virtuous not being distinguished from the vicious."

We find among the officers then sailing in the *United States* the familiar names of H. Paulding, C. H. Davis, William C. Nicholson, Thomas T. Craven, H. K. Thatcher, and James Armstrong.

Returning to New York in the *United States* from this three-years' service, April 25, 1827, Andrew successfully underwent his examination for passed midshipman. He had been laboriously preparing himself for this by availing himself of all opportunities of study and observation in his reach; and Admiral Davis says of this examination that Foote and himself got news of it together, and the question was how to get ready? They at once set about their preparation with great earnestness, consulting what books they had access to, but chiefly making practical observations, and reducing the science of their profession to a regular working system.

Foote had been up to this time four years and five months constantly at sea. It would seem as if he had earned the right to a little rest at home; but, as if it were expressly so planned by his superiors, he was to be allowed no time to display his midshipman's uniform ashore; and on the 26th of August, 1827, to his sore disappointment, he was sent off a second time to the West Indies for a brief cruise, first in the *Natchez* and afterward in the *Hornet*, to which he was transferred October 8, 1827. He had set his heart upon making a cruise with the Mediterranean squadron, for which station he applied. His hopes were not realized. Something better, however, than the gratification of his desires, or even the education of his mind, was in store for him. A change of character that raised him to a higher level of manhood awaited him on this short West India voyage. After he had been at sea some six weeks or two months, his mother received a letter from him, in which are these words: "You may discharge your mind from anxiety about your wayward son." The letter then went on to relate that one of the lieutenants of the ship had spoken to him soon after joining the *Natchez* on religious subjects, and, as his expression was, he had "bluffed him off" by saying that he had aimed to be honorable and honest in all things, and that would do for him. But, after getting on the station, upon a beautiful moonlight night, while riding quietly at anchor, the same officer and himself being on duty, the lieutenant spoke to him again about the subject of religion, and with such earnestness that, as he said, his "knees for the first time bowed to his Maker;" and as soon as he was released from duty, he took his Bible and went into the steerage, and read it under great agitation of mind. This he did for two weeks, when, upon going on deck one day, he came to the resolution that "henceforth, under all circumstances, he would act for God;" upon which his mental anguish and trouble vanished.

In this simple manner he recounts that event in his history which made him a new man, and a true Christian hero. It did not make him over into a perfect character, but he was established now on right principles, and a high and pure impulse was given to his life; and take that life through, at sea and on shore, in battle and at peace, in success and adversity, in life and death, we shall find that, by divine aid, he carried out the resolution made in his youth that "*he would act for God.*"

It should be said here, so that it need not be misunderstood by the reader, that this is the biography of a Christian officer. He thought himself to be, and his life proved that he was right in thinking himself to be, a religious man. His faith, in some respects, took the stamp of his Puritan training. His religious phraseology was that which was in ordinary use in New England homes and literature; but it was a pure Christianity, that showed itself by its fruits. In the case of Admiral Foote, his free and genial temperament, his extensive acquaintance with men, and his constant voyaging up and down in all parts of the world, served to make him catholic in his opinions; but none of these influences ever succeeded in effacing the strong Puritanic stamp with which he began his religious life; and, as a reformer in the naval service, it is a matter of thankfulness that they never did, for here was nourished the invincible will in right-doing that never turned back in any good enterprise, but went, like an iron prow, often roughly enough, through the most time-honored customs, and always straight to the end.

The following letter, written about this time by the commanding officer of the *Natchez*, though but a simple letter of introduction, seems prophetic in its expression in regard to the future character and career of our hero:

"United States Ship 'Natchez,' Pensacola Bay.

"Sir,—It is with great pleasure that I have it in my power to state that Midshipman A. H. Foote served on board this ship, and I found him to be a young gentleman of great merit, being always competent and attentive to his duty; and I am impressed with the belief that he will become a very valuable officer. Mr. Foote is a young gentleman of the first respectability, and of the finest principles and feelings; and his whole conduct while he was attached to this ship has met my cordial approbation—therefore beg leave to recommend him to your favorable consideration. With very much respect, I remain your obedient servant,

"George Budd.

"Commodore Isaac Chauncey, Commanding Naval Officer, N. Y."

The Christian consciousness which had been awakened in the youth soon, of course, as in the case of many others in like position both in the Navy and Army, led him to raise the question of the rightfulness of the military profession as a calling, and whether he could consistently remain in the Navy. When he came home (which he did in the *Hornet* on the 6th of December, 1827) he made known his scruples to his father, who asked him if he did not suppose a Navy to be necessary, and, considering it to be necessary, if there should not be good men and Christian men in it. This sensible and practical way of putting the matter seems to have entirely removed his doubts, as he never appeared to be afterward troubled upon this point.

Foote was detached, January 1, 1828, from the West India squadron, and during his brief stay on shore he was married, June 22, 1828, to his first wife, Caroline Flagg, the daughter of Bethuel Flagg, of Cheshire, Connecticut, who was permitted to cheer his arduous life but a comparatively short time. She died in the year 1838, having borne him two children, the first of whom, named Josephine, lived but four years; and the second, of the same name, was born in 1837.

We very soon find our hero afloat again in the sloop-of-war *St. Louis*, twenty-four guns, to which he was appointed October 5, 1828, as sailing-master, under the command of Captain John D. Sloat. They sailed from Norfolk to the Pacific on the 14th of February, 1829. Three years were passed in this cruise upon his old station in the Pacific, comprising the coasts of Chili, Peru, and Central America, during which period he was appointed acting-lieutenant; and on his return to the United States, on the 9th of December, 1831, he found awaiting him a commission as lieutenant, the commission bearing date May 27, 1830. Thus slowly, by hard work and good conduct, he was creeping up the ladder of official preferment; though in after-years promotion seemed all too slow to his ardent mind thirsting for honorable distinction.

In January, 1832, he was detached from the *St. Louis*; and

on May 1, 1833, he was assigned to the *Delaware*, seventy-four ship of the line, bearing the pennant of Commodore Patterson, then on the Mediterranean station, and was appointed to the honorable post of flag-lieutenant of the squadron. The *Delaware* sailed from Norfolk to the Mediterranean on the 30th of July, 1833. During this trip the ship touched at the principal European, Asiatic, and African Mediterranean ports; and a party of its crew, of which Lieutenant Foote was one, obtained leave to visit many of the historic points up the Nile, in Egypt, and also in the Holy Land. They landed at Joppa, and went to Jerusalem, explored the valley of the Jordan, sailed on the Dead Sea, and climbed Mount Lebanon; and we may be sure that none of that light-hearted company of young officers looked on these sacred scenes with fresher delight than he did, who had been a constant reader of the Bible, and who had devoted his life to the Master whose footsteps once glorified these rocks and vales. A lovely daughter of Admiral Patterson, who with her two sisters accompanied the party, was so deeply impressed by her visit to Jerusalem, and the places where were the head-springs of our Christian faith, that the commencement of her religious life was dated by herself from that period; it was brief, however, for before the ship reached the shores of America, although within sight of them, Miss Patterson died, and was buried at Norfolk, at which port the *Delaware* ended her voyage.

This pleasant cruise of the splendid ship *Delaware* was a kind of triumphal progress all the way, bearing as she did the flag of our young Republic, that was every where recognized and welcomed as the emblem of freedom; and we may, indeed, regard this voyage of pleasure and of glory through the classic waters of the Mediterranean, shared by our hero in the prime of his young manhood, with health, a sound, active mind, an honorable position, and, above all, a good conscience toward God and man, and made as it was before he had a great burden of official responsibility laid upon him, as the acme of his free youth's enjoyment and proud satisfaction.

In a private letter to a friend in Cheshire, dated Mahon, November 28, 1833, he, in an animated, sketchy manner, describes the first portion of the cruise:

"I presume you have caught an occasional glimpse of my letters to Caroline, and to them I refer you for a detailed account of what has occurred since we left the United States. Our passage across the Atlantic to Cherbourg and in the English Channel was unusually pleasant, as much so, in fact, as a large, comfortable ship, pleasant messmates, fine weather, and the agreeable company of our minister, Mr. Livingstone, and his family, could render it. On our arrival, several of the officers went to Paris, were presented at court, dined with the king, and were received with similar marks of respect by his ministry. Our chaplain, Mr. Stewart, who is a man of fine personal appearance, an accomplished scholar, and a polite gentleman, made one of the party. He told me, on his return, that it was the third court at which he had been presented. I believe Mr. S. to be a good and pious man, notwithstanding I have heard when at home he was extravagant in dress and courted polished society. Yet this opinion has doubtless arisen in consequence of his having a handsome person and pleasing manners. He proposed and carried out his resolution to have evening prayers on board, which, except with him in the frigate *Guerriere*, stands without a precedent in our service. Yet do not imagine from this a better state of things with regard to religion existing among us. Candor, indeed, compels me to state that but three or four out of nearly one thousand souls are professing Christians; and at present there appears to be no more interest on the subject than when we sailed from New York. Our evening prayers are rarely held, and sometimes there is no Sunday service; yet this is not attributable to unreadiness on the part of Mr. Stewart.

"On the return of the officers from Paris we left Cherbourg, and on the following morning were close to the English coast. The beautiful hedges and fine appearance of the country, and the associations with it as the land of our fathers, gave it a lively and exciting interest with me. I felt disappointed that I could not go to London; but the Paris party were absent so long that this was rendered impracticable. A few days after leaving the coast of England we encountered a severe gale in the Bay of Biscay; after which we ran down the coast of Portugal in sight of Lisbon Rock. The wind being strong and fair, two days brought us off Cadiz, in Spain, and not far from the place where Lord Admiral Nelson captured the combined fleets of France and Spain, near Trafalgar. The Sunday following we anchored at Gibraltar, a place you know replete with interest. We remained there three days, and then proceeded up the Mediterranean, passing in sight of Malaga and several other places of note, and arrived here the early part of this month.

"In Mahon is the second largest organ in the world. I went with several other officers to hear it. That we might have an idea of the power of the instrument, a tempest was represented so well—thunder, wind, and rain—that it seemed to be real; and the church, whose walls are eight feet thick, had a tremulous motion. We shall probably begin to cruise in April. Report says that the commodore will devote the summer to pleasure, and we shall probably visit Naples, Carthage, Smyrna, perhaps Constantinople, and other points of interest."

CHAPTER III.

CRUISE OF THE "JOHN ADAMS."

The native aptitude of Americans for the sea is abundantly proved in the history of the American Navy. The history of England has not been more wonderful in its proofs of national genius for maritime operations than that of the United States. In the War of the Revolution there were no two-decked American frigates, properly so called; and yet the small ships in use, imperfectly equipped, with insignificantly light metal compared with their adversaries, manned with hastily collected crews, gave important aid in that great struggle. The early exploits of John Paul Jones, Dale, Manley, Barry, Nicholson, Barney, Rathburne, and Biddle, in their active little ships, cutting off English transports, carrying the war into English seas, and by alertness and audacity making up for want of force and organization—these should not be lost sight of, for they were the first efforts of a power that has since then contested the empire of the seas with Great Britain herself. The actual Navy of the Revolution—an emanation from the sea—sank back as suddenly into the sea. Nothing was left of it. For the exigencies of the naval war with France, and for the Algerine and Tripolitan wars, new ships had to be built, and an entirely new system organized. Then arose another brood of naval heroes, who, almost by their individual exertions, redeemed our country from the imbecility into which it sank when it paid tribute to the Dey of Algiers, and was powerless to reclaim its hundreds of American prisoners rotting in his dungeons. The names of Decatur, Preble, Truxton, Somers, Barron, Bainbridge, Chauncey, Hull, Porter, are now with us as household words. Some of these continued to be names of inspiration in the two-years' contest of the War of 1812, in which others of equal if not greater celebrity—such as Lawrence, Stewart, Perry, and Macdonough—were added to the splendid constellation. In the War of 1812, our Navy for the first time assumed something like organization and concentrated efficiency. But at the beginning of the War of 1812 we were worse off than in 1801, at the end of the Revolutionary War. We had actually but seventeen cruising vessels, nine of which were frigates; while Great Britain had more than a thousand ships of war, of which between seven and eight hundred were efficient cruisers. But new frigates were at once built, immense activity was infused into the Navy, and the government devoted its special attention to this department. And the Navy also became at that time more popular, and was sought for by the youth of the best families in the country. Many of these were introduced almost at once from the quiet of home to the horrors and carnage of the naval combat. "Perhaps one half of the lieutenants in the service at the peace of 1815 had gone on board ship for the first time within six years from the declaration of the war, and many of them within three or four. So far from the midshipmen having been masters and mates of merchantmen, as was reported at the time, they were generally youths that first quitted the ease and comforts of the paternal home when they appeared on the quarter-deck of the man-of-war."* Young Foote might be numbered among these. He went from the bosom of well-regulated family life in the quiet country village to the hardships and rough realities of the naval service. It is true, his youth had fallen upon reactionary, peaceful times; but doubtless he would have been all the more ardent to join the Navy had there been hard fight-

* Cooper's Naval History, vol. ii., p. 395.

ing and the chance of winning distinction. As it was, the first years of his sea-life were spent in long cruises (like the one we are now to relate), which have in them little of the stir of warlike achievement, but which are, on the contrary, as this one proved to be, in the immediate interest of peace.

On the 4th of November, 1837, Lieutenant Foote was assigned to the East India squadron, under command of Commodore Read, in the sloop-of-war *John Adams*, and Captain Wyman, in the capacity of first-lieutenant, or executive officer. The *John Adams* was an old ship that had done good service in the Barbary wars, when she was commanded by that able officer, Captain John Rodgers. She was built at Charleston, South Carolina, and underwent many changes. She was constructed for a small frigate, carrying 24 twelves on her gun-deck; was then cut down to a sloop; next raised upon to be a frigate; and finally once more cut down. It is said that the ship was built by contract, and that the original contractor let out one side of her to a sub-contractor, who, in a spirit of economy, so much reduced her moulds that the ship had actually several inches more beam on one side than the other. As a consequence, she both bore her canvas and sailed better on one tack than on the other. The *John Adams* was rebuilt entirely, and became one of the most beautiful ships in the Navy.* Ships acquire a certain kind of personality, and through every spar, timber, and bolt there seems to run an individual life. Thus the old *Constitution* was called "a lucky ship;" and she never lost this character. "In all her service, as well before Tripoli as in this war (1812), her good-fortune was remarkable. She never was dismasted, never got ashore, or scarcely ever suffered any of the usual accidents of the sea. Though so often in battle, no very serious slaughter ever took place on board of her. One of her commanders was wounded,

* Cooper's Naval History, vol. ii., p. 31, note.

and four of her lieutenants were killed, two on her own decks, and two in the *Intrepid;* but, on the whole, her entire career had been that of what is usually called 'a lucky ship.' Her fortune, however, may perhaps be explained by the simple fact that she had always been well commanded. In her last two cruises she had probably possessed as fine a crew as ever manned a frigate. They were principally New England men: and it has been said of them that they were almost qualified to fight the ship without her officers."* The *John Adams* had no such brilliant record as the "old *Ironsides*," but had been nevertheless a serviceable and fortunate ship; and the name of this vessel serves to connect the different epochs of our naval history, and to bring down the past into the present, as Admiral Foote himself unites the old and the new, and forms a connecting link between the ancient and modern periods of the American Navy. He belongs to both periods, although his most famous actions lie in the circle of very recent events. The voyage of the *John Adams*, in which we are now particularly interested, was really one of the circumnavigation of the globe. They sailed around the Cape of Good Hope to Bombay, Canton, Manilla, the Sandwich and Society Islands, the coast of Chili, and doubled Cape Horn; during which cruise the ship was engaged in an attack on the pirates of Sumatra, and especially in an assault upon the Asiatic towns of Quallahbattoo and Arbucloo, burning the latter, the inhabitants of which had treacherously murdered the captain of an American pepper-ship. But the chief interest of this cruise is concentrated in the visit to the Sandwich Islands, on which occasion Lieutenant Foote, now thirty-two years old and a man of matured character, displayed a prompt energy and a loyalty to cherished principles of duty.

Many English ships had in previous years exerted a most

* Cooper's Naval History, vol. ii., p. 378.

deleterious influence upon the natives of the islands by introducing intemperance and other vices; but in July, 1839, Captain Laplace, of the French frigate *L'Artemise*, arrived at Honolulu. He came in the interest of the Romish mission, representing the queen of Louis Philippe as a patron of the missions of her Church, and saying that he had come by order of the French government to put an end to the ill-treatment the French had suffered at the islands. He demanded that the Roman Catholic faith should be granted all the privileges that the Protestant faith enjoyed; that the King of the Sandwich Islands should make a special treaty with France, and should deposit in the hands of the captain of *L'Artemise* twenty thousand dollars as a guarantee of his future conduct; and that if these and other equally peremptory conditions were not complied with, Captain Laplace declared his intention to make immediate war upon the islands. He sent letters to the English and American consuls, informing them of his intention to commence hostilities in case his terms were not agreed to, and offered an asylum to the citizens of the two nations if war should arise; but in the letter to the American consul was this singular language: "I do not include in this class the individuals who, although born, it is said, in the United States, make a part of the Protestant clergy of this archipelago, direct the counsels of the king, influence his conduct, and are the true authors of the insults given by him to France. For me they compose a part of the native population, and must undergo the unhappy consequences of a war which they shall have brought on this country." He referred, of course, to the American missionaries, who, for the reasons alleged, were not to be recognized and treated as American citizens.*

The upshot of all this was that the king was forced to com-

* Dr. Anderson's History of the Sandwich Islands Mission, p. 159.

ply with the conditions above mentioned, and to sign a treaty, one of whose articles was that French wines and brandies should not be prohibited, and should pay a duty of only five per cent. on their value. The French frigate sailed away on the 20th of July; and the French consul, taking advantage of the treaty, used his efforts so successfully to introduce wine, brandy, and tobacco, that the port was flooded with these articles, and the morals of the native population were greatly depraved. A violent Romanist party was raised up, and the Protestant missionaries, who had not injuriously influenced the government in their special measures against the Roman Catholics, were nevertheless defamed, and in many ways greatly annoyed and harassed. In the following October the United States East India squadron arrived at Honolulu; and the rest of the story will be told nearly in the words of Lieutenant Foote, who wrote out a statement of his own share in this transaction.

On the arrival of the squadron, the officers heard of the influence which the late visit of the French frigate *L'Artemise* had exerted upon the government, the mission, and foreign residents. Their first impressions were unfavorable to the missionaries; and the reports in circulation were of such a character as to induce many of them scarcely to question the propriety of the proceedings of the French commander. It was said that the missionaries had an agency in framing many of the penal laws of the government, in urging persecution even to torture against Roman Catholics, and, in fact, all the mistakes and evils in the political and social condition of the islands were ascribed to them.

At the expiration of the first week, Lieutenants Turner and Foote were in possession of facts which left no doubt of the innocence of the missionaries in regard to the motives, and, with but few exceptions, the judiciousness of their acts. With this view of the case, Lieutenant Foote met the members of the mission, and urged upon them the necessity of applying at once to Commodore Read to order a court of inquiry, composed of the officers of the squadron, with power to summon witnesses, enter the proceedings on record, and pronounce an opinion, or at least to put on record all the facts bearing upon the case. The suggestion was immediately adopted: a letter was drawn up and laid before the commodore, urging an investigation. Several days having elapsed without an answer, Foote again met the mission, urging them to reiterate their request. This was done, and on the 30th the commodore replied to the communications from the mission, declining to act. This put a new aspect on the question. Lieutenants Turner and Foote at once formed a plan to give currency to the correspondence and action thus far secured, feeling that in the lack of an investigation it was important to do something to place the real merits of this question before the public. It was determined to make an effort to induce the officers generally to subscribe their names to a letter prefixed to Mr. Castle's article, and to the correspondence with the commodore, the king, the consul, and the mission. A letter was drawn up and was signed unanimously by the wardroom officers of the *John Adams*, and, as no others were asked, it was then sent to the *Columbia*, where it received the signatures of the officers, with two or three exceptions.

This is a copy of the letter:

"We, the undersigned officers of the United States East India squadron, having upon our arrival at this place heard various rumors in relation and derogatory to the American mission at these islands, feel it to be due not only to the missionaries themselves, but to the cause of truth and justice, that the most unqualified testimony should be given in the case, and do therefore order one thousand copies of the annexed article and correspondence to be printed for gratuitous distribution, as the most effectual method of settling this agitated question in the minds of an intelligent and liberal public.

"Being most decidedly of the opinion that the persons composing the

Protestant mission of these islands are American citizens, and as such entitled to that protection which our government has never withheld, and with unwavering confidence in the justice which has ever characterized it, we rest assured that any insult offered to this unoffending class will be promptly redressed. It is readily admitted that there may be in the operation of this, as well as in other systems in which fallible man has an agency, some objectionable peculiarities; still as a system it is deemed comparatively unexceptionable, and believed to have been pursued with the professed principles of the society which it represents; and it would seem that the salutary influence exerted by the mission on the native population ought to commend it to the confidence and kind feelings of all interested in the dissemination of good principles.

"GEORGE A. MAGRUDER, Lieutenant.
ANDREW H. FOOTE, Lieutenant.
JOHN W. TURK, Lieutenant.
THOMAS TURNER, Lieutenant.
JAMES S. PALMER, Lieutenant.
EDWARD R. THOMSON, Lieutenant.
AUGUSTUS H. KILTY, Lieutenant.
GEORGE B. MINOR, Lieutenant.
JOHN HAZLETT, Surgeon of the Fleet.
JOHN A. LOCKWOOD, Surgeon.
DANGERFIELD FONTLEROY, Purser.
ROBERT B. PEGRAM, Master.
FITCH W. TAYLOR, Chaplain.
JOSEPH BEALE, Assistant Surgeon.
J. H. BELCHER, Professor of Mathematics.
A. G. PENDLETON, Professor of Mathematics."

The "article" referred to in the letter, to be printed with the correspondence, was an able article written by Mr. Castle, a leading member of the mission, and published in the *Hawaiian Spectator*, which contained the evidence upon which the unqualified expressions of the letter were based. It furnished many facts in reference to the history of the American mission in the Sandwich Islands, and especially in regard to the relations of the mission with the Roman Catholics, proving that the missionaries had opposed all means of contending against the Roman Catholics other than those of reason and truth. The rigid ecclesiastical discipline, the uncompromising opposition to intoxicating liquors, the exposing of the vice and evils of licentiousness, and the marked preference given to the Protestant faith, were really the head and front of the missionaries' offending. The mission had no doubt represented the tenets of the Roman Catholic Church to be hostile to the religious and political welfare of a nation, and, whether this were true or untrue, the missionaries were justified in a free expression of opinion on the subject.

Fifty copies of these papers were privately struck off; but it appeared that an imprudent gentleman had walked into the office and taken away one of the copies, and it was soon noised abroad that the officers of the United States squadron had published a severe and abusive letter in the interest of the mission against the French government. The excitement at Honolulu was very great. The French consul applied to the commodore for a copy of the offensive letter, that he might forward it to his government.

On Lieutenant Foote's meeting with the commodore, the latter refused to read the letter or to sanction its publication. He was, however, finally convinced by the firm arguments of Foote that he had misconstrued entirely the character of the letter; that it contained no offensive assault upon the French government, but that it was a calm statement of opinion absolutely required by the circumstances. In a conversation which followed with the French consul himself, he was led to admit frankly that the letter was unobjectionable in substance and tone. The English consul concurred in this; and a paper was drawn up and signed to that effect.

By these conversations and explanations the excitement was allayed, and at the same time the desired immediate publicity was given to the dignified statement of the American officers in support of the mission, and all ground of renewing the opposition to the mission in future was taken away. Real service was done to the mission, and at the same time no offense was given to the French government, while its agents received a salutary check.

Lieutenant Foote's spirited conduct received the formal as well as hearty thanks of the missionaries. It was all that he, a subordinate officer in the squadron, could do; but it was done—promptly, thoroughly, and at the personal risk of official disgrace, and perhaps of summary dismissal from the Navy. It may by some be thought to have been an irregular proceeding and an unjustifiable interference, but the risk was foreseen and deliberately assumed. It was the act of a man who placed duty before every thing else. The action which was taken maintained the important principle, now so well recognized, that American missionaries are American citizens, and that wherever they are, they are under the full and complete protection of their country's flag.

CHAPTER IV.

CRUISE OF THE "JOHN ADAMS."—CONTINUED.

FROM the Sandwich Islands the *John Adams* sailed to the Society Islands, and as there are some things of interest in Lieutenant Foote's journal of the voyage, the account will be continued in his own words:

TAHITI, *December* 18, 1839.

"We arrived at these islands after a long passage of thirty-one days, running a distance of twenty-five hundred miles, and found the frigate *Columbia*, bearing the broad pennant of Commodore Read, which came in the day preceding. These islanders have made less advance in civilization than the people of the Sandwich Islands; for although churches are large and Christianity is the religion of the land, still it is a sad fact that licentiousness to a frightful degree prevails, and scenes of the most revolting kind occur.

"The men are larger and better proportioned than in the Sandwich Islands, and the women are beautiful. Nature has been so bountiful that labor is not necessary to support life. All vegetable production is of spontaneous growth. Cattle roam in the mountains. Streams gush from the hills. The climate is healthful during the year. So seductive are these islands that one almost ceases to wonder at the mutiny of the *Bounty*.

"*L'Artemise* had also visited these islands, and imposed restrictions scarcely less intolerable than at the Sandwich Islands. Captain Laplace had not only demanded the free introduction of Romanism, but had imposed on the queen the tax of building Catholic churches.

"As the mission here is English, and no tangible act of which we could complain had been committed, of course we had nothing to do.

"The object of our visit is to investigate a supposed outrage on the American flag. The former American consul had protected, against the laws of the country, some French Catholic priests, who were forcibly expelled from the country, wherein he transcended his powers, and an attack was made upon him, in which he received a severe wound, and his wife met her death.

"I can imagine no greater obstacle to the progress of religion than is to be found in those persons who, coming from different parts of Christendom, pass for Christians, and yet behave so badly. There are some creditable exceptions among the residents, and far be it from me to say that the guilty are found among them alone. No; transient visitors are in the condemnation, and, until quite recently, even vessels of war of all nations were the scenes of nocturnal orgies too bad to relate. This explains the cause why there is so little reciprocity of feeling among missionaries and their countrymen and foreign visitors; and this shows also that little weight should be attached to the opinions and censures of men whose real motive in decrying attempts to diffuse the blessings of Christianity is to be judged of by their own manner of life.

"As to the Catholic question, this is briefly the history of it: At the Society Islands, where the London Missionary Society has for forty years been successfully employed in teaching the Christian faith, frequent arrivals of Catholic priests, and French men-of-war to enforce their claims, have disturbed the mission and held the native government in constant terror. Several years since two French priests came to Tahiti to propagate Roman Catholicism. Queen Pomare and her chiefs peremptorily ordered them to leave the islands, assigning as a reason that it was contrary to her laws and desires that any other religion than the Protestant should be taught in her kingdom. They persisted in remaining until it was perfectly convenient for them to leave, the American consul sustaining them in this. He placed them in a house just beyond the precincts of the consulate. They were frequently warned to re-embark in the same vessel which brought them, and, still refusing to do so, the queen's order to put them on board was executed, and the ship proceeded to her destination, Botany Bay. Some weeks after they returned in an American vessel, and made attempts to land, which were resisted by the natives. The French frigate *Venus*, Captain Petit Thouars, arrived at Tahiti soon after, and exacted two thousand dollars from the London mission, probably to reimburse the captain of the American vessel for his detention, and for the necessity of his going to Valparaiso in consequence of the priests not being permitted to land. It was demanded also that the French Catholics should be put on the same footing with the Protestants. The *Venus* was followed by *L'Artemise*, Captain Laplace, who left the islands but a few months since. This frigate having run on a coral reef, was with difficulty, by the assistance of the natives, got into port, when she underwent extensive repairs, having timber and all necessaries gratuitously furnished by the queen. At the expiration of six weeks she was drawn up and presented her broadside toward the town, and a message was sent to Pomare that a Catholic church must be built at her expense wherever there was a Protestant church, and that the same facilities must be extended to Catholic priests as to Protestant clergymen. Fear for the destruction of life and property prevailed, and the terms were submitted to. How this will be viewed in England, time will disclose. It is to be hoped that the English and our own government will take measures to prevent such outrages in the future.

"A scene took place in the wardroom of the ship which bears on this subject. While at Tahiti, on remarking to our new consul that I could not see the object of the squadron's being detained for the arrival of the queen, he said: 'Oh, it is exceedingly important; the queen has been duped by the English, and regards us as a feeble nation. British influence will try to prevent her coming. I wish her to see the ships. Their order and beauty will make a good impression. I have serious fault to find with the English consul, and also with Commodore Wilkes and the exploring expedition, who were, however, also deceived by the English, and made presents to the children of the English mission, totally disregarding the insult to our flag.' After running on in a rapid manner, I told him I was willing to read any documents he might bring forward, and if Commodore Wilkes had acted improperly, it was his duty to prove it. No man should shrink from doing his duty, cut where it may. As for the missionaries, if they had been guilty of the charges brought against them, of all persons they were the last who should escape with impunity. The next day the consul produced his documents. They consisted of three short letters between Queen Pomare and Commodore Wilkes.

"The letter of Commodore Wilkes contained his directions from the President of the United States to touch at Tahiti, and assure the queen of the good feeling toward her on the part of our government, and to distribute presents among her subjects; and that the President expected the queen to treat our consul kindly, to give him a lot for his consulate, and to regard him as the supervisor of our commercial interests; and that the present consul had been sent to supersede the one of whom she had complained as protecting French priests against her laws. The reply of the queen was short and in a conciliatory tone, she evidently wishing to be on good terms with our government, and stated that the

Roman Catholics were not Americans, for which reason she insisted upon their being taken from the consul, who transcended his powers in protecting them. These were the only points touched upon in the correspondence; and, on remarking that they were not enough to sustain the allegations made in his conversation of yesterday, he said that Commodore Read had the other papers, which he would procure; but he never presented them. I candidly told him that the data were not sufficient to enable me to form an opinion; but from what I had read and heard, I was convinced that no consul had a right to throw our flag around foreign Catholics to shield them from the laws of a government within his consulate."

The events of this cruise entered deeply into the religious feelings of Lieutenant Foote, and his private journal gives indications of great mental trials and heart-searchings.

A few quotations will doubtless prove interesting to the readers of this book, for, as has been said, though not a perfect man, the springs of our hero's character are to be found in his religious nature, and in his intense and unvarying desire to "act for God." These meditations show that, while above all a man of action, he did not live a shallow, surface life, but that the roots of his actions had their nourishment in a more hidden life:

"U. S. Ship 'John Adams,' Valparaiso, *January* 7, 1840.

"Discard the secret whisperings of pride. It is Christ himself that must be formed in the soul the hope of glory. Therefore, my soul, look to Jesus your Redeemer, and the Holy Spirit your Sanctifier, and give God all the glory for every good impulse of the affections.

"This day I renewedly dedicate myself to God; and although trials and temptations await me in a man-of-war, still grace is sufficient to overcome all, if I am faithful to the means which the Holy Scriptures furnish. Enlighten my mind to cherish clear conceptions of thy character, oh God. Communicate thy grace to my dear orphan daughter, that she may early be prepared to serve thee."

"Valparaiso, *February* 7.

"This day I observe as one of prayer and humiliation for the manifold evils of my heart. I deplore the ascendency of my passions and my pride. The world appears to be too much in a heart that is dedicated to God. Blessed Jesus! show me my true character. Give me a view of spiritual things.

"I resolve to watch and pray, to bear in mind that the Christian life is a warfare, that one must be uncompromising in his principles. I resolve to guard my tongue from speaking injuriously of others; to avoid levity of manner, on the one hand, and moroseness on the other; to perform the executive duties of the ship with impartiality, feeling that my official acts will be closely criticised on account of my profession of Christian principles; to devote every day suitable time to meditation and prayer, letting no day pass without one hour being wholly spent in religious reading and devotion."

"AT SEA, *March* 19th.

"Who shall deliver me from the body of this death? Why with the fruits of holiness can not the Christian be satisfied? Alas! in my own case, the world, its honors and varied sources of gratification, steal upon me and are incorporated into all my plans."

"AT SEA, *April* 2.

"My mind being in an unusual state this day, induces me to note the circumstance notwithstanding the gale. Some trials belonging to the service cause me unpleasant feelings, but especially the singular deportment of a friend. Earthly ties bind us to the world, and when they are sundered we should throw ourselves on Him who is without variableness or shadow of turning.

"Oh, enable me to become less sensitive to mortal friendships, and transfer my affections to my Redeemer; and, Heavenly Father, give me influence, that souls may be weaned from the world and placed supremely on thee. Bless this ship, her officers and men."

"AT SEA, *April* 22.

"Doubts as to the Christian religion suddenly flashed across my mind last evening. Why are these things? I know not, unless it is to show us our weakness, and that we must ever in this warfare rely on Christ."

"AT SEA, *May* 21.

"I could give wings to my faith, such are my views and feelings to-day. But, alas! what have they been the last month? Such as to condemn me, for the pride and vanity about the appearance of the ship, instances of passion, and coldness in my devotions. I would humble myself before God this day."

"At Sea, *June* 9.

"We are rapidly drawing to the end of our cruise, a good emblem of life; and it becomes me to look back to the cruise of my life for the evidences that Christ has been formed in the soul.

"The coming week is likely to be one of excitement to me. May my weakness prove my strength! Blessed Redeemer, to thee I look for grace according to temptation.

"Our Father, I renew to thee this day my obligations and vows to be thine—wholly thine. I come to deplore the levity of my character, and yet I come blessing thee. I come with the desire to be taught of God through Christ and the Holy Spirit, so to live and act in my situation as to thy glory, and that my highest ambition may ever lie in being conformed to the will of God. Amen."

Upon the thirty-fourth anniversary of his birth, September 12, 1840, he wrote:

"Oh how mingled are the emotions of my mind. It seems as if love, joy, gratitude, on the one hand, with sorrow and contrition of soul on the other, were all at work within me. The Christian is told in the Word of God that Christ is an all-sufficient Saviour, and he is able and ready in all circumstances to sustain us in a life of *perfect obedience*, if we exercise faith in him. May this year be so passed as to meet thy acceptance; and if I am to leave this world before its expiration, enable me cheerfully to acquiesce."

CHAPTER V.

NAVAL ASYLUM AT PHILADELPHIA.—CRUISE OF THE "CUMBERLAND."—NAVAL ACADEMY AT BOSTON.

Having been detached from the *John Adams* June 24, 1840, Lieutenant Foote was appointed Nov. 22, 1841, to the Naval Asylum in Philadelphia, and after Commodore Barron's resignation the full charge of that institution during the last two years of the administration of Secretary Upshur, was placed in his hands. This establishment at that time combined the character of half hospital and half school, and was, in fact, the first of our home institutions of a like kind that sprang up to meet the necessities of the service. The Naval Academy at Annapolis grew out of this, the purely educational part of it having been transferred to Annapolis. To Lieutenant Foote was especially assigned the care and education of midshipmen.

"By scraps of laws, regulations, and departmental instructions, a Naval Academy has grown up, and a naval policy become established for the United States, without the legislative wisdom of the country having passed upon that policy, and contrary to its previous policy, and against its interest and welfare. A Naval Academy, with two hundred and fifty pupils, and annually coming off in scores, makes perpetual demands for ships and commissions, and these must be furnished, whether required by the public service or not; and thus the idea of a limited Navy, or a naval peace establishment, is extinguished, and a perpetual war establishment in time of peace is growing upon our hands. Prone to imitate every thing that is English, there was a party among us from the beginning which wished to make the Union, like Great Britain, a great naval power, without considering that England was an island, with foreign possessions, which made a Navy a necessity of her position and her policy; while we were a continent, without foreign possessions, to whom a Navy would be an expensive and idle incumbrance; without considering that

England is often by her policy required to be aggressive, the United States never; without considering that England is a part of the European system, and subject to wars (to her always maritime) in which she has no interest; while the United States, in the isolation of its geographical position, and the independence of its policy, can have no wars but its own, and those defensive."*

These remarks are interesting as bearing upon a department of the Navy with which Lieutenant Foote, in the course of his active life, came to be closely identified. He did an important work in organizing and building up these infant establishments and naval schools, which — the distinguished senator to the contrary notwithstanding—are essential to the existence of a strong naval power. It is true we shall never need again a great Navy to protect our territory. The invention of iron-clads, the facility of sea-coast fortifications, the telegraph, the vast extension of the railroad system, make us, so long as no internal dissensions prey upon and weaken us, impregnable without a great Navy, which, if not needed, is a source of expense and foreign menace. But what would we have done at the breaking out of the last war without some military and naval organization, and some actual material of preparation? To say nothing also of our extended commercial interests, the fact that there are such great numbers of Americans residing in Europe and all parts of the world, makes a naval home establishment—with its boards, bureaus, and schools—a necessity.

It is doubtless true that there will be no more sea-actions like those off Brest and Trafalgar, where nation met nation in conflict.

The necessity of maintaining large squadrons, and building costly ships only to go to ruin, when the whole system of warfare and of naval architecture is undergoing such continual

* Benton's "Thirty Years in the U. S. Senate," vol. ii., p. 57.

changes, has, with us at least, ceased. Still there must be a peace establishment as a nucleus for naval operations; and the good order, high discipline, and moral tone of our naval schools, asylums, and ship-yards at this moment are due as much to the efforts and character of Admiral Foote as to any other man.

At the Philadelphia Asylum, during a period of considerable excitement owing to certain local controversies and unsettled questions in relation to organization and government, he began that course of thorough moral reform which he carried through his whole career. By dint of unceasing persuasion, he prevailed upon the pensioners of the asylum to take the temperance pledge, or, as an "old salt" would say, "stop their grog." He was one of the first to introduce the reform of total abstinence from intoxicating drinks into the Navy; and it was well understood that he was in thorough earnest in this matter, so that officers and men who were devoted to the use of liquor fairly understood that it would go hard with them if Foote was on judgment in cases of delinquency. Whether he sometimes carried this too far or not, all knew where he stood, and all were aware of the inflexible resolution he had taken to introduce the temperance reform into the Navy, in which determination he was successful. The Naval Asylum, in fact, made him a thorough temperance man. He said once in Philadelphia to his brother John: "I made up my mind that as a naval officer I could not be a temperance man. I met with persons of all nations. I was obliged to conform to their customs. But when I came here I found these old sailors dreadful drunkards. Whenever I gave them any privilege, they invariably got drunk. I could do nothing with them. At last I signed the pledge myself, and then they followed me." In a certain petition of the pensioners of the Naval Academy to the Honorable Secretary of the Navy—a characteristic sailors' document—Lieutenant Foote is thus spoken of:

"The gallant Commodore Biddle was our first governor. A brave man like him knew what old sailors wanted. He indulged the good men, and brought the bad men into good order; and when he left us, we all to a man wished he had been left alone. The proper rooms were allotted by him to us, and the officers treated us like men. When he went away, Commodore Barron came, who commanded us as an old commodore ought to command old seamen like himself. He was ready to listen to us and to see our wants supplied, and may God bless him, and Biddle too, for both were old sailors' friends, which we put into the newspapers which you have read. When Commodore Barron left us, he left Lieutenant Foote to command. He has done us a great deal of good in making us all sober men. We once thought that old sailors could not do without grog. Now there is not a man in the house who draws his grog, and we feel like human beings, and hate the sin of getting drunk. We now understand the Word of God as it is written in the Bible, with which we are supplied, and hope our latter days will be better than our former lives have been. As old men, we wanted and have had quiet and peace of mind and body."

In all matters of strictly professional education and culture, the principles of navigation, practical seamanship, gunnery, naval tactics, and ship-building, he was, by the testimony of his contemporaries, for his time, a thorough master, leaving nothing to subordinates that he could do himself.

In the year 1842 (Jan. 27) Lieutenant Foote married for his second wife Caroline Augusta (his second cousin), the eldest daughter of Augustus Russel Street, of New Haven, a gentleman of wealth and high cultivation, now well-known as the generous founder of the art-school in Yale College.*

* Mrs. Caroline Augusta Foote died in New Haven, August 27, 1863, just two months after the death of her husband. She bore to him five children, three sons and two daughters, of whom two, Augustus Russel Street and John Samuel, survive their parents. Under the careful and scholarly training of her father, Miss Street's fine mind and lovely character were developed into a rare and beautiful womanhood, fitting her to become the true wife and counselor of a heroic man. She shared patiently his labors and sorrows, and rejoiced in his triumphs with a calm joy that intelligently appreciated their greatness, but was attempered by a higher hope.

But he enjoyed for a short time only the sweets of domestic repose on shore. His whole life was destined to be one of constant hard service in his profession.

In the summer of 1843 (Aug. 26) he was ordered, as first-lieutenant, to the flag-ship *Cumberland*, fifty guns, under Captain Breese. J. A. Dahlgren and others who have since won for themselves distinction were lieutenants and fellow-officers with Foote in this cruise of the *Cumberland*. This vessel bore at her peak the pennant of Commodore Joseph Smith, who on his return from this cruise was made Chief of the Bureau of Yards and Docks at Washington, and who, with Captain Breese, bore a distinguished part in the last war with Great Britain, especially in the battle of Lake Champlain. Commodore Smith proved to be Foote's life-long and perhaps his most loved and trusted friend, and is himself a genial and noble-hearted Christian man. Commodore Smith soon appreciated Foote's working qualities, and in one of his earliest letters he says: "Would you be willing to go to Norfolk if I should go there? as that is a place of *work*, and requires energetic officers." He told Foote that he wished him to be always associated with himself, and he regarded him "as his *mainmast*."

The *Cumberland* sailed from Boston for the Mediterranean on the 20th of November, 1843. When taking the stores on board for the voyage, some of the men got an opportunity to tap a barrel of whisky, and made themselves drunk. Trouble ensued: some of them insulted and attacked one of the officers, and were consequently flogged. Foote took the opportunity to form a temperance society, beginning with the officers, and being sustained and encouraged by the commodore. The movement became popular, and soon all the sailors but one consented to commute their grog-rations for money; and that solitary one, coming up every day to receive his grog, became a laughing-stock, and was soon got rid of.

The spirit-room was emptied of its contents, and the whole

crew, with the exception of the one veteran toper, joined the movement, so that the *Cumberland* became the first temperance ship in the United States Navy; and how interesting is this, when we think of the future fate of this vessel, selected to be the martyr ship of our civil war; when, in the terrible fight with the iron-clad and iron-beaked *Merrimack*, with her flag flying and her crew cheering, she delivered her last fire at her country's foes, and went down unconquered and unsullied in her pure renown.

The effects of the temperance reform on the *Cumberland* were visible in the excellent discipline of the ship, showing that the moral element is the basis of the highest and most efficient military discipline. Lieutenant Foote delivered a parting temperance address before the crew of the *Cumberland*, November 1, 1845, from which the following are extracts:

"To illustrate the correctness of the position which I have taken, let us look at the changes within the last few years. See how the temperance movement has changed the aspect of things. Look around, and we see ourselves in a ship where that great enemy of man—the enemy to his hopes and happiness—ardent spirits, is abolished. Who would have believed a man, thirty years ago, had he predicted that a ship, a frigate—a flag-ship, too, of the squadron—would cruise a year without the grog-tub? But it has been done, and I have strong hopes that in thirty years hence every man-of-war will cruise without a grog-tub, and that liberty in almost every port, and money every month, as has been the case in this ship, with many other changes, will also take place, rendering life in a man-of-war comparatively respectable and happy. But the credit of taking the lead in this reform, this matter which will prove so great a blessing to so many generations of seamen, will ever belong to the *Cumberland*—to the crew of the *Cumberland*. They did it; they also sent a petition to Congress to abolish the whisky-ration—did it voluntarily, of their own accord—no coercion, no force was used. The subject was placed before them—they chose, they acted for themselves; and by it have not only astonished people abroad, but the papers at home are resounding with their praise, and the good effects of their choice have been witnessed in the good order and condition of the ship:

in her snugness aloft and cleanliness below; in her rapid exercise of battery, and no less rapid evolutions of getting under way, furling sails, and, I may now add, of beating every thing which we have met. Of such a ship we may well be proud, and no doubt we shall all, long after the cruise, recur to the *Cumberland* with the most pleasurable feelings. * * *

"I say that temperance has done good, and I believe its good effects will long be felt by many poor deserted mothers, who for ten and fifteen years have not been visited by their sons, but who will in a few months share the gatherings of a two years' cruise. Will they not thank God for the temperance movement in the *Cumberland?* Yes; and I trust that in eternity, as well as in time, many of you will bless the Lord for sending you on board this ship. But now is the crisis—now is the time to make a stand. Now the time has come to decide the great question, whether seamen shall become a rational, long-lived, and respectable class of men, or whether they shall continue to be imposed upon by land-sharks, and madly rush into the grave in the middle age of life. I speak strongly, because I feel strongly on this subject; and here, at the termination of the cruise, still feeling a deep interest in the crew of this ship for their general behavior and efficiency, and hoping at some future day to sail with many of them, I conclude by saying, as a true friend, neither touch, taste, nor handle any thing that can intoxicate. I have practiced and will practice myself these doctrines which I advocate, and so let every man now determine for himself, or he is in danger of rushing, with his eyes open, upon the dreadful alternative—a drunkard's grave and the drunkard's endless doom; which may God avert from us. Farewell!"

Returning from this cruise of the *Cumberland* to Boston, November 10, 1845, after a leave of absence for six months, suffering as he was from ophthalmia, contracted while acting as captain of the boating-service of the *Cumberland* in Egypt and on the dazzling waters of the Mediterranean, he was ordered (June 1, 1846) to the Navy Yard at Boston, where he remained in comparative quiet, though strenuous as ever in the line of professional duty, as executive officer of that establishment, until June 1, 1848.

A few extracts from the familiar letters of Commodore Joseph Smith, at Washington, to Lieutenant Foote, while the latter was in charge of the Boston Yard, relative chiefly to professional matters, and especially to the subject of naval reform, in which both were engaged heart and soul, will prove interesting as reflecting some of the marked personal characteristics of his correspondent. One of Foote's own letters on the subject of the "spirit-ration" to a Connecticut senator we insert among these:

"*January* 30, 1846.

"I conversed with many persons on the feasibility of carrying through Congress our project of abolishing the spirit-ration. I do not believe the committees in both houses would report in its favor; and if they should, I do not believe this Congress will ratify the measure. There is a strong opposition to it, and a good many wires would be pulled to check it. I heard by Dahlgren that your eyes continued bad. The *Cumberland* sailed yesterday for Mexico."

"*February* 20, 1846.

"You have done a good thing for the service by 'putting in your oar' to keep all the bureaus in the Navy. You are not alone in this work; still I learn from reliable sources that your townsman (Gideon Welles) will be confirmed. It is strange that the Navy can not furnish a head to a bureau capable of knowing what seamen want and how to furnish the stores. I trust your eyes will soon be well. I see by the prints that the crew of the *Boston* broke into her spirit-room and got drunk, and caused much trouble. That would be a good spoke in our wheel of reform, and a good commentary upon the effect of whisky in the Navy. The *Cumberland* lay fourteen days in the dry-dock, and no such conduct was enacted there. I have talked with Mr. Choate about the matter. He told me Mr. Calhoun voted against the reform, and that he could not carry it. We have some officers high in rank who will oppose it; nevertheless, I think it will come round by-and-by."

"*February* 22, 1847.

"I fear the six cents' commutation is in danger in the House of Representatives. The bill has been returned with amendments, and I fear the six cents will be attacked, as I know a good many who think much of the difference between the cost of whisky made from potatoes and money; and Mr. Welles has asked and received the assent of the Senate for an appropriation of $200,000 to pay this commutation, and that is what will endanger the bill in the House. God knows when the war (with Mexico) will end. I see no prospect at present. After Vera Cruz and the Castle have surrendered, the chances for peace will be better."

"NAVY YARD, BOSTON, *June* 15, 1847.

"DEAR SIR,—Agreeably to the request contained in your letter of the 24th ultimo, I submit the following reasons, as among the most prominent, why whisky should be stricken from the Navy ration-table:

"In the mercantile marine generally the spirit-ration has been abolished, and its effect upon the *morale* and efficiency of that service has exceeded the expectations of the most sanguine. Similar effects were so manifest in the case of the United States frigate *Cumberland*, bearing the flag of Commodore Joseph Smith, now Chief of the Bureau of Yards and Docks, that all the commissioned officers, although at the outset of the cruise regarding the idea of abolishing the whisky-ration as wholly impracticable, with two hundred and fifty of the crew, subsequently sent a petition to Congress, praying its abolishment. Lieutenant-Commandant Charles H. Davis, of the United States surveying schooner *Gallatin*, and formerly in command of the *Nautilus*, has not for several years served out to his crew the daily allowance of whisky. One of his lieutenants informs me that now they can send their men on shore without apprehension of drunkenness and desertion, which were rife previously to adopting this measure. I inclose herewith a letter from Lieutenant-Commandant Davis, giving his views and mode of proceeding more in detail in relation to this matter. Commander John Pope, of the United States brig *Dolphin*, now cruising on the coast of Africa, in a letter to a friend, just received, says: 'I hope most truly to see the day when the spirit-ration will be done away. We can do as well without liquor as the men in the merchant service.' Commander John C. Long, United States Navy, says: 'It is practicable, it is expedient to abolish the whisky-ration, and it ought to be done forthwith. I tested this matter to my entire satisfaction when in command of the schooner *Dolphin*.' I am aware, notwithstanding this testimony, that there are quite a number of officers in the Navy opposed to its abolishment, and so were the officers of the *Cumberland*, and also of the mercantile marine, until the experiment was fairly tested, when the sentiment changed entirely.

"These facts seem to show conclusively that the abolishment of the whisky-ration would materially advance the moral tone of seamen and the efficiency of the service, but the proposed measure has met with objections, the most prominent of which is that it would be coercive; on the other hand, I would ask in the premises, Is not serving it out a positive encouragement to drunkenness? I have never been able myself to see the force of this objection—coercion. It simply takes away a portion of the ration and gives a full equivalent, which will be far more satisfactory to the men in service generally. It does not forbid the sailor's drinking. It merely ceases to parade by authority the grog-tub daily before his eyes: placing its contents in the same table with beef, pork, and other parts of the ration necessary to sustain his physical being—a sly incentive to his becoming a drunkard. The officer when he draws his ration is not permitted to receive his whisky; the minor is also debarred this portion of his ration. Why not, then, extend the prohibition to the remainder of the crew, especially as it has led them to advocate its abolishment who previously to sailing without it regarded its continuance essential?

"I can not regard the commutation at even $1 80 per month, leaving it optional with the crew, as calculated to have the desired effect. This would leave it still an open, unsettled, exciting question, enabling a few old seamen, most of them foreigners, to influence many of the younger and inexperienced men to use this portion of their ration against their better judgment. In this case, also, the expense to the government, and inconvenience to the ship of filling the spirit-room without knowing what portion would be required, is another objection. On the other hand, strike the whisky unqualifiedly from the ration-table; pay the men $1 per month in lieu thereof, and it will prove acceptable to the men, economical to the government, and in all respects beneficial to the service.

"Respectfully your obedient servant,

"A. H. Foote, Lieutenant U. S. Navy.

"Hon. Geo. P. Rockwell."

To continue the extracts from Commodore Smith's letters:

"*August* 20, 1847.

"I have yours of the 18th inst.; am glad to hear you are getting on so well at your station, and particularly of your successful progress with your improved propeller. You will have a host of competitors from the engineers, I fear; but if the improvement is valuable, it will put down opposition. I fear you have not calculated the effect of the centrifugal force, or rather the *spiral force* of the water after leaving the propeller and coming in opposing contact with the vessel. However, experiment is the only proper test in such matters."

"*December* 29, 1847.

"From Tattnall I received your model of a scull—not *skull.* You are right about the Indian paddles. The shape of these paddles, or floats, or sculls, should be of the same shape as Indian paddles, instead of being circular. But you are behind the times, my friend, in this, for in England this kind of paddle has been in use, or rather experimented upon, for five years, on each quarter instead of the bow, as yours is intended.

"Dahlgren is at home on a visit. He is in tall grass now; has full swing, and will make for himself an enviable reputation. He has won golden opinions from the whole eighty-five middies at the school for the manner and course of his instructions."

"*April* 13, 1848.

"I trust you will have full credit for all your exertions in bringing and keeping the Yard in good order and wholesome discipline, and much is due to you for the excellent state it is in, as all say. You must be a commodore, at least, before the retired list brings you up."

"*April* 25, 1848.

"Your organization of the fire department is excellent, as almost every thing you do is. The only fault, or rather imperfection in the system, is your too great zeal. When I see you with a project in hand to develop its usefulness, I think of the *black stain*, and call to mind, or rather it comes instinctively, what the pastor of the parish where I was reared used to say—'What is violent can not be lasting.'"*

"*August* 31, 1848.

"Go on in your course of talking and writing in the cause of temperance and all good things. While doing those good deeds, God will bless the means to restore your eyes to perfect health. Dahlgren is pro-

* This reference to "the black stain," which occurs in many of Admiral Smith's letters, is thus explained by him: "The story of the 'black stain' originated in the *Cumberland*, by Foote's (who was executive officer) scraping the paint off the gun-carriages to the bare oak wood, and applying a black dye or stain. This caused many quaint remarks from officers and sailors, as it did not at first promise success. Characteristic of the man, whose will was indomitable, Foote persisted in his experiment, and by oiling and frequently rubbing, a beautiful black polish was produced, which, after all the jokes which had been employed to dampen the inventor's ardor, was much admired; hence the frequent quotation afterward, 'Like Foote's black stain,' when a doubtful experiment was in question."

gressing finely, and will give the Navy some interesting results in ordnance."

"*October* 31, 1848.

"I trust your Dr. Elliott will effect a perfect cure, and that your eyes, which were always bright and sharp, will not be less effective and useful to you than any other of your faculties. The political horizon looks as if the wind would change and haul around in favor of old 'Rough and Ready.' He heads up for the White House, and if no unfavorable flaw strike, he will fetch the mark."

"*June* 25, 1849.

"I trust the chastisement will be a lesson to you not to carry things to *excess*, as you, in your zeal to do good and work righteousness, are, or have been, prone to do. I may speak plainly now that you are on your pins again, and say I fear you have been a victim to your 'water cure.' Bless God for his unbounded mercies. You have a new lease of life, and have much more to see of this wicked world than you have seen, and more good to do than you have done."

In regard to the invention of the bow-propeller, to which reference is made in these extracts, there was a correspondence on the subject in the years 1846 and 1847, between Lieutenant Foote and Commodore Morris, Chief of the Bureau of Construction, which correspondence is recorded in the minute-book of the bureau, but does not seem to have led to an adoption of Foote's invention. As explained by the inventor, the object of placing the propeller in the bow is to produce by its motion a partial vacuum or eddy, throwing the water aside that would otherwise rise in front and around, and offer resistance to the bow of the vessel in proportion to the vessel's velocity; which theory, he maintained, was fully sustained by actual experiment, and one fourth, or at least a fifth more velocity was secured by the bow-propeller over the stern-propeller; as in the first the water which offers such resistance to the bow is thrown aside or broken up, while the stern-propeller takes the water from the stern, where it is needed to buoy the vessel, and causes her to go, as it were, upon an inclined plane.

CHAPTER VI.

CRUISE OF THE "PERRY" ON THE AFRICAN COAST.

On September 28, 1849, Lieutenant Foote was assigned to the command of the brig *Perry*, and ordered to the coast of Africa, for the protection of American commerce and the suppression of the slave-trade. The squadron to which the *Perry* belonged was under the command of Commodore Gregory, whose flag-ship was the *John Adams*, and with whom, it will be remembered, he made his first voyage as a midshipman in 1823.

As this was one of the notable periods of his life, and had decisive results upon the infamous slave-trade, it should be treated deliberately; and for this purpose free use will be made of Lieutenant Foote's own papers, log-book, private journal, and especially of his work entitled "Africa and the American Flag."

A good idea of the nature and extent of the cruising-ground of the *Perry* is given in the following extract from Admiral Foote's book, and this will also serve as a sample of the style and character of that work:

"If a chart of the Atlantic is spread out, and a line drawn from the Cape Verde Islands toward the southeastern coast of Brazil; if we then pass to the Cape of Good Hope, and draw another from that point by the Island of St. Helena, crossing the former north of the equator, the great tracks of commerce will be traced. Vessels outward bound follow the track toward the South American shore, and the homeward bound are found on the other. The vessels often meet in the centre of the Atlantic; and the crossing of these lines off the projecting shores of Central Africa renders the coasts of that region of great naval importance.

"The wide triangular space of sea between the homeward-bound line and the retiring African sea-board around the Gulf of Guinea constituted the area on which the vigilance of the squadron was to be exercised. Here is the region of crime, suffering, cruelty, and death from the slave-trade; and here has been at different ages, when the police of the sea happened to be little cared for, the scene of the worst piracies which have ever disgraced human nature.

"Vessels running out from the African coast fall here and there into these lines traced on the chart, or sometimes across them. No one can tell what they contain from the graceful hull, well-proportioned masts, neatly trimmed yards, and the gallant bearing of the vessel. This deceitful beauty may conceal wrong, violence, and crime—the theft of living men, the foulness and corruption of the steaming slave-deck, and the charnel-house of wretchedness and despair.

"It is difficult in looking over the ship's side to conceive the transparency of the sea. The reflection of the blue sky in these tropic regions colors it like an opaque sapphire, till some fish startles one by suddenly appearing far beneath, seeming to carry daylight down with him into the depths below. One is then reminded that the vessel is suspended over a transparent abyss. There for ages has sunk the dark-skinned sufferer from 'the horrors of the middle passage,' carrying that ghastly daylight down with him, to rest until 'the sea shall give up its dead,' and the slaver and his merchant come up from their places to be confronted with their victim."*

The seventeenth and eighteenth centuries were the era of the greatest woe in the slave-trade. Then it became cruelly and murderously systematic. The question what nation should be most enriched by the abominable traffic was a subject of diplomacy. England secured the greatest share of the criminality and of the profit, by gaining from her other competitors the right by contract to supply the colonies of Spain with negroes. But our own country entered largely into this business, and in later times chiefly by means of small and ill-found vessels, which, as they were watched by the cruisers, were crowded and packed with negroes, at any risk of loss by death,

* "Africa and the American Flag," p. 14–16. The ending of this passage calls to mind Ruskin's powerful description of Turner's still more powerful picture of the "Slave-ship," in his "Modern Painters.

so that a successful voyage might compensate for many captures. In olden times there were vessels fitted expressly for the purpose—large Indiamen or whalers. Lieutenant Foote says:

"If ever there were any thing on earth which, for revolting, filthy, heartless atrocity, might make the devil wonder and hell recognize its own likeness, it was on one of the decks of an old slaver. The sordid cupidity of the older, as it is meaner, was also more callous than the hurried ruffianism of the present age. In fact, a slaver now has but one deck; in the last century they had two or three. Any one of the decks of the larger vessels was rather worse, if it could be, than the single deck of the brigs and schooners now employed in the trade. Then the number of decks rendered the suffocating and pestilential hold a scene of unparalleled wretchedness."*

In bad weather, when the hatches were closed, the death of numbers from suffocation would necessarily occur, and in the efforts of the more athletic to get at the air, the weaker would be strangled. The height between decks was so small that a man of ordinary size could hardly sit upright. The slaves were obliged to lie on their backs, and were shackled by their ankles, the left of one being fettered to the right of the next, so that the whole number, in one line, formed a single living chain. When one died, the body remained—during the night, or in stormy weather for a longer time, and until it was in a putrid state—secured to two living bodies.

We are not, however, to suppose that the horrors of "the middle passage" were essentially diminished in modern times; and the diabolical atrocity of those who, in the middle of this century, dealt in "ebony"—some of them New England captains, from homes where the religion of Christ was taught—was increased tenfold by the light of humanity diffused abroad. Here was the fountain-head of the slave-supply in the Southern States; and it is a cause of gratitude that our hero

* "Africa and the American Flag," p. 27.

was enabled to do some serious work toward the permanent destruction of this original evil before he actually came to contend with the slave-power in its final assault upon the life of the government.

In Lieutenant Foote's notices of Africa, before entering upon the detail of his special work, there is much that shows an observing and penetrative, we might almost say, scientific mind; for example, he thus discourses at length of the philosophy of storms on the West African coast:

"The vast radiator formed by the sun beating vertically on the plains of tropical Africa, heats and expands the air, and thus constitutes a sort of central trough, into which gravitation brings compensating currents, by producing a lateral sliding inward of the great trade-wind streams. Thus, as a general rule, winds which would normally diverge from the shores are drawn in toward them. They have been gathering moisture in their progress; and when pressed upward, as they expand under the vertical sun, lose their heat in the upper regions, let go their moisture, and spread over the interior terraces and mountains a sheet of heavily depositing cloud. This constitutes the rainy season, which necessarily, from the causes producing it, accompanies the sun in its apparent oscillations across the equator.

"The Gulf of Guinea has in its own bosom a system of hurricanes and squalls, of which little is known but their existence and their danger. A description of them, of rather old date, specifies as a fact that they begin by the appearance of a small mass of clouds in the zenith, which widens and extends till the canopy covers the horizon. Now if this were true of any given spot, it would indicate that the hurricane always began there. The appearance of a patch of cloud in the zenith could be true of only one place out of all those which the hurricane influenced. If it is meant that *wherever* the phenomenon originated, *there* a mass of cloud gradually formed in the zenith, this would be a most important particular in regard to the proximate cause of the phenomenon, for it would mark a rapid direction upward of the atmosphere at that spot as the first observable incident of the series. That the movements produced would subsequently become whirling, or circumvolant, is a mechanical necessity; but the force of the movement ought not to be strongest at the place where the movement had its origin.

"The squalls, with high towering clouds, which rise like a wall on the horizon, involve the same principles as to the formation of the vapor, and are easily explicable. They are not necessarily connected with circular hurricanes; but the principles of their formation may modify the intensity of the blasts in a circumvolant tornado. Since in the Gulf of Guinea they come from the eastward, it is to be inferred that they are ripples or undulations in an air current. In regard to all of this, it is necessary to speak doubtfully, for there is a great lack of accurate and detailed observation on these points.

"Its position and physical characteristics give to this continent great influence over the rest of the earth. Africa, America, and Australia have nearly similar relations to the great oceans interposed respectively between them. Against the eastern sides of these regions are carried from the ocean those strange, furious whirlwinds on the shallow film of the earth's atmosphere which constitute hurricanes. It is evident that these oceans are mainly the channels in which the surface winds move which are drawn from colder regions toward the equator. The shores are the banks of these air streams. The return currents above flow over every thing. They are thus prevalent in the interior, so that the climatic conditions there are different from those on the sea-board. These circumstances in the southern extra-tropical regions are accompanied by corresponding differences in the character of the vegetable world.

"These winds are sometimes drawn aside across the coast-lines, constituting the Mediterranean sirocco and the African harmattan. Vessels far off at sea, sailing to the northward, are covered or stained on the weather-side of their rigging (that next to the African coast) with a fine, light-yellow powder. A reddish-brown dust sometimes tinges the sails and rigging. An instance of this occurred on board the *Perry* on her outward-bound passage when five hundred miles from the African coast."*

In another place Lieutenant Foote happily describes the physical conformation of the African sea-coast, which has had, and will ever have, its influence upon the commerce of that continent:

"The sea-shore is generally low, except as influenced by Atlas, or the Abyssinian ranges, or the mountains of the southern extremity. There is not uncommonly a flat, swampy plain bordering on the sea, where the

* "Africa and the American Flag," p. 32–34.

rivers push out their deltas, or form lagoons by their conflict with the fierce surge upon the shore. The sea does not deal kindly with Africa, for it wastes or guards the shores with an almost unconquerable surf. Tides are small, and rivers are not safely penetrable. The ocean offered to the negro nothing but a little food, procured with some trouble and much danger. Hence ocean commerce was unknown to them."

But it is time that the real business should be spoken of which the commander of the little brig *Perry* took in hand to do.

After the great European war, when, in the language of Lieutenant Foote, "the matured villainy of the world" was assembled on the African coast to re-establish the slave-trade, England commenced a vigorous system of cruising by her war-ships to suppress the trade. In 1839 the corrective was still more stringently applied. Permission had then been wrung from the slave-trading powers to capture vessels outward bound for Africa when fitted for the slave-trade. The treaties provided that vessels equipped for the traffic might be captured. A slaver was to be taken because she was a slaver: just as it is better to shoot the wolf before he has killed the sheep than afterward. If a vessel, therefore, were found on the African coast with slave-irons, water in sufficient quantity for a slave-cargo, with a slave-deck laid for packing slaves, she was seized and condemned before committing the overt act. Under this arrangement double the number of captures was made during the next ten years than in the twenty years previous. The efforts of the English squadron were conjoined with those of France and the United States, although England took the laboring oar, and was, it must be confessed, the most in earnest in this business. A treaty with Great Britain was signed at Washington in the year 1842, stipulating that each nation should maintain on the African coast a force of naval vessels of suitable numbers and description, to carry in all not less than eighty guns, to enforce, separately and respectively, the laws, rights, and obligations of each of the two countries, for the suppression of the slave-trade. These, together with other subsidiary means (such as the substitution of legal trade, the conversion of old slave-factories and forts into positions defensive against their former purpose, etc.), reduced the export of slaves in 1849 from one hundred and five thousand to about thirty-seven thousand. Still the evil was great, and the laxity on the part of the American government to fulfill its portion of the treaty was sorely felt; and since the American flag was inviolable to any foreign nation, in the case of falling in with a British cruiser, an American slaver, on presenting her register, or sea-letter, as a proof of nationality, could not be searched nor detained. The American flag came thus to be greatly abused, and was deeply involved in the slave-traffic. This was further aided by the artful device of legal trading: with a cargo corresponding to the manifest, and all the ship's papers being made out in form. American slavers, under the disguise of doing a legal business, swarmed on the African coast, and escaped almost with impunity. There was sometimes a pretended sale when the slaver was ready to start from the African coast: the American captain and his crew going on shore as the slaves were coming off, while the Portuguese or Italian *passengers*, who came out in her, all at once, as by a kind of devilish jugglery, became the master and crew of the vessel. There is evidence in the records of the Consulate of slaves having started from the shore, and at the same time the master and crew from the vessel, carrying with them the flag and ship's papers; when, the parties becoming frightened, both pulled back; the slaves were returned to the shore, and the American master and crew went on board the vessel. The stars and stripes were again hoisted over her, and kept flying until the cause of the alarm (an English cruiser) departed from the coast, and the embarkation was safely effected. The American minister at the court of Brazil in 1844 wrote to the Secretary of State:

> "I regret to say this, but it is a fact not to be disguised nor denied that the slave-trade is almost entirely carried on under our flag in American-built vessels, sold to slavers here, chartered for the coast of Africa, and there sold, or sold here—delivered on the coast. And, indeed, the scandalous traffic could not be carried on to any great extent were it not for the use made of our flag, and the facilities given for the chartering of American vessels to carry to the coast of Africa the outfit for the trade and the material for purchasing slaves."

The question as to the deplorable effects arising from the abuse of the American flag was brought into discussion in 1842 between England and America, and the treaty before referred to was established; but the question was still left unsettled—How is a vessel to be ascertained to be American? The plea that any vessel hoisting any flag is thereby secured against all interference in *all* circumstances never could be seriously maintained as a principle of international law. Neither the United States nor any other power has ever acted on a dogma of this breadth. The United States government, while asserting the inviolability of its flag (this very question being the origin of the War of 1812), did not claim that its flag should give immunity to those who were not American; for such a claim would render it a cover to piracy, and to acts of the greatest atrocity. "But any vessel which hoists the American flag claims to be American, and therefore, while she may be boarded and examined by an American cruiser, this right is not conceded to a foreign cruiser; for the flag is *prima facie* evidence, although not conclusive proof of nationality; and if such vessel be really American, the boarding officer will be regarded in the light of a trespasser, and the vessel will have all the protection which that flag supplies. If, on the other hand, the vessel prove not to be American, the flag illegally worn will afford her no protection. Therefore a foreign officer boarding a vessel under the flag of the United States, does it on his own responsibility for all consequences."*

Thus complicated and unsatisfactory was the condition of things; and although after the treaty the United States government sent an organized naval force to the coast of Africa, which was the means of capturing many slavers and of releasing hundreds of wretched negroes, yet the evil was not checked; and at the time the *Perry* came on the coast the trade was at its height, and perhaps was never more brisk. A kind of immunity was given to British cruisers to search American vessels by this implied permission to do so on the responsibility of the searching party. Blundering mistakes and arrogant assumptions on the part of British war-vessels not unfrequently occurred; while the greater evil still remained, that the slavers themselves continued to escape in great numbers even from British vigilance and determination to root out the infamous traffic carried on under the protection of the banner of the United States.

* "Africa and the American Flag," p. 233.

CHAPTER VII.

CRUISE OF THE "PERRY"—CONTINUED.

There is reason to think that Lieutenant Foote, after so much hard sea-service, did not greatly desire to go to this harassing post of duty on the African coast, but he was always ready for honest work; and where there was a disagreeable piece of work to do, or a difficult post to fill, it was quite the custom of the Navy Department, instead of sending a reluctant officer, or of running the risk of an absolute refusal, to say, "Why, send Foote; he will go." When Foote did go, it was to do good work, putting heart and soul into it. Thus it fell out that a great deal of the hard service of the Navy in his day came upon this energetic officer; and perhaps, in the end, though full of labor and care, no work that he ever did gave him more satisfaction than the effective part he performed in the suppression of the African slave-trade, for it was directly in the line of his own character and convictions as a fighter against every form of evil. The following letter, dated October 15, 1849, was written to him before sailing, by his old commodore, Joseph Smith:

"I have your two letters of the 12th instant. I have done my best with the Secretary for your brig and for your own convenience, but I can't make a dent upon him. He says he will order a purser this day; but no person whatever, and nothing not on the allowance-book, will be granted to you. I wished to have Kelly—you remember him in the *Cumberland* as quartermaster—ordered to you as acting-boatswain. He was in the *Perry* when she was stranded, and never let go the helm for twenty-nine hours. He has been through the Gulf war as acting-boatswain of a small craft. I am a little selfish in your orders to the *Perry*, for I wished to hold you back on shore duty till I went to sea; but the

Secretary jumped at you the moment he discovered you were well enough to command. We want such persons as yourself to represent us abroad (and at home, too), and your aid to Gregory will be peculiarly opportune. You are a better man and a better Christian than I am, therefore it would be useless for me to tender you advice. Before you take your crew from the receiving ship, beat up for volunteers to commute the spirit-ration; if you can, get them entirely to relinquish it. Leave the poison behind you; if not, get as many as you can to start fair with, if you must lay in the devil's fuel. Keep up your regular Sunday service, and oftener if convenient; Saturday for mending day, and Sunday for meditation and reading. Each officer and man to have his place and duty. Impose as much responsibility upon the petty officers as they will bear. Your command will be happy, healthy, and efficient in proportion as those under you engage with all their mind in their duties, and are made to feel that reliance is placed in them. Do not spare the lash when the exigency demands it, but throw as many guards around it as will make its use a matter of absolute necessity. As to etiquette, you are as *au fait* in it as I am. Should you meet a flag-ship at sea, haul up courses, down jib, and salute. When you arrive in port, send a boat to our consul, and offer him a conveyance on board; and salute him when he arrives with seven guns—the consul-general with nine. When a foreign ship sends a boat and offers services, etc., send a boat to acknowledge the compliment, and afterward pay your respects to him in person. The last arrived salutes first (except our own flag-officers) and calls first. Salute the place first, and afterward the flag-officer, if any is in port."

How much good advice in a short space (excepting the "lash," which belonged to the older and more barbarous days of the Navy) is contained in this letter! It is a kind of marine pastoral epistle—rough, indeed, but sound, honest, apostolic. A letter written at this time by his friend Dahlgren is also interesting:

"WASHINGTON, *October* 30, 1849.

"MY DEAR FRIEND,—Your very acceptable letter of the 17th reached me to-day, for which I am much indebted to you.

"The impression remained on my mind that the last letter between us was by myself, and that the condition of your sight forbade your writing.

"In two instances I was on the point of visiting you at New Haven (the last time in May of this year), when, being in Boston on duty, Dr.

Wheeler and myself had arranged to make the trip together, for you were often the subject of our conversation, and we felt sorrowful for the state of your health. By the way, there is no one in whose love and regard your remembrance is more fixed than in that of the doctor.

"I regret to see the desponding tone of your letter. Five or six years passed with me in mental torture that no one can understand save a fellow-sufferer; and yet my eyes now are so unexpectedly changed that last summer I dispensed with glasses for the first time in ten years. They are still weak, and unequal to much exertion; but think how much better. Homœopathy has been the agent of this beyond doubt, and I regret truly that you had not been induced to try this at an early period.

"If the master is inefficient, you had better get him out of the vessel as soon as you can without trouble to yourself. And now let me advise you—whether the master is good or bad—to procure a ship's book of suitable size, and cause the master there to record and work every observation. I do not mean the clean copy of either, but the original figures just as made and corrected—not in pencil, but ink. This, with any memoranda showing the ship's position from other sources, should be presented daily. As the case now stands, a commander takes a result without knowing the data. First the master is to mention the chronometer with the observation rates. Before leaving them he verifies these rates by other observations with the sextant. These are to be recorded; at sea, the time and latitude, the rate and error, and so on. In almost every department of a ship save this the record has been systematized.

"I have little doubt of the action of Congress in respect to flogging, and I am utterly at a loss to imagine a substitute. Last session it would have been brought about, but that a few doubtless, like the Dutch governor, felt alarmed. On one occasion the chairman of the Senate Naval Committee spoke to me about it. I told him that there seemed to be an impression that naval officers were partial to the system for its own sake. This was not so—it was a most unpleasant duty; and the fact that they submitted to the painful necessity of inflicting it proved how strong the necessity was. I told him that demagogues argued as if the Navy were created for the special benefit of officers—not as if it were an institution for the common good. For great as might be the personal interest of any officer, it was slight in comparison to that which the planter, the farmer, and the merchant had in the existence of a force afloat competent to protect national and individual rights.

"I wish I could say something in favor of the force of a vessel like the

Perry. Her battery is perhaps as good as she can carry. Unless the change were radical, I would prefer to arm her with two heavy pivot-guns (say 8-inch).

"Your largest pieces are 32-pounders of 33 cwt. If so, they are good guns, and at half a mile would tell effectively;* even beyond that they would not be comfortable customers for an enemy. Always ricochet the shot when the water is smooth enough; but with the shells keep the gun up about half a degree, so that the shot may not touch first nearer than 500 yards, as the water is apt to extinguish the priming of the fuse. In a second this is accomplished, and then neither water nor wood will put out the fuse.

"I wish much that I had known earlier of your appointment to the *Perry*, as I should have liked a boat howitzer to go with you on trial. Now I have none suitable, and there is not time to cast and finish one.

"The kind which I have proposed is now intended by the Bureau to be essayed in such vessels as have boats to carry them. They consist of 12-pounders of two sizes, 400 lbs. and 800 lbs., and 24-pounders of 1300 lbs., for launches of sloops, frigates, and liners respectively. The model is after my own notion, and I am allowed to make them. The ammunition is spherical case (that is, a thin iron shell charged with musket-balls, and burst near the boats or men fired at by a fuse and bursting charge). The English term is shrapnel. They were used at Buena Vista and Palo Alto, and alone saved our forces. I have so arranged the carriage that no breaching is required, and this facilitates the use, so that a howitzer can be fired seven times in a minute. This has been done often in the presence of the Secretary of the Navy, Dupont, Buchanan, and others; though it would not be practicable in a boat for want of room.

"I have now a very important proposition on hand, which, in my view, will work great changes. I shall soon be furnished with pieces of the right character required to prove it, and at some future time you will hear of it.

"And now, my valued friend, you have in these two sheets some evidence of my pleasure in hearing from you. While you are absent you shall continue to have some remembrance from me. Let me entreat you to take good care of your health, and be cheerful and hopeful. When you get wet, have the circulation assisted by a good rubbing, and never

* That is, will strike almost every shot.

lay aside flannel—change it often. Use no more meat than is absolutely necessary when the breathing organs are tender. With you goes every wish that a friend can offer. Ever affectionately,

"JOHN A. DAHLGREN."

On the 21st of December, 1849, the *Perry* arrived at Porto Praya, Cape de Verde Islands, the rendezvous of the American squadron. She was immediately ordered on a cruise south of the equator; and after the vessel had reached the southern point of destination, she was to cruise along the coast, examining the principal points or slave-stations, such as the Salinas, Benguela, Loanda, Ambriz, River Congo, and intermediate places, back toward Monrovia. She reached St. Philip de Benguela after a passage of forty-one days, and none too soon, since but five days previous an English cruiser had captured near this place a brig with eight hundred slaves on board. This vessel came from Rio de Janeiro, under American colors and papers, with an American captain and crew, and had been transferred, when on the coast, to a Brazilian captain and crew. Still other captures were announced of similar character.

Lieutenant Foote, who was heartily welcomed to the station by the English commanders, set about at once to right matters, and began active cruising off Ambriz, a noted slave-mart, in company with the English war-steamer *Cyclops*. He instituted prompt inquiries in relation to those slavers captured under American colors and adjudicated upon in English courts. In the case of the *Louisa Beaton* he acted with independence and energy. This was an American brigantine, which had been boarded and examined by the *Perry*, and proved to be a legal trader. She afterward ran out of Ambriz under American colors, having awakened suspicion that she had stealthily shipped a cargo of slaves. Two boats from the *Perry* were immediately dispatched in pursuit. They did not succeed in overhauling the vessel. Thereupon Lieutenant Foote request-

F

ed the commander of the *Cyclops* to take his (Foote's) second lieutenant on board and steam after her. The proposal was readily complied with; but after running out forty miles without obtaining sight of the *Beaton*, she returned. The commander of the *Cyclops* addressed a letter to Lieutenant Foote, saying that he had noticed the sailing of the *Louisa Beaton*; that he had suspected her of being a disguised slaver; and had there been no American man-of-war present, he should have considered it his duty to have overhauled her and satisfied himself that her nationality had not been changed by sale at Ambriz—not taking it for granted that the flag displayed by any vessel was a sufficient evidence of her nationality. Lieutenant Foote replied, stating that he had in the mean time found the *Louisa Beaton* at St. Paul de Loanda, and ascertained her legal character; and that the principle assumed by the British commander could not for a moment be allowed, but that, in words which have been already quoted, the flag which a vessel wears is *prima facie* though not conclusive proof of her nationality; that those who lawfully displayed the flag of the United States should have all the protection it supplies; and when a cruiser boarded a vessel under this flag, she did it upon her own responsibility. Again, a few months afterward, in the case of the same *Louisa Beaton*, the commander of the *Perry* insisted upon the principle in respect to the inviolability of the flag in an instance of palpable outrage, when the British cruiser *Dolphin* boarded and detained the *Louisa Beaton*, seventy miles off land, sailing under American colors, and having a proper national register and all her papers good, with the exception of the absence of a sea-letter, usually given by consular officers to legal traders after transfer of masters.

The protracted correspondence of nearly a year which ensued between Lieutenant Foote and the British commander of the southern division, Hon. Captain Hastings, was published

ST. PAUL DE LOANDA.

in the "Blue-Book," or Parliamentary Papers of 1851, and resulted in the British commander's disavowal of the act of the captain of the *Dolphin*, his offer to make pecuniary restitution, and his apology to the master of the *Louisa Beaton* for the detention; and, above all, the important principle of the inviolability of the flag was established. English commanders abstained from even going alongside a legal American trader without the assent of an American naval commander.

Lieutenant Foote was thus called upon to settle nice points of international law without help from any quarter. In his own words: "We have cruised ten months on this southern coast, where, with the exception of two months by the ship *John Adams* and one month by the *Portsmouth*, there has been no American man-of-war; neither has there been a consul, nor any public functionary but myself to supervise our commercial interests and suppress the slave-trade as carried on by American vessels and American citizens; while the English, French, and Portuguese, with less commerce, have their commissioned consuls, commodores, and squadrons, with whom I have been in frequent correspondence; and many new and delicate points, which might have been more appropriately assigned to an experienced diplomatist, than added to the cares and responsibilities of a lieutenant in command of the only national vessel on the coast."*

But Lieutenant Foote did not spend his time in diplomatic correspondence; he was at the same time actively engaged in real work. The *Perry* and her boats were constantly at sea in search of slavers, boarding many legal traders, and chasing suspicious vessels, the boats sometimes being absent for a long time, lost in fog and overtaken by squalls, the commander sharing the severest hardships with his men in this laborious service; oftentimes approaching shore where the roar of the

* Private letter to Hon. Truman Smith.

tremendous surf on the low African coast could be heard for twenty miles, passing the breakers, and running up unhealthy, jungle-bordered rivers to the slave-barracoons.

Provisions being nearly exhausted, the *Perry* went north coastwise to Prince's Island, and there had orders from the commodore to make requisitions upon the flag-ship for provisions, and prepare again for service on the southern coast. After a stay of a few days, the brave little brig turned her prow southward a second time to resume her cruising-ground. On the 7th of June, 1850, between Ambriz and Loanda, a large ship, with two tiers of painted ports, was made to windward, standing in for the land. The vessel was overhauled, having the name *Martha*, New York, registered on her stern. The *Perry* had no colors flying. The ship, when in range of the guns, hoisted the American ensign, shortened sail, and backed her maintop-sail. The first lieutenant, Mr. Rush, was sent to board her. As he was rounding her stern, the people on board observed, by the uniform of the boarding-officer, that the vessel was an American cruiser. The ship then hauled down the American, and hoisted Brazilian colors. The officer went on board, and asked for papers and other proofs of nationality. The captain denied having papers, or log, or any thing else. At the same time something was thrown overboard, which was picked up by another boat sent from the *Perry*, and proved to be the writing-desk of the captain, containing sundry papers and letters identifying the captain as an American citizen; also proving the owner of three fifths of the vessel to be an American merchant, resident in Rio de Janeiro. After obtaining satisfactory proof that the ship *Martha* was a slaver, she was seized as a prize.

There were found on board this vessel one hundred and seventy-six casks filled with water, containing from one hundred to one hundred and fifty gallons each; one hundred and fifty barrels of farina for slave-food; several sacks of beans; slave-deck laid; four iron boilers for cooking slave-provisions; iron bars, with the necessary wood-work for securing slaves to the deck; four hundred spoons for feeding them; between thirty and forty muskets, and a written agreement between the owner and captain, with the receipt of the owner for two thousand milreis.

The captain claimed that the vessel could not lawfully be subjected to search by an American man-of-war while under Brazilian colors. But on being informed that he would be seized as a pirate for sailing without papers even were he not a slaver, he admitted that she was on a slave voyage; adding that, had he not fallen in with the *Perry*, he would during that night have shipped eighteen hundred slaves, and before daylight in the morning been clear of the coast.

The crew of the *Martha* were immediately put in irons; a force of twenty-five men, with the first and second lieutenants, was placed on board, the ship provisioned, and in twenty-four hours after her capture the vessels exchanged three cheers, and the *Martha* was on her way to New York, where she was condemned in the United States District Court as a slaver.

The British commissioner soon afterward at Loanda offered his congratulations on the capture of the *Martha*, remarking that she was the largest slaver that had been on the coast for many years; and the effect of sending all hands on her to the United States would prove a severe blow to the iniquitous traffic.

In the neighborhood of Ambriz the *Perry* chased and captured the American brigantine *Chatsworth*, bearing every proof of being a slaver, but evidence which would be required in the United States courts essential to her condemnation being wanting, she was reluctantly released. She was afterward boarded by the *Perry* under still more suspicious circumstances; and additional proofs being obtained of her true character, notwithstanding her having two sets of papers, passing alternately under different nationalities, eluding detection from papers being in form, and trading with an assorted cargo, she was pronounced a prize, and was sent to America, where, after a long trial, she was condemned as a slaver in the United States District Court of Maryland. By the capture of the *Chatsworth*, in whose case the ingenuity of these unscrupulous villains had taxed itself to the utmost as far as the American flag was concerned, a severe and unexpected blow was struck at the slave-trade. Four thousand slaves were waiting at the barracoons of Ambriz, ready for shipment, at the time of the seizure; and Lieutenant Foote in his private journal relates that the captain of the *Louisa Beaton*, who had given information respecting the true character of the *Chatsworth*, went on shore at Ambriz, at the request of Foote, to procure some papers, and from the time elapsing before his return there was reason to suspect foul play from the slavers in revenge for his informing upon them. Mr. Foote adds: "My plan would have been, had there been foul play, to march at the head of my men out four miles to the slave-barracoons, and let four thousand of the 'oppressed go free,' and thus made free soil and free-soilers."

In a private letter to a friend in Cheshire, dated September 25, 1850, Lieutenant Foote remarks: "Our orders are so stringent that no commander will capture a slaver unless he assume great responsibility. I took the *Chatsworth* in the face of a protest of $22,000 from her captain and supercargo; still she and the *Martha* must be condemned."

A visit was made at this time by the commander and officers of the *Perry* to a native potentate in the interior, the Queen of Ambrizette, who is thus described: "A little withered woman then appeared, having, in addition to her native costume, an old red cloak, drawn tight around her throat, and so worn as to make her look like a loose umbrella with two handles." After a long palaver, the prime-minister of the queen, wearing as his chief garment an old French full-dress navy uniform coat, suggested that he considered his services on the occasion to be worth two bottles of rum. Compliance with this request was totally impracticable, as the spirit-room casks of the *Perry* had been filled only with water.

The cruises of the *Perry* were made upon the total-abstinence principle; and this probably will account for the good health of the crew on that unwholesome coast.

On the 8th of January, 1851, the *Perry* again reported herself to the commander-in-chief at Porto Praya, after one year's service on the African coast. Here she made preparations for a third southern cruise. As the slave-trade had been pretty much driven out of Ambriz, and had shifted itself to the Congo River, the *Perry* proceeded thither, encountering on the passage a heavy tornado. Lieutenant Foote thus describes the Congo River:

"The river is more than two leagues broad at its mouth. At the distance of eight or ten miles seaward, in a northeasterly direction, the water preserves its freshness; and at the distance of fifty and even sixty miles it has a black tinge. Here are often seen small islands floating seaward, formed of fibrous roots, bamboo, rushes, and long grass, and covered with birds. The banks of the Congo are lined with low mangrove bushes, with clumps of a taller species interspersed, growing to the height of seventy feet. Palm-trees, and other trees of a smaller growth, are seen with a rich and beautiful foliage. In going up the river, the southern shore should be hugged, where there is plenty of water close to the land. The current is so strong—often running six miles an hour off Shark's Point—that an exceedingly fresh sea-breeze is necessary in order to stem the stream. The greatest strength of this current, however, is superficial, not extending more than six or eight feet in depth. The Congo, like all the rivers of Africa, except the Nile, is navigable but a short distance before reaching the rapids. The great central region being probably not less than three thousand feet in altitude above the sea, these rapids are formed by a sudden depression of the surface of the country toward the sea, or by a bed of hard rock stretching across the basin of the river."*

* "Africa and the American Flag," p. 346.

A paper of considerable hydrographical interest in relation to the Congo River and the navigation of the southern equatorial coast of Africa was drawn up by the first lieutenant of the ship, Mr. Porter, and, after having been carefully supervised by the commander, was dispatched to the United States National Observatory, and has since been published in "Maury's Sailing Directions."

This third cruise of the *Perry* revealed the fact that the slave-trade had received an effectual check within the past year. Only one suspected American vessel had been seen on the south coast since the capture of the *Chatsworth.*

In a letter from Sir George Jackson, British commissioner at Loanda, addressed about this time to Lord Palmerston, it was stated that the languishing state of the slave-trade was owing to the activity of British cruisers, the co-operation of part of the American squadron on the southern coast, within the year the capture of two or three slavers bearing the flag of that nation, together with the measures adopted by the Brazilian government; so that it might be said that the trade on this southern coast was now confined to a few vessels bearing the Sardinian flag. How much of this was due to the energetic efforts of Lieutenant Foote, the reader himself is now, it is hoped, capable of judging.

In a private letter of Sir George Jackson to Lieutenant Foote this direct personal allusion is made:

"The zeal and activity displayed by yourself and brother officers, and the seizures which were the results of them, at once changed the face of things. The actual loss which the traffic has sustained, and still more the dread of those further losses which they anticipated on seeing the United States squadron prepared to confront them at those very haunts to which they had been accustomed to repair with impunity, and determined to vindicate the honor of their insulted flag, which they had too long been allowed to prostitute, struck terror into those miscreants on both sides of the Atlantic. And from the date of those very opportune captures not a vessel illicitly assuming American colors has been seen on the coast."

The *Perry* continued to cruise vigilantly for some months, only varying the hard monotony of the service by a visit to St. Helena, where Lieutenant Foote and his officers, like sea-worn Ulysses and his crew at some pleasant isle of the ocean, were treated with marked kindness and courtesy.

Late in the autumn the *Perry* sailed for the north coast to her old rendezvous at Porto Praya, where she awaited the coming of the American squadron, one at least of whose vessels, the *John Adams*, had done good service also on the coast. Commodore Gregory, in an official letter to Lieutenant Foote, wrote: "The course you have pursued meets my fullest commendation; and the zeal, ability, and energy with which you have discharged the important duties assigned you, commands my highest respect, and I have no doubt will be most favorably considered by the Secretary of the Navy."

Upon the commodore's arrival, the *Perry* was relieved of her duty upon the African station and ordered home, arriving at New York, after a rough winter passage, on the 26th of December, 1851. The appreciation of the services of the commander by the Navy Department was expressed to him through the Secretary (Hon. J. C. Dobbin) in high terms of satisfaction.

Commodore (now Rear-Admiral) Smith, who ever rejoiced in an opportunity to award his friend praise, thus writes to him from Washington:

> "It affords me great pleasure to say that the Department, so far as I can learn, is highly gratified with your doings. Your vigilance, discretion, activity, and talents are duly appreciated, and, not least of all, your moral training of those under your orders is, and ought to be regarded as reflecting honor upon the Navy. You have won honor and glory enough to rest upon your laurels for some time."

Mr. Webster also officially signified his approval of the course pursued by the captain of the *Perry* in his negotiations with the English and other foreign powers in the delicate and difficult business intrusted to his hands.

A few additional observations of a personal nature respecting this service on the African coast, drawn from the journal and notes of Lieutenant Foote, are reserved for the next chapter. It was so cold and stormy when the brig came upon the American coast that, supposing he might be driven off to sea again if he waited for a pilot, the commander, assuming the responsibility, acted as his own pilot, and brought the vessel into port without assistance. It might here be added that our hero reaped more fame than money from his prizes, since he once told a friend that one gold watch was all the material fruit, over and above his regular pay, of his two anxious years' cruising on the coast of Africa.

CHAPTER VIII.

PRIVATE JOURNAL ON THE "PERRY."

In an address, delivered January 18, 1855, by Commander Foote before the American Colonization Society, he sums up what was done by the *Perry* in these words: "In my own vessel—the *Perry*—we were cruising for two years, much of the time exposed in boats—frequently absent from the vessel days and nights; boarded seventy vessels, and captured two or three slavers, yet not a single death occurred among the officers and crew. The only sanitary measures adopted were—not to be on shore during the night, and issuing no grog-rations during the cruise."

Upon a fever-smitten coast where it is thought to be death for any but the black man to live; exposed to a blazing sun by day and malarious exhalations by night; tossed about in the open sea, and sometimes caught in the hurricane sweeping down from the African highlands over the Gulf of Guinea—in all these varied perils and hardships for two long years, there was not a death on board the *Perry*.

It was not only a temperance ship, but a ship where the rulership of the Most High was acknowledged in public worship and private devotion; and, above all, in the care of its master for the best good of his men.

A few extracts from his "sea-journal"—evidently meant for no eye but his own—give us a glimpse into the economy of the good ship, and of the good man's heart who commanded her. These are not always cheerful extracts. They sometimes reveal conflict; but is the real hero one who has no warfare?

November 29, 1849.—"Carried all studding-sails and royals from the time the pilot left us. Vessel behaving as well as a frigate; perfectly easy in her roll and decks dry, although quite a heavy sea on. Officers and men contented and happy; the latter believed to be more so from having all of them stopped their whisky-ration."

December 4, 1849.—"Sea heavy, and vessel very uneasy. Thus far the passage has been exceedingly rough, except in crossing the Gulf Stream. All the officers are sea-sick, and a great number of the men. Surgeon has been reading to me Neander's Church History. We have frequent conversations on the subject of religion. This day have been twenty-seven years in the Navy."

December 5, 1849.—"Fresh gales and squalls. Carried sail very heavily to ascertain the qualities of the brig, which stood up uncommonly well under a large press. Toward night close-reefed the top-sails. From eight to twelve, very heavy sea, with thunder, lightning, and rain. Vessel very uncomfortable all night; I did not get more than four hours' sleep, being on deck until after 1 A.M. My eyes suffer from great exposure and watching."

December 9, 1849.—"Gale increasing and sea very heavy, but the brig exceedingly comfortable under the circumstances; takes in a great deal of spray, but not as much sea as when the wind was ahead. At three called all hands on deck to witness punishment, when I was under the painful necessity of giving seaman ——— twelve lashes with the cats for having gone below when it was his watch on deck. I said a few words to the crew in relation to duty, etc. Made eight inches of water in one hour, which excited apprehension lest the leak might increase as fast as the pumps could free her; but after midnight the gale abated and the leak diminished, showing it to have been in a measure produced by the heavy weather."

December 16, 1849.—"I read divine service to all hands, during which time a quantity of spray came over me, and the wind was so fresh that I was obliged to read very loud."

December 31, 1849.—"Climate affecting my eyes, and debilitating the system generally."

January 1, 1850. Porto Praya.—"A new year has commenced. May God forgive, for his Son's sake, all my sins, and grant me his continual presence during the year to come. One year ago an illness of the most painful and dangerous character confined me to my bed for five months. Now the next five months are to be spent in a most unhealthy climate in the most unhealthy season."

January 8, 1850.—"On Sunday I had one of my severe headaches. I was in consequence unable to read the service, although I had invited several officers from the flag-ship to be present."

January 12, 1850. At sea.—"Found bottom in one hundred fathoms. The master had the morning watch, and ought to have reported the discoloration of the water; but he is ill-qualified to perform his duty (especially in taking reckoning), which imposes a severe tax upon my eyes. Carried away, or parted, the lead-line, which was an old one, and the only deep-sea line we have, except one much smaller of sixty fathoms. We were fitted out miserably in Norfolk. The master and passed midshipman differed much in their reckoning. Found we were farther east than I had anticipated. Spent an anxious and uncomfortable day. Such a command is no sinecure. Ah! this life in its most enviable state satisfies not the soul. May God enable me in faith to look to him for help in all things.

"This is the anniversary of my dear mother's death. I have not dwelt much upon it, as my mind has been necessarily occupied with the vessel. She was a lovely character, and her life was a labor of love. How blessed and happy she is now—how enviable her state compared with mine! If our friends who are gone look down upon us, I trust that her smiles may encourage me in the path of duty. I may lose this vessel and lose much of my professional reputation, or I may succeed in taking slavers, and do humanity some service; but, with the exception of doing good to my fellow-men, of how little value is every thing in this life. May God make me to live near him from love to him."

January 14, 1850.—"Yesterday, Sunday, we had service, when I read a sermon by Rev. Sydney Smith on 'Self-examination.' The day was warm, but not oppressive. All was quiet, and I hope it was a profitable Sunday for me. This morning, in fact during the night, the weather was unsettled; but having seen so much thunder and lightning and heavy rain so near the equator, I thought but little of it. At eight, going on deck in Lieutenant Rush's watch, I saw ahead a dark, ugly looking cloud, with the arch just above the horizon, denoting a tornado. By the time we could get studding-sails and all sail in it struck us—blew heavily, but rained more so, with the heaviest peals of thunder and more vivid forks of lightning than are ever seen out of the tropics, away from Africa. The weather prevented our taking observation; for which we were very sorry, as we are so near Cape Ann Shoals. Accomplished nothing more than looking out for the vessels."

January 29, 1850.—"My views are not carried out. While the greater part of the officers are ready to sustain me, and do all in their power to render the vessel effective, and all hands comfortable and happy, a few are adverse and derange every thing; and this, added to the intolerable climate, makes the situation unenviable. I am determined, however, to carry out my own system where I command."

February 27, 1850.—"Progressing favorably, and much relieved in relation to the passage; but very anxious about the coast, as we are in want of proper charts, and have to run in close to examine all places where there are slavers."

April 3, 1850.—"I am quite ill with lumbago and fever. I write this as I may not be able to write any thing more, for I feel that my health is failing me. I have had too much excitement of late; but I trust in God, if it is his will that I die in this foreign land or at sea. I have tried to act well my part, but fear that as a follower of the Lord I have been sadly remiss; still, I cling to him."

April 5, 1850.—"I went out in chase of a vessel, passed the *Cyclops*, and stood for an American brig; fired two guns, not shotted; but on kept the trader till I overhauled and boarded him. He was from New London, loaded with Yankee notions. The English steamer *Pluto* attempted to cut off the chase for us, but our boats had reached her. Thus we have caught every thing which we have seen."

May 29, 1850.—"Some days since my pains were so excessive that I literally gave up and took to my bed. The doctor administered quinine and blisters. I have obtained no relief for many days, but I have still exercised in bed the duties of captain. I feel satisfied that God does for us better than we could do for ourselves. My illness and disappointments have had a good effect upon me in a spiritual sense."

June 17, 1850.—"I wished to remain in port but four days; and, going into my old business of first lieutenant, I had upward of three thousand gallons of water brought on board, ship painted, and rigging overhauled on the fourth day. Double the work in half the time was performed by the vessel's officers and men, who were reduced nearly one half on account of captures, showing how effective my system is compared with the driving system adopted by one of the first lieutenants. I shall in future insist upon my own system being followed. The *Martha* produced quite a sensation here. Our men did not taste a drop of liquor, but all behaved like good men. Hon. Captain Hastings, of the *Cyclops*, called on me, and congratulated me on taking a big prize, and said: 'I am delighted; it is the heaviest blow given to the slave-traders since I have been on the coast.' He thought the moral effect upon Brazilian and American slave-traders, of my having sent all hands to America, would be great. I cruised off Ambriz for a day or two, and was boarded by the captain of H. M. steamer *Pluto*, with whom I had an hour's pleasant chat. My health is improving physically, and I pray it may be spiritually also."

June 28, 1850.—"Employed in getting up cappings, whipping hawsers, etc. Am contented and happy—the doctor reading to me Neander. Lumbago worse than usual to-day, but health and spirits, thank God, much better. All hands are happy, and brig efficient."

July 23, 1850.—"On the morning of the 2d of July, at half-past three o'clock, I was called and informed that a vessel was standing down for us. I at once sent word to the officer of the deck to clear away the battery and send the men to the guns. While dressing I heard a musket fire, and at once ordered a return fire. The brig passed our stern, when we exchanged names and a few words in a courteous manner. I felt as if the commander of the other vessel, having fired first (although we returned it), ought to have explained himself; and, on reflection, concluded to go after him for the purpose of demanding an explanation. I proceeded to Benguela, and remained two days, and then sailed for the *Flying Fish*, the name of H. M. brig for which I was in search. We spoke the *Water Witch*, and were told that she was cruising but a short distance to the northward. Had our guns all cast loose ready for firing, and cruised for the vessel two or three days, when I was informed by the captain of the brig *Spy* that he had relieved the *Flying Fish*, and that she had gone north of the equator. I then proceeded to Ambriz; and supposing that the *Flying Fish* had really gone north, I wrote the following letter to her captain, which I read to Hon. Captain Hastings, and requested him to forward it to Captain Paty:

"'SIR,—On the morning of the 2d of July, as you approached us, a musket was fired from the brig under your command, which was returned by a similar fire from this vessel.

"'I regarded the occurrence as a mistake on your part arising from the obscurity of the night, and supposed that you would avail yourself of the earliest opportunity to explain it.

"'Subsequently, as the vessels passed each other, you made no offer of explanation.

"'I therefore now call upon you for an apology, explaining the circumstances which led to your exceptionable course toward a national vessel of the United States.'

"Captain Hastings informed me that Captain Paty was cruising but a short distance to the northward, and I could see him myself. He asked me if Commander Paty fired after I did. I told him no; if he had, I would have opened our battery upon him. I then left Captain Hastings and cruised for the *Flying Fish* several days, and at length fell in with the object of my search. I sent the purser, Mr. Watmough, on board to ask an apology and an explanation, telling him if it were not promptly made, to hand my letter to Commander Paty. The commander, on receiving Mr. W., at once expressed his regrets that he had fired first, and said he would go on board and see Captain Foote, which he did; and in my cabin apologized fully, and stated that as we had accidentally come up in the wind and were going round, he thought we were trying to get clear of him; and, suspecting that we were a slaver, fired to bring us to, and he stopped when we fired. He said all that he could have said, and fully satisfied me that he regretted the affair, and was ready to make any amend in his power; and this, together with our having returned his musket-fire, satisfied me."

September 28, 1850.—"One year ago to-day I was ordered to the command of the *Perry*. Much has been endured and accomplished. I do not regret having accepted the command; still no one can imagine what

I have been through. In God may my trust be for guidance; and I hope, if it be his will, that on the next anniversary I shall be at home with those I most love."

July 14, 1851.—"Our men, or at least a large part of them, wish to have their grog on account of their bad treatment for hard service and good conduct, and the officers also are in a great state of excitement and indignation. In fact, if we had done nothing we should have fared better. But I am satisfied to go without credit, as I did not act on that principle, but a higher one.

"After staying ten days at Porto Praya, I took the store-keeper aboard, who was almost dead with fever, and sailed for Madeira. I ran through the islands some distance, and went near the wreck of the *Yorktown.* We beat some six or eight vessels in sailing. I feel jaded, worn out, disheartened, and truly 'tired, sad, and weary.' Oh, I am glad that nearly forty-five years of my life have passed. God grant that I may be prepared for a better world."

September 17, 1851.—"I feel great relief on the dark blue sea, away from the sultry coast of Africa, its dangerous reefs and pestilential vapors."

October 25, 1851.—"Last night at sunset saw nine islands, one of them one hundred and ten miles distant. The atmosphere was perfectly clear —a rare phenomenon."

December 12, 1851.—"Thus adieu to the coast of Africa. I hope from my heart to realize the goodness of our heavenly Father in directing me thus far in my course of duty. I shall never perhaps in life be called upon to act again so responsible a part on my own judgment."

These extracts might be multiplied. In their groanings and bitter cries they show the man's inmost spirit. They prove him to be jealous of his country's honor, but noble withal—

"As the flint bears fire,
Which much enforced shows a hasty spark,
And straight is cold again."

They prove him indomitable in sickness, in weariness, in the incompetence and opposition of subordinates, in every difficulty, peril, and discouragement. He had a "system," and he carried it out. He had principles, and he stuck to them "off soundings." He might have erred in over-zeal, but never in cowardly laxness. These extracts prove him to be a first-rate seaman and a most energetic commander. They prove, more than all, that his motives were high and unselfish. He loved the reputation of doing a great deed; he was vividly sensible to the fame it brought, but duty was deeper with him than fame; and from the manner in which he ever afterward spoke of and dwelt upon this African service, it was evidently the thing that gave him most pleasure in life. He had done some good. He had aided the cause of humanity. He had "let the oppressed go free." And however the approval of his superiors in rank caused him lively gratification, and however much he enjoyed the public praise which he had deservedly won, he cherished more than all the simple thought that he had done his duty to his Master, and wrought deliverance for his suffering poor.

CHAPTER IX.

LITERARY LABORS.

THE beginning of the year 1852 found Lieutenant Foote at home with his family in New Haven; and for a period of more than four years he remained ashore, being the longest time up to that date that he had spent on land since he had been in the service. It was a time of general inactivity in naval matters, disturbed only by a little breeze now and then on the fishery question, but not enough to produce a serious movement in the way of naval preparation or reform. Congress had an economical fit; there was much talk about reducing the Navy, naval boards and bureaus were cut down, salaries of officers were discussed, and promotion was slow. Under these circumstances the active mind of Foote sought employment in writing, and in lecturing to public bodies upon temperance and kindred themes. His old friend Commodore Smith thus writes to him: "I congratulate you on your success in your lecture. Being perfectly familiar with the subject, your genius had full scope. No doubt while on the way you made good preparation for the meeting; in traveling one has time to *charge his battery* for the occasion. You could tell the old Jacks how the high officials who legislate for them are disposed to kill King Alcohol." The following is the newspaper report of this, or of a similar lecture:

"Captain A. H. Foote, of the United States Navy, apologized for his lack of preparation for speaking.

"He sketched the character of seamen in the Navy, as affected by various causes under his own observation. He remembered when every seaman was allowed a half-pint of whisky, and he himself proposed the reduction of the allowance to one gill, which was at last effected, and money being paid in place of grog to such as did not draw it, the amount consumed became much reduced. The greatest barrier to the improvement of the moral and spiritual condition of the sailor was intemperance. That sailors would not work without their grog was a great mistake. He had had command in ten vessels of war: for the first six there were no religious services, and they had the 'liquor-rations;' in the remainder they had religious services, and in two of them every man had voluntarily given up his rations of spirits. There were not better organized or more orderly and efficient crews on the ocean. He regretted that while merchantmen were doing away with the grog allowance, our government continues to deal out intoxicating drinks to sailors in its employ, and he called upon the press to present the condition of affairs in the strongest light possible."

The following is also a newspaper report of a lecture he delivered before the American Colonization Society:

"Captain Foote of the United States Navy then addressed the audience at length, stating what he knew of Liberia, from having visited it and spent considerable time there and on the coast of Africa. He spoke highly of President Roberts, and said that when he was in Washington the President asked him how President Roberts succeeded; and he was about to say, in reply, as well as any president; but he thought that would institute too direct a comparison, and he therefore said as well as governors generally. The trade of Liberia amounts to half a million annually. No white man is eligible to office there. Iron ore is found at a distance of twenty miles from the coast in abundance, which is malleable without smelting. The climate is healthy for blacks, and the state of morals such that on one occasion, a short time since, while walking home from church in the city of New Haven in company with a gentleman who had spent some time in Liberia, his friend remarked that he knew no place where the Sabbath was so well observed as it was in New Haven, except at Monrovia, in Liberia. He visited President Roberts often, and had seen the whole people in their various avocations, and he was struck with the great change which they exhibit for the better. There is no person whom he would more cordially welcome to his hospitality and home than President Roberts. He spoke of the interest Great Britain had taken in the colony, and of the fact that its independence has been acknowledged by her as well as by France, Prussia, and Brazil, while we refuse still to acknowledge it. He thought that the squadrons which our government kept on the coast had done much good, and should be continued there. Colonization had destroyed the slave-trade for five hundred miles. The English are acting in good faith in keeping their squadrons on the coast. Colonization and the keeping of an efficient coasting squadron must go together, in order to sustain Liberia and suppress the African slave-trade."

From a more elaborately written lecture upon Christian missions delivered during this period, this extract is taken: "Such are the grounds, my friends, upon which I expressed the opinion that in a few years the Christian religion would rise upon the view of the heathen mind in India; and such also was the impression conveyed to me by the governor-general and several other officers of high intelligence." When we read the accounts of the progress of Christianity in India, and the enlarged and hopeful operations of Christian missions in that vast peninsula; and when we read, too, the words and doings of the disciples of the Brahmo Somaj, although their faith lacks the divine light, we feel that the prophecy of this earnest lover of Christ was not groundless, but that Christian ideas are penetrating the deepest thought of India, and that the popular heart must soon follow the lead of the higher intelligence. Captain Foote was true to the cause of Christian missions, although he had seen their imperfections and discouragements, and was by no means backward in expressing his criticisms; but he cast the whole weight of his influence in favor of this work, and the single-minded, faithful missionary of the Cross always knew where to look, while he was living, for a strong friend and champion of the good cause.

During this period of home life Captain Foote wrote the book to which reference has been made, entitled "Africa and the American Flag."* This volume was dedicated to his true

* Published by the Appletons of New York in 1854.

and loving friend Commodore Smith, who acknowledged the compliment in the following note:

"BUREAU OF YARDS AND DOCKS, *May* 13, 1854.

"MY DEAR SIR,—I received your book two days since, and was sensibly struck with the Dedication, which I had not anticipated. For this modest but kind manifestation of your friendship and regard for me, accept my unfeigned acknowledgments.

"I have but cursorily run through the book. I pronounce it to be excellent in matter and arrangement. This to me will place you in high standing both in and out of the Navy. My kindest regards to your household. I am very truly yours, JOSEPH SMITH.

"Commander A. H. Foote, U. S. Navy,
Naval Asylum, Philadelphia, Pa."

Commodore Smith's estimate of the work is in the main well sustained by the book itself. Although Captain Foote's forte was not writing, but fighting, he succeeded in making a clearly methodized and valuable book, that interweaves in a quiet way the narrative of his own achievements on the African coast with much that is of general interest respecting Africa and the slave-trade, and that has been cited as authority from the bench of United States Courts. The following are some brief extracts from the many criticisms and encomiums which the book brought forth from the press, and which are here introduced as bearing testimony to the public estimation in which the author was held at that time:

"The work is written in excellent spirit, and in an unpretending style that does much credit to the author's good taste, while the religious regard for truth, and the liberality of sentiment manifest in every chapter, win the reader's confidence and esteem. A considerable portion of the volume is devoted to an account of the operations of the American Colonization Society, and all who take an interest in the colonization cause will derive satisfaction from the strongly favorable testimony which Commander Foote bears to the condition of Liberia as a nation."*

* *N. Y. Commercial Advertiser.*

"The speculations of the author regarding the future of Africa are more cheering than those we are accustomed to hear, and as they are based on positive facts and investigations, they are not merely prophecies of a philanthropic heart, but conclusions of a logical mind."*

"The American people may well be proud of their naval officers. Such men as Ingraham, Maury, Kane, Lynch, Foote, and others who might be named, confer honor upon the flag under which they sail, and which their gallantry is ever ready to protect. While looking after the interests of commerce, they have proved themselves awake to the interests of humanity; and while familiar with the arts of war, they have shown themselves equally familiar with the sciences by which the horrors of war may be mitigated or prevented."†

"The ethnographical chapter in this work is worth the books of some authors we might name. The poor despised Bushman, forming to himself with sticks and grass a lair among the low-spreading branches of a shrub, or nestling at sunset in a shallow hole amid the warm sands of the desert, with wife and little ones, like a covey of birds, sheltered by some ragged sheepskins from the dew of the clear sky, has an ancestral and mental relationship to the builders of the pyramids and the colossal temples of Egypt, and to the artists who adorned them."‡

"It contains, in a compendious shape, a complete account of the continent of Africa in all its relations to the United States, physical, commercial, political, and religious. The account of the active cruise in which Commander Foote was engaged for two years is full and circumstantial —too much so, perhaps, for one who reads merely for amusement, but very satisfactory to one who wishes to get complete and reliable information on the important question touching the value of our African squadron. The book has been published in an evil hour for those who are designing, whether by a cowardly connivance or by open and direct sanction, to revive the African slave-trade; but most opportunely for the cause of justice and philanthropy, and (we intend no irony) national honor and faith. We agree with most of the criticisms upon the book which we have seen in commending its literary execution. Commander Foote's style has a sailor-like simplicity, but is wanting neither in elegance nor

* *Graham's Magazine.* † *Philadelphia Presbyterian Banner.*
‡ *N. Y. Independent.*

liveliness. Some of his descriptions, indeed, are full of humor and quiet satire."*

Lieutenant W. B. S. Porter, U. S. N., thus writes in a private letter:

"I am surprised at the amount of information contained in so small a compass, which at the same time forms a complete exposition of the devices of the slave-trader for conducting the traffic and escaping the vigilance of our cruisers. If taken as a guide, it will relieve our commanders of many difficulties in their intercourse with suspected vessels under the American flag. The difficulty which our officers had was to interpret their instructions, which seemed contradictory; but in your work they have the true spirit and the practical illustration of the conduct to be pursued."

Commander Davis, U. S. N., writes:

"To have brought out such a result from an African cruise, from which so many bring nothing, is a proof that your thoughts and sympathies are expanded far beyond the narrow sphere of ship duties—it is proof of an enlarged comprehension and an elevated spirit. Our old friendship gives me the right to praise you without the suspicion of flattery."

A letter from the Rev. Geo. W. Bethune and a notice from the London *Spectator* are all we will add to these extracts. Dr. Bethune says:

"Your notice of Buchanan† is a just tribute to his worth. I knew him well—better than any one else knew him—and he has never yet received an estimation sufficiently high for a combination of admirable qualities mingled with but few faults. You have correctly estimated the difficulty and danger of his acting against the slavers, as he did without legal or any authority, and when he was liable to extreme prosecution before any admiralty court. The last night I saw Buchanan he bade me farewell at midnight. He came, he said, to state his difficulty and ask my advice, which he said he was determined to follow, as to his assuming or not the responsibility of seizing and punishing slavers. My answer was, 'Buchanan, authority or no authority, if you find a slaver on land or on sea, *blow him sky high!*'

* *The New-Englander.*

† Buchanan was one of the black founders and presidents of the colony of Liberia.

"He grasped my hand, looked me steadily in the face for at least a minute, and then, without a word, left me. I never saw him again; but among the earliest letters I had from him was one inclosing an account of the battle of the barracoons, and these words, 'Dear Dominie, I have blown him sky high.'

"I thank you again for your capital book, which is, I trust, designed for great usefulness."

The opening and concluding paragraphs of the critical article from the London *Spectator* are these:

"This quaint-looking title indicates the contents of the volume exactly. The book contains a geographical and historical sketch of Africa, or rather of Negroland, and an account of the doings of the American squadron on the slave-coast. It is the result of much African experience, which infuses into the volume living knowledge, definite ideas, and a certain degree of vigor. * * *

"Captain Foote lays it down broadly that unless the American squadron is efficiently kept up, the slave-trade will become as active as ever under the American flag. The best mode of proceeding is for a British and an American ship to sail together, so as always to be within easy communication. In this way every thing can be overhauled: the American taking vessels sailing under the American flag, the British those of her own or any other nation with which she has right-of-search treaties; for the Americans only meddle with their own people. Indications frequently turn up of the delicacy required in dealing with American vessels, from the difficulties springing from the techiness of their naval officers, and the over-zeal of British officers, not always free from a desire to make prizes."

It is not necessary to speak further in detail of the book itself, but only to say that, with some faults of repetition and of ambitiousness of style, and here and there of an appearance of its having been compiled rather than created, it is work well done—surprisingly well done—considering that its author had studied ships and gunnery more than making books; and it is a genuine and manly contribution to the literature of an important subject from personal observation; and when the names of those who have thought and suffered for Africa shall be gathered into a bright crown, the name of Andrew Hull Foote will not be forgotten.

We also find Commander Foote, in January, 1855, delivering an address upon the "Ashburton Treaty" and "Consular Sea-letters," which was afterward published in pamphlet form, and which gained him much credit as a brief, forcible, and pointed argument setting forth and sustaining these propositions: 1st. That our consuls abroad should not be allowed to give *sea-letters*, as they are called, to American vessels sold abroad, when such vessels are bound to Africa. 2d. That the expense of our African squadron is not nearly so large as has been commonly represented. 3d. That most beneficial results may be expected from a cordial co-operation between our own and British cruisers for the suppression of the slave-trade, and that in no other way can the disgraceful abuse of the American flag be suppressed. 4th. That if any change in the Ashburton Treaty is to be made, it should be to alter the terms, so that instead of a stipulated number of guns to be kept by us upon that coast, we should employ a number of small steamers, as being much better adapted to that service; but that in any case, treaty or no treaty, a hearty co-operation with the British squadron is all important.

It is needful that a word should be said in regard to the official rank and special professional services of Captain Foote during this four years' period of life ashore, which interval appears to have been by no means uselessly spent when viewed in a purely professional light. In December (19) of 1852 Lieutenant Foote was promoted to the rank of commander; and in the year 1854 (March 9) he was ordered to the Naval Asylum in Philadelphia as executive officer under Commodore Storer, governor of the asylum, where he remained for fifteen months; and he is said to have introduced some valuable reforms in the practical working and discipline of the institution. In 1855 (June 20) he was appointed to a membership of the "Naval Efficiency Board" at Washington, under Act of February 28th, 1855, together with Shubrick, Perry, McCowley, Stribling, Bigelow, Pendergrast, Missroon, Buchanan, Dupont, Barron, Godon, Page, W. L. Maury, and Biddle. He attended to the duties of that office until he took command of the *Portsmouth*. During all this time his correspondence indicates a desire for sea-service, although there is abundant proof of his activity for good in the more quiet positions which for a time he then occupied.

Hon. John A. Foote relates that he once rather unexpectedly visited his brother while he was stationed at the Naval Asylum in Philadelphia. He was told by the sentinel that at that hour Commander Foote was at his regular weekly religious meeting. Before reaching the door of the apartment, he caught the voice of the speaker, and listened outside to hear what he was saying. He was speaking plainly and earnestly of the peculiar temptations of the sailor, and telling his audience that he himself was as a brand plucked from the burning; but that happily there was room and time for repentance given to all, and that they who were now in this snug harbor had a most favorable opportunity for reformation. He closed his remarks with a fervent prayer. After the meeting, John walked into the room, and received from his brother a friendly but pretty severe blow for not letting himself be known, and was immediately introduced by the commander to the old tars as his brother from Ohio, who would deliver a temperance address to them that evening, to which superimposed appointment he was rigidly held.

During all this comparatively long period of his stay on shore, Foote was not unobservant of public affairs, especially those that related to his own department, as may be seen from a strong letter addressed by him in the winter of 1855 to Senators Seward, Clayton, Chase, and Sumner in regard to the "Navy Efficiency Bill," protesting against this important measure's being killed by amendments, and urging public men to their duty in this regard.

CHAPTER X.

CRUISE OF THE "PORTSMOUTH" AND TAKING OF THE "BARRIER FORTS."

COMMANDER FOOTE received his appointment to the *Portsmouth*—ordered to the East India station to join Commodore Armstrong's fleet—April 5, 1856. He was already tired of life on shore, and longed to see blue water again. He had applied for a Mediterranean station, but, fortunately for his naval reputation, a cruise involving more responsibility and more arduous professional service was now opened to him.

The sloop-of-war *Portsmouth* was one of the finest vessels at that time in the American Navy. She was a ship of splendid qualities, a very fast sailer, and with a new and heavy battery.

In this "battery" of the *Portsmouth*, Dahlgren, who had already developed his talent for scientific gunnery, felt a special pride; and we forestall the order of events a little to insert here a long letter addressed to Foote by Dahlgren upon the subject of ordnance, which, to professional men at least, will prove interesting:

"ORDNANCE OFFICE, WASHINGTON, *January* 8, 1857.

"MY DEAR FOOTE,—Your letter from Hong-Kong came to me in good season, and I was much pleased to hear that you made the trip out so satisfactorily. I had previously seen your letters to the commodore and to the bureaus. From all, I infer that the new battery was so far an improvement as to locate the burden most favorably; for no ship, not even a clipper, could bowl off ten, eleven, twelve knots for days in succession, and reach even fourteen and a half, unless the weights she carried were right in quantity and place. The complaining of the decks only proves that service and time had unfitted it for bearing the burden in guns which it had always carried to this time; and if renewed, as it should have been, would not have complained. The other inconveniences are not so readily disposed of, for I fear the length of the gun is too much for the width of deck, particularly in the gangways, where boats and spars are stowed. One foot between muzzle and side is necessary for a convenient recoil, and eighteen inches would be better still; for the activity of the piece has been inconveniently increased by the use of lignum-vitæ trucks in lieu of ordinary ones; it may yet be requisite to come to the shorter 8-inch (of 55 cwt.). The power of the battery is, however, unquestioned, and with a fair chance for the ship's fine sailing, she would be an ugly customer for many larger ships. The results with the new ships are entirely satisfactory as regards the ordnance. The *Merrimack* was well overhauled in England, and all accounts, private and public, concur that the guns made much impression. Jones, who you know is a competent witness, says they 'were particularly admired, the naval and military men admitting that they were constructed on proper principles.' 'Somehow or other it became known that I knew something of them, and repeated applications were made for their dimensions, etc.' The Chief of Bureau also showed me a letter from Sir Howard Douglas asking information of them. The Navy Department has finally recognized my service in the matter, and in terms which are as complimentary as any one could desire. Still I have had to wait for many weary years, and when the *Merrimack* left the United States, it was not known beyond official circles that I had any particular concern in her battery; so that I am not chargeable with having obtruded myself on the public attention. Jones tells me that he had 'conversed with many of the officers who served actively in the late war, all of whom express themselves very decidedly in favor of heavy calibres, though they differ as to the relative value of shot and shell. I should judge, however, from the changes now taking place, that the shells are gaining favor; for instance, the *Princess Royal* was just recommissioned, having been paid off only a few days before, and her entire gun-deck battery is now composed of eight 65-pounder guns.' Before there were 32-pounders on that deck. There is, moreover, a marked sentiment growing up in England favorable to heavy guns, and a disposition to rival us. In the *Excellent*, Jones saw a long 68-pounder, of 95 cwt., mounted on a broadside carriage. 'Eighteen men worked it with as much ease as the crews of the other guns worked theirs.' He adds, 'Captain Peel, of the *Shannon* (their new crack frigate), told me that he had applied to have his main-deck battery of 8-inch changed for them (68-pounders, of 95 cwt.), gun for gun.' That is going it heavy, and rather bluffs the notion of some of our own officers, who opposed even 9-inch guns, on the ground that they were too heavy, and stick to it still, though they weigh 9000 pounds, and the English 68-pounder weighs 10,600 pounds. 'Prove all things, and hold fast that which is good,' says *the* Book. Mr. Bull is stirred, however, as one would judge, when our officers saw a gun manned in the *Excellent* by lieutenants; their zeal must be rampant. The spirit of inquiry is clearly abroad, and we frequently meet persons sent here by other governments to take note of our progress. Lately I have been visited by a scientific officer from France and two from Russia, besides a commission from England previously, and officers from Sweden, etc. These chaps ask to see every thing without apology, while they are precious particular to show nothing to those (few enough) whom we send. Indeed, it is said that the French Minister of War was rude to our commission.

"The *Merrimack* was five weeks at Portsmouth, ten days at Brest, two weeks at Lisbon, and at the last accounts had reached Cadiz, whence she will come back by way of the West Indies. The *Wabash* gets along well. She has taken a relief to the St. Mary's, at the Isthmus, and will soon be in the United States with the old crew. I am told she is fast under sail. The other ships are gradually being prepared for sea, and the Secretary told me that he would send one to the Pacific. Hudson is to command the *Niagara*, with Pennock as first; but the ship will hardly be ready before April—the steam is behindhand. The French constructor who was here had examined her closely, and told me that he considered her strength ample. Our constructors say not. I wonder who is right? The death of Mr. Steers was most deplorable; a brief moment sealed his plans and his hopes here forever.

The *Niagara* is now in dock to receive the propeller, and has been all in order for some months. I confess she pleases my eye, though officers generally are averse to her entirely. The difference comes of taking a different view of the subject. I agree that she requires much to perfect her as a man-of-war, and no one officer of the Navy did more than myself to remedy the deficiency of the battery, and the result was only prevented by the fact that the original plan had been too far carried out to introduce an armament on the gun-deck. But I go beyond the shortcomings of the *Niagara* herself, in order to consider how far her unquestioned merits can be turned to account in building other ships. Present notions do really proceed on the basis that clipper lines and clipper speed are incompatible with the carrying of a heavy battery. I have believed otherwise, with the proviso that the ends be not loaded with guns or other freight. Now if the *Niagara* have the speed her builder claimed, and will preserve her form as well as other ships, the main point is settled, and any carpenter can raise her gun-deck and pierce ports when the course of service takes the repair so low. With thirty 9-inch guns below, and the twelve 11-inch above, she will have a broadside of 2000 pounds—nearly equal in weight, and superior in all else to any three-decker in the British Navy. It is, indeed, to be regretted that the stiff-neckedness of Navy constructors have forced us outside to solve the problem; but so it is, and officers must take a comprehensive view of the subject, and not admire the *Niagara* for her single deck of heavy guns, nor condemn her for the want of the lower tier. The true question is elsewhere; and had Steers lived, no one would have taken the lesson more aptly, for the man whose *second* sailing-ship was the *Niagara* must have been of no ordinary stamp.

"I have now to tell you somewhat of the *Plymouth*. In course of last summer the Secretary decided to assign her to me as an ordnance ship, and she came up here in October as soon as the midshipmen were landed. I am to have a fair sweep, and have begun. The light deck is to remain, and the new battery is to be four 9-inch guns and one of 11 inches on pivot, giving a broadside of 279 pounds, or one fourth less than before in weight thrown, but much superior in all else. The third, fifth, and eighth ports are occupied, which removes the weight of four 32-pounders forward, and of six abaft. Weight of guns and carriages thirty tons, or just one half that formerly carried. Now if the innovations of the *Portsmouth* have stirred the waters, what may be said of the *Plymouth?* It has to go for all that. As things now look, it will be May before I get into the broad Atlantic, and then—good luck, I hope. The folks are puzzled, probably, that a man with a snug berth should insist on pushing out to sea, when he is not asked to do so. Even the Chief of Bureau thinks the anchors ought to be down; but I would never be content to aim below the mark, and if I am to manage the craft she must take her tour of sea duty. Then I am asked, 'Well, *what* are you going to do?' To which the answer is, 'I will tell you when I come in.' I wish you were nearer—within visiting distance; but I shall not cross the line. * * * The Senate bill to overhaul the retired list has been reported by the House Committee unaltered, but will have a hard fight to get through. Tom Turner is woefully exercised, and wrote to me to stop it right off, instead of voyaging this way and stopping it himself. Very easy to encourage others, as was done before at long range. Let each man take his trick, and Jupiter may help the concern.

"*January* 13.—Well, the bill was taken up yesterday, and so far from a hard fight, as I expected, it passed off-hand by a vote of three to one. Its details I am not acquainted with, but I believe it offers a court of inquiry to any of the retired who may apply. Whatever may be thought of the Efficiency Bill itself, or of its amendment, there can be little doubt that Congress is entirely unfit to deal with the question. First they insisted on a most extreme clause (that of dropping) as a *sine qua non*, and now they wheel right about and eat dirt, as the Turk says. The final effect, as matters now stand, will be the gain for the nonce of those who have actually fingered the parchment; those who have not, may hug the hope of some future reform.

"The disposition of ships in our own waters, or soon to return, are: *Merrimack*, on the way home from Cadiz through the West Indies; *Wabash*, just in New York from the Isthmus—flag-ship of home squadron; *Roanoke*, nearly ready for sea; *Colorado*, about the summer; *Niagara*, in the spring; *Minnesota*, went to Philadelphia by her own steam, to be coppered—not to go to sea till after the others; *Franklin*, not yet launched; *Powhatan*, refitted with new ordnance (9-inch and 11-inch), at Norfolk, nearly ready; *Cumberland*, razeed to carry 9-inch and 10-inch, progressing at Boston. It is supposed that the Ten Sloop Bill will pass the house, in which case we ought to look for something fine. The new French frigates are not so large as ours, with batteries as usual, and a great increase of steam-power; they talk of twelve knots. The English, too, are on the lookout; but as there is no war, will probably feel the way well before going in too largely.

"*January* 21.—After an unusual scarcity of snow, it has come down with a vengeance, as the paper says—twelve inches on the level, and three feet in drifts. Pleasant news from *Wabash:* yards square, ship rolling, the muzzles on gun-deck under—cast loose, and practiced. Captain and first lieutenant report that the 9-inch guns were perfectly under control, though the sea washed in on the deck and wet the cartridges while loading. So another bugbear is disposed of, and it is ascertained that guns of this weight on broadside carriages are not unmanageable, as the growlers would have it. *Per contra*, a fall parted while setting up lower rigging in heavy weather; killed one man, and hurt several others

—captain among them. I wonder that the growlers are not opposed to lower rigging. When new, it is apt to stretch, and if a ship is caught in a gale, and setting up has to be done, why some accident is *possible.* Many applications from the retired list have been made, and there is much speculation as to results. Some supposed that but few would apply, and that fewer will return; others are of the opposite notion. The Secretary is said to be busy in arranging the programme.

"The steamer just in at Halifax telegraphs news of the British attack on Canton, and says also that the *Portsmouth* has been filibustering, which I deny, of course, as you were even opposed to the annexation of Texas. However, they will let you off, if you have made good gunnery. And, my good friend, you have the best evidence in my power that I often think of you. Such a document as a letter of seven pages from me is certainly not extant. Write when you can, and believe me that my best wishes for health and prosperity ever attend you.

"Sincerely and warmly your friend,

"J. A. Dahlgren.

"P. S.—I forgot to say that your kind arrangement for some of the books will be borne in mind—in case I should be driven to the necessity of looking to dollars and cents; but I hope that they will reach the officers without cost to them. Much to my annoyance, constant attention to other affairs than my own has embarrassed me. Each book has taxed my pocket more or less, while the number taken and price paid by Uncle Sam is but a partial relief. However, the book is complete, and will soon be in the binder's hands; the size of page is equal to that of Douglas's 'Gunnery,' and the number about 450.

"I am much pleased to hear that Mr. Simpson has a turn for gunnery, and I should like much if he were disengaged and near the *Plymouth.* My best regards to all the officers of the *P.*"

To return now to the narrative of the actual cruise of the *Portsmouth.* That vessel sailed from Norfolk, Virginia, May 4, 1856; and after a passage of ninety-five days, in which she encountered heavy gales, reached Batavia, where the officers were most hospitably entertained by the Dutch authorities and people. From Batavia the *Portsmouth* proceeded directly to Hong-Kong, and remained there for a month or so; then, from the fact of not finding Commodore Armstrong at that port, and also from the fact of a difficulty having arisen between the English and Chinese (on account of the contemptuous treatment of the British flag), which threatened to result in war, Commander Foote took his ship up the Canton River to Whampoa. While at Hong-Kong, Captain Foote had a correspondence with Sir John Bowring in regard to the summary trial of an American seaman by British authorities, which, however, needs no further notice.

These were troublous times in the Chinese waters; but, as a proof of the disposition of our officers to avoid difficulty with the Chinese in the war which had already sprung up between them and the English, the following circular, issued by Commander Foote, may be adduced:

> "The undersigned has been informed that the American flag was this day borne on the walls of Canton through the breach effected by the British naval forces. This unauthorized act is wholly disavowed by the undersigned, in order that it may not be regarded as compromising in the least degree the neutrality of the United States.
>
> "The United States naval forces are here for the special protection of American interests; and the display of the American flag in any other connection is hereby forbidden.
>
> "ANDREW H. FOOTE,
>
> "Senior Officer, commanding U. S. Naval Forces at Canton.
>
> "CANTON, *October* 29, 1856."

On arriving at Whampoa, Commander Foote, in view of the unsettled state of affairs, at once organized a force of eighty men into companies, and established and fortified posts in Canton in a manner best fitted to protect the lives and property of American residents of that city. He was also enabled incidentally to afford aid and protection to French residents, for which he was formally thanked by the French *Chargé d'Affaires* at Macao. He issued an order to American sentinels to avoid firing upon the Chinese except when directly assailed; and he enjoined upon all under his command scrupulously to keep the peace. He seems, indeed, to have done what he could to prevent Americans from being drawn into the English and Chinese imbroglio, although fighting was going on all around him, and his own ship was endangered from flying shots and combustibles; and thus for three weeks he preserved an armed neutrality, and protected American interests. In the mean time Commodore Armstrong had arrived at Hong-Kong from Shang-Haï. In order to avoid the danger of compromising our neutrality, the commodore ordered the removal of the American force from the city of Canton. To expedite these arrangements, Commander Foote was actively engaged; and on one occasion, while returning from Canton to the *San Jacinto,* then lying at Whampoa, his boat was fired upon by the Chinese, which uncalled-for and outrageous act resulted in the capture and destruction of the Chinese "Barrier Forts" in the Canton River. A detailed though modest account of this affair, in which the fiery bravery and military skill of Commander Foote were so conspicuous, is given in his own words in an official report to his commanding officer. It contains some unimportant particulars, but we have preferred to give the whole letter on account of its intrinsic interest to American readers:

"UNITED STATES SHIP 'PORTSMOUTH,'
Off the 'Barrier Forts,' near Canton, *Nov.* 26, 1856.

"SIR,—Agreeably to your orders of the 15th instant to return to Canton and resume my duties in command of the force placed there for the protection of American residents in their persons and property, I proceeded the same day, with one of our boats, in company with Lieutenant Macomb of this ship, Assistant-Surgeon Gibson of the *Levant,* and Messrs. Sturgis and Macy of Canton, for the purpose of directing Commander Smith to return and take his ship (the *Levant*) to that city, preparatory to the withdrawal of our force from the foreign factories.

"When within point-blank range of the fort commanding the passage, a shot was fired, which fell a short distance from the boat; this was soon followed by another, which struck still nearer the boat, and ricochetted far beyond it—Mr. Sturgis in the mean time waving the flag that it might be fully displayed, and I firing my revolver toward the fort, and giving the order to pull away. We soon passed beyond range of the fort; and

THE "BARRIER FORTS."

when within two hundred yards of the next, it opened upon us with two successive discharges of round shot and grape, which fell thick and fast around us, one of them striking the water within two blades of the oars; the last discharge was made after the boat's head was turned toward the ship. I then returned and reported the occurrence verbally to you.

"As the removal of this ship and the *Levant* to this place was under your own orders and personal supervision, and as you yourself were an eye-witness of the cannonading between the *Portsmouth* and the forts on Sunday, the 16th instant, it is unnecessary in this report to make further allusion to those events.

"During the day succeeding your departure to Whampoa, the two ships were in position to open upon the forts on the recommencement of active hostilities on the part of the enemy—although the narrow channel and strong tide rendered it necessary to move them abreast of, instead of in a line with each other.

"Your last communication of the 19th instant contained the following clause:

"'I am glad to hear that you are at this instant strong enough to accomplish any thing I may direct; and although, pending negotiation, I do not wish to take aggressive steps without a sufficient cause, yet I repeat my wish to have the enemy prevented from increasing his means of defense or assault, in the most expedient and efficient manner your judgment and means may warrant, even though you may be led to the capture of the forts.'

"As there were no other means in my power effectually to prevent the enemy from strengthening his defenses, I immediately determined to storm his forts, and would have done so the same evening if it had been possible to complete the necessary arrangements before dark.

"At 6.30 on the morning of the 20th instant, both ships being in position and in all respects ready for action, we beat to quarters, and simultaneously opened on the two nearest forts. After an interval of five minutes the fire was briskly returned until 7.45, when it materially slackened. The storming-party, consisting of two hundred and eighty-seven persons—officers, seamen, and marines—with four howitzers, commanded by myself—Commanders Bell and Smith leading respectively detachments from the *San Jacinto* and *Levant*—then left the ships, and pulled in three columns for the shore. The company of marines was most efficiently led by Captain Simms. While landing, Louis Hetzel and Thomas Krouse (apprentice boys) were killed by the accidental discharge of a Minie rifle. The party formed, and marched toward the fort, dragging three howitzers with them across the rice-fields, and wading a creek waist deep. In order to attack the fort in the rear it was necessary to pass through a village, in which several shots were fired upon us, till the howitzers cleared the streets, and secured for us an unobstructed progress. When near the fort the soldiers were seen fleeing from it, many of them swimming for the opposite shore. The marines, being in advance, opened fire upon the fugitives with deadly effect, killing some forty or fifty. The American flag was planted on the walls of the fort by a lieutenant from the *Portsmouth*. As the fort opposite was playing upon us, the guns we had captured—fifty-three in number—were several of them brought to bear upon and soon silenced it, but not before a shot had struck the *Portsmouth's* launch and sunk her. She floated, however, at the flood, and was soon rendered efficient for further service. The city of Canton being only four miles distant, a portion of its army, variously estimated at from five to fifteen thousand, and which I believe to have numbered at least three thousand, was stationed near. This force twice advanced; but they were both times repulsed by the marines, with ten or twelve killed; and, as they were retreating, a deadly fire was opened upon them from one of the howitzers. During one of these skirmishes a man belonging to the *Portsmouth* received a shot-wound in the leg. While firing at the opposite fort, a boatswain's mate from the *Portsmouth* was wounded in the head and foot by the bursting of a gun.

"A small portion of the force was withdrawn at night, and the fort was occupied by the commander of the *San Jacinto* with the remaining force till morning.

"At three A.M. the next day an 8-inch shot from one of the forts struck the *Portsmouth* and lodged in the bends. This was instantly returned by three of her shells, and the fort was at once silenced. At four A.M. the commander of the *San Jacinto*, with the force which had occupied the captured fort during the night, embarked and returned to the ship. At six o'clock both ships opened their fire on the three remaining forts, which was at first briskly returned. During the action Edward Riley (O. S.) was mortally wounded aboard the *Levant*, and died this evening. The fort nearest the ships having been silenced, at seven o'clock the boats in tow of the American steamer *Cum Fa*, temporarily in the charge of Mr. Robinet, left the ship and proceeded toward the object of attack. While passing the barrier, a ricochet 64-pound shot from the farthest fort struck the boat abreast of my own, completely raking it, and instantly killing James Hoagland, carpenter's mate, and mortally wounding William Mackie and Alfred Turner, who died soon after. Seven others were also wounded more or less severely. The boat struck was the launch of the *San Jacinto*, in charge of the first lieutenant of that ship. The steamer stood in with the boats in tow, till they were covered by an intervening neck of land, on which the party landed. After wading a ditch waist deep, and receiving several shots from gingals and rockets, the fort was carried, with one of the marines severely wounded, in presence of a thousand or more Chinese soldiers just beyond howitzer range. A corporal of marines, the standard-bearer of the company, planted the American flag upon the walls. Several of the guns of the fort, with our own howitzers, were brought to bear upon the centre fort, commanding the river, which had opened fire upon us. It was soon silenced. The other guns in the fort we had captured, which were altogether forty-one in number, were spiked, their carriages burned, and every thing destructible, by the means in our power, destroyed.

"At four P.M. the marines advanced on the bank of the river and captured a breastwork mounting six guns; a party of Chinese soldiers, some hundreds in number, advanced toward them, but were soon repulsed by two companies of sailors, led by their lieutenants. In the mean time one of the howitzers played upon a still greater number, who were drawn up in front of and around a pagoda, until they were dispersed, and retreated carrying off their killed and wounded. The boats, under fire from the fort on the opposite side of the river, had been tracked up to the breastwork, and now, under cover of its guns and those of the fort just captured, they crossed with the party to the island, and took possession of its fort, containing thirty-eight guns; one of these was a brass gun, of 8-inch calibre, and twenty-two feet five inches in length. The standard-bearer of marines was again the first to plant the American flag upon the walls. The same work of destruction was here renewed. The only fort remaining in the possession of the enemy on the Canton side of the river at once opened upon us. Accordingly the guns in the fort we occupied were brought to bear, and, with the assistance of the howitzers, silenced it in the course of half an hour. It now being dark, it was thought expedient to suspend further operations till morning. Active preparations were making by the enemy during the night, showing a determination to make a vigorous resistance.

"The following morning, Saturday, the 22d instant, at four o'clock, all hands were called, and arrangements made preparatory to the attack in front of the fourth and last fort. At early daylight, every thing being ready, the first lieutenant of the *San Jacinto*, who was left in charge of the fort, was directed to fire a single howitzer, for the purpose of drawing the fire of the enemy. As this did not succeed, another discharge was made, with no better result. Three howitzers were left in the fort to cover the landing, and prevent the enemy from firing the guns trained on the point which we were to double. Our launch, with the howitzers, preceded the other boats, which followed in three columns. The howitzers commenced playing briskly to divert the fire of the fort from us. But, from the moment we doubled the point, and during the time intervening until we reached within musket-shot and gave three cheers—notwithstanding the rapid and effective fire of the howitzers in the fort and the launch—the hostile fort opened and continued a brisk fire upon the boats with round shot, grape, and gingals. The shot passed closely over our heads, with the exception of three, one of which passed between the two boats, and each of the others striking an oar.

"As the boats could not be brought close to the shore, our party jumped into the water, and thus entered and took possession of the fort, just in time to fire upon the last of the enemy in their retreat. It was discovered that they had, before evacuating, loaded the guns, and trained them upon the boats with a slow match ignited. Those of our men who were in advance cut the train. A boatswain's mate from the *Portsmouth* was the first to enter the fort and plant the American flag upon its walls. The number of guns which it contained was thirty-eight. The fort was demolished.

"The forts contained a total of 176 guns, many of them of the largest calibre. I am told that they have always been considered as among the strongest defenses of the empire, as well as the key to the city of Canton.

"The commander of the *San Jacinto* is to-day at work in the fort last captured, preparing utterly to demolish that part of the walls facing the river; these are of massive granite, and eight feet in thickness. As soon as this work is accomplished, we shall proceed in the same way with the other forts. An attack was made upon the rear of the fort occupied by our force at three o'clock this morning by a body of Chinese, who threw several rockets and stink-pots. The assailants were provided with scaling-ladders. They were soon dispersed by a brisk fire of musketry and the howitzers, leaving two ladders behind them in their retreat.

"The ships received during the cannonading of the 16th, 20th, and 21st instants forty shots in their hulls and rigging—the *Portsmouth* eighteen, the *Levant* twenty-two; and their fire was most satisfactorily effective, as may be witnessed on the demolished parapets of the nearest forts and their appearance within the walls.

"Previous to all the attacks I counseled freely with the commanders of the *San Jacinto* and *Levant;* and as the latter's officer performed such effective service by the cannonading of his ship previous to the storming, and as the other was present without his ship, I may be permitted to say of the former that I found him ready to suggest and to execute at any moment and in all exigencies. I ought to mention that the commander of the *Levant*, previous to the action of the 20th and 21st instants, had brought his ship into position nearer the forts, so that she received the hottest of their fire, and he has now brought her close to the fort which we are undermining. From the other officers also I received very important suggestions. In short, the bearing of all the officers, sailors, and marines was creditable to them in the highest degree.

"The readiness and coolness with which Captain Curry, of the American steamer *Willamette*, towed this ship into position, on the 16th instant, under fire from the nearest fort, exposing himself and his vessel, and not 'casting off' till so ordered, excites our highest admiration. Mr. William

M. Robinet, of Maryland, now a resident merchant in Canton, gave his services as pilot and commander of the *Cum Fa*, when that steamer towed the boats inshore to attack the second fort. This gentleman also, by his knowledge of the country, was able to point out the course adopted in the attack of the second and third forts, and suggested the time of the attack upon the third and last.

"Captain Henry Devens, of Charlestown, Massachusetts, voluntarily acted as my aid in the capture of the last three forts, and was ready to render good service. Captain Sewall, of the American ship *Flyaway*, occasionally took charge of the steamer *Cum Fa*, and repeatedly volunteered to serve in any capacity wherein he could promote the success of the expedition. Several other American gentlemen, whose names have not been mentioned, volunteered their aid, and rendered important assistance.

"It may be seen in this report how efficient our marines are in service of this kind; and the inference is inevitable that an increase of that corps, and of the number of officers and men attached to our ships, would tend to insure success in like expeditions. In all the advances, the men were ready, in perfect order and discipline, to respond to the call of their officers.

"It is but just also to the sailors to say that their order and subordination, as well as their bravery, most favorably impressed me; and I was convinced that when the two bodies acted in co-operation, in skirmishing parties and otherwise, they were capable of successfully resisting any Chinese force which they might encounter.

"The howitzers contributed greatly to—I may say secured—the success of the expedition, not only by their destructive qualities, but by the fear which their appearance inspired among the enemy.

"I can not help believing that the heavy and prolonged cannonading of the *Portsmouth*, on the 16th instant, was most important in preparing the way for the operations which succeeded. The powerful battery of this ship, consisting of sixteen 8-inch shell-guns, each of 63 cwt., so paralyzed the nearest fort, which was within a range of four hundred and eighty yards, that it was never afterward able to do the injury which it might otherwise have inflicted. I am disposed to believe, too, that a ship with guns of smaller calibre could not have sustained alone the hot fire to which this vessel was that day exposed from the four forts combined; and much less could have silenced the two nearest of those forts, as she did after a brisk cannonading of between two and three hours.

I am happy to add that the new elevating screws of Constructor Hartt, with which her guns are fitted, stood the severe test of the heavy firing during the several actions to my entire satisfaction.

"It is, of course, impossible to ascertain definitely what loss the Chinese have sustained. Their own rumors make it, at the least estimate, five hundred—although I am inclined to believe that it will not exceed one half that number. It is said, on good authority, that a hundred and twenty Chinese sailors, recently discharged from a foreign man-of-war, and who have thus had the advantage of European training and discipline, were among those who served the guns of the forts. This accounts for the superior gunnery displayed by the enemy.

"It becomes my painful duty to add the following list of killed and wounded (seven killed and twenty-two wounded); and I can only express in this place my feeling of sorrow for the loss which their own friends have sustained, and which the country and the service to which they belonged have also suffered. It is proper for me to mention that, by request of the fleet-surgeon, the surgeons of the ships were not permitted to accompany the storming-parties on shore, as the most important operations could not be performed on the field, but on board ship. All that medical skill could do to relieve the sufferings and save the lives of the wounded was promptly and successfully accomplished.

(Surgeon's report omitted.)

"I am, very respectfully, your obedient servant,

"(Signed) Andrew H. Foote,

"Commander and Senior Officer present commanding U. S. Naval Forces, off the Barrier Forts, near Canton.

"Commodore James Armstrong, commanding U. S. Naval Forces, East Indies and China Seas.

"P. S.—Subjoined is a list of the officers of the several storming-parties:

"Commander Andrew H. Foote . . . . *Portsmouth*, Commanding.
" Henry H. Bell . . . . . *San Jacinto.*
" William Smith . . . . . *Levant.*
Lieutenant Henry H. Lewis . . . . . *San Jacinto.*
" John Rutledge . . . . . "
" S. P. Carter . . . . . . "
Assistant-Surgeon R. P. Daniel. . . . "
Captain's Clerk William S. Aske . . . "

Brevet-Captain John D. Simms, Marines . *San Jacinto.*
Lieutenant William H. Macomb . . . *Portsmouth.*
" Henry K. Davenport . . . "
" Edward Simpson . . . . "
" Pendleton G. Watmough . . "
" George E. Belknap . . . . "
Master Francis E. Sheppard . . . . . "
2d Lieut., Marines, Wm. W. Kirkland . "
Purser John V. Dobbin . . . . . "
Assistant-Surgeon John Vanzant . . . "
Carpenter Joseph G. Meyers . . . . . "
Master's Mate Peter McAvoy . . . . "
Lieutenant George Colvocoresses . . . *Levant.*
" John J. Guthrie . . . . . "
" Earl English . . . . . . "
Master H. A. Adams . . . . "
Assistant-Surgeon A. S. Gihon . . . . "
2d Lieutenant, Marines, H. Tyler, Jr. . . "
Captain's Clerk S. A. Coale, Jr. . . . . "
Carpenter Edward Williams . . . . "
Gunner H. M. Gordon . . . . "
Master's Mate Fitch Taylor . . . . . "

"A. H. F."

CHAPTER XI.

REMARKS ON THE TAKING OF THE "BARRIER FORTS."—CRUISE OF THE "PORTSMOUTH" CONCLUDED.

THE action narrated in the preceding chapter, in the judgment of competent witnesses, was, in a military point of view, a brilliant one. The English and French were loud in their praises; and as the gallant *Portsmouth* dropped down the river, the ship of the British admiral, Sir Michael Seymour, as well as his commodore's vessel, manned the rigging, and gave three rousing cheers for the *Portsmouth*, while the bands struck up "Hail Columbia" and "Yankee Doodle"—a compliment rarely paid to our ships by rival nations.

This action made a deep impression. In China, to this day, Commander Foote is well remembered; and the storming of the "Barrier Forts" taught the mandarins a lesson which they never forgot, made the American flag respected even by that stolid and peculiar people, and led the way to the advantageous treaties of Mr. Reed and Mr. Burlingame.

The battle was varied in its emergencies by sea and land, and called forth the best judgment as well as courage of the commanding officer; and although he was opposed by semi barbarians, the odds in respect to numbers were great on the side of the Chinese—some 5000 to 280 Americans. The forts were strong, and capable of doing immense mischief if further strengthened. But Foote did not wait for this. He urged upon the commodore the necessity of immediate reprisals for the insult to our flag and the wanton assault upon the boats, feeling that a lesson should be given. The commodore was on board the *Portsmouth* during the first cannonading, but, being ill, he withdrew, leaving all in the hands of Foote. He, in fact, took the responsibility and carried the thing through. The boldness with which his vessels were laid alongside the forts, up to the very teeth of the cannon, and the straight, impetuous storming work which followed their cannonade, remind us of a scene more fresh in our memories, and are characteristic of the man and of his mode of going to work.

The American Government added its approval of the conduct of her Navy on this occasion. The following is an extract from Secretary Dobbin's dispatch to Commodore Armstrong of February 27, 1857:

> "Our national flag was borne by American officers on waters where it was legitimate to show it. The mission of those bearing it in the small boat was peaceful. No notice had been given by the Chinese, no shot of warning was fired over the boat; but shot and shell were fired deliberately at the officers and men, with a view to their destruction. My reflections upon the whole case convince me that it was indispensably necessary promptly to vindicate the sacredness of our national flag, and to inflict a degree of punishment sufficiently impressive to deter these people from again rashly and recklessly insulting us. Had the offensive act been temporarily submitted to and referred to the tardy process of Chinese explanations, this trifling with our flag would probably have been repeated, and led to still more serious consequences.
>
> "I approve, therefore, of the course pursued by you and those under your command. The brave and energetic manner in which the wrong was avenged is worthy of all praise. The gallantry, good order, and 'intelligent subordination' displayed by all engaged in the various conflicts with the enemy; the precision and admirable success with which the guns were managed, are highly creditable to the service. Be pleased, sir, to communicate to the officers, seamen, and marines the Department's high appreciation of their good conduct."

In the "Blue-Book" presented to the British Parliament, the notices of the capture of the "Barrier Forts," made by Consul Parkes and Rear-Admiral Sir Michael Seymour, were in marked terms of commendation both of the skill and the gallantry displayed by the Americans.

There were not wanting those who criticised both privately and publicly the conduct of the American Navy in this affair, as involving itself hastily and unnecessarily in the English and Chinese difficulty. A most indignant and caustic letter, written by Commander Foote himself to Chaplain James Beecher, shows that he could fight with the pen as well as with the sword. In this letter he defends himself from every charge. On the point of the Chinese firing upon the boats, which, it had been intimated, was a natural thing for them to do in their indiscriminate and unintelligent hatred of foreigners, he says:

"The fact of the trade of all nations being suspended; the fact that we are not at war with China; that French armed boats, as well as boats of different nationalities, were passing the 'Barrier Forts' unmolested, as they had a treaty right to do, before and after my own boat was fired upon, show your general views to be as crude as they are perverse where the honor of your country's flag is involved."

It may be that Mr. Beecher and others were right in their criticisms; it may be that Commander Foote was over-ready to fight in this instance (a failing of his); it may be that a longer forbearance would have resulted in more good; but it is difficult, with the facts before us, to see these things. We should be the last to defend him in that which is wrong; but we must in this instance fall back upon his superior knowledge of the facts of the case, and upon his established character as a man of high principle and humanity. His professional duty pressed him to act energetically. He did so act, and we are not aware that by truly competent authority, both civil and military, he has been adjudged to have acted rashly, or to have merited aught but praise.

A letter written about this time makes mention of one of these newspaper notices of his conduct to which reference has been made; and as it bears directly on the main point in the case, it is quoted in full:

"U. S. Ship 'Portsmouth,' Hong-Kong, *June* 27, 1858.

"My dear Bradford,—I have read your letter published in the Philadelphia *Press*. It does you intellectually great credit, and certainly I believe it to have been written, notwithstanding its wholesale errors about our force in Canton, with that moral sentiment which I always have considered as a feature in your character.

"You were not in Canton when our force was there. Consequently the assertion in your letter that it was not asked, but, on the contrary, that a request was made that it might be withdrawn, as it was unnecessary for protection, must have been made on other authority than your personal knowledge. The credibility of that authority may be seen by the inclosed copy of a letter addressed to me by Consul Perry, showing that the force was officially and immediately urged by the highest American functionary in Canton—Dr. Parker, the commissioner, being with you at that time in Shang-Haï. And so far from the force not being wanted by the Americans, and they having requested its withdrawal, I need only to remark that, after having been in Canton a fortnight, I received orders from the commodore to proceed with the ship to Shang-Haï. On making these orders known, one of the merchants said that he hoped I would not leave them; that a letter signed by the Americans, showing the necessity of a force for their protection, would, if I wished it, readily be furnished. I declined the proposal, remarking that in the existing state of affairs I should not leave Canton, and had no doubt but that the commodore would, as he afterward did, fully approve my course. Besides this, every American house in Canton—I do not remember a single exception—importuned me for sentinels to be posted within their premises. And still further, I call upon your informant, or any American then in Canton, to say that he gave me the slightest intimation that our force might be withdrawn, until it had been there more than a fortnight, and accomplished fully the object for which it was placed there—for the protection of our citizens, and their persons and property; when I announced my intention of conferring with the commodore on the propriety of withdrawing the men, and having the *Levant* brought up to the city as a place of refuge in case of emergency.

"Although the government has unqualifiedly approved our course, as may be seen in the copy of a letter in my possession, still, if there remain a doubt on the subject in the minds of persons whose opinions are worthy of my regard, I hope that the whole matter may be reopened by agitation, investigation, probing, and sifting, so far as my own agency in taking the force to Canton is involved, as well as the subsequent course of the squadron at the 'Barrier Forts.'

"I still feel, as I often have expressed myself, that had I not promptly taken the force to Canton, and in counsel and deed approved the capture of the 'Barrier Forts' for having on three different occasions fired upon our flag, I ought to be turned out of the Navy as one wholly unworthy of holding a commander's commission in it. Had you been there, holding my commission, I believe also that your course would have corresponded with my own.

"I thus have freely commented, as I am justified in doing, on that part of your letter referring to acts in which I bore a prominent part; and now take the liberty of a friend in remarking that our sentiments toward the English are antipodal. I hold them to be a nation altogether in advance of any European in promoting Christian civilization and the highest interests of mankind. Your Anglophobia, pardon the expression, often leads you, though no doubt unintentionally, to do them an injustice. I am quite proud of our ancestry, even with all their faults, when I compare them with the other nations of Europe.

"I am truly yours,

"(Signed) A. H. FOOTE."

The *Portsmouth* lay off the "Barrier Forts" for some days, to carry out the work of demolition. In one of his dispatches to the commodore, Foote says, "We don't work, of course, today. I have preached aboard and in the fort." The destruction of the forts was completed in ten working days. Some men were unfortunately killed, and others wounded, by a premature explosion. Of this work of demolition, Commander Foote writes to a friend:

"The governor (Yeh) in his correspondence with the commodore has given no satisfaction, and therefore we have taken it by utterly demolishing his forts. He now says that he also desires peace, and matters look more pacific, at least till the pleasure of our government is known. American merchants here, and missionaries too, unanimously regard our course as having been necessary to show the Chinese that the Americans are as powerful as some other nations with whom they have been in conflict. It is the first display of American force in China, and it was desirable that it should be effectual."

In certification of what Commander Foote here says of the opinion of other Americans then in Canton and vicinity in regard to his course of action, the following letter to Captain Foote, signed by influential American residents in China, is of value:

"MACAO, *February* 9, 1858.

"DEAR SIR,—We have been informed that in some of the American newspapers it has been stated in a communication from China that the force taken by you to the factories at Canton, in the month of October, 1856, while difficulties existed between the English and Chinese authorities, was not only not necessary there, but that you were requested to withdraw it. In justice to yourself, we beg to say that of the necessity for the force there, at the period in question, we are fully satisfied, and that it imparted great confidence and security to the Americans generally in Canton. We, of course, can not know if you were requested to remove it, but are convinced that had you done so, the danger to life and property would have been greatly increased.

"We are happy also to avail ourselves of this opportunity to express to you our acknowledgment for the prompt and willing manner in which you have given your assistance and support to your countrymen in this part of China, whenever it seemed to you that you could be of any possible service or that circumstances required them. We remain, dear sir, your friends and countrymen,

"JAMES PURDON & Co. (of Canton)," and others.

The remainder of the cruise of the *Portsmouth* must be more briefly treated. She dropped down to Hong-Kong, and stayed there until the 1st of January, 1857, when she was sent north to Shang-Haï; and after remaining twenty days at that port, she came south to Ningpo, on account of alleged disturbances there. Commander Foote and his officers were invited to an entertainment by the governor, or *Taontai*, who pledged himself to protect American lives and property. From Ningpo the *Portsmouth* proceeded to Foo-Chow, where it was found that the Canton difficulties had not extended to the detriment of our interests. Amoy was the next stopping-place; thence they returned to Hong-Kong on March 14th, having visited all the Chinese ports north of Canton opened by treaty.

On the 11th of April the *Portsmouth* sailed once more from Hong Kong to Singapore, her commander being charged with orders to obtain full information in regard to the case of the Dutch bark *Henrietta Maria*, that had been abandoned at sea by her officers and most of her men, and brought into that port by the American ship *Cœur de Lion*, in a perilous and constructively piratical condition, for adjudication. The difficulty was one of salvage with the British civil officer, and involved a somewhat lengthened correspondence between the Governor of Singapore, Edward A. Blundell, Esq., and the commander of the *Portsmouth*. This business being attended to with his usual thoroughness, Foote set sail May 21st for Bangkok, taking on board Dr. Bradley, bearer of the treaty to the King of Siam. While at Bangkok the officers of the *Portsmouth* were presented to both kings, and were treated with the highest consideration.

The second king of Siam having made many inquiries about the ship, and manifesting a good deal of interest in ordnance and fire-arms, Commander Foote invited him to visit the vessel, which he did, although this was the first time that a king of Siam had been aboard a foreign man-of-war. The king came down from Bangkok, forty miles, to where the *Portsmouth* was anchored, with a suite of twenty princes and nobles, and remained during the day. A grand banquet, taxing the artistic powers of the *Portsmouth* in this line to the utmost, was got up for the occasion.

The treaties of Siam with the United States, England, and France are fast developing the agricultural resources of the country, especially the culture of sugar; and Commander Foote remarks: "It is due to the American missionaries to say that, owing to their indirect influence, favorable treaties have been negotiated. Previously to their coming, the Siamese were almost as exclusive in their commercial policy as the Japanese. Our consul, the Rev. Mr. Mattoon, in consequence of his personal popularity with the kings and officers of state, his knowledge of the language and business habits, has exercised a stronger influence upon the government and people than any other foreigner, and to him we are chiefly indebted for the good opinion of Americans which prevails in Siam." While in Siam, Foote visited the missionaries *in state*, in order that the natives might be led to pay them more respect.

The *Portsmouth* returned to Hong-Kong, arriving on the 26th of June, whence she departed a second time for Shang-Haï, to carry Consul Bradley to that post. After dry-docking and repairs at Shang-Haï, the good ship, which had seen such continual service, meeting in these long voyages in the China seas many severe storms and typhoons, and once being aground in a dangerous condition in the Min River, set sail from Shang-Haï on the 22d of August for Simoda and Hakodadi in Japan. The day before reaching Simoda, breakers ahead were discovered in latitude 34° 14′ N., longitude 138° 17′ E., not laid down in the charts, and were named "Portsmouth Breakers." If they had been running at night, the cruise of the *Portsmouth* would have been brought to an abrupt termination. Commander Foote says of Simoda:

"The appearance of Simoda, in fact the entire country around, is beautiful. Deep ravines lie between the mountain ranges, while the highly cultivated terraced fields stretch up to the very hill-tops. Again, green thickets were seen creeping up the valleys; and lawns of verdant turf here and there overlapped the precipices. The town added no beauty to the scenery. As soon as we had anchored, a large boat came alongside, with four officials high in rank, who in the name of the governors—bear in mind the duality of the Japanese—gave us a courteous and cordial welcome. These representatives were inquisitive, and manifested a degree of intelligence corresponding to their courtesy. We were favorably impressed with the cleanliness of the officials and of their men and boat, which their 'celestial' neighbors might do well to copy."

Many incidental remarks occur in Foote's journal respecting the Japanese, whom he seems to have studied, and their history, with great interest in the brief time he was in Japan —some of which seem almost to have suggested the wonderful development of that people in these late years. He writes that on a visit to the Governor of Simoda, "one of them remarked that he hoped the day was not far distant when the Japanese would visit America; they readily admit our superiority, and seem to be strongly impressed by our country." Hakodadi was also visited, which place pleased the commander even better than Simoda. He remarks upon its spacious harbor, completely land-locked, and capable of containing two hundred sail in an anchorage of from five to twelve fathoms. He thought it the most desirable harbor, in point of security and health, for a man-of-war that he had ever visited. Its position in relation to California, and to Russia and the Amoor River, make it a port of trade and supply of great importance to our government, far preferable to Simoda, whose harbor is too small to admit of more than five or six vessels obtaining a good anchorage. A feast was given to the Governor of Hakodadi and his suite on board ship, where the oblique-eyed natives did straight justice to their fare, and handled knife and fork with an intuitive dexterity. The hospitality was not, however, very generously returned. The supply of bullocks fell short, and since, as Commander Foote remarks, "beef sometimes involves a principle," a peremptory demand for fresh beef, with the guns of the *Portsmouth* to back it, brought at once an abundant supply. Our hero was shorter than some in his diplomacy with the Orientals, and, it may be added, more successful. After placing a buoy at the termination of the spit which forms the harbor of Hakodadi, rendering the entrance easier than when Commodore Perry visited this port, Foote sailed for Hong-Kong, which he reached October 26th, after a passage of sixteen days. On his passage, he speaks of the phosphorescent appearance of the sea in a heavy gale of wind at night as resembling immense banks or shoals of snow in constant motion. At Hong-Kong he learned of the fall of Delhi, and of the approaching end of the Indian rebellion. While lying here he also received an interesting letter from the second king of Siam, the English of which is remarkably good. In his answer to this royal epistle, he says: "It is impossible to say where we shall cruise for the future. We all hope to go home in the course of five or six months. A sea-life is monotonous as well as dangerous in these seas of typhoons and currents and shoals. I presume that your majesty will cruise about the Gulf of Siam in the man-of-war yacht. You will certainly work chronometer and meridian observations well. You will also take lunar observations. The vessel will be as well navigated as any in the China seas should your majesty handle the instruments." Our bluff sailor knew how to pay a compliment when the time for it came. A letter was addressed by him to the first king of Siam in acknowledgment of the gift of a gold and silver cigar-case, which was accompanied by an autograph letter; and still another epistle to the second king, dated January 11, 1858, informing him of the bombardment and capture of Canton by the combined forces of the English and French, with a stately letter from the first king, received during the civil war in America, deploring the war, but giving all his sympathies to the cause of the Union, closed this curious correspondence, which seems to have originated purely from personal liking or friendship, and had nothing of an official character.

In December, 1857, the *Portsmouth* ran twice over to Macao, once to carry Mr. Reed, the American minister, and suite, and a second time to protect American citizens during the assault of the English forces on Canton. In February, Commander Foote left Hong-Kong for Manilla, and there quite unexpectedly received orders for home. He sailed March 5th for Anjer, island of Java, where the ship took in water and supplies; thence to St. Helena; and from St. Helena to Portsmouth, New Hampshire, United States, where they arrived on Sunday, June 13th, 1858, having sailed since leaving the United States more than forty-nine thousand miles.

A few letters, written and received during her home voyage, will conclude the narrative of the eventful cruise of the *Portsmouth.*

"U. S. SHIP 'PORTSMOUTH,'
"At sea, lat. 5° S., long. 107° E., *March* 23, 1858.

"MY DEAR WIFE,—We ought three days ago to have been in Anjer, and been ready with our water and chickens to leave 'Java Head,' homeward bound *via* St. Helena. We hurried off from Manilla in order to save the monsoon and avoid the coming typhoons. The latter we must be exposed to when off the Mauritius, Isle of France. The commodore and Mr. Reed sent me two handsome letters. I left the squadron on the best of terms. We ran under the commodore's stern, and gave him three cheers, and then hauled up the courses and fired a salute; then ran under the *Minnesota's* stern, and they gave us three cheers, which we heartily answered; and then, in the dark night, we stood out for the narrow entrance into the bay, and passed it at daylight next morning. I had but little sleep. We have had light winds, making only one hundred miles on an average daily. I was up all night in running through Gaspar Strait—intricate navigation. Next day, Sunday, read service and a sermon on deck, and delivered a lecture at berth-deck service. We hope to anchor to-morrow, when I will resume this. Write on the 20th of June, and address the letter to me at Portsmouth Navy Yard, New Hampshire. Tell Mr. Bacon that I have written to have his things sent on to New York by the *San Jacinto.* Of course, we did not expect to go home before returning to Hong-Kong, or I should have taken his things on board. I wished myself to return to Hong-Kong in order to buy some china, grass-cloth handkerchiefs, and other things. But if we had gone back, it would have delayed us three months. I feel very anxious to have to wait until six months expire without hearing from you. I commend you all to God's grace. I would have addressed this to Josephine, but your name was down before I was aware of it. Tell her it is for you both. You will receive a bill in my name for seven hundred dollars. I have certainly economized to the utmost this cruise—hardly keeping up my position."

"*Anjer*, *March* 25, 1858.—We arrived early this morning, and, as you may imagine, in these straits of tacks and shoals I was up most of the squally night. We are nineteen and a half days from Manilla, but have beaten the clipper ships, one of which I wrote you sailed eight days before us, and is not here yet. I ran inside of all the shipping, and the captain of the port says I am rather close to the shore.

"We hear that an attempt has been made on Louis Napoleon's life, also that Paulding has seized Walker. I go ashore to breakfast with the port officer. We sail to-night or at daylight in the morning. May God watch over you and the dear children, and enable us to meet and see each other. I wish the boys were here to see the monkeys and parrots, and eat the pine-apples and other fruit. A splendid banyan-tree that would cover your garden is close at hand. There is a delicious sensation in this balmy climate and tropical scenery."

"'San Jacinto,' Manilla, *March* 4, 1858.

"My dear Foote,—Our association afloat on duty has been very short, but has been rendered by you so agreeable that I could wish it were to be longer; but the wish could be scarcely generous, as you leave the arid shores of China for happy old Connecticut and your family. I wish you with all my heart a happy reunion with them, and I trust that your good ship, in which you have so long and so faithfully served, may prove true to you to the last.

"My kindest regards and remembrance to your family, and believe me, very sincerely your friend,

"Josiah Tatnall, Commodore.

"Captain Andrew H. Foote, U. S. Ship *Portsmouth*."

"Dear Sir,—Pray add to your autographs this most earnest expression of my gratitude for all you have done and all you are going to do for me and mine. I am a good deal disturbed at parting with my son—more than I thought I should be; but my decision is a wise one, for all reasoning fails if three months' association with you, and such as you have about you, do not do him good. He is a good-natured boy, with no defects of temper. Treat him, for my sake, as a son, and correct him if he do wrong, which I think he will not do intentionally. If you are in Philadelphia, try to see Mrs. Reed, who will welcome you as my friend. The record of my good opinion is of little value, but you shall have it. It is no flattery, but exact truth, that the service has not an officer better worthy of confidence for any duty than him to whom these few words of earnest farewell are written. God bless you, my dear sir.

"Ever truly yours, WILLIAM B. REED.

"To Captain A. H. Foote, MANILLA, *March 4th*, 1858."

These are extracts from Commander H. H. Bell's letters from Whampoa, dated April and May:

"I have visited the burying-grounds three or four times, and could not discover that the graves of our dead had been molested otherwise than by the removal of the wooden head-boards—except in one instance, where three graves bordering upon a paddy-field had been dug away for the extension of said field; the wretches betraying themselves in this peculiarly Chinese theft by leaving the heads of the graves—say six inches deep—showing in the bank which they had cut away, though no part of the coffins remain—this does not look like malicious desecration. Mr. Everett's monument remains intact, having Chinese characters written on it; yet the grave of ——— ———'s little boy is said to have been broken up. ———, they say, was much disliked by the natives. The tombs of the English were entirely destroyed."

"I accompanied our consul as a passenger and guest; the 'Barrier Forts' are as we left them, no attempt having been made to renew them. The French frigate *Capricieuse* lay there. The city of Canton, along the line of the river as well as in the interior, is a sad spectacle, most of the houses having been deserted, and presenting nothing but ruins and desolation to the view—the broken walls and torn roofs giving melancholy evidence of the ruthless bombardments in the several attacks on the city. I found the streets quite deserted for a Chinese city, the people looking cowed and dejected, and apparently of the worst class. All who were able have retired to the neighboring cities and villages, under the terror of British guns."

"Wentworth, the leper, whom you left here, is said to be a putrid mass. It is feared we shall have to receive him, for your charities excite no little feeling on the part of those who have to do the nursing."

We close these two fighting *Portsmouth* chapters with an extract of a pleasant letter of Commander Foote to his eldest son, Augustus, then a little boy, dated Bangkok, June 7, 1857:

"It is not every young gentleman who can say he has a correspondent in this far land. Our sitting or reception room here is sixty feet square and thirty-five feet high, with a great deal of gilding about it, and some twenty large mirrors on its walls. We have every thing furnished us by the king. The attendants come in crawling on all fours, much as Willie did when he was a baby, and then they knock their heads on the floor as they approach you. The king lately lost five hundred out of fifteen hundred elephants in a fight. We have put up a flag-pole in our yard as high as the one on the New Haven Green, and have hoisted the American flag upon it."

Recent occurrences in China have cast a new light on the policy of foreign nations with that empire. It is the testimony of intelligent residents in China who have watched the course of events, that the failure of England and France to exact reparation on the spot for injuries done by the Chinese, and the reference of these to the slow action of diplomacy, has been totally misunderstood; has given the impression to the Chinese that foreign nations were afraid of them, and without doubt was the real cause of the late terrible massacre. This tends indirectly to the justification (if aught more were needed) of the prompt action of the commander of the *Portsmouth* in attacking the Chinese forts in Canton River.

CHAPTER XII.

CORRESPONDENCE.—BROOKLYN NAVY YARD.—BEGINNINGS OF STRIFE.

JUDGED by the estimate of ordinary lives, a period had now come when the subject of this memoir might have retired honorably from public service to a well-earned repose. After twenty-one years and three months of wearisome sea-service, under all suns and climes, reaping little more from the barren fields of ocean than bare reputation, this veteran wanderer and fighter might have said—

> "Is there any peace
> In ever climbing up the climbing wave?"

It is true that the end had come of his actual sea-life, but something remained for him to do that was still worthier and greater:

> "Old age hath yet his honor and his toil;
> Death closes all: but something ere the end,
> Some work of noble note, may yet be done,
> Not unbecoming men that strove with gods."

A hearty letter from his true friend, Commodore Smith, greeted him in Portsmouth, N. H., on his return, congratulating him "on the termination of a successful cruise, reflecting additional honor upon your commission and character."

He did not yet have, and probably never did have, a dream of idle ease. He was really too restlessly ambitious a man to be inactive; though his ambition was of a fine quality, ending not in self, but in the public good. After a few months' rest he received an appointment to the command of the United

States Navy Yard in Brooklyn, N. Y., October 26, 1858. Before he entered upon the duties of this station, while at his home in New Haven, and also during the time he lived in Brooklyn, his thoughts were much engrossed in public affairs —benevolent, religious, and political. His correspondence, which was naturally for the most part professional, and concerned itself with matters which had engaged his mind in the past, still had the great objects of the public welfare in view. He wrote and spoke much on the subject of the suppression of the slave-trade.

His grand panacea, which was good as far as it went, and to which he clung until, with thousands of others, he was taught a better lesson, was African colonization. He was, however, persevering in his collection of facts, and in his appeals to the government on the subject of a vigorous suppression of the trade at its original source, the African coast. He thought that the responsibility rested in a great measure with our country. He would have our government, like England, cleanse its hands of all that iniquity, and, having clean hands, it could act with power with other nations in its negotiations on this subject. One of his correspondents, Captain Le Roy, commanding the steamer *Mystic*, then cruising off the African coast, seems to have had less confidence than himself in the pure benevolence of England. This officer thus writes:

"I like your article much, and when I fall in with Calhoun and Godon, will send it to them. I believe a few more such articles will have the effect of drawing public attention in such a way toward this nefarious traffic as may cause the establishing of measures to break it up. I regret that my response to your inquiry about the palm-oil in the Congo should have been incorrect; but, as I subsequently stated, palm-oil within the last year has begun to be an article of manufacture and export from the Congo. With regard to the 'right of search,' as a general rule I am opposed to its exercise by foreign vessels, especially by our English brethren. I must confess that, with all my regard for John Bull, I am not so perfectly satisfied that he would *always* do the clean thing, and unless he were held to a strict accountability, our legitimate traders might be subjected to great annoyances.

"As to the idea of the suppression of the slave-trade being a matter of philanthropy with Master John, I don't believe it, and I do not believe one hundredth part of the zeal would be exhibited by him if he did not receive so much per ton for every vessel captured, and so much a head for every slave; in fact, I have known an English captain honestly to confess that he came out here to make money; and when it has been suggested that it would be a good plan to put an officer and boat's crew from an English man-of-war aboard of our ships, and the opposite, so as to make possible the more complete identification and interruption of the illegal traffic, the response has been, 'But will you share prize-money with us?' Prize-money is what they are after, and without it poor nig may be a slave to the end of his life for all they care. As to cruising in company with our vessels, they do not wish it. If there is a suspicious craft about that will not deny its American nationality, so as to enable Master John to seize him, he will possibly, in the exercise of his magnanimity, discover that 'the grapes are sour,' and inform one of our cruisers; but if the fellow has cargo aboard, he will endeavor to persuade him to haul down his flag and deny his nationality by promising to let him land, or work upon his fears by threatening to hand him over to some American man-of-war. Of course, knowing his offense is punishable by our laws with death, the slaver does not long hesitate. We must change our laws upon the subject. It must no longer be declared piracy, and punishable with death, but a penal offense. Does it ever occur to the vaunters of British philanthropy that few or none of all the slaves captured by British cruisers ever return to their native soil—that they are taken to British colonies and apprenticed? And what is the nature of that apprenticeship? Poor abused Brother Jonathan puts his big hand into his pocket and sends captured slaves back to Africa, and supports them there until they can do something for themselves; yet honest old John, who steals the slaves from the slavers, and calls them apprentices, rolls up his eyes and groans over American insincerity in countenancing the slave-trade, and thinks complacently of how much he is doing for the suffering negro race. Our friend Monsieur goes to work systematically, and has extensive and comfortable barracoons put up; *buys* his *apprentices*, and has them decently cared for, and sent in a regular way to his colonies. Though called apprentices, they are still slaves. For some time past a great rivalry has existed between the French factories and the slave-traders, which has resulted in the price of slaves advancing some fifty or a hundred per cent."

This writer, as well as Captain (afterward Commodore) Dornen, his other correspondent from Africa, constantly express to Captain Foote the obligations of those actually engaged in the work of putting a stop to the African slave-trade to himself for what he had done, and evidently regard him as authority on all these questions. He did what he could. He worked and watched at sea, and wrote and agitated on shore; and if his views were not always the most comprehensive, he must be looked upon as one who with an untiring life-long zeal labored for the happiness of the colored race.

In the temperance reform, especially among seamen, and in purely religious matters, he remained true to his convictions; and he seemed to delight in the opportunity of being at home once more, in order to throw himself into these good works. In private religious meetings his voice was heard in exhortation. One of his warm-hearted naval friends writes to him from Cincinnati in the midst of the revival scenes of 1858:

"While voices from multitudes are going up from this goodly land in praise and blessing for the outpourings of His Holy Spirit in these days on our country, I was sure you would be glad to hear mingling with them a voice from the ocean. I was enabled this morning by strength from above to stand up and speak—to speak about our glorious ship; to do what you, sir, have done and are doing. I should like to receive from you a letter on the subject of religion among us sea-faring men—of this new and wonderful working of God's Spirit with us as well as ashore. How they would rejoice to hear from an experienced head and Christian heart tidings of these things, and would thank God and take courage."

While in charge at Brooklyn, Commander Foote established and carried on, as he did in former years at the Philadelphia and Boston Yards, a regular system of religious instruction and of mission-schools among the operatives of the Yard, and in the neglected outlying districts; and there are many poor families, sailors, and workingmen now living in and about that neighborhood to testify of the good that he did to their bodies and souls during his brief military rule at the New York harbor. In the winter of 1859–60 there was quite an interest in religious matters on board the receiving-ship *North Carolina*, and a prayer-meeting was held nightly for months on the orlop-deck of that vessel, upon which meeting Foote was a regular attendant; and so frank, cordial, and confiding, as well as energetic, was the tone of his piety, and his efforts for the spiritual good of others were so earnest, that he was thought to be immediately instrumental in the conversion of many. He believed in George Herbert's words—

"Be useful where thou livest."

He did not wait for impossibilities to clear up like mists, but he steered straight into and through them. He began to do what he could. He saw no impossibilities. Difficulties acted upon him like stimulants. His methods were old and unvaried, but he believed in them, and he applied them unhesitatingly. He meant to regulate matters, to begin the work of improvement, to clear away old abuses, and leave the world better than he found it; and his grand principle of action was to begin at once at the religious nature, and try to implant a new life there.

One of his old *Portsmouth* officers (Pendleton G. Watmough), about to leave the Navy, writes:

"It is a long parting from one who represents all that is good in a service where I have spent seventeen years; and though about leaving it, I shall always cherish a remembrance, and a fond one, of my associations with many in it—particularly of our brilliant cruise in the 'saucy *Portsmouth*.'"*

* In the same year of the return of the *Portsmouth*, a neat and handsome monument, designed by a New York artist, costing $1000, which was contributed "by their shipmates" of the *San Jacinto*, *Portsmouth*, and

Another fellow-officer of the East India cruise, Captain Macomb, writes:

"The men like to hear of you. They know that you afforded them all the 'pigeon,' as they call it, on the cruise, and that you had full swing in that squadron. The old *Portsmouthers* are proud of being remembered by Captain Foote. Could you not write to them, and give them some of your good advice?"

Commodore Smith sends a characteristic letter, which may serve to diversify this uneventful but by no means unprofitable portion of Commander Foote's life:

"WASHINGTON, *February* 4, 1860.

"MY DEAR CAPTAIN,—Yours of yesterday's date, with a *douceur* for Anna, just received. She is a sturdy beggar, and seems to think the orphans are especially under her charge. The object is good—none better; but I have cautioned her against troubling *my* non-Catholic friends to contribute to *her* Catholic charities. She gets enough out of me to suffice for the Protestant part of the Navy. But as you seem to be so popular with the ladies, it emboldens them to take liberties. You are more liberal than I should be under similar circumstances. My opinion is favorable to the institution of widows' and orphans' homes of all religions. Nevertheless I bear in mind what my priest reads at our offertory—'Never turn your face from any poor man. If you have no penny to give, hear his story and judge charitably.' You are a good Samaritan. You not only give the pennies, but you pour the oil and wine of consolation into the wounds of the conscience and heart. I wish I were so endowed; but I am not. I do not possess the quality of pathos which brings the stray sheep into the fold again. Such *sacred oratory* is rare. It is not taught at the forum nor learned in the pulpit, but in private, with 'labor and intercourse with men.' Go on in your course. If your military commission should fail you in any sense, your zeal and ability to teach and speak will not. At last a Speaker is chosen. Next

Levant, was erected in the Brooklyn Navy Yard to the memory of those who fell in the capture of the Canton "Barrier Forts." The names of these are inscribed upon the monument, with a representation of the ships and the forts, with flags, wreaths, and other appropriate devices. It is one of the finest marine monuments in the country, and forms an interesting feature of the Yard.

week I presume Congress will proceed to business, after squandering two months in nonsensical squabbling. We hope a calm may succeed the storm; in the nature of things it must; but the storm will not subside until after March, 1861. I have no Navy news. I hear a vessel is to sail next Tuesday for Brazil. You must be getting slack of work at your Yard, which will make you uneasy. Yours truly, in haste,

"JOSEPH SMITH.

"Captain A. H. Foote, U. S. Navy Yard, New York."

There is a new and separate phase of Admiral Foote's life which it would be interesting to dwell upon, but which we would only indicate here. A large portion of the documentary matter left by him is taken up with bulky notes of court-martials in which he was personally engaged, both while stationed on shore and while at sea. Owing to his great practical energy and executive talent, he was often called upon to act as the presiding officer in these courts; and owing also, it must be confessed, to his exceptionally rigid ideas of discipline, he was, in his own command, sometimes involved in bitter controversies and litigations with officers. While he went to the root of matters—while he was searching and unsparing, and perhaps even at times erring in severity whenever insubordination, disrespect, and wrong was to be dealt with, never swerving for fear of making an enemy—he was unusually humane where infirmities of character were involved, especially among common sailors, so that he was considered to be quite democratic, or too much inclined to take the part of the seaman, or apprentice, or petty officer who was delinquent. He was, in fact, rather too popular among the men for the aristocratic standard of the officers of the Navy. He befriended, encouraged, and defended those whom he thought had no friends. This trait is noticed by one of his brother-officers, who says:

"I am very much grieved that your purser is 'infirm of purpose.' I feel assured you have done your duty toward him, and that your kind feeling for the weaknesses of the weak—a characteristic point in you—has rather prompted you to go further in covering this vulnerable spot than many others would."

As it is not desirable to stir up old controversies which have now entirely passed away, it does not seem necessary to mention particular instances of court-martial trials in which Foote was conspicuous at the time; merely saying that his firmness and general impartiality, with now and then a singular display of roundabout good sense and kindly tact, are noticeable in the history of these oftentimes protracted and difficult cases; and from the testimony of all, in this judicial or juridical department of his profession he was very valuable, having, indeed, from a natural love of controversy, a partiality for its excitements, and for all its elaborate forms and details, though he was kept by his sound head and good heart from widely erring in judgment.

Admiral Foote was a friend of education. In a correspondence with Lieutenant (now Commodore) Simpson, who was then stationed as a teacher of gunnery at the Naval Academy in Annapolis, he defends the system of professional instruction against the vigorous assaults of that young officer, who was in favor of a more practical teaching by purely naval men who had seen actual service at sea. Foote expresses himself in favor of a proper and equal combination of the two kinds of teachers, thereby securing a thorough and scientific training, as a basis upon which to build practical seamanship. This intelligent view, coming from one so intensely practical as Captain Foote was, certainly shows comprehensiveness and breadth of mind. He was, in fact, a progressive man in all matters of education, and was never so superstitiously in love with the old as not to seize with eagerness upon new methods and ideas, as he did, for example, upon the use of iron in naval warfare. In fitting out the *Portsmouth* for her East India cruise, the following letter was addressed by him to the Secretary of the Navy, which goes to prove his hearty interest in scientific investigations:

> "During the cruise of the *Portsmouth* abundant opportunities are likely to occur to make collections in natural history. The surgeon of the ship, Dr. Henderson, will collect specimens for the Academy of Natural Sciences in Philadelphia, and perhaps also for Yale College. It is desirable, therefore, that a copy of Professor Dana's 'Report on Crustacea' (Exploring Expedition under Captain Wilkes) should be in the vessel. Believing myself, in common with two or three scientific gentlemen here, that it will meet the views of the government to encourage officers to contribute when abroad to the cause of science, I respectfully request that it may be purchased for the use of the *Portsmouth* during her approaching cruise."

The letter of Lieutenant Simpson, shortly before referred to, seems to have been sent for perusal by Foote to his friend Dupont, and called forth this expression in his reply:

> "But let me say how rejoiced I should be to see you, my dear Foote, take hold of this establishment (Annapolis Naval Academy), from which the last hope must spring of our giving the country an efficient Navy by rearing officers of capacity and moral worth. I have ever followed the fortunes of the academy with deep interest, increased perhaps by the fact that I was a member of the first two boards which organized the school. It has steadily progressed, like West Point, which is the creation of over half a century. Yet you would find an abundant scope for your active and intelligent energies in developing improvements still needed, and which no one man could cover heretofore in the brief period allotted him there."

Both of these gallant men were soon to be summoned to a more stirring and arduous service.

We have called this brief period of Commander Foote's life—when he had in charge the New York Navy Yard—an "uneventful" one; but this is not literally true. The period of great events was rapidly drawing on, and they had already begun to cast their shadows over the scene. It was a time of agitation and popular excitement. Those especially who held offices of responsibility under the government were compelled to the exercise of constant watchfulness from foes within and without. The trial time, in fact, of this government was approaching. It was to be proved whether a republic was a strong or a weak government. It was to be proved whether there existed a principle of vital national unity, or whether this nation was but a loose confederation of independent States, bound together by a mere selfish tie easily dissolved. There is a principle of growth in a nation as in a man—an aspiration toward a higher civilization; in fact, a true moral life—and it was to be seen if a century's apparent growth were no true life after all, but a false existence and progress. Was it a social compact or a living state? Could the republic die by simple disintegration or falling away of disaffected portions? Had it a life which was strong enough to throw off corruption, and which contained within itself the means of its own cure and preservation?

The election of Abraham Lincoln on the 6th of November, 1860, to the Presidency, brought an end to the hopes of plotters in regard to the future control of the national government; but they had still six months to work out their schemes during the waning administration of an imbecile executive, who held the view that it was constitutionally forbidden to protect the government against rebellion. Men in high official position were busily engaged in secretly undermining the national power. While faithful servants, of whom Commander Foote was one, were almost despairingly striving for the upbuilding and concentration of the Navy, the Secretary of the Navy was sending off our ships to distant regions, or rendering them useless for defense, and an easy prey to conspirators. Both in the Army and in the Navy there were treacherous men, who at heart were traitors while they nominally remained in the pay of a government they had deliberately resolved to destroy. Then came in rapid succession the actual events of the

Secession drama—the withdrawal of the Southern States one after another from the Union; the seizing upon navy yards, arsenals, and forts; the inauguration of a Southern Confederacy; and the open insults offered to the national flag. At the North as well as the South the atmosphere was surcharged with disloyal sentiment. Even good men were in a state of hallucination in regard to duty. One hardly knew his neighbor for a friend or a foe. Compromise was still the cry when the sacred treasures and household gods were stolen away by bold enemies of the state.

President Lincoln was inaugurated on the 4th of March, 1861, in the deepest period of gloom. He came to the administration of a government whose resources were crippled, and which, indeed, had been rendered almost powerless in every department. Not to speak of the Army, the Navy was at an extremely low ebb. Its vessels of war were either away at foreign ports, or those at home were unready for action and but half-manned. "At the beginning of the year 1861, the total Navy of the United States was ninety vessels, carrying, or designed to carry, 2415 guns. Of this number only forty-two were in commission. Twenty-eight ships, bearing in the aggregate 874 guns, were lying in ports dismantled, and none of them could be made ready for sea in less than several weeks' time; some of them would require at least six months."* The most of those in commission had been sent away to distant seas, and, with the exception of the store-ship *Relief*, of 2 guns, the steam-frigate *Brooklyn*, of 25 guns, which had just before arrived at Norfolk after a three-years' cruise, was absolutely the only armed vessel on the Atlantic coast; and the *Brooklyn*, moreover, drew too much water to enter Southern harbors, or to operate with efficiency in the first scenes of the war. Many of the naval officers, who were born at the South

* "Lossing's Civil War in America," vol. i., p. 299.

left their posts at the critical moment. No less than sixty, including eleven at the Naval Academy at Annapolis, resigned their commissions; and there were also continual desertions. In the Report of the Secretary of the Navy for the next year there were two hundred and fifty-nine desertions and dismissals of officers from the Navy alone. At length the thirteenth of April and the surrender of Sumter awoke the country, and the war began. These are facts fresh in the memory of this generation; and we live now to bless the day when the first gun was fired on Sumter, whose flash opened the eyes of the nation to see its peril.

We subjoin two or three letters addressed to Commander Foote while at the Brooklyn Navy Yard, from fellow-officers, which go to show the intense disturbance in the Navy before the war had actually commenced and at its earliest beginning, and which also show that there were noble and loyal souls in the Navy as well as in the Army:

"NAVY YARD, PHILADELPHIA, *January* 25, 1861.

"MY DEAR FOOTE,—I had intended writing you a 'New-Year's' letter, but about that time I had many irons in the fire.

"A previous order to that which brought me here carried me immediately after to Annapolis as president of an examination board. From this duty I only returned home last Saturday, finding our whole family circle in deep grief from the loss of Mrs. Dupont's eldest sister, who had been for many years a second mother to her.

"On reaching here on Tuesday I found your letter of the 16th instant, which should have been forwarded to me at Annapolis. At that place I saw your friends the Rodgerses and Simpson, who always spoke of you with earnest admiration, and seemed to think the coast was clear for you to come to the academy when Blake left.

"But, alas! my dear friend, are we to have any academy? My own belief is that the drift is all one way. I have very little more faith in the Border States than in the Cotton States; there are any number of traitors in Maryland. The Chief Justice is a Secessionist.

"I still hope against conviction, and that is about all that is left for a man to do.

"We have been living under a delusion that we had a national government, which has toppled over at the first breeze; and secession, disunion, and treachery are made the rule instead of the exception—so safe has it been made for a state to go out that the novelty alone encourages the attempt.

"What has made me most sick at heart is to see the resignations from the Navy. I had occasion to go to Washington the last week in November, and was astounded to find the extent of the demoralization, not only in every department of the government, but among the officers of the Navy. I spoke out plainly, I tell you; told them I had never believed that I had been serving two masters; that I had been nourished, fed, and clothed by the general government for over forty years; paid whether employed or not; and for what?—why, to stand by the country, whether assailed by enemies from without or from within; that my state had had no part or lot in this support; that my oath declared allegiance to the United States as one to support the Constitution.

"But if I feel sore at these resignations, what should a decent man feel at the doings in the Pensacola Navy Yard? Here I can not trust myself to speak; and the Department accepting these resignations, not waiting for a single particular after hearing that the Yard had been surrendered! So that, on a reconstruction, these two affairs will come back into the Navy by treaty, of course.

"Thank you for your kind congratulations about my orders here; they are very acceptable, particularly if we hold together.

"I stick by the flag and the national government as long as we have one, whether my state do or not, and well she knows it.

"I have Lardner and Drayton in the Yard with me—nice men; there is no nonsense about the latter, though he is from South Carolina.

"I have a thousand things to tell you, but must close for the present. Please remember me to Commodore Breese.

"Ever yours most truly, S. F. DUPONT.

"Captain Foote, U. S. N.

"I see you had no idea of being surprised by mobs. Oh, why was not some one like you at Pensacola? I pass no judgment on the old commodore; he was in a tight place, and if he had only ironed well the traitors under him before he gave up, I should have been thankful."

"U. S. FRIGATE 'WABASH,' HAMPTON ROADS, *August* 7, 1861.

"MY DEAR FOOTE,—I received your kind and very welcome letter by the *Rhode Island*, and am thankful to you for it. We met the *Rhode Island* off the Frying-Pan Shoals, while we were securing two vessels by getting prize-masters and crews on board of them. One was the *Mary Allen*, a prize to the rebel privateer *Dixie*, and the other an American vessel under English colors, just out from Wilmington, North Carolina. These Englishmen in the rebel states are playing a deep game. The consuls of Her Majesty are giving American vessels provisional registers, and are loading them for English ports with the products of these Southern States. I sent both vessels to New York, but fear they will be recaptured before they get there. The papers we received previous to these captures led me to believe that our coast from the capes of Virginia to Cape Fear was lined with our cruisers in consequence of the excitement occasioned by the depredations of the *Jeff Davis.* But on my arrival here I learn such is not the case. Acting under my false impression, I directed the vessels to keep in shore, and if they are not captured it will be a miracle, as I learn that small privateers are ready at every inlet along the whole coast of North Carolina to run out in a moment and capture any poor devil who may show himself along the coast. I begin to believe that our press is a curse to our country. It was its malign influence which caused our disaster at Bull Run. These two captures and touching on Frying-Pan Shoals without damage are the events of the passage from Charleston. I think if we could hang about half a dozen editors and as many members of Congress, we should get along better. I am afraid our President is not equal to the times, and I begin to think the Cabinet is badly constructed. Seward seems to be disposed to truckle to the English, and the President made a great mistake that he did not close all the rebel ports entirely by an edict forbidding all commercial intercourse with them whatever. This would have prevented Lord Lyons and Mr. Mercier troubling us about the blockade. It seems to me that the results of our exertions are by no means commensurate with the enthusiasm of our people and the unlimited means placed at the disposition of our government. But I will growl no more.

"I congratulate you most heartily, my dear Foote, on your promotion. Get a smart, active vessel at once, and come and help us. I wish you would give my love to Mrs. Foote and Miss Josephine, not forgetting the smaller fry, and believe me most truly your friend,

"SAMUEL MERCER.

"To Captain A. H. Foote, Navy Yard, New York."

These letters, which do honor to the Navy, might, if we had the room, be greatly multiplied; but we will only add the following extracts from letters of a little earlier date than the preceding, from an officer who a short time before had retired from the service to become a farmer at the West:

"Events which have followed each other for the last month so rapidly, and all tending to the disruption of our government, and even the bonds of society itself, have naturally turned every one's attention to the appalling state of affairs likely to arise in the future. You will not be surprised to hear that my desires look back to my profession. My faith in the Union gives me an intense desire to lend my service, such as it is, to the support of the Constitution. I am most satisfactorily situated here, with excellent promise of future content and of a peaceful and prosperous life, and the idea of returning to the Navy would otherwise never have suggested itself. I want to hear from you and get your advice. I am inclined to view the failure of the *Star of the West* to get to her destination as a circumstance reflecting discredit upon the government. I must confess to having wished, with all my heart, that your old command had been commissioned with that job. My father says, 'Oh that Foote had had command of that *Star of the West!*' He feels keenly the shade of indignity put upon his old arm of the service, the artillery, and hardly allows himself to speak of the outrage upon the flag by those crazy men at Charleston. If you hear of any thing which would argue a solid and great action of the Executive in defense of the government which he holds in his weak hands, let me know, and I will take steps." * * *

"I was much gratified, my dear captain, by the receipt of your card, which appeared in the *Tribune* a few days since. I heard of it, and was anxious to see it. Our papers here, as well as your own, were filled with accounts of the 'Navy Yard excitement,' and just such exaggerated sensational articles as appear in reference to any matter of our day. I was quite persuaded, and told my friends, that in a few days we would probably arrive at the truth, and we would then find that 'our Navy' had done nothing subjecting them to ridicule or censure. I had almost determined to write to you myself and get the truth, when your letter came. Allow me to say it is a characteristic letter, just such a one as you can write—frank, good-humored, truthful, and fearless—the case made clear, and criticism itself disarmed.* Yesterday I sent a letter to the President, tendering my services to the government in my old position as lieutenant; but I will give you the letter. My object is to have it on file. It was as follows: 'In the spring of 1859, when the government was at peace and seemed secure in the loyalty of the people, I resigned my commission as lieutenant in the Navy, after a service of eighteen years. Recent revolutionary acts in portions of the territory, and the many cases of desertion from the service, fill me with a desire to assist in maintaining the integrity of the Union and the honor of its flag, and impel me to tender my services to the government. I am ready at a moment's notice to return to the Navy, should contingencies arise which shall make my services needed.' The letter has not been acknowledged; but as the feeble individual at the head of the government seems to have lost his head, this carries no special sting. I suppose a few days will decide our fate now. I await them with intense impatience. A great fear for Sumter possesses the public mind here. Should it fall, woe to that old man in his native community!"

"The eve of the eventful day has arrived, and millions have read the inaugural of our new President. I need hardly say that many in this our city lament its tone, and show no disposition to recognize or support the high, and, in my view, the only true position assumed by him. For my part, I should heartily despise a government which took other grounds, and should despair of the people who failed to support it. My letter to Buchanan has been passed by without notice. I am ready to renew the offer—in truth, feel that it is a duty for every citizen to uphold, to the whole extent of his ability, the high position assumed by the President. I am willing to risk life and all in what seems to me the only salvation of the nation when its integrity is attacked. If we shrink from the execution of laws the moment they are rebelled against, what is to become of us? I despise such a course, which causes a bitterness of feeling in me which I never fancied I could have. Under any party, I would take the same course to give my services to uphold the government."

"It would be a happy day in my life to find myself once again associated with you in upholding the honor and integrity of our beloved

* Reference here to a letter of Captain Foote's published in the Brooklyn *Eagle* (January 30th), in reference to a little flurry in regard to the alleged exceeding of his official authority for the protection of the Navy Yard.

flag. Selfishness, cowardice, and depraved party necessities seem to be arrayed against the purity and unity of our once glorious nation."

This has the true ring. It must have gone home to the heart of his former commander. While it can not be denied that Foote struggled for a time, as a great many did, with the political problems of the hour, and even strove, as did Crittenden and others, to discover some impossible compromise-ground, yet when the time for action came he was found at his post of duty. He had no hesitation as to his own course. That was clear as the sun in heaven. One day, while discussing these matters with his brother John, he said : "Well, brother John, tell me plainly, do you mean to fight? If you don't mean to fight, then don't express your opinions so loudly. As for me, I intend to fight."

Although he had now held for some time the title of captain, yet he did not receive his actual commission to the captaincy until June 29, 1861. His worth and capacity were then also fully recognized. In this hour of need the government gladly turned to him and to the few who were like him. He received an order, August 23d, to proceed to Washington, and report in person to the Naval Department. He was removed from the Navy Yard August 26th, and was appointed to the command of the naval operations in the Western waters. The following is the order of his appointment:

"NAVY DEPARTMENT, WASHINGTON, *August* 30, 1861.

"SIR,—You have been selected to take command of the naval operations upon the Western waters, now organizing under the direction of the War Department.

"You will therefore proceed to St. Louis, Missouri, with all practical dispatch, and place yourself in communication with Major-General John C. Fremont, United States Army, who commands the Army of the West. You will co-operate fully and freely with him as to your movements.

"Requisitions must be made upon the War Department through General Fremont, and whatever the Army can not furnish the Navy will endeavor to supply, having due regard to the operations on the coast.

"The Western movement is of the greatest importance, and the Department assigns you this duty, having full confidence in your zeal, fidelity, and judgment. I am, respectfully,

"GIDEON WELLES, Secretary of the Navy.

"Captain Andrew H. Foote, U. S. Navy, Washington, D. C."

As we now commence a new period, by far the most important and brilliant one of Admiral Foote's life, we reserve further details respecting the new field for the next chapter.

CHAPTER XIII.

APPOINTMENT TO COMMAND OF NAVAL OPERATIONS AT THE WEST. —THE WESTERN FLOTILLA.

THE official account of Captain Foote's appointment to the command of naval operations on the Western waters is thus briefly given in Secretary Welles's Report of December 1, 1862:

"Besides these large squadrons on our maritime frontier, it became a necessity at an early period of the insurrection to have an organized naval force on the Mississippi and its tributaries. On May 16, 1861, Commander John Rodgers was directed to report to the War Department, which in the preliminary stages assumed the chief expense, for the purpose of initiating an armed flotilla on the Western waters, and immediately entered upon his duties. Proceeding to the West, he purchased steamers which, under his supervision, were fitted, armed, and armored as gun-boats, and thus was commenced the organization of the Mississippi flotilla, which a few months later made itself felt in a succession of achievements that electrified the country. But before Commander Rodgers had an opportunity of completing his arrangements and taking his vessels into action, he was succeeded by Captain A. H. Foote, whose energies and talents were exerted in creating and preparing that Navy on the Western waters which he soon made so serviceable to the country. Painfully wounded at Fort Donelson, he was relieved the 9th of May by Captain Charles H. Davis, who was soon after appointed Chief of the Bureau of Navigation, and in October relinquished the command. By order of Congress the gun-boat fleet was transferred to the Navy, and now constitutes an important squadron, under the command of Acting Rear-Admiral D. D. Porter, who entered upon his duties the 15th of October.

"When Flag-Officer Foote arrived at St. Louis, and on the 6th of September, 1861, assumed command of the Western flotilla, the forces consisted of three wooden vessels in commission, which had been purchased, equipped, and armed as gun-boats by Commander John Rodgers; and there were nine iron-clad gun-boats and thirty-eight mortar-boats in course of construction.

"The service was anomalous in its character, and there was with many great incredulity as to the utility and practicability of gun-boats in carrying on hostilities on the rivers, where it was believed batteries on the banks could prevent their passage. There were also embarrassments for want of funds and of material for naval purposes, there being no Navy Yard or naval dépôt on the Western waters. All these difficulties were met and surmounted by the energetic and efficient officer to whom the duty was intrusted, whose perseverance and courage in overcoming the obstacles that impeded and retarded his operations in creating a river Navy were scarcely surpassed by the heroic qualities displayed in subsequent well-fought actions on the decks of the gun-boats he had, under so many discouragements, prepared."

The disasters with which the beginnings of the war were signalized aroused the government to a sense of the vastness of the work which was before them; and preparations both for the increase of the Army and Navy were begun on a scale of commensurate magnitude. Additions were made to all the squadrons, the outlying ships were called in, a fleet of steam gun-boats was built, armed steamers, constructed for speed,* were added to the blockade service, and the recruiting for the Navy was carried forward with an enthusiasm and a success that never before were witnessed in the history of the American Navy.

But the marked feature in the history of our Navy in the

---

* In reference to swift steamers of light draught, the following order was sent to the commanding officer of the New York Navy Yard:

"NAVY DEPARTMENT, *April* 21, 1861.

"COMMODORE SAMUEL L. BREESE, Navy Yard, New York:

"SIR,—By order of the President of the United States, you will forthwith procure ten steamers capable of mounting a 9-inch pivot gun, with light draught, about nine or twelve feet, having particular reference to strength and speed. You will consult with Commodore Foote, the naval constructor, and such other persons as are capable of giving information and advice. Charter on the best possible terms for three months, with the option of the government purchasing them within that time at a year 1861 was the introduction of iron-plated steam-ships, armed with a few guns of the very heaviest calibre—the genuinely American idea of uniting the smallest vulnerable surface with the greatest destructive power. On the 3d of August, 1861, Congress passed an act authorizing the Secretary of the Navy "to appoint a board of three skillful naval officers to investigate the plans and specifications that may be submitted for the construction and completion of iron-clad steam-ships or steam-batteries, and on their report, should it be favorable, the Secretary of the Navy will cause one or more armored, or iron or steel clad steam-ships or floating steam-batteries to be built; and there is hereby appropriated, out of any money in the treasury not otherwise appropriated, the sum of $1,500,000." Commodores Joseph Smith and H. Paulding, with Captain C. H. Davis, were appointed to this board, and their report was presented of the date of September 15. The result of this was the construction of those armored vessels and monitors contracted for by Ericsson, Merrick & Sons, and S. C. Bushnell & Co., whose services were so wonderfully timely. It is altogether possible that iron-plated vessels and batteries will be superseded, since already projectiles have been invented under whose impact solid 4½-inch armor splits like glass, and nothing in the shape of iron or

---

stipulated price; these vessels to be immediately removed to the Navy or private yards, with the necessary alterations and equipments to render them efficient for the service required.

"I am your obedient servant,

"GIDEON WELLES, Secretary of the Navy."

Similar letters were sent to Boston and Philadelphia. When it is considered that, comparatively speaking, with no Navy, or material for one to begin with, the immense number of six hundred vessels—most of them steamers—required to close up three thousand five hundred miles of blockade, and the fleets for outlying service and upon the Western waters, were, in a space of time to be reckoned by months, made ready for efficient service, we are justly amazed at the energy exhibited by the Naval Department during the war.

steel can resist them; but for the emergency of our war, the original genius that adapted iron to the system of naval attack and defense can not be too gratefully remembered. Upon the little turreted monitor of Ericsson on the 9th of March, 1862—an untried craft, at which old sailors looked askant, and about which the most hopeful had serious doubts—the fate of the Navy, the safety of the national capital, and the existence of the republic, seemed to be suspended; but after that four-hours' fight with the *Merrimack*, the question was settled, and a total revolution was wrought in the defensive capacity and relative strength of nations. The vast crop of monitors and their huge contemporaries, such as the *New Ironsides*, *Weehawken*, *Dictator*, *Monadnock*, and *Miantonomah*, clad with invulnerable scales, and pointed with destructive rams, swarmed our Atlantic waters, and made the threat of foreign invasion an empty breath. They literally "warned off" all intermeddlers. But the same principle was also applied to operations on our Western rivers and waters. Soon after taking charge of the Western Department, Major-General Fremont became convinced of the necessity of preparing a fleet of gun-boats for the purpose of acting with the Army, and of commanding the Mississippi and its tributaries. The fleet, when finally completed, under the successive commands of Rodgers and Foote, especially the last, who brought it to perfection and carried it into operation, consisted of twelve gun-boats, seven of them iron-clad, and able to resist all except the heaviest solid shot, and costing on an average $89,000 each. The boats were built very wide in proportion to their length, so that on the smooth river waters they might have almost the steadiness of stationary land batteries when discharging their heavy guns.* This flotilla, carrying one hundred and forty-three guns, was as follows:

* Lossing's "Civil War in America," vol. ii., p. 198.

Benton	16 guns.	*St. Louis*	13 guns.
Essex	9 "	*Cairo*	13 "
Mound City	13 "	*Pittsburg.*	13 "
Cincinnati	13 "	*Lexington*	9 "
Louisville	13 "	*Conestoga*	9 "
Carondelet	13 "	*Taylor*	9 "

Some of these guns were 64-pounders, some were 42-pounders,* and none were less than 32-pounders. Each boat also carried a Dahlgren 10-inch shell gun, the *Benton*, Foote's flag-ship, having two of these in her forward battery. But we will speak more particularly of the construction and history of these boats before the close of the chapter.

When Captain Foote went to his head-quarters at St. Louis, on the 6th of September, 1861, he at once took up the work which had been commenced by his predecessors. It can not be denied that he went to this Western field from a simple sense of duty, his decided preference being to have a purely naval command, in which he doubtless would soon have made his mark on the Southern coast. He loved blue water and plenty of sea-room. He was every inch a sailor, and had little taste for soldiering and for amphibious operations in swamps and rivers. This work on Western waters was a "hybrid service," part on land and part on water—something demanding totally new expedients. It was an untried field, involving in every part and aspect of it immense perplexities, difficulties, and, to any but the most energetic man, impossibilities. Of course the preparation of the boats was his first care. He could do nothing until these were ready, and fitted for their work on waters of a peculiar character and beset with peculiar obstacles. The creation of this fleet, which be-

* Wherever 42-pounders are spoken of, it should be understood that they were really 7-inch rifle guns; the guns were old 42-pounders, smooth bore, that had been rifled, and the shells used in them weighed some eighty pounds.

came the terror of rebeldom on the Mississippi, Cumberland, and Tennessee rivers, he himself regarded as the greatest achievement of his life. The fighting of them he looked upon as a secondary matter.

The work already done upon these boats, such as the *Lexington* and the *Conestoga*, which were handed over to him when he assumed the command, was, in some important respects, bungling and imperfect. Captain Foote, in a letter addressed to the Secretary of the Navy, thus speaks of the condition of the fleet at that time:

"On assuming the command, September 6, 1861, the force consisted of three wooden vessels in commission, purchased, equipped, and armed as gun-boats by Commander Rodgers. There were also nine iron-clad gun-boats and thirty-eight mortar-boats in process of building. Seven of these gun-boats had been contracted for by Quartermaster-General Meigs, under authority of the War Department; and the two remaining boats were purchased and converted into gun-boats by order of Major-General Fremont. The thirty-eight mortar-boats were also built by order of General Fremont; these were built of solid timber, without motive power, and were each designed to carry a single mortar. The iron-clad boats had less than one half of the vessel plated, while its most vulnerable part had on it but two and a half inches of plate."

In consequence of wanting money, credit, and material, neither gun nor mortar boats could be completed within the time specified by contract. "If they had been finished two months earlier than they were," says Captain Pennock, "there would have been no Columbus, no Island No. Ten, no Memphis, no Vicksburg, and the Western forces might all have been sent East. Every thing turned on those two months."

But new vigor was now infused into the work. Every thing was left in Foote's hands, as the following letter testifies:

"St. Louis, *September* 16, 1861.

"Sir,—In consequence of the duties which press upon my attention, I am necessarily forced to trust much to your discretion. You will, therefore, in the duty confided to you, use your own judgment in carrying out the ends of government.

"Spare no effort to accomplish the object in view with the least possible delay. J. C. FREMONT, Major-General Commanding.

"Captain A. H. Foote, Commanding U. S. Naval Forces on the Western Waters, St. Louis."

Material improvements were made in the plating and arming of the vessels; the casting of the guns at the Fort Pitt Foundery, Pittsburg, was expedited; mortars and shells were largely contracted for, although at first Foote was somewhat doubtful in regard to mortar-boats without motive power, as being unserviceable in waters with rapid current; but he seems to have been convinced by the arguments of Assistant-Secretary Fox and of his experienced subordinates, and, more than all, afterward by actual use. Some more vivid idea of the questions, small and great, that had to be settled may be obtained from the business letters of those under his command, especially the letters of that active officer Lieutenant S. L. Phelps, who, in Rodgers's as well as in Foote's time, had an important part in getting the fleet ready. Lieutenant Phelps says, writing from Louisville before the boats were floated down the Ohio:

"The carpenters have left the *Lexington* and the *Conestoga*. There is no paint for the boats. The *Lexington* has exhausted the supply put on board by contractors. I find the people have got an idea that there is a chance for contract—upon which our country has gone mad, and about which it is worse than dishonest—to get the vessels over the bars. Any one of these river men is ready to enter into a contract to do it, even if there is not a particle of chance to succeed, knowing well that it is an easy matter to get relief from Congress for two or three times the amount of their outlay, whether successful or not, as the government is liberal, and only needs the show of having undertaken to serve it for a good basis to recover largely. I make it my business to gather all the information I can about the river below, and I am satisfied the steamers can not now be floated out in any manner. The officers have not a cent to send to market and start the messes. What shall be done?"

At another time the lieutenant writes:

"The more I examine the work on the *Conestoga*, the more disgraceful patching it seems to be. The *Lexington* is best done, but none well; and the joiner-work all around is more like the work of common laborers than of mechanics. The boat davits are not up, and no attempt made to put them up; the same of the iron ties and bars over the boilers. In the *Taylor* you can not get from aft forward without walking over the boilers. No attempt has been made to deck over for a gangway. The contract calls for swinging booms—none are provided. I am persuaded that you will find it necessary to get authority to issue navy rations, and to have navy regulations in regard to commutation, etc. It will be the only way to save annoyances and losses to us. The army is not fit for shipboard, and won't do at all."

"U. S. GUN-BOAT 'TAYLOR,' MOUND CITY, *October* 3, 1861.

"SIR,—A draft on the assistant-quartermaster of St. Louis for two thousand dollars, indorsed by me and discounted by the Cairo City Bank, enabled me to pay a small amount to the officers and some of the more needy of our crew; but we are sadly in want of funds to complete and equip our boats for service, and pay the bills already incurred in alterations and repairs. Mr. Hamilton complains that the burden is more than he can bear. Government has failed to pay him toward the construction of the new gun-boats according to contract, and the bills for the repairs of the *Lexington* and *Conestoga* are still unpaid. I hope, therefore, for his sake as well as our own necessities, you may succeed in obtaining some money forthwith.

"Commander Stembel called at the bank to have a draft discounted, the same as ours, and was informed by Mr. Safford that the one we sent had not been honored, and until it was he should not feel as if he could extend the amount. He, however, after some arguing, consented to let Commander Stembel have one thousand dollars, but refuses further accommodation until our draft is paid, and so the matter stands. Mr. Safford accommodated us more on the faith of the Navy than from any confidence he had in the Quartermaster's Department; and I trust through your influence, and for the benefit of the others, that our draft will be met immediately.

"May I ask of you the trouble to ascertain if our requisitions for sundry articles—countersigned by General Grant, and forwarded from the

Quartermaster's Department at Cairo—reached the Department at St. Louis? and, if so, if they have been attended to? We need the articles for immediate use, and are suffering without them. The articles of lard and coal-oil are selling at Cincinnati at prices far below the range here, and it would be a great saving to government if we could make immediate requisition for a supply for the three vessels.

"Matters are very quiet about Cairo. The *Conestoga* has gone up the river under orders to Owensboro. General Grant informed Commander Stembel that he had nothing for him to do, and desired that he might cruise up and down the river a few miles either way, to let the rebels know we were moving. Under these circumstances I shall remain here till the vessel is completed, unless otherwise ordered.

"It is approaching winter; it will be necessary to have some means of heating our apartments. I would suggest the use of steam-pipes. The main supply could come from the escape-pipe, and thus appropriate to good use what would be lost. Very respectfully, your obedient servant,

"H. WALKE, Commander U. S. N.

"Captain A. H. Foote, commanding Naval Forces on Western Waters, St. Louis, Mo."

(Telegram.)

"CAIRO, *November* 22, 1861.

"To COMMODORE FOOTE,—I would inform you that the Mississippi is falling, with scant six feet. Would it not be well to send the gun-boats while it is possible? U. S. GRANT."

(Telegram.)

"CAIRO, *November* 30, 1861.

"To COMMODORE FOOTE,—Two or three rebel gun-boats have made a reconnoissance down the Tennessee. General Small requests that a gun-boat from here be sent. I have none. U. S. GRANT."

(Telegram.)

"WASHINGTON, *December* 23, 1861.

"To CAPTAIN A. H. FOOTE,—The general-in-chief has directed General Halleck to send to the gun-boats eleven hundred men from unarmed regiments. M. C. MEIGS."

(Telegram.)

"CAIRO, *December* 17, 1861.

"TO A. H. FOOTE,—General McClellan will order to-day eleven hundred men to be detailed for your boats. We have vessels waiting for men. A great many of our ships go to sea without any Navy officer on board; but we can give you Lieutenants Bryant and Thompson, dates of eighteen hundred and thirty-seven, and possibly some commanders.

"G. A. FOX, Assistant-Secretary of Navy."

(Telegram.)

"WASHINGTON, *December* 30, 1861.

"TO FLAG-OFFICER FOOTE,—After waiting four days, I have had an interview with Meigs, presenting accounts for more than three hundred thousand dollars. I can obtain no assurance of receiving a dollar, and must return as I came. Will leave this evening for Cairo.

"JAMES B. EADS."

(Telegram.)

"WASHINGTON, *January* 10, 1862.

"TO A. H. FOOTE,—The President desires immediately a full report of the number of your gun-boats, armament, crew, etc., and full particulars in relation to the mortar-boats, the number in commission, number of mortars mounted, number of mortars ready to mount, and the time of completion of all the boats.

"G. V. FOX, Assistant-Secretary of Navy."

(Telegram.)

"CAIRO, *January* 29, 1862.

"TO CAPTAIN A. H. FOOTE,—The President orders if Flag-Officer Foote can find a suitable boat which he can purchase at a fair price, let him purchase it at once. You will be governed accordingly in procuring a boat for the mortar-flotilla. M. C. MEIGS."

(Telegram.)

"CINCINNATI, *February* 3, 1862.

"TO FLAG-OFFICER A. H. FOOTE,—Can not buy *Western* for less than twenty thousand dollars. Shall I buy her? It is absolutely necessary that Mr. Magee come here immediately. How many men and shells is the steamboat to be fitted for? Answer immediately.

"J. P. SANFORD."

These are specimens of the great number of such letters, telegrams, and communications—some of them still more urgent, and relating to more important and difficult matters—that might be given, showing the multiplicity of detail, and the perplexing questions of all kinds that were constantly coming up and requiring immediate decision—questions in regard to ordnance, to money supplies, to the obtaining of fit mechanics, to the equipping and manning of the vessels, and especially in relation to the work to be done upon the vessels themselves, which, peculiar in their build and novel in their adaptation of iron-plating to river steamboats, required close watching and the greatest scientific skill. It remains only to speak more definitely than has yet been done of the origin of this famous flotilla.

As early as April, 1861, the government was convinced of the military importance of the Western rivers and waters. Attorney-General Bates wrote to James B. Eads, of St. Louis, a man of great mechanical genius and energy of character, who had been engaged in removing obstructions from the Mississippi and its great tributaries, respecting the use of steam gun-boats upon the rivers. Mr. Eads's plan was referred to Commodore Paulding, who reported favorably upon it, and a naval officer, Captain John Rodgers, was detailed to go to the West and consult with Mr. Eads. The result of this consultation was that in the latter part of May and in June the freight-and-passenger Ohio steamers *Conestoga*, *Taylor*, and *Lexington* were altered at Cincinnati, and armed as gun-boats. These vessels were not plated, but were protected by oak bulwarks against musket-balls.

During the month of July following, the quartermaster-general advertised for proposals to construct a number of entirely new iron-clad gun-boats for the service of the Mississippi River. The same Mr. Eads was the successful bidder. "The Department decided to construct seven of these vessels, each of about six hundred tons, to draw six feet, to carry thirteen heavy guns, to be plated with iron two and a half inches thick, and to steam nine miles per hour. They were one hundred and seventy-five feet long, and fifty-one and a half feet wide; the hulls of wood; their sides projected from the bottom of the boat to the water-line at an angle of about thirty-five degrees, and from the water-line the sides fell back at about the same angle to form a slanting casemate, the gun-deck being but a foot above water. This slanting casemate extended across the hull, near the bow and stern, forming a quadrilateral gun-deck. Three 9 or 10 inch guns were placed in the bow, four similar ones on each side, and two smaller ones astern. The casemate inclosed the wheel, which was placed in a recess on the stern of the vessel. The plating was two and a half inches thick, thirteen inches wide, and was rabbeted on the edges to make a more perfect joint."*

These seven vessels were begun and carried forward with immense energy, and were finished and ready for armament within one hundred days after the signing of the contract. The first of them, and, indeed, the first United States iron-clad, with her boilers and engines on board, was launched in Carondelet, Missouri, on the 12th of October, 1861. She was named the *St. Louis* by Admiral Foote; but when the fleet was transferred from the War Department to the Navy, this name was changed to the *De Kalb*, there being another commissioned vessel at that time named the *St. Louis.* Then followed the *Carondelet*, *Cincinnati*, *Louisville*, *Mound City*, *Cairo*, and *Pittsburg*. Shortly after, the most powerful vessel of them all, and which played an important part in the war as the flag-ship of Admiral Foote—the *Benton*—was altered and plated from the basis of a very large and stout snag-boat that had borne the same name. Some smaller

* Boynton's "History of the Navy during the Rebellion," vol. i., p. 501.

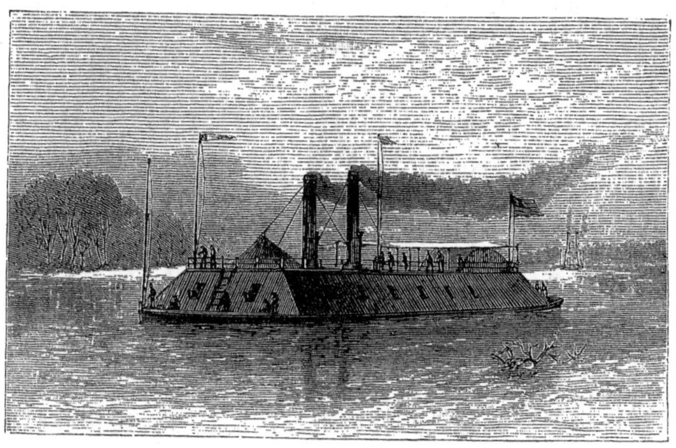

THE "BENTON."

boats, partially armored, were added, and thus, in an incredibly short time, there was prepared "a powerful squadron, aggregating five thousand tons, capable of steaming at nine knots per hour, each heavily armored, fully equipped, and ready for their armament of one hundred and seven large guns."

This rapid generalization does not convey any conception of the incessant detail and the wearing toil, night and day, week-days and Sundays, of those who were chiefly concerned in the getting up, or extemporizing, as it were, of this fleet, whose peculiar character necessitated the invention of new machinery, and the establishment of new navy yards, dock yards, rolling-mills, machine-shops, foundries, forges, and saw-mills. "The timber to form the hulls of the vessels was as yet uncut in the forests, and the engines to drive them were unbuilt." Of course the general supervision of this work—certainly during the latter half of it—and the impelling will that carried it all forward, and brought it up to a point where it was wrought into a most complete and formidable instrumentality of destruction, without which the power of rebeldom at the West could not have been broken—this undoubtedly was his who mainly bore its responsibility; but, like the labors of Perry in constructing his gun-boat fleet on Lake Erie, while the work was arduous, it was the sure means of final success.

The letters of Captain Foote betray the intense anxiety that he felt, but they bespeak at the same time the unflinching spirit of the man in carrying on this anomalous work, which was, as has been remarkod, wholly uncongenial to him. He wished to surround himself with naval men, and he succeeded in doing so to a considerable extent; but his sailor soul was harassed by having to operate through the Army Department, through Army agents and civil contractors, and landsmen and river men of all kinds, some of the latter being most finished specimens of Western Yankees intensified.

But there were some encouraging features. The whole country was looking on with interest; and at Washington Secretary Welles, and, above all, Foote's warm personal friends, Gustavus Vasa Fox, the Assistant-Secretary of the Navy, one of the most able and far-sighted men in the government, and Commodore Joseph Smith, who from the earliest was a main promoter of the iron-clad innovation—these, as far as they had time and opportunity, were unwearied in their aid.

A few extracts from Commodore Smith's letters, written at this period, will close the chapter. Under the date of October 25, 1861, he writes:

"Great excitement prevails on account of the fall of Lexington, and it seems that General Fremont has incurred the displeasure of many for not supporting Colonel Mulligan better. What the result may be is yet to be seen. We are behind in equipment, for want of guns of the proper kind. Rifled cannon may be very useful in certain positions and cases, but my opinion is that heavy shot from smooth bores will be more destructive than the rifled projectiles. Some of each may be well. Missouri and Kentucky seem now to be the most interesting points, and we should have double the men in those regions that we have. I think the Department will be disposed to favor you, for none in the Navy stand before you. You see what changes in squadrons have been made—a lieutenant in command of one of our largest ships! It is said that our Navy officers are too old—be it so; I am ready to be put into the hopper to be ground over again. Don't know what the Board will do, and care less.

"Pity our *élite* of the Navy could not have let well enough alone, and left the Department to furlough inefficient officers while it had the power to do so. Oh, my country! I feel for her misfortune and fear for her destiny. But there is a higher Power, and I trust after He has sufficiently scourged us we shall return to our duty and to peace. We are too sordid for patriotism, and until the selfish principle shall be eradicated we shall continue to suffer."

Under October 31st he writes:

"I understand all your embarrassments; but if any man can overcome them, you can. I spoke to the Secretary about sending men to you, and I understand they will be taken from Fort Ellsworth, near Alexandria, and sent to you forthwith—and good men they are. We are pressed here for supplies, all transportation being cut off except by the Baltimore Railroad. Supplies now are at a most ruinous price, but we hope soon to open the Potomac by upsetting the batteries studded on the Virginia bank of that river. What are to be the next movements of the Army of the Potomac I do not know. I hope when they do move they will sweep clean as they go. I have seen the man here who furnished the iron for plating your boats; it is sufficient to break, or stop, or turn the enemy's shot, I think."

He says, December 31:

"I submitted your general orders to Dahlgren, who said they could not be criticised. It is difficult to prepare a flotilla in the circumstances in which you are placed; but you will master it, and come out all right. We are going at the rate of $200,000 per diem, and upon the rag system. You have read Seward's reply to Lord John Russell's demand. It is ingenious, *gassy*, too long, but able. Our diplomacy with England stands 'Wilkes, *vs.* Apology.' We shall, I trust, strike a death-blow to the Confederate hopes before many months pass; if we do not, our country will be in a lamentable condition. The black clouds around us look threatening; but I trust they have a silver lining which will dispel them after a time."

CHAPTER XIV.

FIRST OPERATIONS OF "FOOTE'S FLOTILLA."—THE ACTION AT LUCAS'S BEND, AND RECONNOITRING EXPEDITIONS.

Now that the war is over, we can afford to give our whilom Southern foes the credit of great ability in military affairs, and to recognize the truly formidable nature of the rebellion that was organized against the national life. They certainly far surpassed us at the more calm and sluggish North in the force, rapidity, and skill of the early operations and dispositions of the war. From the fact also that there was a real despotism at the South, and a spirit of intense, passionate concentration upon one subject, the Southerners hurled themselves with desperate energy into the struggle. In point of territory, also, the country was about equally divided; for the Ohio River really formed the northern defensive line of the rebel states. Kentucky's neutrality was of such a nature as to give free scope to the enemy's operations; the Mississippi River below Columbus was entirely sealed up; in Missouri the rebellion had a strong basis for attack upon the Northwestern States; and, in fact, the rebel line presented an almost unbroken front of fortified posts from the mouth of the Ohio to the mouth of the Potomac. Success in Virginia alone could avail but little to break this line of defense unless at the West it was penetrated and cut in two. Vast masses of Southern troops were concentrated in Tennessee between Nashville and the Mississippi River, and also in Eastern Tennessee; but how to come at these, and how to project and maintain Northern armies in hostile states, so far from the base of supplies, was a difficult question, and, at the time, one wholly incapable of being answered so long as the great river communications of the West were in the power of the enemy. The Ohio River was to be kept open through its entire length; the Cumberland and Tennessee rivers were to be cleared of their formidable fortifications; Kentucky and Tennessee were to be held possession of with a strong grasp; Columbus was to be flanked, and the Mississippi River to be opened to its mouth—these were the problems that presented themselves to our government to be solved before it could hope to deal successfully with the rebellion at the West, or with the rebellion at all in its essential strength.

We have in this country been put to school by the hard schoolmistress, War, and have learned a great deal of the geography of our own country that we did not know before; and, above all, we have come to understand better than before the magnificent system of inland water communication that traverses our vast territory, and makes it available, not only to the peaceful offices of commerce, but the sterner uses of war. The inhabitants of the rebel states grasped the idea sooner than we at the North did, and they promptly seized upon the Western rivers as they had done upon the Potomac; but they evidently did not anticipate the creation and powerful character of the Northern gun-boats, although upon the Mississippi they themselves had commenced at an early date the construction of iron-clads and the armoring of river steamers already in use.

The first operations of "Foote's Flotilla," now that the gunboats were fast becoming prepared for action, were wholly tentative, and chiefly directed to exploring expeditions and reconnoissances on the Ohio, Cumberland, and Tennessee rivers. They were at this time under the immediate control of the War Department, and were more especially to act in co-operation with the army force under General Grant, whose head-quarters were at Cairo; but Captain Foote, strenuous for

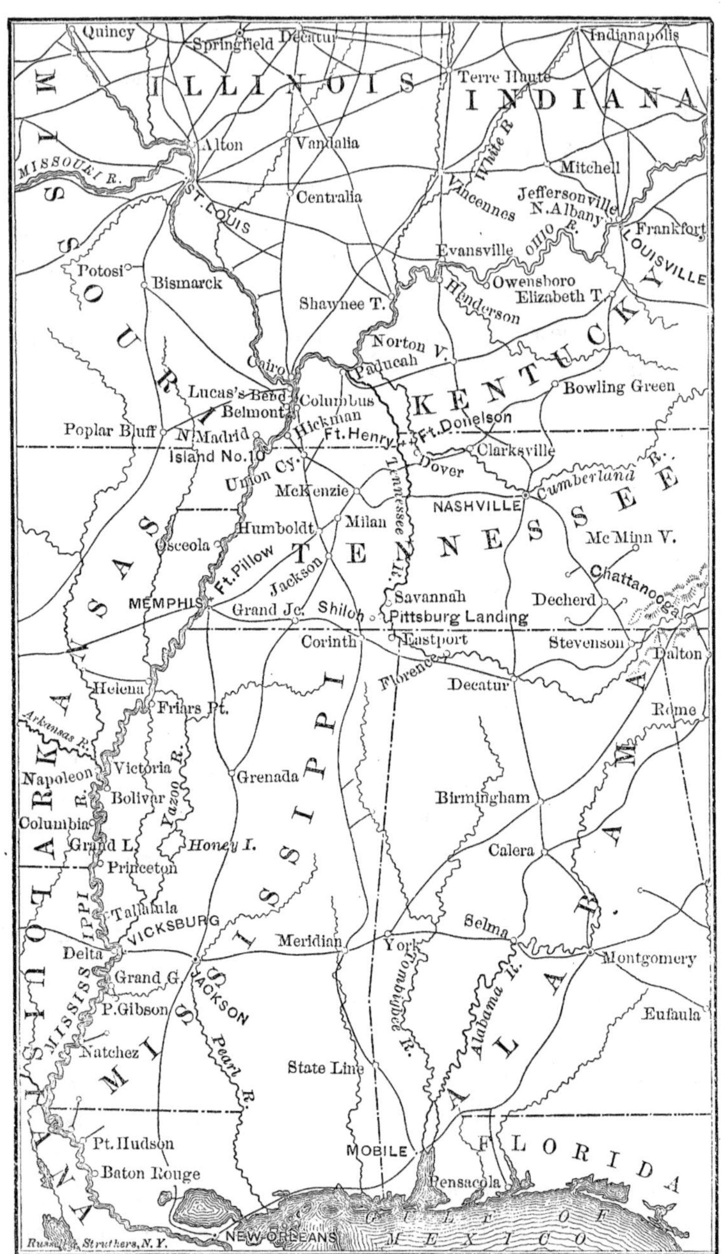

SCENE OF OPERATIONS AT THE WEST.

the independence and freedom of his command, while at the same time prompt to co-operate with the Army, seemed at first to be busy in trying the capacities of his fleet before attempting great things. He sent his grim river-dogs, singly or two in company, up and down these waters on short excursions to spy out the enemy's position, and sometimes to give them a little taste of what was to come. It was characteristic of him not to attempt any thing important until he was perfectly ready, and then he moved swiftly.

One of these early minor but not unimportant expeditions, made in conjunction with the land forces, is what is called the fight of "Lucas's Bend." Eight miles below Cairo, at Norfolk, a town in Missouri, there was a body of rebel troops whom General Grant determined to dislodge, and two vessels of the flotilla—the *Lexington* and the *Conestoga*—were at once put in requisition. The narrative of this action is briefly given in the following letter, written by Lieutenant Phelps, commanding the *Conestoga*:

"U. S. Gun-boat 'Conestoga,' Cairo, Ill.,
September 10, 1861.

"Captain A. H. Foote, U. S. N., commanding Naval Forces, Western Rivers:

"Sir,—I have to inform you that this morning I got under way with this vessel, in company with the *Lexington*, at the request of Colonel Waggoner, and went down the river to cover an advance of troops from Norfolk in that direction. After passing considerably below the forces on shore, the *Lexington* turned back to be nearer them. I proceeded on farther down to examine the head of Island No. Two for a reported battery, but failed to find it. I, however, discovered the enemy in force on the Missouri side at Lucas's Bend, and at once opened fire upon their artillery and cavalry. The enemy had about sixteen pieces of field artillery, and, it is believed, one heavy piece in battery. Several of their pieces were rifled cannon, and ranged to and beyond this vessel, striking all about her. In a short time Commander Stembel, hearing our guns, came down with the *Lexington*, and joined in the fight. The rebels moved their batteries from point to point, while we availed ourselves of our motive power to move up stream as the enemy would attempt to move up, back from the banks, and bring their several batteries out at different places to fire a few rounds, and then gallop to some other point. Their force of cavalry was considerable, and I fired several shells among them with great apparent effect. The shell and shot of both our vessels were lodged among their batteries. Both the *Lexington* and this vessel retired out of range for a short time about one o'clock, hoping to lead the enemy up higher, to where our land forces were. Two steamers of the enemy had come up from Columbus, one of them the gun-boat *Yankee*, which also opened fire on us; but I found our guns could not reach them where they lay below the batteries. At about two o'clock I again dropped down with this vessel, determined to try a shot again at the rebel gun-boat. The first shot must have struck her on the ricochet, as it touched the water close alongside, and she at once started down stream.

"The *Lexington* again came up, and, it is believed, succeeded in landing an 8-inch shell in the *Yankee's* wheel-house and side, where it burst. At all events, the vessel appeared to be greatly injured, and went off with but one engine working. She retired under the batteries at Columbus, where the other one had previously gone. Our boats again opened fire upon the enemy's batteries, and before five o'clock we had silenced them entirely, driven their force out of reach, and without any injury to ourselves. I am satisfied we did great damage to the enemy. While retiring, this boat was fired upon with musketry by an enemy concealed in a thicket, and one man, Nelson Castle, quartermaster, was shot through the arm and in the forehead. I think he will recover, but an operation will be required upon his skull. I at once opened with canister upon the thicket, and quickly cleared it of the rebels. Some of them were shot by our small-arms men. I can not speak too highly of the spirit and will of the crew, scarcely one of whom had been under fire before. I am, respectfully, your obedient servant,

"S. L. PHELPS, Lieutenant U. S. N."

Captain Foote makes the following report to General Fremont of a reconnoitring expedition which he himself conducted:

"OWENSBORO, KY., *Sept.* 25, 1861.

"GENERAL,—Agreeably to your orders per telegram of the 22d instant, and further instructions from General Grant, commanding at Cairo, to proceed to Owensboro with the gun-boats for the purpose of keeping the

Ohio River open, and to dislodge the rebels supposed to have been in possession of that place, I proceeded to Paducah on the morning of the 23d in the steamer *Bee*, before the gun-boat *Lexington*, Commander Stembel, was ready to leave Cairo, for the purpose of calling on General Smith, and of having the gun-boat *Conestoga*, Lieutenant Phelps commanding, ready on the arrival of the *Lexington* to accompany me up the river.

"On reaching Paducah, I ascertained from General Smith that the *Conestoga* had gone on a short cruise; consequently, on the arrival of the *Lexington*, I immediately proceeded with her alone up the river, taking with us the steamer *Bee*, as the water was low and the river falling, that we might have the means, if necessary, of getting afloat more readily. I also sent the *Bee* up the Cumberland River fifteen miles in a vain search for the *Conestoga*. After grounding twice, at one o'clock on the morning of the 24th we were compelled to anchor and lie over till 8 A.M., when, in company with the *Bee*, and she towing us, we proceeded up the river to Evansville, from whence I telegraphed you at 11 P.M.

"This morning we reached Owensboro; found no batteries, but were boarded by Colonel McHenry, who, with Colonel Hawkins, had a skeleton Kentucky regiment, which had arrived the previous morning. I sent for the authorities of the place, and directed them to prevent the display of secession flags. A strong disunion sentiment is manifest in the place, but no disrespect was shown me, although I have been much among the people; but I directed Commander Stembel to hold as little communication with the shore as practicable. The colonels, with their force, as previously designed, left the town during the day, although I strongly importuned them to remain, as I did the Cincinnati company; but they declined on the ground of not being properly equipped, nor having been mustered into the service. Under these circumstances, and the water requiring the *Lexington* soon to leave, I ran down to Evansville on the *Bee*, and telegraphed to General Morton at Vincennes, Indiana, asking for five hundred men for Owensboro. If I get no answer, I purpose telegraphing General Anderson at Louisville for the same number. On returning to Owensboro in the evening, I again communicated with the shore; after which, and giving my orders to Commander Stembel to remain till the low water required him to leave in order to reach Cairo safely, I ran down to Evansville, meeting and boarding the *Conestoga* on the way, and giving her instructions; and here have telegraphed to General Anderson for five hundred men to be sent to Owensboro. Having done all in my power in this quarter, and the preparations of the gun-boats in St. Louis demanding my immediate attention, I leave for that place at 10 A.M. to-morrow, and trust that I may personally communicate with you in the evening. In haste.

"I am, very respectfully, your obedient servant, A. H. FOOTE.

"Major-General Fremont, Commanding Western Army,
St. Louis, Mo."

The *Conestoga* proceeded to Owensboro, and remained there as long as it was safe to do so, even going farther up to Hawsville and Cannelton, quelling by her presence some symptoms of disturbance, but leaving suddenly on account of the alarmingly low state of the river, and having great difficulty in getting over the bars, there being three inches too little of water. The commander of this vessel, Lieutenant Phelps, was, as has been remarked, one of the most energetic of Foote's officers. He ably seconded his chief's incessant labors to bring the gunboats to a higher state of efficiency. He writes (October 5):

"I would ask your attention to the armament of this vessel. Had there been a rifled cannon, or even a heavy 32-pounder on board on the evening of the 1st, we could, in all probability, have destroyed the rebel gun-boat *Jeff Davis*, near the batteries above Columbus, under which she found protection. The rifled 32 or 42 pounder, one on either end, would render this vessel infinitely more efficient. General Grant offered to exchange a heavy 32-pounder for one light one carried aft, but the carriage we have will not answer. I would quite as soon have the 32-pounder at present on board as the 64-pounder shell-guns on the other boats. With solid shot our range is better. I feel confident that this change of armament—especially for one heavy rifled piece—is of importance enough to justify my urging it upon your attention."

In another letter (October 18), Lieutenant Phelps gives an interesting account of a reconnoissance up the Tennessee River, even as far as Fort Henry. He says:

"On the following day (12th) we ascended the Tennessee River to near Fort Henry, where we lay over night. The next morning I examined the fort carefully at a distance of two to two and a half miles, the rebels not opening fire upon us.

"One mile below a small body of men had fired at the vessel with small-arms; but a shot put an end to further demonstrations of the kind. The fortification is quite an extensive work, and armed with heavy guns, mounted 'en barbette,' and garrisoned by a considerable force. It is situated about half a mile above the head of Panther Creek Island, and where the Tennessee state-line leaves the right bank and crosses the river. There is no channel upon one side of the island (western), and a narrow and somewhat crooked one upon the other, which continues so till within a mile of the fort, where the water becomes a good depth from bank to bank—some six hundred yards. It is credibly reported that the rebels, at a point about five miles above the fort, are converting three steamers into gun-boats, and are plating them with iron. There are extensive iron works on the river. They have one of the finest and fastest steamers in the West—the *Eastport.* If desirable, it will be an easy matter to render their boats almost useless by obstructing the channel in a narrow spot a few miles above Paducah. On the 14th instant I entered the Cumberland, and ascended it sixty miles, where the water became shoal, and then dropped down to anchor over night at Eddyville—a strong secession town, and a neighborhood where Union men have been driven from their homes. It was reported that the rebels were building a battery below the town. I found it necessary to use strong language to the citizens in regard to the persecution of Union people. The more active Secessionists fled at the approach of the gun-boat.

"I yesterday again ascended the Tennessee to Aurora, where the state-road from Columbus east, passing through Hopkinsville, etc., crosses the river, and seized the steam ferry-boat *Henry*, bringing it to this port (Paducah). It is evident that each time this boat is shown along these waters there is an increased confidence and sense of security on the part of the Unionists."

The new flotilla was thus feeling its way to more important results, exciting alarm among the ranks of secession people along the banks of the great rivers, and giving new strength to the enfeebled national cause, while at the same time it was gradually finding out its own deficiencies and its own power. It was not as yet clearly defined where the Western flotilla belonged—to the Army or to the Navy—and this continued to be a cause of great embarrassment; but Captain

Foote, by constant and strenuous requisitions, as far as his authority went, on the credit of the government, for men, money, and supplies, finally succeeded in equipping his fleet. If, instead of continual appeals to Washington, and now and then unfortunate interferences on the part of civil and army authorities, the whole thing had been left in his hands, and the power and the money intrusted to him unconditionally, there would have been more rapid progress; but, under the circumstances, that could not well be done; and, as it was, patience and will wore through all difficulties, and the time was now near at hand when all these anxious and wearing toils were to be rewarded with important and even splendid success.

CHAPTER XV.

ACTION AT EDDYVILLE.—DOCUMENTS RESPECTING THE FLOTILLA.
—DEFECTIVE GUNS.—BATTLE OF BELMONT.—
CORRESPONDENCE.

That the gun-boats, or those that were prepared for action, were not suffered to remain idle, the following letter will testify; and this is one of many written during the closing months of the year 1861, giving accounts of similar expeditions by different officers in command of vessels of the Western Navy. Many of the details may seem unimportant, but they afford a true view of the character of the service in which these vessels were engaged:

"U. S. Gun-boat 'Conestoga,' Paducah, Ky.,
October 28, 1861.

"Captain A. H. Foote, U. S. Navy, commanding Naval Forces, Western Rivers:

"Sir,—On the afternoon of the 26th instant, by order of General Smith, I left this place in company with the steamer *Lake Erie*, No. 2, on board of which were three companies of the Ninth Illinois Regiment, under command of Major Phillips, and proceeded up the Cumberland River upon an expedition to surprise a rebel camp near Eddyville, Kentucky, and have the honor to make known to you that the result was in the main successful.

"I went, with Major Phillips on board, in advance to Smithfield, to procure guides and pilots, expecting that the transport would not approach the wharf-boat; but the captain ran her to it, which rendered a change of plan necessary, and caused the force to reach the rebel camp at a later hour than was designed. The distance from Smithland to Eddyville by land is not half that by water; and the rebels have a complete system of runners established in that section of the country. The transport was, therefore, sent up the Ohio a few miles, and the *Conestoga* followed, an hour later, with two heavy barges in tow. These were cast off on reaching the transport, which was then taken in tow, with all lights out, fires screened, and engines stopped, by which precautions we succeeded in dropping down to Smithland and passing into the Cumberland, without its being suspected, in the darkness of the night, that we had the steamer in tow. The two boats, after passing to a safe distance, made all speed up the narrow and crooked stream, but did not reach and disembark the troops at the point selected, two miles below Eddyville, till half-past three o'clock A.M. I then had the transport moved to near the town and concealed behind a wooded point, while this boat was quietly anchored off the main street, as had been done several times before in the past few weeks.

"As soon as I felt satisfied that Major Phillips had had time to reach the rebel camp—a march of seven miles over an exceedingly rough country, and in lanes and foot-paths—and that information of the force was reaching the citizens, I threw a force on shore and surrounded the town with picket-guards, to prevent the escape of rebel citizens, or the entrance and concealment of refugees from the rebel camp.

"About 10 A.M., Major Phillips reached town with a number of prisoners, horses, wagons, arms, etc. He had got to within four hundred yards of the enemy after daylight before being discovered, when the rebels formed in line. Our troops were moved at a double-quick to within one hundred yards, when they delivered their fire and charged bayonets upon the rebels, who broke and fled in every direction, leaving seven killed on the field. Two of our soldiers were severely wounded, and one or two slightly—among these a captain of a company.

"I seized a flat-boat belonging to a noted Secessionist, and it was freighted with the prisoners and plunder and towed to this place. The horses and mules were first placed on the wharf-boat at the town, also Secession property; but the boat was found to be too leaky and rotten for towing, and the animals were embarked on the transport, and one hundred of the troops were transferred to the *Conestoga*. There were taken in the rebel camp and brought to this place, where we returned last evening, twenty-four prisoners, seven negroes, thirty-four horses, eleven mules, two transport wagons, a large number of saddles, muskets, rifles, shot-guns, sabres, knives, etc. A number of valuable horses were unavoidably killed in the skirmish at the camp.

"Eddyville is sixty-two miles from Paducah, and the camp was four miles back of the town, at a place known as Saratoga Springs. We were absent from Paducah twenty-nine hours.

"Major Phillips and the volunteers deserve the greatest credit for their successful daylight surprise. I am, respectfully, your obedient servant,

"S. L. Phelps, Lieutenant Commanding U. S. Navy."

While services like the above were being rendered by the boats, before we relate their further operations it would be well to present some additional documents having special relation to the business matters of the fleet. Great difficulty continued to be experienced in raising men to man the fleet, and, at last, strenuous requisitions had to be made upon the West, upon barge-men, river-men, lake-men, and landsmen of all sorts (and some of the worst), to fill up the vacancies; the clothing and supplies of the crews were still greatly deficient, and the pay of officers and men was woefully in arrears; some of the boats were as yet unfit for service; good subordinate officers, foremen, firemen, engineers, and pilots were scarce; and, from the parting of a hawser to the buying of a steamboat, every thing had to go through the head and hands of the commanding officer. That all was done with the greatest economy might be proved from the competent testimony of Paymaster Captain George D. Wise (May 25, 1862): "Notwithstanding all this, our gun-boat flotilla has not cost, including the building of the gun-boats, $3,000,000 to this date. When we look at the results it has accomplished, the money has been well laid out; and if we balance it by the destruction and capture of the enemy's property, we shall be largely in pocket."

"Navy Department, *October* 28, 1861.

"My dear Sir,—We have been drilling some three hundred men here for you, and will send them when you so write or telegraph. We have also given orders to ship landsmen in New England for you. They are good men—mostly fishermen—but without drill. If you wish any of your officers ordered away, or can spare any of them, write me word.

"Respectfully, G. V. Fox, Assistant-Secretary.

"Captain A. H. Foote, U. S. N."

"WASHINGTON, D. C., *November* 17, 1861.

"MY DEAR FLAG-OFFICER,—We have sent you off five hundred men, but I am inclined to think it is all we can do. Every means is being used to recruit, but the large number of vessels put afloat absorbs them. Be sure that you shall have the first fifty men to spare from this coast; but it looks now as if it would be impossible to do more. If you wish or can spare any officer, drop me a private note, for we are ashore for commanders. We shall not disturb you unless you agree, but rather go to the merchant service. I made several calls upon the War Department about the money, and they tell me it was remitted. What a magnificent piece of seamanship Dupont has given us—it wipes out the disgraceful transaction on board the *Richard* in the Mississippi. Wise showed me your note about the gun-boats. I suppose if they barely float they may do, unless they draw too much water. It will be a blow upon the Navy if they fail. Can't camels be made of rubber to lift them over?

"Most truly your friend, G. V. FOX."

"U. S. GUN-BOAT 'LEXINGTON,' CAIRO, ILL.,
November 22, 1861.

"SIR,—I have the honor herewith to inclose duplicate requisitions for $1250. I am induced to make this requisition, in addition to the $5000 already received, in order to pay my crew the two thirds of their wages faithfully promised them at the time of their enlistment. Most of my men are married, and have families to provide for, and are in great need of their wages. I was forced, by the necessity of the case, to reduce the payment twenty-five per cent., in order to make the $5000 hold out, and give each an equal proportion; their clothing and small stores account was also deducted from the two thirds, and this left but a small amount to each. Some of my men have been shipped now nearly five months, and have received but one small payment previous to this. I should be much pleased if you can consistently approve this requisition, and much oblige, Very respectfully, your obedient servant,

"R. N. STEMBEL, Commander U. S. N.

"To Commodore A. H. Foote."

It is pleasing to learn from other sources how willingly and faithfully these ill-provided and ill-paid men continued to work, with rare instances of desertion. The men sent at various times from the East also came, with very few losses, promptly to their posts, and served with that heartiness which characterized all departments of our patriotic forces in the great struggle.

"WASHINGTON, *November* 1, 1861.

"COMMODORE A. H. FOOTE, U. S. N., commanding Gun-boats, St. Louis:

"I am instructed to say that General Halleck has instructions in regard to the gun-boats.

"The appropriation not being sufficient to complete and equip more than three altered and seven built gun-boats, the Department is embarrassed by the action of the commanding general West in ordering so many mortar-rafts, tugs, and altered boats, in addition to those contracted for by this Department. All can not be completed without further appropriations, and, for the present, at least, this Department can not remit money except for those contracted for under its authority.

"Respectfully, M. C. MEIGS, Quartermaster-General."

The complete outfit of the mortar-boat department, requiring a great many implements and needing a long time to manufacture them, gave rise to a long correspondence both with officials at Washington and ordnance officers and manufacturers at Pittsburg. It will not be necessary to give this correspondence; but the following is a private letter of Captain Foote's, which sets forth some of the facts of the case from his point of view:

"CAIRO, *January* 11, 1862.

"MY DEAR SIR,—I send the report herewith which your telegram of the 10th, but not received till this morning, required for the President. I have endeavored to keep the Department fully informed of our progress, with all incidental circumstances. I have worked incessantly since I have joined or assumed command here. The contractor, in not being up to time, and for want of men, has kept the gun-boats from being commissioned. I have had all things in my power, and over which I had control, in readiness long since. With reference to the mortar-boats, I only wish that you could see them. Their magazines are merely square holes in the timbers, banded together, forming the boat, and of course most of them leak. The mortar-boats would require, if all fitted out, about eight hundred men. There are no conveniences for living aboard.

They will leak more and more. Some of our best officers have no better opinion of these rafts or boats than I have; still this is unofficial. It is my business to let the government judge, and I am to obey orders; and while I can not consider these boats as well adapted to the purposes for which they were designed, still, as I said to General Meigs, so much has been expended upon them, they ought not to be cast aside, or 'words to that effect,' and I certainly would not presume to throw obstacles in the way of having them fitted, armed, and equipped. I obtained authority to this effect from General Fremont; but General Curtiss, when he sent for me and asked for my orders and instructions (which I reported, to show how every brigadier might interfere with me, and by way of illustrating the necessity of the appointment of a flag-officer), said that General Fremont's orders were, or would be, now of no avail. Still, on General Halleck's arrival, I called on him, and said that I had selected Captain Constable, who, with Lieutenant Sanford, under my direction, could have good mortar-boats made in fourteen days in St. Louis, while I could send Captain Pike, who had been an engineer appointed by Fremont, to Pittsburg, to have the mortars there made, and sent or shipped here before navigation closed. I asked General Halleck to allow me to do this, and I would have the mortar-boats armed in twenty days. He declined, as he had no authority, and in a few days sent Captain Constable to join his company. He was averse to helping me at all. General Meigs, on referring to him, said that General Halleck had instructions with reference to gun and mortar boats, as shown in his letter to me. I left St. Louis under those circumstances, while afterward the quartermaster sent down the mortar-boats, asking me to receive them. Such is a brief history of these boats. I have here had no men nor officers, nor means to attend to them; yet had I supposed that it was the intention of the Department for me to fit them out or to move in the matter, I would have found a way of doing it. But under the circumstances it could not be expected of me to have done differently from what I have done. I am aware that an officer in command is considered culpable by the public when any thing is wanting in the Department where he is the chief, irrespective of the question of his right or power to do it, but I trust you judge otherwise. I have to-day telegraphed to Pittsburg to learn how many beds and mortars are or can soon be ready, and I am ready—as I have always been. I know that an officer of great resources can overcome almost insuperable obstacles; but away from a navy yard, and with the limited means I have at hand in this wilderness of naval wants, I must say that no one could have done more than I have done. Very truly yours, A. H. FOOTE.

"G. V. Fox, Assistant-Secretary of the Navy.

"I have made every effort to ship men in the West, but have secured only about two hundred. The river-men enlisted in June, or went South; and as our pay is eighteen dollars per month, and their old pay thirty dollars, the remaining men are indisposed to ship in the gun-boats.

"A. H. F."

The following letters are interesting as showing the straits into which the government was forced in the early periods of the war. Most of the defective guns mentioned were thrown out; but some of them continued to be a source of annoyance and actual damage from bursting during the operations of the gun-boats under Flag-officer Foote and Captain Davis, who succeeded him.

"COMMANDANT'S OFFICE, U. S. NAVY YARD,
January 20, 1862.

"CAPTAIN A. A. HARWOOD, Chief of Bureau of Ordnance and Hydrography:

"SIR,—I beg leave to call the attention of the Bureau to the fact that certain 9-inch guns have been sent to the Western flotilla which were made for the Navy in 1855, and rejected for want of strength. As one of these guns burst as low as 121 fires, it is evident they are unsafe. I am aware that at the time they were sent West there seemed to be an immediate need of some ordnance, and it not being possible to procure any others, there was a justification for the risk incurred. But this is no longer the case; and as the gun-boats on which these guns are may be in action before long, I would urge the Bureau to lose no time in replacing the 9-inch guns sent West by others which have been fully proved.

"I have the honor to be, very respectfully, your obedient servant,

"JOHN A. DAHLGREN, Commandant."

"BUREAU OF HYDROGRAPHY, NAVY DEPARTMENT,
WASHINGTON, *January* 23, 1862.

"SIR,—You were telegraphed on the 21st instant (1) not to send more 9-inch guns to New York until further orders, and to get ready with all possible dispatch sixteen of the same class for a special purpose. (2) The Bureau now informs you that the sixteen guns are intended for the gun-boat flotilla at Cairo; and you will please forward the guns by the quickest means of transportation, one by one, as fast as they can be delivered. (3) You will please inform the Fort Pitt founders that the Bureau especially and urgently requests that every possible exertion may be made to expedite the work for the purpose indicated at the earliest practicable moment. I am, very respectfully, your obedient servant,

"ANDREW A. HARWOOD, Chief of Bureau.

"Commander J. R. M. Mullany, U. S. N.,
Asst. Ins. Ordnance, Pittsburg."

But it is time that we should speak of the remaining operations of the gun-boats during the year 1861, from the date of the action at Eddyville, October 26th.

It should be borne in mind that the whole Western military field, comprising both land and water, was up to this time under the command of Major-General Fremont, and thus, generally speaking, of the Army Department. General Grant, having seized upon Paducah, gained a footing near the mouth of the Ohio River, and established his head-quarters at Cairo, with a force rapidly increasing in numbers. Combined with him in the control of operations in the Mississippi Valley was that very able commander, General C. F. Smith; and with these two army leaders Foote, with the title and authority of flag-officer,* which ranked him with a major-general in the army, was appointed specially to co-operate with his gun-boat fleet; having, it is true, an independent command, but at the same time being more or less under the direction of the army, and his subordinate commands being liable at any moment to be peremptorily ordered to perform some duty required in carrying out the plans of General Smith or General Grant. This state of things, in which the authority and responsibility

* His official naval rank as "flag-officer" dates actually from November 13th, 1861, although before this he was the regularly appointed commander-in-chief of the Western waters.

were at best but vaguely defined, was, as has been more than once hinted, a source of annoyance to so high-spirited a man as Foote; and it grew to its height under General Halleck, who, two days after the battle of Belmont, succeeded Fremont in the control of the Western Department. Foote felt this to be so great a grievance that he at one time solicited a transference to a separate naval coast command; but his value at the post where he had been placed was so great that the government refused his request, having unlimited confidence in his ability and his adaptation to the work assigned him. The wisdom of its choice was confirmed by the result; but the subject of it nevertheless was subjected to a cruel trial, which, however, he nobly bore, suffering it to have no evil influence upon his actions. He went straight on in spite of all obstacles, sacrificing his personal feelings to the public good.

On the 1st of November, 1861, Major-General Fremont ordered Grant to make demonstrations on both sides of the Mississippi River. This order was countermanded; but was renewed on the 5th, and was carried into effect by Grant. Having learned on the 7th that there was a movement of the rebels from Columbus to Belmont, to cut off Colonel Oglesby, whom he had sent with three thousand men toward the St. Francis River, Grant immediately resolved to attack Belmont, and to surprise General Polk, who was there with a force of seven thousand men, thus preventing him from sending reinforcements into Missouri. Grant's troops, consisting of about three thousand men, were swiftly embarked on transports at Cairo; and the gun-boats *Taylor* and *Lexington* were ordered to convoy them down the river to a point two miles above Belmont, where they were landed; but as we do not intend to give an account of the battle of Belmont, but only of the part that the flotilla, which had been prepared for action and, as it were, created by Foote, took in it, we simply subjoin Commander Walke's report:

"U. S. Gun-boat 'Taylor,' Mound City, *Nov.* 9, 1861.

"Sir,—I have the honor to report that on the evening of the 6th instant I received instructions from General Grant to proceed down the river, in company with the *Lexington*, under Commander Stembel, for a reconnoissance and as convoy to some half-dozen transport steamers. We proceeded opposite to Norfolk, near the Kentucky shore, where we rounded to, and anchored for the night. I then learned for the first time the extent of the reconnoissance.

"At three o'clock the following morning, at the request of General Grant, the *Taylor* and *Lexington* started down the river for the purpose of engaging the rebel batteries at Columbus; but after proceeding a few miles we were met with such a dense fog as to render any farther progress hazardous; we therefore rounded to, and returned to the point from whence we started. At six o'clock we all got under way, our two gunboats taking the lead, and convoying the steamers containing Generals Grant and McClernand and their aids, and some three thousand troops, two companies of cavalry, and some artillery. We proceeded down the river to the extreme end of Lucas's Bend, and just without, as I thought, the range of their guns on Iron Banks. After the troops had disembarked, and were under marching orders (half-past eight o'clock), our two boats proceeded to engage their batteries on Iron Banks, each expending several rounds of shell, and returning to the transports. Their shot passed over us, though in some instances coming very close to us. At this time, with their long-range rifled cannon, they sent a large number of shot half a mile above the transports. I requested the captains of the transports to move up and out of the range of their shot, which they did. At ten o'clock, the engagement having commenced at Belmont, we again engaged the Iron Bank batteries, expending still more shell, their shot flying around us, but doing no harm, while our shells seemed to go where they could be effective. We returned, after an engagement of about twenty minutes, to the transports.

"At about noon, hearing the battle of Belmont still going on, our two gun-boats made a third attack upon their batteries, this time going nearly a quarter of a mile nearer to them. We opened a brisk fire of shell, and seemingly with good effect. While in this engagement one of their 24-pounders struck us on the starboard bulwarks, and, continuing obliquely through the spar-deck, took off the head of Michael Adams, seaman, and broke the arm and otherwise seriously injured James Wolfe, seaman, and slightly wounding a third. Acting-Surgeon Kearney, who was cool and

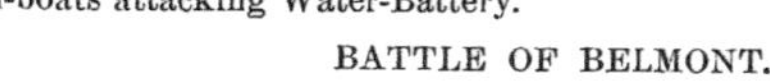

Gun-boats attacking Water-Battery. General Grant's Transports.

BATTLE OF BELMONT.

assiduous in the discharge of his duties, immediately dressed Wolfe's wound, but considers him in a critical condition. We fired a few more shell and returned, keeping up the fire from our stern guns as long as we were within reach of them.

"It is providential that we have escaped with so little damage. A fragment of one of their shells struck us on the stern, but doing little damage.

"When nearly all our troops had re-embarked, or were about ready to start, a sudden attack was made upon the transport vessels by a large force coming in from above. Our gun-boats being in good position, we opened a brisk fire of grape, canister, and 5″-shells, silencing the enemy with great slaughter. After the transports were under way we followed them, throwing a shell occasionally to repel the enemy's approach to the banks. When a few miles up the river, we met one of the transports (*Chancellor*) with Brigadier-General McClernand on board, who stated that some of their men were left behind, and asked that we might return with our gun-boats, and see if we could find them. We did so, the *Lexington* accompanying us, and between us we succeeded in securing nearly all that were left behind, together with about forty prisoners, including some badly wounded.

"We then proceeded up to Island No. One, when the *Rob Roy* met us, with instructions from General Grant to turn over all the troops and prisoners, and to remain until Colonel Cook, who was down the Kentucky shore on a reconnoissance, should return. He returned at ten o'clock, and at eleven I weighed anchor and returned to Cairo, having sent the *Lexington* on before me.

"It is but an act of justice to the officers and crew to state that they acted throughout all our engagements with perfect coolness, ability, and courage, the crew answering the calls to quarters with an alacrity becoming earnest co-operators for the government. I was astonished, with the apparently new materials we have, to see with what zeal and efficiency they all performed their parts.

"The *Lexington*, under Commander Stembel, as consort, supported me throughout the day with the most commendable energy and efficiency.

"Very respectfully, your obedient servant,

"H. Walke, Commander U. S. N.

"Captain A. H. Foote, U. S. N., commanding
Naval Forces on Western Waters."

There is no doubt but that the gun-boats performed a signal service at Belmont, and by covering with well-directed fire the final retreat, prevented our troops from being almost, if not entirely, cut to pieces. The action of the boats was by no means intended to be an assault upon Columbus—a fortification containing 40,000 men, and more than one hundred guns of large calibre—but it was simply to reconnoitre the enemy's position and to convoy the transports; yet, as it turned out, the gun-boats proved to be, in this instance, the salvation of the Army. Our loss, notwithstanding the early brilliant success of the attack, was five hundred men; and what might it not have been, with an overwhelmingly superior force from Columbus coming down suddenly upon our troops hastily re-embarking, if the watchful gun-boats had not been at hand to keep the foe at bay with their slaughterous discharges of grape and canister?

In the flag-officer's correspondence about this time with his active officers there are many interesting things mentioned, and facts that bring before us vividly the state of the times. Running up the rivers, coming suddenly upon small villages, surprising farm-houses, and appearing without announcement in secession districts, the gun-boats gained a sort of omnipresent reputation. One of the lieutenants writes:

"On arriving at Linton, two signal guns were fired, and about sixty loyal refugees came in during the night, in small parties, from the back country. Just before dark a negro ran down to the river bank, near the boat, chased by blood-hounds in full cry after him, and begged to be taken on board. I sent a boat to his rescue, and learning by his statement, confirmed by Kentuckians on board, that he was being chased by rebel cavalry—he had run eighteen miles—I received him on board and brought him away. His master is a Secessionist. The cavalry did not show themselves, and the hounds were taken from the track; but we saw three of them."

This poor fellow must truly have blessed the hour

"Wen de Linkum gun-boats cum."

A letter of Captain Foote to his wife, dated December 13, 1861, written upon the back of a letter of General Grant to himself, asking his aid in an anticipated attack by the rebels upon Fort Holt, and addressing him as "Dear Commodore," breathes the weary, anxious, yet brave spirit of a man almost overborne by cares, but still hopeful:

"CAIRO, *December* 17, 1861.

"MY DEAR WIFE,—Weary days are my lot. Sanford is better to-day, and may be up and about in a week. Pennock, the only one left good for any thing, is on the Board examining mortar and gun boats with two generals and a colonel. I have been hard at work all day, but the Board have capsized every thing, and will keep us back for several days. If I could be fitted out at a navy yard, I would not care; but this fitting out vessels where no one knows any thing is discouraging. But I can now and then see light aloft. I feel clearer of head oppression than usual, though I may be prostrated at any minute. I sleep nicely at night, which is a blessing, and I don't mean to fret. General McClellan is to give us 1100 men—have just heard of it by telegram from Fox. Things brighten a little ahead. Ever affectionately, A. H. F."

CHAPTER XVI.

PREPARATIONS FOR ATTACKING FORT HENRY.—THE ASSAULT AND CAPTURE.

ALTHOUGH the history of the Western flotilla is part and parcel of the biography of Admiral Foote, and although its achievements belong, in a true sense, to his renown, and all that it was and did is thoroughly identified with him, who was the main cause and promoter of its efficiency, yet we do not think it necessary to dwell further upon those minor movements and expeditions in which he was not present or personally engaged, and which were undertaken at the suggestion of the Army Department; and we turn now to those greater and more splendid operations where Foote himself was the prime directing and inspiring force.

The first strong line of the rebel defense at the West stretched from the Mississippi River at Columbus to the Cumberland Mountains. It was necessary to break through this at the most feasible point, which could not be on the Mississippi River on account of the immense strength of the fortifications at Columbus, neither could it be done by sending an Army across the Ohio into Kentucky, so far from the base of supply; and Foote, as well as the two Army commanders, Grant and Smith, early appreciated the strategic importance of seizing the strongholds on the Tennessee and Cumberland rivers, thus letting them far into the Southern line, and establishing a base whereby both Columbus and Bowling Green could be made untenable to the enemy, the railroad communications cut, and the rebel line of defense pushed farther down, leaving Kentucky and Tennessee at the command of the Union forces. Foote was earnestly bent upon this idea, and hastened forward his preparations during the month of January, 1862. He was particularly careful as to the perfect condition of his gun-boats. The whole thing was novel and untried. It had not yet been ascertained how iron-clads would compete with land-batteries. This, in fact, was the first trial of iron-clad vessels. The strength of forts Henry and Donelson in guns and men was known only by rumor. It was therefore necessary to make cautious reconnoissances, without awakening the least suspicion of what was intended to be done. One of these expeditions, undertaken January 7th, is thus reported by Lieutenant Phelps of the *Conestoga:*

"Yesterday I ascended the Tennessee River to the state line, returning in the night. The water was barely sufficient to float this boat, drawing five feet four inches, and in coming down we dragged heavily in places. The Cumberland is also too low above Eddyville.

"The rebels are industriously perfecting their means of defense both at Dover and Fort Henry. At Fort Donelson (near Dover) they have placed obstructions in the river, one and a half miles below their battery on the left bank, and in the bend where the battery comes in sight. These obstructions consist of trees chained together and sunk across the river, with the butts up stream, the heads floating near the surface, and pointed. Placed as they are reported to be, any attempt to remove them must be made under a severe fire, and where there is very little room for covering boats. The bend is a very sharp one, and the river not more than one hundred and fifty yards wide. The battery upon the right bank is upon a hill half a mile back from the river, and considerably below the fort upon the left bank. It can be seen, I am told, but one mile. Four weeks since they had four 32-pounders mounted on the hill, and had a large force of negroes at work. The fire of gun-boats here would be at a bad angle. On these narrow streams, with their usually contracted channels, it would appear to one very necessary to have the assistance of mortars in reducing earth-works as strong and complete as those on the Tennessee and Cumberland have been made. The forts are placed, especially on the Cumberland, where no very great range can be had; and they can only be attacked in one narrow and fixed line. Shot can dislodge their guns (all *en barbette*)—nothing more. The shells must burst at the moment, or they pass harmless, while there is little room to regulate distance nicely. There is no advantage to be gained by moving in circles or otherwise. Some of the disadvantages of narrow streams would be partially removed by a high stage of water.

"Fort Henry I have examined, and the work is formidable. Fort Donelson can only be seen from an easy range of its guns. There are a thousand rumors; but I conclude that the batteries upon both sides—their situation, the character and location of the obstructions—may be considered as known. It is now too late to move against the works on either river, except with a well-appointed and powerful naval force."

Another still more important and extensive reconnoissance was undertaken on the 16th of January by the gun-boats, accompanied by an Army force, in which a feigned assault was made upon Fort Henry. It is thus narrated by Lieutenant Phelps:

"On the 16th we proceeded up the river, accompanied by the transport-steamer *Wilson*, having on board a force of five hundred men—infantry and artillery—under command of Major Ellston, and anchored for the night near where the Tennessee line strikes the right bank of the river. A few miles above Paducah the *Lexington* struck a rock, and lay upon it over an hour, but was not apparently much injured. In the morning (17th) we proceeded up to near Fort Henry—the transport remaining a little below—and shelled the river bank at a point where all informants have uniformly reported a masked battery of two rifled guns; but we did not succeed in drawing its fire, although we approached to abreast the place. We also fired a few shells at Fort Henry—two and a half miles—too distant for effect. Having complied with General Smith's wish in feigning an attack, at early morn, with the whole force in view, we dropped below to Aurora, where the troops disembarked and marched for Murray. The transport returned down stream, while the two gun-boats again returned to the neighborhood of Fort Henry, and remained overnight at anchor about three and a half miles by water below the fort. The rebels made numbers of signals in the evening. In the morning we left there, coming directly down. A charge of slugs was fired yesterday at a group of officers, and Mr. Hamilton, gunner, was slightly wounded in the neck.

"There was a coal-barge lying at a landing some three miles below Fort Henry, on the Kentucky side, evidently taken there to freight a quantity of wood thrown down from the banks in readiness, and the wood could only have been intended for use at the fort. I therefore seized the barge, loaded the wood on it, and brought it down. The barge, or flat, is a very fine one, and might be of service at Cairo. I also cut adrift a small wood-boat at the same landing, to prevent its use in transporting supplies to the rebels."

The use of mortar-boats for the reduction of the forts on the Cumberland and Tennessee rivers became now an earnest question between Foote and the government. General Halleck, who had been appointed to the command of the Western Department, was the medium of communication.

"ST. LOUIS, *January* 17, 1862.

"FLAG-OFFICER FOOTE, Cairo:

"COMMODORE,—General McClellan wishes to know if it would be of much advantage in any expedition up the Tennessee and Cumberland to have the mortar-boats armed. Can they be used with advantage on such an expedition? Very respectfully, your obedient servant,

"H. W. HALLECK, Major-General."

The flag-officer replied in favor of the effectiveness of mortar-boats; but the difficulty seemed to lie in the Ordnance Department, which, for some reason or other, was behindhand in its preparations—so much so that Fox, the Assistant-Secretary, writes (January 27th):

"The President is very much exercised in the matter, and I do not blame him. He telegraphed to Pittsburg, and they replied that two beds were ready. I doubt if the history of any war ever furnished such an exposure. The plan matured and commenced last summer, the boats built, the gun-boats in good condition, the river high, the time come to make the movement coincide with others, and only two beds ready. The President has determined to remove ——— from the Ordnance, and it has shaken his confidence in many others. The result of the whole matter is a delay and change of programme. Our twenty mortar vessels have partly sailed, and will probably all be off in the course of ten days.

I think their success under Porter will shame the Army people for their great crime in neglecting these boats. Halleck seems to take no interest in your part of the expedition, but I advise him to obey orders about furnishing you with men. Your daily telegraph to Wise goes to the President, who very wisely has taken this matter into his own hands."

Quartermaster H. A. Wise also writes (January 31st):

"With respect to the mortar-rafts, and the amount of shells required, the President remarked that he thought it would be expedient to receive all the mortars and shells sent to Cairo, so as to be able to meet any probable amount of work that may be demanded; that he wished you to be sure, when you opened fire on Columbus, 'to rain the rebels out,' as he desired to 'treat them to a refreshing shower of sulphur and brimstone.' The President added his commendation of the energy you have displayed in the matters intrusted to your charge. He is evidently a practical man, understands precisely what he wants, and is not turned aside by any one when he has his work before him. He knows and appreciates your past and present ardent services, and is firmly resolved to afford you every aid in the work in hand."

The question of the use of mortar-boats on the Tennessee and Cumberland rivers was practically decided by Foote's attacking the forts without waiting for their assistance.

When all was ready, the following dispatch was sent, the proposition contained in it having come from Foote to Grant:

"CAIRO, *January* 28, 1862.

"General Grant and myself are of the opinion that Fort Henry, on the Tennessee River, can be carried with four iron-clad gun-boats and troops, and be permanently occupied. Have we your authority to move for that purpose when ready? (Signed) A. H. FOOTE, Flag-Officer.

"Major-General Halleck."

Information had come that there were five thousand men at Fort Henry, it having been reinforced; add to these the force at Dover, and there would be about six thousand men. Evidently there was an expectation of an attack, although many movements on the Mississippi and the other rivers had served to confuse and blind the enemy. They did not know where the blow would be struck; but they felt that it must come soon and come heavily, and great anxiety was manifested to be ready for it.

Fort Henry* was situated on low, marshy land on the eastern or right bank of the Tennessee River, in Stewart County, Tennessee, about sixty miles above Paducah. It lay in a bend of the stream, and was at times almost surrounded by water; its guns commanded a reach of the river below, toward "Panther Island," for about two miles. It was a strong earth-work, constructed with much scientific skill, covering ten acres, with five bastions from four to six feet high, the embrasures knitted together firmly with sand-bags; and its armament consisted of seventeen heavy guns, one of them a 10-inch columbiad (120-pounder), one 24-pounder rifle, twelve 32-pounders, one 24-pounder siege-gun, and two 12-pounders.† The fort had accommodations for an army of fifteen thousand men, but at the time of its capture was defended by probably about three thousand troops, including those that were encamped outside of the main works, who, during the battle, retreated precipitately to Fort Donelson. It was commanded by Brigadier-General Lloyd Tilghman, a Marylander, and a graduate of West Point.

On the 30th, an order came from General Halleck to the combined forces to proceed to the attack of Fort Henry. Active operations were immediately commenced, and on the morning of Sunday, 2d of February, Foote left Cairo with a small fleet of seven vessels, four armored and three wooden. The fleet moved up the Ohio to Paducah, and that evening was in the Tennessee River.

Grant's army, composed of the divisions of Generals

---

* For map of Fort Henry, see p. 200.

† Authorities differ in some particulars in their description of the fort. I have mainly followed Lossing's account of the fort and the battle, together with the official reports issued by the Secretary of the Navy.

McClernand and C. F. Smith, were embarked in transports, and proceeded to Paducah, whence they were convoyed the next day by the gun-boats to a point a few miles below the fortification, out of range of its guns, where they were landed. From Paducah, Foote wrote to the Secretary of the Navy a letter which gives some idea of his own view of his state of preparation for the contest:

"U. S. GUN-BOAT 'TAYLOR,' PADUCAH, *February* 3, 1862.

"SIR,—I have the honor to inform you that I left Cairo yesterday with this vessel, having ordered the armored gun-boats *Essex*, *Carondelet*, *Cincinnati*, and *St. Louis* to precede me to Paducah, and arrived here last evening.

"To-day I propose ascending the Tennessee River with the four new armored boats, and the old gun-boats *Taylor*, *Conestoga*, and *Lexington*, in convoy of the troops under General Grant, for the purpose of conjointly attacking and occupying Fort Henry and the railroad bridge connecting Bowling Green with Columbus. The transports have not yet arrived, although expected last night from Cairo, which causes detention; while, in the mean time, unfortunately, the river is falling. I am ready with the seven gun-boats to act offensively whenever the Army is in condition to advance; and have every confidence, under God, that we shall be able to silence the guns of Fort Henry and its surroundings, notwithstanding I have been obliged, for want of men, to take from the five boats remaining at Cairo all their men, except a sufficient number to man one gun-boat for the protection of that important point.

"I have left Commander Kilty as senior officer in charge of the gun and mortar boats at Cairo, ordering him, with the assistance of Fleet-Captain Pennock, to use every effort in obtaining more men and forwarding the early equipment of the mortar-boats. It is peculiarly unfortunate that we have not been able to obtain men for the flotilla, as they only are wanting to enable me to have at this moment eleven full-manned, instead of seven partially manned gun-boats, ready for efficient operations at any point. The volunteers from the Army to go in the gun-boats exceed the number of men required; but the derangement of companies and regiments, in permitting them to leave, is the reason assigned for not more than fifty of the number having been thus far transferred to the flotilla.

"I inclose a copy of my orders to the commanders of the gun-boats, in anticipation of the attack on Fort Henry; also a copy of orders to Lieutenant-Commanding Phelps, who will have more especial charge of the old gun-boats, and operate in a less exposed condition than the armored boats. I have the honor to be, etc.,

"A. H. FOOTE, Flag-Officer.

"The Hon. Gideon Welles, Secretary of the Navy."

The orders referred to are the following, which, as they were strictly carried out, form, as it were, Foote's plan of operations:

(Order No. 1.)

"U. S. GUN-BOAT 'TAYLOR,' OHIO RIVER, *February* 2, 1862.

"The captains of the gun-boats, before going into action, will always see that the hoods covering the gratings of the hatches at the bows and sterns, and elsewhere, are taken off; otherwise great injury will result from the concussion of the guns in firing. The anchors also must be unstocked if they interfere with the range of the bow guns.

"In attacking the fort, the first order of steaming will be observed, as by the vessels being parallel they will be much less exposed to the enemy's range than if not in a parallel line; and by moving ahead or astern, which all the vessels will do by following the motions of the flag-ship, it will be difficult for the enemy to get an accurate range of the gun-boats.

"Equal distances from one another must be observed by all the vessels in action. The flag-ship will, of course, open the fire first, and then others will follow when good sight of the enemy's guns in the fort can be obtained. There must be no firing until correct sights can be obtained, as this would be not only throwing away ammunition, but it would encourage the enemy to see us firing wildly. The captains will enforce upon their men the absolute necessity of observing this order; and let it be also impressed upon every man firing a gun that, while the first shot may be either of too much elevation or too little, there is no excuse for a second wild fire, as the first will indicate the inaccuracy of the aim of the gun. Let it be reiterated that random firing is not a mere waste of ammunition, but it encourages the enemy when he sees shot and shell falling harmlessly.

"The great object is to dismount the guns in the fort by the accuracy of our fire, although a shell in the mean time may occasionally be thrown in among a body of the enemy's troops.

"When the flag-ship ceases firing, it will be a signal for the other vessels also to cease. As the vessels will be all so near one another, verbal communication will be held with the commander-in-chief when it is wanted. The commander-in-chief has every confidence in the spirit and valor of the officers and men under his command, and his only solicitude arises lest the firing should be too rapid for precision, and that coolness and order, so essential to complete success, should not be observed; and hence he has, in this general order, expressed his views, which must be observed by all under his command. A. H. FOOTE,

"Flag-Officer Commanding Naval Forces on Western Waters."

(Order No. 2.)

"U. S. GUN-BOAT 'TAYLOR,' OHIO RIVER, *February* 2, 1862.

"The division of the three gun-boats not armored, and, consequently, not prepared to encounter at so short a range the batteries of the fort as the four armored boats, will take a position astern, and, if practicable, inshore of the right of the main division. Lieutenant-Commanding Phelps, in charge of this division, from his great experience and successful charge of our interest for most of the time on the Tennessee and Cumberland rivers, will, I trust, be enabled to throw shells into Fort Henry, with no greater exposure of his division, comparatively, than to that of the armored boats, while the main division, more directly in the face of the fort, attempts to dismount its guns in close range. The captains of this division will also see that no gun is fired without accurate aim, as we have no ammunition to throw away.

"Great care must be observed lest our troops should be mistaken for the enemy. When the main division ceases firing, it will be an indication that the fort is ready to surrender. A. H. FOOTE."

(Order No. 3.)

"U. S. GUN-BOAT 'TAYLOR,' PADUCAH, *February* 2, 1862.

"Lieutenant-Commanding Phelps will, as soon as the fort shall have surrendered, and upon signal from the flag-ship, proceed with the *Conestoga*, *Taylor*, and *Lexington* up the river to where the railroad bridge crosses, and if the Army shall not already have got possession, he will destroy so much of the track as will entirely prevent its use by the rebels.

"He will then proceed as far up the river as the stage of water will admit, and capture the enemy's gun-boats, and other vessels which might prove available to the enemy. A. H. FOOTE."

It was necessary to move cautiously up the Tennessee on account of torpedoes. After some delay from this source, under the skillful direction of Lieutenant Phelps, eight of these "floating mines" were successfully fished up in the channel off Panther Island. "They were cylinders of sheet-iron, five feet and a half long, pointed at each end, each containing in a canvas bag seventy-five pounds of gunpowder, with a simple apparatus for exploding it by means of a percussion-cap, to be operated upon by means of a lever, extending to the outside, and moved by its striking a vessel. These were anchored in the river a little below the surface."*

As the vessels moved on, the woods were shelled to discover concealed batteries.

On the night of the 5th there was a severe storm, which put the troops who had been landed to great inconvenience and suffering, and also flooded the neighboring region, causing the river to rise rapidly.

But on the morning of the 6th all was in readiness for the attack of the combined forces.

McClernand's division moved first, up the eastern side of the Tennessee, to get into position between forts Henry and Donelson, and be in readiness to storm the former from the rear, or to intercept the retreat of the Confederates, while two brigades of Smith's division, that were to make the attack, marched up the west side of the river, to assist and capture half-finished Fort Hieman, situated upon a great hill, and from that commanding point to bring artillery to bear upon Fort Henry.†

The rain of the preceding night had swollen every little stream, so that it was necessary to build bridges to get the artillery over, and the roads were in such a condition that,

---

* Lossing's "Civil War in America," vol. ii., p. 202, note.

† *Ibid.*, vol. ii., p. 203.

though the distance was but five miles, and never men worked harder, they were still some considerable distance from their destination when the battle had commenced. General Lewis Wallace, who was with Smith's division, wrote: "The guns of the fleet opened while we were yet quite a mile from our objective. Our line of march was nearly parallel with the line of fire to and from the gun-boats. Not more than seven hundred yards separated us from the great shells, in their roaring, fiery passage. Without suffering from their effect, we had the full benefit of their indescribable and terrible noise. Several times I heard the shots of the fort crash against the iron sides of the boats. You can imagine the excitement and martial furor the circumstances were calculated to inspire our men with."

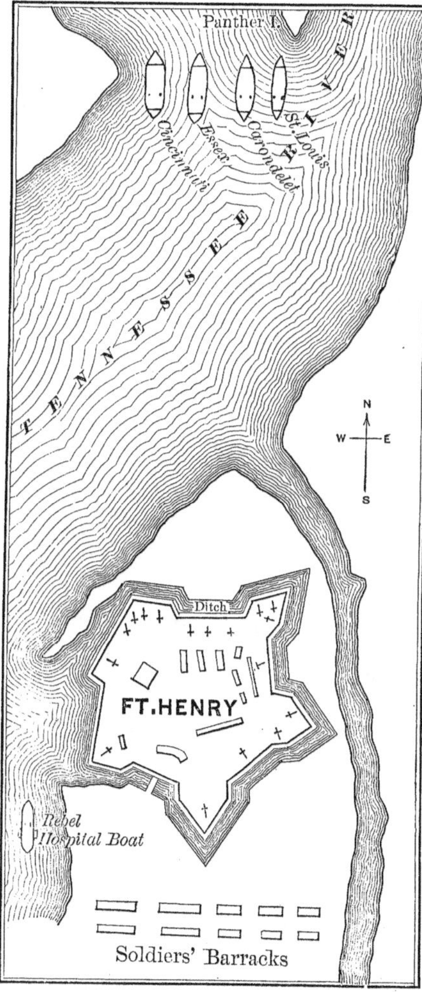

At about ten o'clock on Thursday morning, February 6th, the little flotilla started slowly and steadily up the river, along the west channel, by Panther Island, the four iron-clads leading abreast—the flag-ship in the centre—and as they drew near the fort firing

Fort Henry. United States Gun-boats.

BATTLE OF FORT HENRY.

occasionally from their bow guns. The three wooden boats, according to Foote's orders, ranged themselves abreast, and followed half a mile or so to the rear. At half-past twelve the armored boats steamed up to a position just diagonally across the river, within six hundred yards of the batteries, and opened their bombardment. This was responded to vigorously from the fort. The firing, at so short a distance, was destructively accurate, especially on the side of the gun-boats. It was, in fact, terrific. An officer within the fort relates that it exceeded in terror any thing that the imagination had pictured of the power of shot and shell, plowing complete roads through the earth-works and sand-bags, dismounting heavy guns and crippling others, setting on fire and bringing down buildings within the fortification, and cutting in two as with a scythe large trees in the neighborhood. Such a hurtling tempest of shot and shell was rained incessantly upon the enemy's works from those black floating batteries, which, however, in their turn were exposed to a hot fire from heavy guns well worked. Perceiving by her broad pennant that the *Cincinnati* was the flag-ship, and that her range and firing were better than that of the other boats, the rebels concentrated upon her a storm of solid shot, striking her thirty times. One 68-pound conical shot struck, bounding in the centre of the front part of the pilot-house, in which Commodore Foote, Captain Stembel, a midshipman, and the two pilots were standing; it did not perforate the vessel, but indented its side deeply. The shot that pierced or took effect were chiefly in the front sides of the vessel, which were not sheathed, and in the chimneys and works of the upper deck. The chimneys were perforated by eight or ten cannon-balls, but were still serviceable after the fight. A 32-pound ball came through the forward angle of the starboard side, killing one seaman, and passed through the whole length of the lower deck without further damage. Many sailors were seriously wounded, and why no more were killed is extraordinary, as the *Cincinnati* stood up nearest the batteries—one account says within four hundred yards—and took their full brunt.

The other vessels also were frequently hit with serious effect; and at about twenty minutes before one o'clock a 32-pound shot struck the *Essex* just above one of her bow guns, killing a young officer, Samuel B. Brittan, master's mate; then going through the bulkhead in front of the boiler, it passed into the flue of the centre boiler, occasioning an escape of the steam and hot water, and dreadfully scalding all on the forward gun-deck, and the two pilots, who were almost immediately over the front of the boilers. Twenty men and officers were instantly killed or scalded by this explosion; and, among them, the brave Captain Porter himself was severely injured. The *Essex* was completely disabled, and was obliged at once to withdraw from the combat.

But the fire from the fleet, both of the armored and wooden vessels, was so tremendous that the gunners of the enemy were driven from their posts; the 10-inch columbiad and other heavy guns silenced, and nothing could withstand its fury; and after a hot conflict, lasting an hour and twenty minutes, in which the forces under General Tilghman made a most determined resistance, the rebel flag was lowered, and, amid the wildest excitement and cheers of the crews, the victory was declared for the gun-boats.

It was indeed a brilliant naval victory. By the force of circumstances that could not be foreseen nor prevented, the glory as well as the suffering of this battle belonged entirely to the naval forces. The Army strove earnestly to share in the fight, but the impetuosity of the sailors, combined with the heavy state of the roads, rendered it impossible for them to come up in time; and when they did come up, the thing was accomplished, and the fort, with all that it contained, was quietly handed over by Commodore Foote to General Grant.

"A few minutes before the surrender," says the Southern historian, Pollard, "the scene in and around the fort exhibited a spectacle of fierce grandeur. Many of the cabins were in flames. Added to this were the curling and dense wreaths of smoke from the guns; the constant whizzing of fragments of crashing and bursting shells; the deafening roar of artillery; the black sides of five or six gun-boats, belching fire at every port-hole; the volumes of smoke settled in dense masses around the surrounding back-waters; and up and over that fog on the heights, the army of General Grant deploying around our small army, attempting to cut off its retreat. In the midst of the storm of shot and shell, the small force outside of the fort had succeeded in gaining the upper road, the gun-boats having failed to notice their movements until they were out of reach. To give them further time, the gallant Tilghman, exhausted and begrimed with powder and smoke, stood erect at the middle battery, and pointed gun after gun. It was clear, however, that the fort could not hold out much longer. A white flag was raised by the order of General Tilghman, who remarked, 'It is vain to fight longer. Our gunners are disabled—our guns dismounted. We can't hold out five minutes longer.' As soon as the token of submission was hoisted, the gun-boats came alongside the fort and took possession of it, their crews giving three cheers for the Union."

It is related that, on meeting Foote, the rebel general remarked, "I am glad to surrender to so gallant an officer." Foote replied, "You do perfectly right, sir, in surrendering; but you should have blown my boat out of the water before I would have surrendered to you." This is the newspaper account; but Foote's own account of the interview, as related to a friend,* is different from this. "The facts are these," he

* Mr. E. H. Leffingwell.

said: "General Tilghman came on board my boat, evidently in deep distress, wringing his hands and exclaiming, 'I am in despair; my reputation is gone forever.' I replied, 'General, there is no reason that you should feel thus. More than two thirds of your battery is disabled, while I have lost less than one third of mine. To continue the action would only involve a needless sacrifice of life, and, under the circumstances, you have done right in surrendering. Moreover, I shall always be ready to testify that you have defended your post like a brave man.' I then added, 'Come, general, you have lost your dinner, and the steward has just told me that mine is ready;' and, taking him by the arm, we walked together into the cabin. This is all that passed between us." Admiral Foote rarely, if ever, forgot that he was a gentleman, and especially with those whom the fate of war had made prisoners.

We subjoin the modest report of the commander of the victorious fleet, giving the authentic details of the battle, and which may serve to correct errors in the foregoing brief account, that has been drawn mostly from other sources:

"CAIRO, ILL., *February* 7, 1862.

"SIR,—I have the honor to report that on the 6th instant, at half-past twelve o'clock P.M., I made an attack on Fort Henry, on the Tennessee River, with the iron-clad gun-boats *Cincinnati*, Commander Stembel; the *Essex*, Commander Porter; the *Carondelet*, Commander Walke; and *St. Louis*, Lieutenant-Commanding Paulding; also taking with me the three old gun-boats *Conestoga*, Lieutenant-Commanding Phelps; the *Taylor*, Lieutenant-Commanding Gwin, and the *Lexington*, Lieutenant-Commanding Shirk, as a second division, in charge of Lieutenant-Commanding Phelps, which took position astern and inshore of the armored boats, doing good execution there in the action, while the armored boats were placed in the first order of steaming, approaching the fort in a parallel line.

"The fire was opened at seventeen hundred yards' distance from the flag-ship, which was followed by the other gun-boats, and responded to by the fort. As we approached the fort under slow steaming till we reached within six hundred yards of the rebel batteries, the fire, both from the gun-boats and forts, increased in rapidity and accuracy of aim. At twenty minutes before the rebel flag was struck, the *Essex*, unfortunately, received a shot in her boiler, which resulted in the wounding, by scalding, of twenty-nine officers and men, including Commander Porter, as will be seen in the inclosed list of casualties. The *Essex* then necessarily dropped out of line astern, entirely disabled, and unable to continue the fight, in which she had so gallantly participated until the sad catastrophe. The firing continued with unabated rapidity and effect upon the three gun-boats as they continued still to approach the fort with their destructive fire, until the rebel flag was hauled down, after a severe and closely contested action of one hour and fifteen minutes.

"A boat, containing the adjutant-general and a captain of engineers, came alongside after the flag was lowered, and reported that General Lloyd Tilghman, the commander of the fort, wished to communicate with the flag-officer, when I dispatched Commander Stembel and Lieutenant-Commanding Phelps, with orders to hoist the American flag where the Secession ensign had been flying, and to inform General Tilghman that I would see him on board the flag-ship. He came on board soon after the Union had been substituted by Commander Stembel for the rebel flag on the fort, and possession taken.

"I received the general, his staff, and some sixty or seventy men as prisoners; and a hospital ship containing sixty invalids, together with the fort and its effects, mounting twenty guns, mostly of heavy calibre, with barracks and tents capable of accommodating fifteen thousand men, and sundry articles, which, as I turned the fort and its effects over to General Grant, commanding the army, on his arrival in an hour after we had made the capture, he will be enabled to give the government a more correct statement of than I am enabled to communicate from the short time I had possession of the fort.* The plan of the attack, so far as the army reaching the rear of the fort to make a demonstration simultaneously with the Navy, was frustrated by the excessively muddy roads and high stage of water preventing the arrival of our troops until some time after I had taken possession of the fort.

"On securing the prisoners and making necessary preliminary arrangements, I dispatched Lieutenant-Commanding Phelps, with his division, up the Tennessee River, as I had previously directed, and, as will be seen in the inclosed orders to him, to remove the rails, and so far render the

* It was estimated that more than a million dollars' worth of property was captured at Fort Henry.

bridge incapable of railroad transportation and communication between Bowling Green and Columbus, and afterward to pursue the rebel gun-boats, and secure their capture, if possible. This being accomplished, and the army in possession of the fort, and my services being indispensable at Cairo, I left Fort Henry in the evening of the same day with the *Cincinnati*, *Essex*, and *St. Louis*, and arrived here this morning.

"The armored gun-boats resisted effectively the shot of the enemy when striking the casemate. The *Cincinnati* (flag-ship) received thirty-one shots; the *Essex* fifteen; the *St. Louis* seven; and the *Carondelet* six; killing one and wounding nine in the *Cincinnati*, and killing one in the *Essex;* while the casualties in the latter amounted to twenty-eight in number. The *Carondelet* and *St. Louis* met with no casualties.

"The steamers were admirably handled by their commanders and officers, presenting only their bow guns to the enemy, to avoid exposure of the vulnerable parts of their vessels. Lieutenant-Commanding Phelps, with his division, also executed my orders very effectually, and promptly proceeded up the river in their further execution after the capture of the fort. In fact, all the officers and men gallantly performed their duty; and, considering the little experience they have had under fire, far more than realized my expectations.

"Fort Henry was defended with the most determined gallantry by General Tilghman, worthy of a better cause, who, from his own account, went into action with eleven guns of heavy calibre bearing upon our boats, which he fought until seven of the number were dismounted or otherwise rendered useless. I have the honor to be, etc.,

"A. H. Foote, Flag-Officer.

"The Hon. Gideon Welles, Secretary of the Navy."

CHAPTER XVII.

RESULTS OF THE CAPTURE OF FORT HENRY. — FURTHER MOVEMENTS OF THE GUN-BOATS.—PREACHING AT CAIRO.

THERE were far greater battles during the war, both on land and water, than that sharp fight on the narrow river which resulted in the fall of the earth-work of Fort Henry—there was the siege and taking of the almost impregnable Vicksburg, and there was the splendid crowning naval victory of Admiral Farragut at New Orleans—but there were few battles of more vital importance to the Union arms than this earliest success of the Western flotilla. It was a moment of great gloom and uncertainty in the country's affairs; and this was almost the first marked success—success of such a kind as had a sure prophecy of the future in it—or, as a Confederate officer, Colonel Gilmer, said in his report, "it was for the enemy a great success, as it emboldened him to make the attack on Fort Donelson." It was the triumph of a new agency in war—of a power the development of which was of incalculable value, not only to the Northern cause, but to the cause of all peoples who were called upon to fight for their freedom. The people who had iron and coal at their command were hereafter to be deemed unconquerable—they could not be subjected or destroyed. Above all, Fort Henry was the key of the rebel position in the West. Its subdual, with that of Fort Donelson, unlocked to our armies the states of Kentucky and Tennessee, leading General Halleck (who, though bigoted in favor of the Army, was an earnest patriot) to express himself in his bulletin of the victory in these words: "The flag of the Union is re-established on the soil of Kentucky. It will never be removed." By it the first strong rebel line of defense—the spinal column, as it were—was broken. The control of the direct line of railroad which connected the great rebel force of Columbus with that at Bowling Green was secured, a point far in the rear of both of these was seized, and the road was opened for the southward advance of our armies. Bowling Green was soon after evacuated. The desperate battles of Pittsburg Landing, Shiloh, and Corinth were the logical consequence of the capture of Fort Henry, being the struggle on the part of the rebels to establish a new line of defense running from Memphis and Island No. Ten to Pittsburg Landing, on the Tennessee, and Chattanooga. Foote was happy in taking the initiative of victory. The movement was begun which, with wavering and alternate success, and after many severe conflicts, was in the end slowly to bear down and crush the power of the rebellion at the Southwest, where its greatest and final strength lay.

The military qualities and skill which were displayed in the battle of Fort Henry need not be dwelt upon, for they were very simple and thoroughly characteristic of the commander, in whose conduct of the affair we are vividly reminded of the past, and especially of the qualities exhibited in the Chinese "Barrier Forts" engagement, viz., a cool, scrupulous, perhaps over-cautious preparation, and rapid, concentrated, desperately close fighting. The boats drew nearer and nearer to the batteries in a fiercer death-hug. It was the Connecticut sailor calculating every chance and every mishap, and then throwing away all care and fear, and fighting with incredible fury. It was undoubtedly anticipated by Grant and the Army that if the gun-boats were capable of weakening or even reducing the fort, that it would be only after many hours, in which time they would have ample opportunity to bear an equal if not predominant part; but the matter was settled in somewhat over an hour; while the forces engaged were about equally balanced, since, in the whole conflict, Foote brought to bear but eleven heavy guns against as many or more of the same weight on the part of the enemy.

The country and the government received the news of the fall of Fort Henry with enthusiasm. The loyal papers over the whole country were full of the details of the conflict and congratulations upon the happy event—which was one of those events not in itself of great proportions, but whose "singular felicity" depends upon its time, circumstances, and consequences. One of the most generous acknowledgments of the victory, and one that must have been personally gratifying to Foote, was the letter of General McClernand, written the day after the battle:

"HEAD-QUARTERS, FIRST DIVISION, FORT FOOTE (LATE HENRY), TENN., *Feb.*, 1862.

"COMMODORE FOOTE, Flag-Officer, Western Waters:

"DEAR SIR,—As an acknowledgment of the consummate skill with which you brought your gun-boats into action yesterday, and of the address and bravery displayed by yourself and your command, I have taken the liberty of giving the late 'Fort Henry' the new and more appropriate name of 'Fort Foote.'

"Please pardon the liberty I have taken without first securing your concurrence, as I am hardly disposed to do, considering the liberty which you took in capturing the fort without my co-operation.

"Very respectfully yours, etc.,

"JOHN A. MCCLERNAND, Brig.-Gen., Com. First Division."

From the mass of other letters and testimonials of honor and gratitude which speedily flowed in, we select but these two, as expressive at the same time of the value set by the government upon our commander's services and of warm personal friendship:

"NAVY DEPARTMENT, *February* 13, 1862.

"SIR,—Your letter of the 7th instant, communicating the details of your great success in the capture of Fort Henry, is just received. I had previously informed you of the reception of your telegraphic dispatch announcing the event, which gave the highest satisfaction to the country.

"We have to-day the report of Lieutenant-Commanding S. L. Phelps, with the gratifying result of his successful pursuit and capture and destruction of the rebel steamers, and the dispersion of the hostile camps as far up the Tennessee River as Florence.

"I most cordially and sincerely congratulate you, and the officers and men under your command, on these heroic achievements, accomplished under extraordinary circumstances, and after surmounting great and almost insuperable difficulties. The labor you have performed, and the services you have rendered in creating the armed flotilla of gun-boats on the Western waters, and in bringing together for effective operation the force which has already earned such renown, can never be overestimated. The Department has observed with no ordinary solicitude the armament that has so suddenly been called into existence, and which under your well-directed management has been so gloriously effective.

"I am, respectfully, your obedient servant,

"GIDEON WELLES.

"Flag-Officer A. H. Foote, U. S. N., commanding Gun-boat Flotilla, etc., Cairo, Ill."

"NAVY DEPARTMENT, *February* 8, 1862.

"DEAR FLAG-OFFICER,—You have been rewarded for the trials and sublime patience of the labors you have given to your work, and crowned with victory. Of yourself, we all knew that the hour of trial for you was but the hour of success. Another fort knocked over by the Navy is my reward. The victory is very important, as this stage of the river, I presume, gives you access even to Nashville if you take the Cumberland. You will also strengthen the branch of the service with the great West, where the empire soon will be. Your telegraph came at noon, and we sent it immediately to Congress, where it gave intense satisfaction. Believing that you will carry our arms wherever your flag can penetrate, I am sincerely yours, G. V. FOX.

"Flag-Officer A. H. Foote, U. S. N., commanding Western Flotilla."

The following letter shows on the part of Commodore Foote a characteristic courtesy, as well as a positive assertion of principles:

"CAIRO, *February* 10, 1862.

"SIR,—Your note of the 9th instant, referring to my official telegram to the Navy Department, and requesting me to correct an error where mortars are referred to, has been received.

"I have, as you will see by the inclosed letter to the Secretary of the Navy, stated to him that I did not speak of mortars at all in my telegram, which was probably introduced by the printer by mistake.

"The haste in which my dispatch was prepared, or, rather, the short time I remained after the fort surrendered, I find has led me into several little errors referred to in my letter to the Secretary. Still, to show that I intended to represent matters fairly, I did not, either in my telegram or report, speak of our four armed boats having, I believe with a single exception, fired or used but the eleven bow guns—two in the *Essex*, and three in the other three boats. I appreciate your high qualities of courage and other characteristics (always excepting your disunion views and conduct) too highly not to wish to do you every justice.

"I am, very respectfully, your obedient servant, A. H. FOOTE.

"General Lloyd Tilghman, Paducah, Kentucky."

In accordance with the special order of his chief, Lieutenant Phelps, when the surrender of Fort Henry took place, started at once up the Tennessee to cut the railroad track between Memphis and Bowling Green, and to capture rebel gun-boats and steamers upon the river. His report, as showing the state of the country, and in many other respects, though long, is so interesting and valuable, that we give it in full:

"UNITED STATES GUN-BOAT 'CONESTOGA,' TENNESSEE RIVER, *February* 10, 1862.

"SIR,—Soon after the surrender of Fort Henry, on the 6th instant, I proceeded, in obedience to your orders, up the Tennessee River, with the *Taylor*, Lieutenant-Commanding Gwin; *Lexington*, Lieutenant-Commanding Shirk, and this vessel, forming a division of the flotilla, and arrived after dark at the railroad crossing, twenty-five miles above the fort, having on the way destroyed a small amount of camp equipage abandoned by the flying rebels. The draw of the bridge was found closed, and the machinery for turning it disabled. About a mile and a half above were several rebel transport steamers escaping up stream.

"A party was landed, and in one hour I had the satisfaction to see the draw open. The *Taylor* being the slowest of the gun-boats, Lieutenant-Commanding Gwin landed a force to destroy a portion of the railroad track, and to secure such military stores as might be found, while I directed Lieutenant-Commanding Shirk to follow me with all speed in chase of the fleeing boats. In five hours this boat succeeded in forcing the rebels to abandon and burn three of their boats loaded with military stores. The first one fired (*Samuel Orr*) had on board a quantity of submarine batteries, which very soon exploded. The second was freighted with powder, cannon, shot, grape, balls, etc. Fearing an explosion from the fired boats—there were two together—I had stopped at a distance of one thousand yards; but even there our skylights were broken by the concussion, the light upper deck was raised bodily, doors were forced open, and locks and fastenings every where broken.

"The whole river, for half a mile about, was completely 'beaten up' by the falling fragments and the shower of shot, grape, balls, etc. The house of a reported Union man was blown to pieces, and it is suspected that there was design in landing the boats in front of the doomed house. The *Lexington* having fallen astern, and being without a pilot, I concluded to wait for both of the boats to come up. Joined by them, we proceeded up the river. Lieutenant-Commanding Gwin had destroyed some of the trestle-work at the end of the bridge, burning with them a lot of camp equipage. L. N. Brown, formerly a lieutenant in the Navy, now signing himself 'Lieutenant C. S. N.,' had fled with such precipitation as to leave his papers behind. These Lieutenant-Commanding Gwin brought away, and I send them to you, as they give an official history of the rebel floating preparations on the Mississippi, Cumberland, and Tennessee. Lieutenant Brown had charge of the construction of gun-boats.

"At night, on the 7th, we arrived at a landing in Hardin County, Tennessee, known as Cerro Gordo, where we found the steamer *Eastport* being converted into a gun-boat. Armed boat crews were immediately sent on board, and search made for the means of destruction that might have been devised. She had been scuttled and the suction-pipes broken. These leaks were soon stopped. A number of rifle-shots were fired at our vessels, but a couple of shells dispersed the rebels. On examination I found that there were large quantities of timber and lumber prepared for fitting up the *Eastport;* that the vessel itself—some 280 feet long—was in excellent condition, and already half finished; considerable of the plating designed for her was lying on the bank, and every thing at hand to complete her. I therefore directed Lieutenant-Commanding Gwin to remain with the *Taylor*, to guard the prize and to load the lumber, etc., while the *Lexington* and the *Conestoga* should proceed still higher up.

"Soon after daylight, on the 8th, we passed Eastport, Mississippi; and at Chickasaw, farther up, near the state-line, seized two steamers—the *Sallie Wood* and *Muscle*—the former laid up, and the latter freighted with iron destined for Richmond and for rebel use. We then proceeded on up the river, entering the State of Alabama, and ascending to Florence, at the foot of the Muscle Shoals. On coming in sight of the town, three steamers were discovered, which were immediately set on fire by the rebels. Some shots were fired from the opposite side of the river below. A force was landed, and considerable quantities of supplies, marked 'Fort Henry,' were secured from the burning wrecks. Some had been landed and stored. These I seized, putting such as we could bring away on our vessels, and destroying the remainder. No flats or other craft could be found. I also found more of the iron and plating intended for the *Eastport*.

"A deputation of citizens of Florence waited upon me; first, desiring that they might be able to quiet the fears of their wives and daughters with assurances from me that they would not be molested; and, secondly, praying that I would not destroy their railroad bridge. As for the first, I told them we were neither ruffians nor savages, and that we were there to protect from violence and to enforce the law; and with reference to the second, that if the bridge were away we could ascend no higher, and that it could possess no military importance, so far as I saw, as it simply connected Florence itself with the railroad on the south bank of the river.

"We had seized three of their steamers—one the half-finished gunboat—and had forced the rebels to burn six others loaded with supplies; and their loss, with that of the freight, is a heavy blow to the enemy. Two boats are still known to be on the Tennessee, and are doubtless hidden in some of the creeks, where we shall be able to find them when there is time for the search. We returned on the night of the 8th to where the *Eastport* lay. The crew of the *Taylor* had already got on board of the prize an immense amount of lumber, etc. The crews of the three boats set to work to finish the undertaking, and we have brought away probably 250,000 feet of the best quality of ship and building lumber, and the iron, machinery, spikes, plating, nails, etc., belonging to the rebel gun-boats; and I caused the mill to be destroyed where the lumber had been sawed.

"Lieutenant-Commanding Gwin had, in our absence, enlisted some twenty-five Tennesseans, who gave information of the encampment of Colonel Drew's regiment at Savannah, Tennessee. A portion of the six or seven hundred men were known to be 'pressed' men, and all were badly armed. After consultation with Lieutenants-Commanding Gwin and Shirk, I determined to make a land attack upon the encampment. Lieutenant-Commanding Shirk, with thirty riflemen, came on board the *Conestoga*, leaving his vessel to guard the *Eastport;* and, accompanied by the *Taylor*, we proceeded up to that place, prepared to land 130 riflemen and a 12-pounder rifle howitzer. Lieutenant-Commanding Gwin took command of the force when landed, but had the mortification to find the camp deserted.

"The rebels had fled at one o'clock in the morning, leaving considerable quantities of arms, clothing, shoes, camp utensils, provisions, implements, etc., all of which were secured or destroyed, and their winter-quarters of log-huts were burned. I seized also a large mail-bag, to send you the letters giving military information. The gun-boats were then dropped down to a point where arms, gathered under the rebel 'press-law,' had been stored; and an armed party, under Second-Master Gondy, of the *Taylor*, succeeded in seizing about seventy rifles and fowling-pieces. Returning to Cerro Gordo, we took the *Eastport, Sallie Wood*, and *Muscle* in tow, and came down the river to the railroad crossing. The *Muscle* sprang aleak, and all efforts failing to prevent her sinking, we were forced to abandon her, and with her a considerable quantity of fine lumber. We are having trouble in getting through the draw of the bridge here.

"I now come to the, to me, most interesting part of this report—one which has already become too long; but I must trust you will find some excuse for this in the fact that it embraces a history of labor and movements, day and night, from the 6th to the 10th of the month, all of which details I deem it proper to give you. We have met with the most gratifying proofs of loyalty every where across Tennessee, and in the portions of Mississippi and Alabama which we visited. Most affecting instances greet us almost hourly. Men, women, and children several times gathered in crowds of hundreds, shouted their welcome, and hailed their national flag with an enthusiasm there was no mistaking—it was genuine and heartfelt. These people braved every thing to go to the river bank, where a sight of their flag might once more be enjoyed; and they have experienced, as they related, every possible form of persecution. Tears flowed freely down the cheeks of men as well as of women; and there were those who had fought under the stars and stripes at Moultrie who in this manner testified their joy.

"This display of feeling and sense of gladness at our success, and the hopes it created in the breasts of so many people in the heart of the Confederacy, astonished us not a little; and I assure you, sir, I would not have failed to witness it under any consideration. I trust it has given us all a higher sense of the sacred character of our present duties. I was assured at Savannah that of the several hundred troops there, more than one half, had we gone to the attack in time, would have hailed us as deliverers, and gladly enlisted with the national force.

"In Tennessee the people generally, in their enthusiasm, braved Secessionists, and spoke their views freely; but in Mississippi and Alabama, what was said was guarded. 'If we dared to express ourselves freely, you would hear such a shout greeting your coming as you never heard.' 'We know there are many Unionists among us, but a reign of terror makes us afraid of our shadows.' We are told, too, 'Bring us a small organized force, with arms and ammunition for us, and we can maintain our position and put down rebellion in our midst.' There were, it is true, whole communities who, on our approach, fled to the woods; but these were where there was less of the loyal element, and where the fleeing steamers in advance had spread tales of our coming with firebrands, burning, destroying, ravishing, and plundering.

"The crews of these vessels have had a very laborious time, but have evinced a spirit in the work highly creditable to them. Lieutenants-Commanding Gwin and Shirk have been untiring, and I owe to them and their officers many obligations for entire success.

"I am, respectfully, your obedient servant,

"S. T. Phelps, Lieutenant-Commanding U.S.N.

"Flag-Officer A. H. Foote, commanding
Naval Forces, Western Waters."

It is not surprising that special commendations should have been added to the report of this officer; and it might be said that no man was better supported by his officers than was Foote while at the West. Porter, Phelps, Walke, Gwin, Shirk, Sanford, Pennock, and others, called, as they were, from their business on broad ocean to do unaccustomed work, did the Navy great credit by their patient and courageous services—in storm and fog, cold and heat—on those turbid rivers, in clumsy vessels that seemed, like mud-turtles, made to court sandbanks, snags, low water, rapid currents, to say nothing of torpedoes, ambuscades, and infernal machines.

"U. S. FLAG-STEAMER 'ST. LOUIS,' PADUCAH,
February 12, 1862.

"SIR,—I have the honor and high gratification to forward to the Department the official report of Lieutenant-Commanding Phelps, by which it will be seen that he has, with consummate skill, courage, and judgment, performed a highly beneficial service to the government, which, I doubt not, will appreciate it. I can not too highly commend the conduct of Lieutenant-Commanding Phelps for this his signal service in his long cruise to the head of navigation on the Tennessee River.

"I am now, with three iron-clad steamers, ascending the Cumberland River, to co-operate with General Grant in an attack on Fort Donelson. Lieutenant-Commanding Phelps, with his division, accompanies me. In great haste. I have the honor to be your obedient servant,

"A. H. FOOTE, Flag-Officer.

"The Hon. Gideon Welles, Secretary of the Navy."

We give here a semi-official letter written by Lieutenant J. P. Sanford, ordnance officer of the flotilla, showing the efforts and needs of another branch of the gun-boat service, no less important than others, and, in fact, forming the striking arm of this formidable power:

"CINCINNATI, *February* 12, 1862.

"MY DEAR FLAG-OFFICER,—I have but a few moments in which to write. I am so busy that I have not had the leisure even to take my regular meals. You have my most hearty and cordial congratulations on your recent victory, and I have to regret at the same time that I was not with you.

"I am pushing up the work on the arks, and expect to leave here Saturday evening.

"I telegraphed to Pittsburg and Washington for 8-inch guns immediately on receipt of your telegram, and have them, from Washington, ready to be expressed. One of the guns I intend for the *St. Louis.* She has but two.

"I have just got a telegram from Captain Pennock. About two hundred additional rounds to be put up at Pittsburg Arsenal, making in all five hundred for each gun. I pity the poor guns!

"The ammunition-boats have large and splendid shell-rooms and magazines. I trust that what I have done to these boats will meet with your approval. It is no small matter to fit up such things as these river boats for eight hundred men and magazines. Permit me to suggest the propriety of a guard of thirty soldiers being obtained from the Army to do duty as marines. The boats will, in my judgment, absolutely need them. I shall want about five sentries on mine to make all secure. A lieutenant could be placed over them.

"I wrote to General Ripley a few days since for three hundred more swords—two hundred of them to be distributed to gun-boats, additional to what they have, and fifty to each of the ammunition-boats. I am putting a stiff piece of timber on the guards on either side of forecastle, to receive bolts for breechings, side tackles, etc., for a 32-pounder. If you did not think it absolutely necessary for me to come down with the boats, I would go to Pittsburg about the ammunition; but I suppose it is proper I should come down with them.

"I can't get flat-boatmen. They have all gone into the Army. I propose sending a first-rate man to Pittsburg to drum up some. I am told my best chance is there.

"I shall have to leave nearly all my accounts here unsettled, as the moment I can get stores, etc., on board, I shall be off.

"I have had fifty mess cloths made by Haggerty on a venture for the ammunition-boats—not enough, but Captain Pennock might have some spare ones, as I would not load the government with unnecessary extras.

"Yours sincerely, J. P. Sanford, Ord. Officer of Flotilla."

In regard to the feeling developed at the South after the battle of Fort Henry, the Richmond *Dispatch* of February 13th says: "Our Tennessee exchanges give us gloomy prospects for the future in that part of the Confederacy. Several leading journals intimate plainly that there is really a threatening state of affairs in East Tennessee, growing out of the idolatrous love of many of these people for the old Union.

The correspondent of the Memphis *Avalanche* writes that the condition of the interior provinces is not improved, and the people apprehend an immediate advance of the Northmen."

While the flag-officer was at Cairo, the first Sunday after the capture of Fort Henry, the incident of his "preaching" took place, which caused much remark at the time, and has, indeed, become one of the stock anecdotes of the war. The matter excited no astonishment to those who knew him well; and to the readers of this volume, who have followed him from his youth up, and have become acquainted with his outspoken religious character and habits, it can cause no surprise. On this Sunday he went to attend divine worship at the Presbyterian Church, and found a full congregation assembled, but no preacher present. With his promptitude for business, seeing that no one else took the lead in the emergency, he went to the deacons, and endeavored to persuade them to conduct the service. Failing in this, he himself mounted the pulpit, read the Scriptures, made a prayer, and preached a short discourse from the words, "Let not your hearts be troubled; ye believe in God, believe also in me." When the sermon, which was listened to attentively by a delighted audience, was concluded, an Army chaplain, who had in the mean time entered the house, stepped up to the commodore and expressed himself greatly pleased with the discourse. The commodore replied pleasantly (in no sharp terms of rebuke, as it was represented by some) that the chaplain should have come forward and taken his place. These are the simple facts of the case as given by eye-witnesses; and with such "lay-preaching," by one who showed his faith by his works, we, on our part, are not disposed to find fault. He himself often declared, however, that this was the last time he should ever attempt lay-preaching.

We can not forbear adding one of the letters of his hearty old friend, Commodore (now Rear-Admiral) Joseph Smith:

"*February* 14, 1862.

"MY DEAR FOOTE,—I have yours of the 9th instant. I hardly know for which vocation to award you the meed of greatest praise, as a first-rate flag-officer, or as a 'preacher'—no matter which, as you are in high estimation in both.

"The Burnside expedition has done nobly. Goldsborough got glory enough to satisfy even his longings. Our cause looks cheering, and I apprehend, if only the roads were passable, we should soon be in possession of all Virginia. Porter has departed with his mortar-boats, and expects to meet you with yours at New Orleans. I have but a faint idea of your boats, that they fight end on—only bow and stern guns to be used, and I presume you can use but two at either end. You see a bill reported for reorganizing the Navy Department. Nobody says any thing to me on the subject. Fox is the moving power. I could make a better bill, and organize a Board of Admiralty.

"Your successes will bear you up against all the pressure your position loads you with. Anna thinks her bauble will carry you through victoriously. You are on the top round of the ladder, and therefore you have very little more to do.

"I hope you will make the *Benton* go, as you were authorized to incur the expense to do so. Yours truly, in haste, JOSEPH SMITH."

The following vote of thanks was passed (February 14, 1862) by the General Assembly of the State of Ohio:

"*Resolved*, by the General Assembly of the State of Ohio, that the thanks of the people of Ohio be, and through their representatives are hereby tendered to General Grant and Flag-Officer Foote, and the brave men under their command, for the courage, gallantry, and enterprise exhibited in the bombardment and capture of Fort Henry—a victory no less brilliant in itself than glorious in its results, giving our Army a foothold in Tennessee, and opening the way for an early advance to the capital of that state.

"*Resolved*, That the governor transmit copies of these resolutions to said officers, with the request that the same be read to the men under their command.

"JAMES R. HUBBELL, Speaker of House of Representatives.
B. STANTON, President of the Senate."

CHAPTER XVIII.

THE SHARE TAKEN BY FOOTE'S FLOTILLA IN THE SIEGE OF FORT DONELSON.—HE IS WOUNDED.—CORRESPONDENCE.

As soon as Fort Henry fell into our power, great efforts were made by the rebels, now thoroughly aroused and alarmed, to strengthen the corresponding fortified post upon the Cumberland River. Russelville and Bowling Green were virtually evacuated, and great numbers of troops, to the amount of some twenty-five thousand, were immediately concentrated at Fort Donelson. General Bushrod Johnson, with Buckner, Pillow, and Floyd, threw themselves into the place, and every thing looked like a most determined resistance, as if the fate of the whole war were to be staked upon it. And, in some respects, this was true. The post was one of vast strength, both by nature and art. Floyd wrote to Richmond, with more of sincerity, probably, than was customary with him: "Have no fear about us. The place is impregnable; the enemy can never take it."

Fort Donelson* was situated twelve miles southeast of Fort Henry, upon the west bank of the Cumberland, a mile below Dover, where the stream makes a sudden turn to the westward, and then again to the northward. It is a broken, irregular country, and the hills, or knolls, rise from the river quite abruptly to a hundred or a hundred and fifty feet in height. Upon one of these eminences stood the fort, containing a hundred acres. It was surrounded by creeks and deep ravines. Its own works were strong, and line beyond

---

* For map of Fort Donelson, see p. 222.

line of intrenchments, redoubts, and rifle-pits stretched far around over the neighboring hills and valleys. The water-line of batteries, for commanding the river approaches, with their guns trained down stream, formed the most powerful means of defense, and consisted of three tiers of batteries, the lower one near the water, the second fifty feet above, and the third fifty feet above that, the lower or principal battery being armed with eight 32-pounders and one 10-inch columbiad; another bore a heavy rifled cannon that carried a 128-pound bolt, flanked by two 32-pound carronades.* These were to be tested by the gun-boats in a combat of brief but terrible severity.

On the morning of the 12th of February General Grant set his army in motion upon the three roads leading from Fort Henry to Dover; and in the afternoon, without meeting with resistance, the different bodies came in sight of the fort, drove in its pickets, and took up their several positions, to be ready for the next day's assault. The forces within and without the fort were probably nearly equal. On the same day Foote was moving up the Cumberland with his gun-boats, convoying transports filled with troops that were to constitute Wallace's Third Division.† One boat, however, the *Carondelet*, Captain Walke, had been sent forward two days in advance of the other vessels; and on the morning of the 13th, in connection with a movement by a portion of the land force, this vessel made a gallant diversion in favor of the Army, and had the honor of opening the siege. Although in the rapid current she could use only her bow guns, she fired one hundred and thirty-eight shots, until a 128-pound shot entered one of her ports and injured her machinery, compelling her to withdraw. She renewed firing in the afternoon, but

* Lossing's "Civil War in America," vol. ii., p. 209.

† *Ibid.*, vol. ii., p. 210.

against such heavy batteries, single-handed, and at a comparatively long range, could effect little.

The fighting on the part of the Army during that day was severe and indecisive. There was, indeed, no general attack made, as Grant, feeling the need of all his power, was awaiting the presence of the gun-boats and of Wallace's Third Division; but an assault was ordered by McClernand upon one of the principal redoubts, which developed into a battle of considerable magnitude, with varying fortune, though ending in the repulse of the National forces. That night, in cold and sleet, without tents and without provisions, the weary and dispirited troops lay upon the frozen ground, anxiously looking for the coming light to renew the combat, and for the hoped-for arrival of the flotilla and the transports.

These having come up, and also a reserved force from Fort Henry, Grant proceeded, as well as he was able, to complete the investment of the place, and prepare for the decisive battle.

At about three o'clock on the afternoon of the 14th, the flotilla, consisting of the armored vessels *St. Louis*, *Carondelet*, *Pittsburg*, and *Louisville*, forming the first line, accompanied by the wooden gun-boats *Conestoga*, *Taylor*, and *Lexington*—the flag-ship *St. Louis* taking the lead—made a direct attack upon the water batteries (Foote giving orders not to regard the batteries on the bluff), and steaming straight up, in the usual bold manner of this commander, to be-

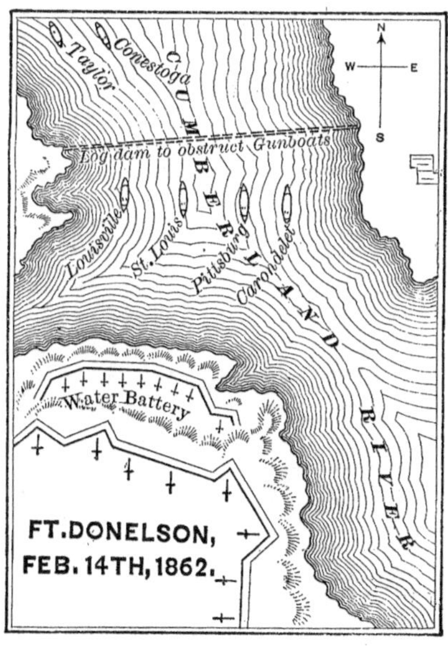

FT. DONELSON, FEB. 14TH, 1862.

Upper Battery. Water-Battery. Gen. Grant's Army in the distance. United States Gun-boats.

BATTLE OF FORT DONELSON.

tween three and four hundred yards of their teeth. His intention was to silence the batteries and pass them, so as to gain a position to enfilade the faces of the fort with broadsides.* The firing on both sides was soon very accurate, rapid, and destructive. The shot and shell from the fleet plowed into the lower batteries, dismounting guns and driving away the gunners, while the heavy cannon of the fort played incessantly upon the sides and decks of the boats. "Never was a little squadron exposed to so terrible a fire. Twenty heavy guns were trained upon it, those from the hill-side hurling plunging shot with awful precision and effect, while the boats could reply with only twelve guns."† Notwithstanding this furious fire from the fort at a higher level, and at so great an advantage, raking the broadsides of the boat obliquely, in which some of the 128-pound shots crushed through the iron armor, carrying destruction with them, the boats held on constantly to their work, until the upper battery of four guns was silenced, and the men were distinctly seen flying from the lower battery, and the vessels were just on the point of shooting by and gaining a favorable position. It is said (and we give this as an unauthenticated report) that at this time of the height of the combat Pillow telegraphed to Governor Harris: "The Federal gun-boats are destroying us. For God's sake, send us all the help you can immediately. I don't care for the land force of the enemy; they can't hurt us if you can keep those iron hell-hounds in check." At this critical moment, when things looked as if victory were almost in their grasp, the *Louisville* was disabled by a shot which cut away her rudder-chains, making her totally unmanageable, so that she drifted with the current out of action. Very soon after the *St. Louis* was disabled by a shot through her pilot-house,

---

* Lossing's "Civil War in America," vol. ii., p. 213.
† *Ibid.*, vol. ii., p. 213.

rendering her steering impossible, so that she also floated down the river. The other two armored vessels were also terribly struck, and a rifled cannon on the *Carondelet* burst, so that these two could no longer, by themselves, sustain the action; and after fighting for more than an hour, the little fleet was forced to withdraw. The immediate object of the attack of the gun-boats, viz., to silence the formidable river batteries, and to obtain a good position to bombard the upper works in co-operation with the assault of the land forces, which was all, in fact, that the flotilla had the power of doing, since there was a whole army within the fortifications to be dislodged and conquered, and the boats could not walk upon land—this object of the attack was on the point of being successfully attained, when the unforeseen casualties that have been related occurred. It was indeed a hard disappointment after such persistent fighting. Foote, it is said, wept like a child when the order to withdraw was given.

The *St. Louis* was struck fifty-nine times; the *Louisville* thirty-six times; the *Carondelet* twenty-six; the *Pittsburg* twenty; and the four vessels receiving no less than one hundred and forty-one wounds. The attack was repulsed, but it was through the imperfection of the boats themselves in not having sufficient protection to their machinery, wheels, and steering apparatus; but the demoralizing influence of their fierce bombardment upon the fort could not have been small, and must have helped toward the great but hard-won success of the next day. At all events, the gun-boats did what they could, and, until rendered entirely helpless for action, drifting like logs in the rapid current, they were fought with a determined energy that looked, even to the last moment, only to victory.

The fleet, gathering itself together, and rendering mutual help to its disabled members, proceeded to Cairo to repair damages, intending to return immediately with a stronger naval force to continue the siege. General Grant decided to await their return, and also the coming of reinforcements to his army; but events took place of sudden and rapid evolution, compelling him to change his plans, and bringing on the general battle of the next day. Early on the morning of the 15th, two grand sorties by the enemy, the one led by Generals Pillow and Johnson, and the other by Buckner, effected a complete surprise of the National forces, caused most sanguinary fighting, and seriously menaced the whole of Grant's right wing. It was only the prompt valor of Generals Wallace and McClernand (in the absence of Grant, who was in consultation with Foote), backed by the dogged bravery of the Western troops, that prevented a total rout. When the whole battle hung in the balance, wavering and uncertain, Grant himself came up, and by a bold inspiration that snatched victory from defeat, he ordered McClernand to retake the hill he had lost, and Smith to make a simultaneous attack on the Confederate right.* By desperate fighting, intrenchment after intrenchment was carried, and that night Grant knew that the ultimate triumph was his. Then took place those extraordinary and hurried councils in the camp of the enemy which resulted in the escape of Floyd and Pillow, and the unconditional surrender the next morning by Buckner of the stronghold with its army of fifteen thousand—or what remained of its army of twenty-five thousand who did not run away—and its immense amount of military stores.

As our business has been to give an account mainly of those operations in which Foote and the naval forces under his command were engaged, we have not entered into a detailed history of the assault and taking of Fort Donelson. It is, however, but just and right to give the flag-officer's own report of his share in that siege:

* Lossing's "Civil War in America," vol. ii., p. 217.

"FLAG-SHIP 'ST. LOUIS,' NEAR FORT DONELSON,
CUMBERLAND RIVER, *February* 15, 1862.

"SIR,—I have the honor to report to the Department that, at the urgent request of General Halleck and General Grant, who regarded the movement as a military necessity, although not, in my opinion, properly prepared, I made an attack on Fort Donelson yesterday, the 14th instant, at three o'clock P.M., with four iron-clad and two wooden gun-boats—the *St. Louis*, *Carondelet*, *Louisville*, and *Pittsburg*, and the *Taylor* and *Conestoga*. After a severe fight of an hour and a half, being in the latter part of the action less than four hundred yards from the fort, the wheel of this vessel, by a shot through her pilot-house, was carried away; the tiller-ropes of the *Louisville* were also disabled by a shot, which rendered the two boats wholly unmanageable, and they drifted down the river, the relieving tackles not being able to steer or control them in the rapid current. The two remaining boats, the *Pittsburg* and *Carondelet*, were also greatly damaged between wind and water, and soon followed us, as the enemy rapidly renewed the fire as we drifted helplessly down the river. This vessel, the *St. Louis*, alone received fifty-nine shots, four of them between wind and water; one in the pilot-house, mortally wounding the pilot; and others, requiring some time to put her in repair. There were fifty-four killed and wounded in the attack, which, notwithstanding our disadvantages, we have every reason to suppose would, in fifteen minutes more, could the action have been continued, have resulted in the capture of the two forts bearing upon us. The enemy's fire had materially slackened, and he was running from his batteries, when the two gun-boats helplessly drifted down the river from disabled steering apparatus, as the relieving tackles could not control the helm in the strong current; and the fleeing enemy, returning to their guns, again boldly opened fire upon us from the river batteries, which we had silenced.

"The enemy must have brought over twenty guns to bear upon our boats from the water-batteries and the main fort on the side of the hill, while we could only return the fire with twelve bow guns from the four boats. One rifle-gun aboard the *Carondelet* burst during the action.

"The officers and men in this hotly contested but unequal fight behaved with the greatest gallantry and determination, all deploring the accident which rendered two gun-boats suddenly helpless in the narrow river and swift current.

"On consultation with General Grant and my own officers, as my services, until we can repair damages by bringing up a competent force from Cairo to attack the fort, are much less required here than they are at Cairo, I shall proceed to that point with two of the disabled boats, leaving the two others here to protect the transports, and with all dispatch prepare the mortar-boats and the *Benton*, with other boats, to make an effectual attack upon Fort Donelson.

"I have sent the *Taylor* to the Tennessee River to render impassable the bridge, so as to prevent the rebels at Columbus reinforcing their army at Fort Donelson. I am informed that the rebel batteries were served with the best gunners from Columbus. I transmit herewith a list of casualties. Very respectfully, your obedient servant,

"A. H. FOOTE,

"Flag-Officer, commanding U. S. N. Forces, Western Waters.

"The Hon. Gideon Welles, Secretary of the Navy, Washington, D. C."

A second dispatch announces the capture of the fort by General Grant:

"CAIRO, *February* 17, 1862.

"TO THE HON. GIDEON WELLES:

"The *Carondelet* has just arrived from Donelson, and brings information of the capture of the fort by the land forces yesterday morning, with fifteen thousand prisoners, including Buckner and Johnson. Loss heavy on both sides. Floyd escaped with five thousand men during the night. I go up as soon as possible with the gun-boats. Will proceed to Clarksville. Eight mortar-boats are on the way, with which I hope to attack Clarksville. My wound is painful, but not dangerous.

"The army behaved gloriously. I shall be able to take but two iron-clad gun-boats with me, as the others are disabled. The trophies are immense. The particulars will soon be given.

"A. H. FOOTE, Flag-Officer."

The commodore's wound was not considered severe at the time, although it was painful, and he made light of it, not suffering it to interfere with his active duties. But as it was the immediate cause of his being compelled some months later to throw up his command at the West, and as it is probable, combined with the great burdens laid on him, that it was a remote cause of aggravating his last fatal disease, therefore, by reason of this and other valuable lives that were forfeited, a mournful interest is attached to the siege of Fort Donelson, the then greatest victory of the war. Commodore Foote was, in fact, twice wounded, both times apparently slightly—though it proved not to be so in the end—in this battle. He had stepped into the pilot-house to see that the boat was kept in position. A solid shot, hurled at a distance of less than four hundred yards, struck the pilot-house at an angle of forty-five degrees—which gives some idea of the fort's elevation and the immense disadvantage at which the gun-boats fought—penetrated the wood, thirteen inches in thickness, and the iron, an inch and a quarter thick, and filled the pilot-house with broken fragments of iron and missiles of destruction. The pilot was instantly killed, and the commodore was struck by a fragment on the foot. At that moment a second shot, fired by the wooden gun-boat *Taylor*, that lay behind, came across the tiller-ropes, disabling the "relieving tackle" at the helm; and it was this shot that rendered the boat unmanageable. One account says that the commodore was taken up senseless, his leg bruised almost to a jelly from his ankle to his hip; but as the versions of this whole affair vary considerably in their details, we give his own brief letter to his wife in which he speaks of the circumstance:

"CAIRO, TELEGRAPH OFFICE, *February* 16, 1862.

"MY DEAR WIFE,—I telegraphed you from Paducah last night that Fort Donelson was not taken, but that I was slightly wounded, once at a gun and once in the pilot-house. It was by a piece of spent shot once, and a splinter once, but only slightly, on my left arm and left foot, which puts me on crutches for a few days; but I will be running about in less time than a week. I will not go so near again, although at Fort Henry I produced an effect by it. We ought to have been victorious at Donelson, as we fought harder than at Henry. I went into it against my judgment by order of Halleck. We had fifty-four killed and wounded, and fifty-nine shots in one vessel—a thing never before heard of in a naval fight. I have sent up four mortars, and hope to go again myself to-night; but we will lay off at a long distance. I shall not go near until the *Benton* is ready, and they can't hurt her; so don't feel uneasy about me. I consider my personal danger almost over. Upon my word, you are cool in response to Fort Henry; but, never mind, 'you are a humbug.'

"I don't feel depressed much about Fort Donelson, only in its effect upon our cause; for I fought desperately, but against my judgment, and I am above all blame. I have an avalanche of complimentary letters from all quarters, from strangers as well as friends; but I suppose that the Donelson affair will check them—but we deserve even more credit for that than for Fort Henry. But God's will be done in all cases.

"I am now at the telegraph office by request of General McClellan, to talk with him by cipher. I send you his first telegram, which you may read if you can. I had a severe headache in the last action, but fought it coolly and determinedly, without a moment's flinching; and officers and men have unbounded confidence in me, and I tell them, 'Not unto us,' etc.

"I will, if I can, add a few words, and do you remain quiet and easy till you hear further from me. To Emily kisses, and love to 'folks' and friends who inquire after me.

"Just as I wrote 'me' I received the inclosed telegram from McClellan. We are now talking. I may go back to-night or to-morrow morning if I can be spared. I have been too much absorbed in war matters for Sunday—still hope in God in all things.

"Ever affectionately yours, A. H. F."

One of the telegrams referred to in the above is the following:

"WASHINGTON, *February* 16, 1862.

"TO FLAG-OFFICER A. H. FOOTE:

"Sorry you are wounded. How seriously? Your conduct was magnificent. With what force do you return? I send six hundred sailors for you to-morrow. Give me details.

"G. B. MCCLELLAN, Com.-in-Chief U. S. A."

These two additional letters of Commodore Foote to his wife at this time, written as they were with unconstrained freedom, let us into his inmost feelings:

"FLAG-STEAMER 'CONESTOGA,' NEAR PADUCAH,
February 17, 1862.

"MY DEAR WIFE,—The steamer trembles as we are pressing her hard up to fourteen knots for Fort Donelson. I take Phelps, a glorious officer, as flag-captain of the *Benton*, and will then have an easy time myself. He is bold and cautious.*

"You need have no fears about us now, as we will keep off a good distance from the fort at Clarksville, and let the mortar-boats do most of the work. I hope to find two of your letters, which are adrift somewhere, as they were sent to me at Fort Donelson. I have but little idea that the rebels will make a stand at Columbus; they will abandon it now that the Tennessee and Cumberland are about being cleanly swept out.

"I hope in a week or two to throw away my crutches and be well again. My two little wounds at the gun and the pilot-house would give me no trouble if one of them had not been on the foot. I can not write, we are so much shaken up.

"I have hosts of papers sent me, as well as letters; but I will be a nine-days' lion only, as this war brings out men too fast for any one to attract attention long.

"I shall have a good sleep to-night with a wet cloth on my left foot, and I hope to be rid of its bother soon.

"May God watch over and preserve you all is the prayer of

"Ever your affectionate husband, A. H. FOOTE."

"U. S. FLAG-STEAMER 'CONESTOGA,' FORT DONELSON,
CUMBERLAND RIVER, *Feb.* 18, 1862.

"MY DEAR WIFE,—Yours of the 7th reached me to-day. I telegraphed at the close of the fight at Fort Donelson, where we so demoralized the rebels that the fort fell a prey to the army the next day, as they are afraid to see the black boats coming into their teeth and belching forth shot and shells. A rebel colonel told one of our officers to-day that the army never could have taken the fort had it not been for the gun-boats. We came within an ace of getting it, as two hundred yards farther would have placed us so that their guns could not bear upon us, and then we would have mowed them down; but I am satisfied and rather glad that the army did take the fort, as they have fought like tigers and lost almost two thousand men. It was a horrid fight; and Aunty would think so if she saw the mutilated dead. It is an exceedingly strong fort, and the rebels had no idea it could be taken. One of the gun-boats has burned John Bell's iron rolling-mill, with property worth two hundred thousand dollars, and took his partner prisoner. I go up with this vessel and an iron-clad to-morrow on a reconnoissance as far as Clarksville.

* A man evidently after his own heart.

Had I had time to do this before I made the attack on Fort Donelson, I should have taken it. On Friday we hope to try our hand on Clarksville with four boats and eight mortars. They can not stand it long. I consider that our danger is past, and you need not in the future be at all uneasy. Generals Grant and Smith have been to see me to-day. We are all friendly as brothers; and I have strong faith and hope, under God, that we now shall have victory upon victory.

"I will not describe the scene here—the taking off of twelve thousand prisoners—the dead and wounded on the shore—the bands playing all the while—the good spirits and life of our people—the number of steamboats—the battered forts and riddled houses in Dover, etc., etc. I have for you a pair of double heavy rebel blankets. I have also for the boys a double-barreled gun. I am tired; still on crutches, but am getting better. Kisses and love to the children. Affectionately, A. H. F."

There can be no doubt, judging from these letters and other evidences, that Foote truly thought he had with his gun-boats nearly accomplished the subdual of the fort, even as he had done in the case of Fort Henry. He said more than once that within ten or fifteen minutes he would have done it. He probably may have erred in this, since the two cases were not entirely parallel, owing to the greatly superior strength of Fort Donelson, and the much larger army force within its walls. But we have his own opinion in the case distinctly averred, and he was certainly no incompetent judge. He went into the fight, as he says, "against his own judgment." He did not consider his boats ready for the conflict, and the event showed he was right; and, moreover, he had not time to get up his mortar-fleet, which he had confidently depended upon in this second more important and difficult service. On the 11th of February he wrote to Secretary Welles:

"I leave again to-night with the *Louisville*, *Pittsburg*, and *St. Louis*, to co-operate with the army in the attack on Fort Donelson. I go reluctantly, as we are very short of men; and transferring men from vessel to vessel, as we have to do, is having a very demoralizing effect upon them. Twenty-eight men ran off to-day, hearing that they were to be sent out of their vessels. I do hope that the six hundred men will be sent immediately. I shall do all in my power to render the gun-boats effective in the fight, although they are not properly manned; but I must go, as General Halleck wishes it. If we could wait ten days, and I had the men, I would go with eight mortar-boats and six armored boats."

If, instead of this thoroughly equipped fleet, with mortar-boats to support at a distance and to shell the upper works, and gun-boats for the lower batteries, we remember that he had but four armored boats, and these not well-fitted and manned, we can not cease to wonder at the audacity of the attack. It was truly a sacrifice to a dire war necessity; and the valor and skill with which the fight was made were the only reasons why they were not wholly destroyed.

The orders of General Halleck, which precipitated the gun-boat attack, were the two following telegrams:

"*February* 11, 1862.

"FLAG-OFFICER FOOTE,—You have gained great distinction by the capture of Fort Henry. Every body recognizes your services. Make your name famous in history by the immediate capture of Fort Donelson and Clarksville. The taking of these places is a military necessity. Delay adds strength to them more than to us. Act quickly, even though only half ready. Troops will soon be ready to support you.

"(Signed) H. W. HALLECK, Major-General."

"*February* 12, 1862.

"FLAG-OFFICER FOOTE,—Push forward the Cumberland expedition with all possible dispatch. In addition to the land forces at Paducah and on their way from Michigan, Ohio, Indiana, and Illinois, I shall send one regiment from here on Thursday, one on Friday, and one on Saturday. Push ahead boldly and quickly. I will give you plenty of support in a few days' time. Now every thing for use. Don't delay an instant.

"(Signed) H. W. HALLECK, Major-General."

But other services remained to be done. With a spirit of cheerful alacrity, in spite of disappointments and sufferings, Foote girded himself anew to the work, and we hear of him shortly after farther up the Cumberland, busily issuing proclamations, and zealous to push on to Nashville and the heart of the Southern Confederacy.

CHAPTER XIX.

CAPTURE OF CLARKSVILLE.—FOOTE'S PROCLAMATION.—NOT PERMITTED TO TAKE NASHVILLE.—ARMED RECONNOISSANCE DOWN THE MISSISSIPPI.—FLAG OF TRUCE.—EVACUATION OF COLUMBUS.

The ablest of the rebel generals who commanded at the Southwest, Albert Sidney Johnston, declared that he "fought for Nashville at Fort Donelson." Commodore Foote was also among the first to perceive the truth of this; and he urged Halleck and Grant, at the moment when the panic occasioned by the fall of the forts was at its height, to send a detachment of troops to Nashville, or to let him go at once with his gun-boats. For some reason this request was not complied with by Halleck, and Foote was not suffered to proceed farther than Clarksville, a fortified post some sixty miles north of Nashville. The river was open above this point, and his fleet, carrying with it so formidable a prestige, might easily have taken possession of the important city of Nashville, with its immense amount of military stores, which was not actually taken possession of until the 25th or 27th of February, when it was entered without opposition by an army force under General Buell, accompanied by two gun-boats.

After burning the "Tennessee Iron Works," six miles from Dover, on the 19th of February the commodore, with two gun-boats, ascended the Cumberland to Clarksville, to attack the rebel fort at that place, situated at the mouth of a small stream called Red River; but the report of the commander will best tell the story:

"U. S. FLAG-STEAMER 'CONESTOGA,' CLARKSVILLE, TENNESSEE, *February* 20, 1862.

"We have possession of Clarksville. The citizens being alarmed, two thirds of them have fled; and having expressed my views and intentions to the mayor and the Hon. Cave Johnson, at their request I have issued a proclamation, assuring all peaceably disposed persons that they may with safety resume their business avocations, requiring only the military stores and equipments to be given up, and holding the authorities responsible that this shall be done without reservation.

"I left Fort Donelson yesterday, with the *Conestoga*, Lieutenant-Commanding Phelps, and the *Cairo*, Lieutenant-Commanding Bryant, on an armed reconnoissance, bringing with me Colonel Webster, of the engineer corps, and chief of General Grant's staff, who, with Lieutenant-Commanding Phelps, took possession of the principal fort, and hoisted the Union flag. A Union sentiment manifested itself as we came up the river. The rebels have retreated to Nashville, having set fire, against the remonstrances of the citizens, to the splendid railroad bridge across the Cumberland River.

"I return to Fort Donelson to-day for another gun-boat and six or eight mortar-boats, with which I propose to proceed up the Cumberland. The rebels all have a terror of the gun-boats. One of them, a short distance above Fort Donelson, had previously fired an iron rolling-mill belonging to the Hon. John Bell, which had been used by the rebels.

"A. H. FOOTE,

"Flag-Officer, commanding Naval Forces, Western Waters.

"The Hon. Gideon Welles, Secretary of the Navy."

The proclamation to the citizens of Clarksville was as follows:

"*To the Inhabitants of Clarksville, Tennessee.*

"At the suggestion of the Hon. Cave Johnson, Judge Wisdom, and the mayor of the city, who called upon me yesterday, after our hoisting of the Union flag and taking possession of the forts, to ascertain my views and intentions toward the citizens and private property, I hereby announce to all peaceably disposed persons that neither in their persons nor in their property shall they suffer molestation by me or the naval force under my command, and that they may in safety resume their business avocations, with the assurance of my protection.

"At the same time, I require that all military stores and army equipments shall be surrendered, no part of them being withheld or destroyed; and further, that no Secession flag, or manifestation of Secession feeling, shall be exhibited; and for the faithful observance of these conditions I shall hold the authorities of the city responsible.

"ANDREW H. FOOTE,

"Flag-Officer, commanding Naval Forces, Western Waters.

"U. S. FLAG-SHIP 'CONESTOGA,' *February* 20, 1862."

This document is, we think, a model of its kind, exhibiting kindness and firmness, brief, modest, positive, and reminding us of the sharp-cut though courteous letters written by our hero in his diplomatic correspondence on the African coast. He refers with considerable self-satisfaction to his Clarksville visit in a letter of the same date to his wife:

"I have just returned from Clarksville—a beautiful city—where I issued the inclosed proclamation. Old Cave Johnson, who knew my father so well, came to me. The Clarksville affair will do me credit. Give one of the proclamations to Dr. Bacon. I am off to Cairo to-night to procure more gun-boats for Nashville. They are held in terror, and we will easily take it."

He assuredly had reason to feel chagrined at not being permitted to carry into execution his feasible plan in regard to East Tennessee and Nashville. He was, in fact, deeply injured in his feelings at what seemed to be a robbery of that opportunity for fair fame that justly belonged to him; and, more than all, for the injury done to the cause. General Halleck's peremptory telegram was as follows:

"TO GENERAL GRANT:

"Don't let the gun-boats go higher than Clarksville; even then they must limit their operations to the destruction of the bridge, and return immediately to Cairo, leaving one at Fort Donelson. Mortar-boats to be sent back to Cairo as soon as possible.

"H. W. HALLECK, Major-General.

"Official.—S. A. Hurlbut, Brigadier-General U. S. A."

The exact truth of the matter is, when Commodore Foote

returned from Clarksville to Fort Donelson (after taking possession of the former place on the 20th of February), an arrangement was made between him and General Grant for a joint movement upon Nashville, and all the troops that could be transported were to have been embarked and ready to leave at 4 A.M. on the 21st, under convoy of the gun-boats. This would have placed them in Nashville by or before noon of the 21st of February—four days before the *Cairo* reached Nashville with Nelson's command. At midnight on the 20th the commodore and General Grant were together—part of the troops had already embarked—when the general received a telegram from Halleck positively ordering him not to push his forces beyond Clarksville, nor to permit the gun-boats to go higher up the river than that place. On receiving the telegram, the general handed it to the commodore without remark; the latter read it, and said, "I suppose this ends our movement." General Grant himself was severely annoyed that the full fruit of his victory at Donelson should not have been gathered. Had it not been for the great number of prisoners to be sent away to places where they could be cared for, and for his limited means of transportation, he would have gone on to Nashville in twenty-four hours after the capitulation of Fort Donelson; and the delay to follow up the victory was of immense value to the rebels. We might say that if it had not been for this unexpected and unfortunate check, Grant's future operations would have been by the way of Nashville, and a wholly different and undoubtedly more advantageous turn would have been given to the war in the Southwest.

At Nashville itself it was confidently expected that Foote would be up immediately with his whole flotilla, and there was great excitement there, and a rapid clearing out of obnoxious Secession leaders. Floyd, on hearing that Foote's gun-boats were coming, gave orders on Monday (it was supposed by the Confederates that the Nationals would push on toward

East Tennessee, and it was for the purpose of opposing such a movement that Johnston took position at Murfreesboro) for the Confederate stores to be thrown open to the public; two steam-packets, which were being changed into gun-boats, to be burned; and the two bridges at Nashville to be destroyed. Against the last act the citizens most vehemently protested, and it was postponed until Tuesday night, when they were both burned by Floyd's order; and he and Pillow literally scampered away southward by the light of the conflagration. During the remainder of the week Nashville was the theatre of the wildest anarchy, and neither public nor private property was safe for an hour. Happily for the well-disposed inhabitants, Colonel Keaner, of the Fourth Ohio Cavalry, of Mitchell's division, entered the city on Sunday evening, the 23d, and endeavored to restore order. He was immediately followed by the remainder of his commander's force, who encamped at Edgefield, opposite Nashville, and there awaited the arrival of General Buell. That officer came on the 25th, and on the same morning the *Cairo* arrived from Clarksville, as a convoy to transports bearing a considerable body of troops under General Nelson. These had not been opposed in their passage up the river, for the only battery on its banks between the two cities was Fort Zollicoffer, on a bluff, four or five miles below Nashville, which was unfinished, and was then abandoned. Pursuant to previous arrangement, the mayor of Nashville (R. B. Cheatham), and a small delegation of citizens, crossed over to Buell's quarters at Edgefield, and there made a formal surrender of the city. General Buell at once issued an order congratulating the troops "that it had been their privilege to restore the national banner to the capitol of Tennessee." On the following day, General Grant and staff arrived, and he and General Buell held a consultation about future movements.*

* Lossing's "Civil War in America," vol. ii., p. 233.

On reading the above, a sensible person would be struck by the fact that there was a totally uncalled for delay in capturing the city, and that if Foote, as he desired, had gone up at once, much property would have been saved, much disorder prevented, and extensive movements of National troops rendered unnecessary. This certainly is the appearance on the face of things, whatever occult reasons there might have existed for a contrary course. These reasons have never transpired.

The final settling up of the Cumberland and Tennessee war matters, as far as Foote and his fleet were concerned, seems to be contained in this general telegraphic order from Halleck:

"St. Louis, *February* 25, 1862.

"To Commodore Foote, Cairo:

"The possession of Nashville by General Buell renders it necessary to countermand the instructions sent to Foote and Sherman yesterday morning, dated 23d. Grant will send no more forces to Clarksville; General Smith's division will come to Fort Henry, or to a point higher up on the Tennessee River; transports will be collected at Paducah and above; all the mortar-boats to be immediately brought back to Cairo; two gun-boats to be left at Clarksville, to precede Nelson's division up the river to Nashville—having done this, they will return to Cairo; two gun-boats to be left in the Tennessee River with General Grant; the latter will immediately have small garrisons detailed for forts Donelson and Henry, and all other forces made ready for the field.

"H. W. Halleck, Major-General."

It may be that the following letter, being that of a warm personal friend, and for that reason, perhaps, somewhat prejudiced, should remain unpublished; but, after due consideration, we have concluded to make it public, although in this biography we have no desire to rake up old jealousies and disputes, which, in the peculiar relations of the Army and Navy at the West, where both were striving to do the most gallant deeds, were unavoidable, and which, among brave men, are now either laid to rest in their silent graves, or are buried in noble and patriotic hearts:

"NAVY DEPARTMENT, *March* 1, 1862.

"FLAG-OFFICER A. H. FOOTE:

"MY DEAR SIR,—As we are just receiving your letters of the 31st of December, 1861, I fancy you never get any of my notes. I observed that you were taken down from Clarksville when bound to Nashville, and I imagined the reason at once. I also noticed your proposition about first going to Fort Henry. I will take care that these matters shall be placed publicly to your credit. Carter has raised you one hundred men at Erie, and fifty seamen go from New York. We do this for five ships waiting for crews, and for the *Narragansett*, not yet relieved, though their time is up. Please keep us posted with official documents and copies of telegrams, as in the Henry and Donelson affairs, so that I can have copies in the hands of naval friends. Your reputation is that of the Navy and the cause, and well you have sustained it under difficulties that placed the entire credit on your head. I wish some trophy of your noble fight at Fort Henry. With the warmest wishes for your health and safety. Success you will win. Yours most truly, G. V. FOX."

Commodore Smith, still more plain-spoken, writes:

"*March* 1, 1862.

"MY DEAR FOOTE,—I have yours of the 24th ult., with its inclosures. Mrs. "Jesse" Benton will be elated, I think, at your notice of her by naming the *Benton's* tender for her.

"I had hoped the excitement would keep away the headache from you; but active brains like yours must have a safety-valve. You are cut out of a dash upon Nashville; but enough is left for you to do yet. I infer you were on better terms with Fremont than with Halleck; but you quarrel with nobody unless the party play foul, and then the 'black-stain' perseverance will be brought to bear on your opponents. Gregory says you 'pray like a saint and fight like a devil.' It seems to me the Army, or some portions of it, are jealous of you. Why should they send such riff-raff to you, that are only in your way. I would not take them, or, if I did, I would place them where David put Uriah. I have no doubt the gun-boats hurt Fort Donelson and created a panic; pity you could not have had your mortar and other boats there. What we have apprehended as a defect in iron-clad boats has been demonstrated by you—that is, the exposure of the rudder and steering gear. What guns have you condemned? The rifled cannon are becoming of doubtful endurance. The 80-pound rifles have been ignored, and 100-pounders substituted where they can be used. Breese is by me, and desires regards. Mrs. Foote is sharing your glory by receiving the applause of your townsmen and a flag.* Congress is tearing the Navy to pieces by a multiplicity of bills. Three more bureaus are proposed, and the pay of all to be cut down alike. I have worked to the full stretch of my brains, and I get no credit for it. I like the idea of promotion for gallant acts, but I do not think the former war-services of officers should be overlooked.

"Our Army of the Potomac is stirring, but I know not the programme. I think we are doing up Secesh, and I hope the rebels will be tired of such an unprofitable and wicked war without justification.

"Yours very truly, JOSEPH SMITH."

On the 21st of February, 1862, the Kentucky House of Representatives passed the following resolutions:

"The nation has been compelled, by every patriotic motive, to call upon her true sons to arrest rebellion and preserve the government. Military men must put down rebellious politicians, who have created the existing evils which threaten our destruction. Reason and entreaty having failed, the sword is now to settle our destiny. While we feel sentiments of the highest admiration for all the brave officers and soldiers engaged in the cause of the Union, wherever their field of operations may be, we entertain a peculiar gratitude to those who are driving our invaders from the soil of Kentucky; therefore,

Resolved, by the General Assembly of the Commonwealth of Kentucky, that General Albin Schœff, General William Nelson, General George H. Thomas, Colonel J. A. Garfield, General U. S. Grant, and Commodore

* This has reference to a pleasant and enthusiastic gathering of the students of Yale College (February 22d) in front of Mrs. Foote's residence, and the presentation to her of a National flag, which was raised soon after on the commodore's house. The Hon. Pelatiah Perrit responded to the address of the students. At the same time a letter was addressed to the commodore, signed by many eminent citizens of New Haven, such as the venerable Jeremiah Day, Professor Benjamin Silliman, President Theodore D. Woolsey, and others, warmly congratulating him, as townsmen, on his successes, and urging him on to greater victories.

A. H. Foote, together with the brave officers and men in their respective commands, deserve the thanks of Kentucky, and the same are hereby most cordially tendered to every man of them for their brilliant victories achieved at Wild Cat, Ivy Mountain, Logan's Fields, Mill Spring, Prestonburg, Fort Henry, and Fort Donelson. While we thus offer our heartfelt tribute to the officers and soldiers who have exposed their lives on the field of battle, we can not withhold the expression of our most grateful thanks to Generals Halleck and Buell, the commanders-in-chief of their respective departments, for their admirable arrangements, which have resulted in these glorious and effective victories.

"*Resolved*, That a copy of these resolutions be forwarded by the clerk to each of the officers herein named, with a request that they have the same read to their respective commands.

"Which were adopted. Attest: W. L. SAMUELS,

"Clerk of House of Representatives."

The Western fleet was now, as a body, quickly recalled from its operations on the Cumberland and Tennessee rivers, and was assembled at Cairo for further services in another quarter. Foote's dispatch of February 21st to his navy commanders urged them to activity, and closed with these words:

"The gun-boats and mortar-boats must leave immediately for Cairo, to be prepared instantly for service. Hasten! hasten! 'bear a hand' to follow me."

The National successes in Tennessee had served to isolate the enemy's stronghold at Columbus, called "the Gibraltar of the West," and in one sense rightly called, for before it was rendered strategically untenable, it was judged impregnable to direct assault. It was situated upon high bluffs, with every advantage that skillful engineering and heavy munitions could add, and had an army of twenty thousand troops in its walls. Of course it was not known but that this formidable fortification would stand siege. Early on the morning of the 23d of February, Commodore Foote, with four iron-clads, two mortar-boats, and five transports partially filled with troops, left Cairo and steamed down the Mississippi on an armed

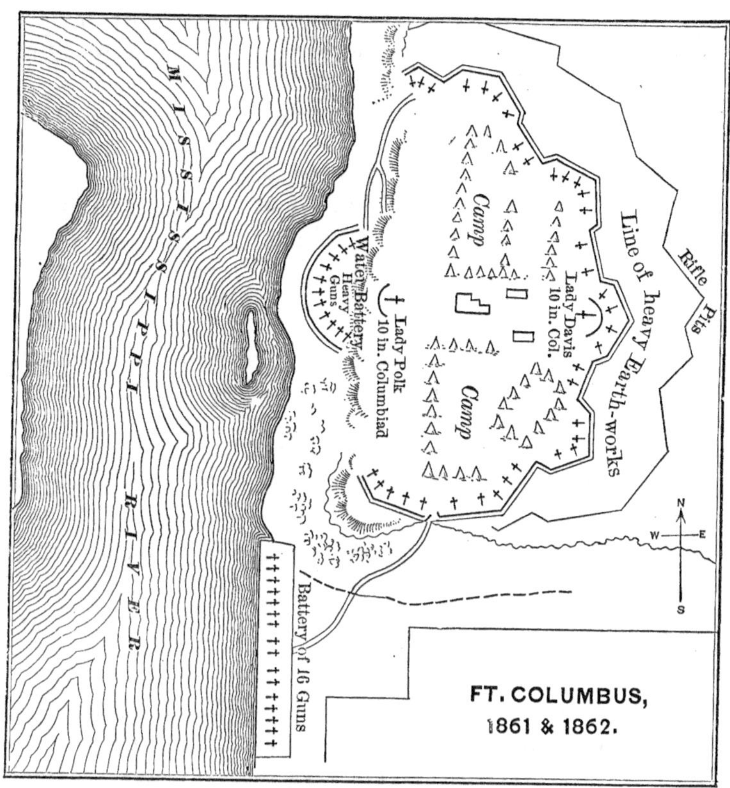

reconnoissance of Columbus. As they drew in sight of the batteries, a steamer bearing a flag of truce from General Polk came out to meet them. The account is given in the following report of the commodore:

"U. S. Flag-Steamer 'Cincinnati,' Mississippi River,
Near Columbus, Ky., *February* 23, 1862.

"Sir,—I have the honor to report that, in company with General Cullum, chief of General Halleck's staff, with four iron-clad boats, two mortar-boats, and three transports, containing one thousand men, I made this day a reconnoissance in force toward Columbus to ascertain its condition; and when near the batteries a flag of truce came out to communicate with us, the result of which will be seen in the inclosed papers. The object of the reconnoissance being attained, and finding that fire from the mortars would lead the enemy to plant guns where they could reach them with their batteries should we again open upon them with a larger number of mortars, I concluded to return to Cairo; and there we must remain until the gun and mortar boats are completed, as otherwise the flotilla will be demoralized for want of time and means to properly prepare for active service. The army will not move without gun-boats, yet the gun-boats are not in a condition to act offensively at present. On this subject I will soon write more fully. A telegram will be sent to the Department on my arrival at Cairo, referring to the events of to-day. I am your obedient servant, A. H. Foote, Flag-Officer.

"The Hon. Gideon Welles, Secretary of the Navy.

"P. S.—Columbus evinces no signs of an evacuation or dismounting of guns. The batteries seem to be intact, and we saw great numbers of tents and troops."

Before noticing a correspondence with General Polk on the subject of a "flag of truce," which forms a curious episode of itself, we introduce a part of the letter of a newspaper correspondent, dated February 24th, which gives a lively, chatty description of this sail down the Mississippi and its sudden termination:

"A little after daylight the gallant Commodore Foote hobbled painfully aboard the *Cincinnati*, and almost immediately after the whole fleet was steaming down the river. From the moment of starting, the regular line of battle was observed, the four iron-clad boats leading, abreast, the *Cincinnati* a mile to the rear, and close behind this the transports and mortars. The five transports seemed more for show than use. However, it was the Sabbath, and beneath the warm beams of the first sun we had seen for weeks, we pushed merrily ahead, absorbed in our devotions and the weather, and not caring to be captious, or to ask too many questions.

"A little before noon we steamed into Lucas's Bend, and saw, two miles below, across a promontory that ran out from the right bank, the tent-crowned bluffs of Columbus. A shot from a heavy gun came booming over the water, conveying to us an invitation seemingly to fight. Another followed, and then another—the latter a cogent invitation of some one hundred and twenty-eight pounds in weight, that plunged into the river a short distance to the left of us, and sent the water splashing skyward like a water-spout. A heavy gong sounding in the boats sent the men to quarters; guns were run in, every thing and every body was in place, the mortar-boats were hugging the shore to gain uninterruptedly a position a little lower; and from all appearance I expected in another instant to witness a repetition of the Fort Henry and Donelson tragedies. However, just as the guns seemed on the eve of belching their sulphureous thunders against Columbus, a rebel transport steamer rounded the point of the promontory with a flag flying from her jackstaff. She rounded the point close under the guns of the iron boats, and commenced whistling, as if asking permission to hold a conference. A whistle from the flag-boat gave the permission; a tug ran down to her, lay alongside a short time, ran back, and then the *Cincinnati* ran down, took position between her and the Columbus batteries, and dropped her anchor.

"A deputation was soon after seen to leave the rebel transport—the *Red River*—and go aboard the National gun-boat. For three long hours the boats lay there, and many and wild were the conjectures as to what was going on. All agreed unanimously that a surrender was going on—none doubted that he would take dinner or supper in Columbus. Finally, a stir was observed in the gun-boat, and the tug put off, carrying back some officers to the transport. 'Now for Columbus,' said every body; and in imagination we had already penetrated the securities of that stronghold, and were rambling among its water batteries, its land batteries, rifle-pits, breastworks, redans, abatis, bastions, redoubts, palisades, lunettes, and the Lord only knows what else, when three flags glided up the staff on the flag-boat, and Master ———, of the *Carondelet*, with the remark, 'That's to close up, probably,' opened his signal-book, and, with a look of incredulity, read, 'Fall in line.'

"But there seemed to be no mistake. The *Cincinnati* bore straight up the river for Cairo—black, grim, and uncommunicative; and shortly after we had all taken our places, and were slowly following our leader.

"Arriving at Cairo, a rush was made for the commodore. No use. Never was a drum tighter than the hero of Henry and Donelson, and the sorrowing crowd departed."

The flag of truce, to all appearance, was simply an expedient to obtain knowledge of the strength of the National forces. Whether it were so or not, its result was favorable to our cause, as it was at once followed by the evacuation of Columbus. The reader can form his own judgment of the case from the facts and the correspondence. General Polk sent by the transport this letter:

"HEAD-QUARTERS, FIRST DIVISION, WESTERN DEPARTMENT,
COLUMBUS, KY., *Feb.* 22, 1862.

"Presuming you will be willing to reciprocate the courtesy shown to the families of officers of the United States Army, after the battle of Belmont, in allowing them to visit those officers who were prisoners within my lines, I take the liberty of sending up, under a flag of truce, the families of several of our officers who were captured at Donelson. These are the families of General Buckner and Colonels Hawson and Medeira. They are accompanied by Colonel Russel and Messrs. Vance and Stockdale as escorts; also by Mr. Mass.

"Hoping you may find it convenient to send these ladies forward to their husbands, I have the honor to remain, respectfully, your obedient servant, L. POLK, Major-General, commanding.

"To Commanding Officer U. S. Forces, Cairo, Ill."

This was answered as follows:

"UNITED STATES FLAG-STEAMER 'CINCINNATI,' MISSISSIPPI
RIVER, NEAR COLUMBUS, KY., *Feb.* 23, 1862.

"GENERAL,—Your letter of the 22d instant, received to-day by the hands of Captain Blake under a flag of truce, *nearly within range of your guns and in the presence of our armed forces*, at half-past twelve o'clock to-day, will be answered to-morrow by a flag of truce at the same point of the river at which this was received.

"Very respectfully, your obedient servants,

"ANDREW H. FOOTE,
"Flag-Officer, commanding Naval Forces, Western Waters;
"GEORGE W. CULLUM,
"Chief of Staff and Engineers, Department of Missouri.

"Major-General L. Polk, commanding at Columbus, Ky."

On the same day came this second letter from General Polk:

"HEAD-QUARTERS, FIRST DIVISION, WESTERN DEPARTMENT,
COLUMBUS, KY, *Feb.* 23, 1862.

"To A. H. FOOTE, Flag-Officer, commanding Naval Forces, Western Waters; GEO. W. CULLUM, Brig.-General, Chief of Staff and Engineers:

"GENTLEMEN,—I have received your note of this date, acknowledging mine of yesterday asking permission for the wives of certain Confederate States officers to visit their husbands who had been made prisoners of war at Fort Donelson.

"The application was based on the fact that I had on a former occasion granted a similar request made of me in behalf of the wives of Colonels Dougherty and McClerkin, captured at Belmont, and the assurance of the commanding general at Cairo that he would reciprocate the courtesy if events should make it desirable.

"I note that you say my letter was received under a flag of truce, '*nearly within range of your* (my) *guns, and in the presence of our* (your) *armed forces.*'

"As to the flag appearing in the presence of your armed forces, and nearly within range of my guns, it was purely accidental. The ladies, whose safe conduct the flag was intended to secure, arrived at this post from Nashville on the evening of the 21st instant. Preparations were made to send them up under a flag on the 22d, and my letter was written and intrusted to Captain Blake. The departure of the flag was prevented by the heavy fall of rain. They left this morning, the boat taking its departure from a point considerably below my batteries, from whence your position in the river (five miles above) was not visible. It appears that several guns were fired from the fort prior to the departure of the boat; but as my artillery officers are constantly practicing, the firing attracted no particular attention; and the presence of your armed forces in the river, it seems, was not known to the officer in charge of the flag until after his boat had passed around the point.

"This statement of facts, I am informed, has already been made to you by Captain Blake; and it is repeated here only because of the remark above quoted, which you have taken pains to underline.

"Allow me to assure myself that officers of your rank and reputation could not impute any improper motive in sending a flag of truce. I would be unwilling to believe such a suspicion could be entertained by any mind except one conscious of its capacity to venture upon such an abuse. I have the honor to be, gentlemen, your obedient servant,

"L. POLK,

"Major-General, commanding Confederate Forces."

The next day this dignified though sharp response was sent by a flag of truce from the National head-quarters:

"CAIRO, ILLINOIS, *February* 24, 1862.

"MAJOR-GENERAL L. POLK, commanding at Columbus, Ky.:

"GENERAL,—In answer to your request 'to reciprocate the courtesy shown to the families and officers of the U. S. A., after the battle of Belmont, in allowing them to visit those officers who were prisoners,' by asking permission to have passed through our lines 'the families of General Buckner and Colonels Hawson and Medeira,' captured at Fort Donelson, accompanied by certain gentlemen as escorts, we have to inform you that we will cheerfully comply with your request, subject to the approval of the President, but limited to the wives and children of those officers, and excluding their escorts; but to provide them with a protector, Colonel Thom, an aid-de-camp of Major-General Halleck, and one of the bearers of our flag of truce, has offered to take them in charge as far as St. Louis, where they will learn the destinations of the captured officers, which are unknown to us.

"The flag of truce will wait, if necessary, long enough to obtain your action on this proposition.

"Before concluding this note, we feel constrained to make some remarks upon your abuse yesterday of the sacred character of a flag of truce.

"Upon approaching the batteries of Columbus with armed forces, and when within supposed range of your artillery, you fired three heavy guns; and, to add to this hostile demonstration, one of your gun-boats rounded Belmont Point apparently to give battle; but immediately, upon discovering our strength and position, retired. Soon after there appeared an armed steamer, with Captain Blake bearing your flag of truce, accompanied by many officers and citizens, upon the frivolous pretext above stated, evidently with the intention of discovering our force and intentions. Under these circumstances, by the usages of war, the dispatch-bearer and those with him were subject to be made prisoners and the steamer captured; and we felt it our duty to inform you that a repetition of such an unwarrantable abuse of a flag of truce will not again be tolerated.

"Your letter, though dated the 22d, evidently was not dispatched till after the firing of your first gun, near eleven o'clock, more than an hour before your flag of truce was seen about two miles from your batteries, and certainly dispatched after the gun was discharged.

"Regretting that we have to animadvert on this flagrant departure from the established usages of flags of truce,

"We are, very respectfully, your obedient servants,

"Andrew H. Foote, Flag-Officer, etc.;

"George W. Cullum, Chief of Staff, etc."

In a letter to his wife, dated the 23d, Commodore Foote

thus speaks of this "flag of truce" affair, which perhaps has already taken up too much space:

"We had been to Columbus, and had got the two mortars in position to open upon Belmont, when a flag of truce came out with several ladies, as you will see by General Polk's letter, and we hoped it was to surrender; but, instead, it was a mere artifice to discover our strength. We shall write a letter to the Right Rev. General to-morrow, charging him with violating all military rules of propriety by his remarkable act. We were glad it was done, however, as we ran within sight of his heavy batteries, and attained the object of our reconnoissance—still, we shall give the bishop a rub."

He says in this same letter:

"I am still on crutches, but my foot is rapidly improving. I have no objection to the wound either in the foot or in the arm, as they are honorable wounds; but the last was a hard fight. I stood one side of a gun when five out of six men were knocked down, and I only escaped serious wounds. I was touching the pilot with my clothes when he was killed."

The following dispatches tell the story of the speedy breaking up of the enemy's strong position at Columbus, which, together with Nashville and Bowling Green, was really conquered at forts Henry and Donelson:

"CAIRO, *March* 1, 1862.

"SIR,—Lieutenant-Commanding Phelps, sent with a flag of truce today to Columbus, has this moment returned, and reports that Columbus is being evacuated. He saw the rebels burning their winter-quarters, and removing their heavy guns on the bluffs; but the guns in the water-batteries remain intact. He also saw a large force of cavalry drawn up ostentatiously on the bluffs, but no infantry were to be seen as heretofore; and the encampment seen in our armed reconnoissance a few days ago has been removed. Large fires were visible in the town of Columbus and upon the river banks below, indicating the destruction of the town, military stores, and equipments.

"I shall consult General Cullum, and we shall probably proceed to Columbus with the force we have already soon after daylight. General Polk informs us that he will send a flag of truce at meridian to-morrow to the point where the flags of truce met to-day, in reference to which we shall be governed according to circumstances. But as General Cullum has not been fully consulted, I can give no particular information of our movements to-morrow. I have the honor to be, etc.,

"A. H. Foote, Flag-Officer.

"The Hon. Gideon Welles, Secretary of the Navy."

"U. S. Flag-Steamer 'Cincinnati,' Columbus,
March 4, 1862.

"Sir,—I have the honor to forward a copy of the telegram sent to the Department to-day announcing the fall of Columbus.

"The fleet not being in a condition to proceed down to Island No. Ten and to New Madrid, where the rebels are represented as fortifying, I leave for Cairo immediately to make the necessary preparation for going down the river with a suitable force of gun-boats and mortar-boats in a proper condition for effective service. I am fully impressed with the importance of proceeding to New Madrid as soon as possible, where General Pope has arrived with ten thousand men; but such is the condition of my command that I shall decline moving, as I informed Generals Sherman and Cullum, unless I am ordered to do so by the Secretary of the Navy, as I must be the judge of the condition of the fleet, and when it is prepared for the service required.

"It is due to Commander Pennock, the fleet captain, and to Mr. Sanford, the ordnance officer of the flotilla, to say to the Department that these efficient officers earnestly entreated me to permit them to go on this expedition, as well as up the Tennessee and Cumberland rivers; but their services in preparing the gun and mortar boats at Cairo being absolutely necessary, I reluctantly denied their application from a sense of duty to the government; yet their services should be regarded as equally important to the object of the expedition as if they had participated in the different actions. A. H. Foote.

"The Hon. Gideon Welles."

In his report of the evacuation, March 4, he says:

"My armed reconnoissance, on the 2d instant, caused a hasty evacuation, the rebels leaving quite a number of guns and carriages, ammunition, and a large quantity of shot and shell, a considerable number of anchors, and the remnant of a chain lately stretched across the river, with a large number of torpedoes. Most of the huts, tents, and quarters are destroyed.

"The works are of very great strength, consisting of formidable tiers of batteries on the water side, and on the land side surrounded by a ditch and abatis.

"General Sherman, with Lieutenant-Commanding Phelps, not knowing that the works were last evening occupied by four hundred of the Second Illinois Cavalry, on a scouting-party sent by General Sherman from Paducah, made a bold dash to the shore under the batteries, hoisting the American flag on the summit of the bluff, greeted by the hearty cheers of our brave tars and soldiers.

"The force consisted of six gun-boats, four mortar-boats, and three transports, having on board two regiments and two battalions of infantry, under command of Colonel Buford—General Cullum and General Sherman being in command of the troops. The former, leaving a sick-bed to go ashore, discovered what was evidently a magazine on fire, and immediately ordered the train to be cut, and thus saved the lives of the garrison.

A. H. Foote.

"The Hon. Gideon Welles."

There was every evidence, in the great amount of ordnance and military property left behind, and the vindictive plan, happily foiled, of destroying the victorious forces, that the enemy suddenly and reluctantly left this strong fortification. The powerful show of grim iron-clads and mortar-boats no doubt hastened this decision. Foote probably felt some disappointment at not being able to try his mortar-boats upon the heavy fortifications of Columbus. The Assistant-Secretary of the Navy, in a private letter, seems to have felt the same disappointment:

"Navy Department, *March* 5, 1862.

"My dear Commodore,—Last night, at a party at Mr. Welles's, your dispatch was received giving an account of the occupation of Columbus after its evacuation by the rebels. I felt a pang that the mortar-boats were thus deprived of a participation in the work. As Fremont started these at my suggestion, I naturally feel a deep interest concerning them, and hoped their first use would have been made in the Western waters by yourself; but the vagabonds have not given you a chance at Columbus. Perhaps Porter will give us the first trial; but, in either case, God speed you. I have no fears of the result. I notice how publicly you praise ———. Will you pardon a friend for observing that he is on the staff of the general who holds you back and ignores you. These engineer officers are puffed up with a contempt for the Navy, and have all their lives been trying to prove impossible what you have demonstrated possible, viz., to attack forts successfully with vessels. If I did not feel for you sincere admiration and friendship, and have your reputation most dear to me, I should not beg of you to be careful and not lavish praise upon any person in your dispatches, unless for distinguished conduct that must also be apparent to those who are distant from the scene. I don't know how the mail now is between here and Cairo, but it has been bad; and Mr. Blair has sent out two agents to right matters. We all feel proud of your work, attained without the efficient co-operation of any one, which renders your labors the more faithful. If you do rain 13-inch shells upon them, be sure to give us full particulars early.

"Very truly yours, G. V. Fox.

"Flag-Officer A. H. Foote."

We have noticed, and shall notice frequently hereafter—what it would be folly to ignore—the soreness that Foote felt at what he considered the great injustice done him, and the false position in which he was placed by those high in command, whose sympathies were wholly given to the other arm of the service—the Army. He had, indeed, come to the decision to obey no more orders issuing from Army officers. The Secretary, whose watchful eye was over the Navy, and who exercised a judicious rule of its affairs, notices with anxiety the development of this feeling, and cautions him against it. Mr. Welles says to him in a letter dated May 7th:

"Step by step I have watched your proceedings, and marked the persistency, patience, and determination, under many and great discouragements, with which yourself and those associated with you have met and surmounted every difficulty. Rest assured the country knows and justly appreciates your services. I am confident you will permit no jealous feeling, or any appearance of such feeling, against our branch of the service to annoy you; and I trust that it will at no time be cause of embarrassment. Under your orders and acts the Navy has vindicated its character before the country, and contributed its full share in planting again the Union standard, and restoring the Union feeling in the great central valley. The rapid and successive blows you have struck with such effect have electrified the nation, and animated our people with higher hopes than I have before witnessed since the outbreak of this rebellion. This very hasty letter I have written, and so send it because of inexcusable delay in saying to you privately and as an old schoolmate—'Friend, how gratified I have been and am with what you have done.'"

CHAPTER XX.

THE MISSISSIPPI AS THE SCENE OF OPERATIONS.—GENERAL POPE'S MOVEMENTS AT NEW MADRID.—CHARACTERISTIC ORDER.—CORRESPONDENCE.

THE two gun-boats *Taylor* and *Lexington* had been sent by the commodore back to the Tennessee River, to guard captured posts and to act as patrols in preventing the enemy from erecting new fortifications upon the shores. A spirited little engagement took place at Pittsburg, Tennessee, on the 1st of March, and another at Chickasaw, Alabama, at a later date, between the gun-boats and small detachments of the enemy's troops, who were attempting to fortify at those places, resulting in the breaking up of their plans, and showing the ability of the iron-clads not only to open the river, but to keep it open. But the vessels belonging to the Western flotilla were now called to a greater achievement—to unlock the Mississippi itself, that it might be a free stream in all its vast extent.

The Mississippi has been frequently described, but we doubt if any powers of description would be equal to convey an impression of this "Great River," as its name signifies. The words of the Psalmist occur to one as he sails upon its broad bosom: "Thou visitest the earth and waterest it; thou greatly enrichest it with the river of God, which is full of water. Thou preparest the corn and wine when thou hast so provided for it." It rolls along its exhaustless abundance of water like a sea, through territories of boundless agricultural wealth, while hundreds of cities, some of them already of considerable magnitude, and many of them destined to be densely populated, stud its banks. When one is at St. Paul, in Minnesota, with a great river still above him, there are more than two thousand miles of river below him; and that part of it which is called the "Upper Mississippi," from Dubuque to St. Paul, where the water is clear and pure, is equal in some respects to the Rhine or the Danube in beauty, and will hereafter be visited and built upon for its noble scenery. At St. Louis, a thousand miles and more above its mouth, and at points where was the chief scene of operations of "Foote's Flotilla," the river at places is more than two miles wide, turbid with the yellow flood of the muddy Missouri, and strong in current with the mingled force of two mighty streams. It is a thoroughly masculine river, an impetuously rolling and uncontrollable flood, sometimes devouring in its insatiate, destructive will large sections of the land, and changing its channel at pleasure. Its banks are like those of the Nile—mud-banks that break off suddenly, not slope off gradually—and one can frequently see great masses of soil detaching themselves and falling into the river. For hundreds of miles continuously there is sometimes nothing but forest—sombre, almost impenetrable primeval forest; and through such as this the men of Foote and Pope had to hew their way at Island No. Ten. The broad current at times separates into three or four channels, now chafing the foot of high bluffs on one side, and losing itself on the other in swampy forests or bayous, in whose endless vistas the eye vainly wanders. Upon the shores of this river an empire is growing, and the dullest mind can see that in the future the great rivers of the East—the Nile, the Euphrates, and the Ganges—will be equaled, perhaps surpassed, in what will probably be here realized in the populousness and magnitude of its magnificent states. It is now comparatively without a history—it runs for hundreds of miles through almost savage and unrecorded wildernesses; but already, since the last war, it is becoming an historic river, and a human interest, romantic and powerful, is blending with the majesty of its natural features. New Orleans, Vicksburg, Island No. Ten, have fastened the charm of valor, faith, and patient endurance, for the sake of great principles and the interests of humanity, upon its shores.

Henceforth—to return to our narrative—the short remaining active career of Commodore Foote is confined to his unremitting efforts to clear away the forts and barriers that the enemy had placed upon this pathway of the nation, which the West had decreed should be free, and had consecrated to freedom forever. He expected to do this with his own fleet. He declared more than once that he intended to descend the Mississippi to its mouth; and this accounts for the deliberateness of all his preparations for a task that he knew, better than others, was so great. He fairly began this work, which was finished by Farragut, together with the blows of Grant at Vicksburg, so that the names of the two naval heroes must hereafter be associated with the mighty stream which they were instrumental in opening anew to freedom, sweeping away every obstruction upon its broad waters. He was not permitted to do all he wished to do, but what he did was genuine work, and was what gave the impulse to final complete success.

After Columbus was made untenable by the breaking up of the first line of the Southern defense, or, in view of this anticipated event, the rebel leaders had pitched upon a position some forty miles below, on the river, at the now famous Island No. Ten, which they fortified with every device of military engineering skill, under the immediate personal supervision of General Beauregard, who had been then recently appointed to the command of the Department of Mississippi.

Island No. Ten* is situated at the turn of a long bend in the

* Below the mouth of the Ohio River the islands in the Mississippi are designated by successive numbers.

river fifty-five miles below Cairo, and by nature and art was perhaps the strongest position on the river. It could not readily be reached by land forces; and field batteries were placed along the shores approaching it for ten or twelve miles commanding the channel, where the current of the Mississippi was so swift and strong that it was with the utmost difficulty that cumbrous iron-clads like those commanded by Commodore Foote, with deficient steam-power, could hold their own; and they had to be managed with the greatest caution, lest, becoming unmanageable, they should drift down under the enemy's batteries. This fighting down stream, with their sterns up stream, or "bow on, and with only the forward guns," in the uncontrollable and sea-like Mississippi, with clumsy arks of boats that were really little more than huge floating batteries, was a very different duty from fighting up stream in the smaller Cumberland and Tennessee rivers, where the boats could be brought into close range, and, if disabled, would of themselves float away from the enemy's reach. Some seventy heavy guns upon the island and its opposite shores were so trained that, though set in batteries wide apart, which necessitated their being assailed separately, they were still enabled to direct their fire simultaneously upon one spot. The whole side of the island fronting the Missouri shore bristled with cannon, and the stream itself narrowed at this point. At Island No. Ten the river, after making a sudden bend, runs to the northwest several miles, and at the turn of the northern bend, where it begins to take once more a southerly direction, at the junction of a large bayou and the Mississippi, is situated New Madrid, on the Missouri shore. In order to prevent the island's being attacked by land forces from the Missouri side, the rebels had strongly fortified at New Madrid, and stationed there a large number of troops, drawn partially from the now abandoned stronghold of Columbus; and they had also fortified a few miles below New Madrid, upon the Tennessee side.

Between New Madrid and Island No. Ten, on both sides of the Mississippi, extend immense swamps or bayous, which forbade military operations, and which also hemmed in the rebel forces themselves, and prevented their escape in case the island should be captured.* It was, in fact, a huge and complicated system of water-locked defenses, at the centre of which, and guarding the channel of the Mississippi, lay the strong and almost unassailable fort of Island No. Ten, like a dragon of fable, coiled in the heart of its swampy fastnesses; and, to carry out the illustration, belching forth sulphureous flames. In order to completely invest this fortification, it was necessary first to obtain possession of New Madrid, and thus cut it off from below, as the river ran, though really above, geographically speaking. This task was assigned to General John Pope, who proved himself an able and energetic commander, with great resources and perseverance. As early as the 22d of February, General Pope was dispatched by General Halleck from St. Louis, with a considerable body of Ohio and Illinois troops, to attack New Madrid. His transports landed at Commerce, in Missouri; and his main column, toiling through miry swamps, on the same day that Columbus was evacuated (March 3d), appeared before New Madrid, where Pope found to oppose him, in addition to a large rebel force, Hollins's flotilla of gun-boats on the river.† He retired out of reach of their cannon, and sent to Cairo for heavy siege-guns. He also planted successfully a battery twelve miles down the river, at Point Pleasant, in the rear of Island No. Ten. As soon as his heavy artillery arrived, being laboriously dragged through the swamps, after "a quick, sharp siege," in which the Confederates suffered greatly, they fled precipitately, leaving New Madrid in Pope's possession.

---

* Boynton's "History of the Navy during the Rebellion," vol. i., p. 535.

† Lossing's "Civil War in America," vol. ii., p. 239.

The morning that the National troops under General Pope entered New Madrid (March 14), Commodore Foote left Cairo with his fleet, to co-operate with him at Island No. Ten; but before giving an account of his operations at that point, there are a few matters of previous occurrence and some correspondence to be taken notice of.

We mentioned the spirited services of the gun-boats *Taylor* and *Lexington* on the Tennessee River, undertaken to prevent the rebels from refortifying at Pittsburg and Chickasaw. This gallant conduct drew forth the lively praise of the flag-officer, who, beyond almost any commander in the war, was generous to render his subordinates their full honor, but it also called forth this sailor-like order:

"CAIRO, *March* 4, 1862.

"SIR,—I have received your report, and have forwarded it to the Secretary of the Navy, with commendatory remarks. But I give a general order that no commander will land men to make an attack ashore. Our gun-boats have no more men than are necessary to man the guns; and as the army must do the shore work, and as the enemy want nothing better than to entice our men ashore and overpower them with superior numbers, the commanders must not operate ashore, but confine themselves to their vessels. In haste, respectfully, A. H. FOOTE.

"Lieutenant-Commanding Gwin.

"P. S.—Be cautious, as it is an element equally necessary to bravery, and life must not be risked without a prospect of success."

It is but right to presume that if Foote had lived long enough he would have organized the Navy Department of the West into a more homogeneous body, doing its own work more exclusively but effectively, and having its own position and rights more clearly understood, so that the Army would have looked upon it in the light of an ally and equal, not of a mere auxiliary, and that something of the high and united spirit of the American Navy would have been breathed into it. We are perhaps even now inclined to think of the Navy as confined wholly to the ocean coast, and to forget the immense extent of inland waters over which a well-regulated naval organization should extend; although it is the desire of every patriotic heart that civil war will never again require the services of fighting vessels so far within our own borders. It is to be fervently hoped that the broad realms of North and South, united by the Mississippi River, by nature, by origin, by kinship, by liberty, shall be evermore one happy nation.

The two following letters at this time relating to things immediately past and present betoken much anxiety and despondency of mind, and we insert them for the reason that this is not intended to be a eulogy, but a real life, with its lights and shadows. Yet some of the statements in these letters are important, as coming from a man of strict truth and honesty. The first is addressed to a relative of his family:

"CAIRO, *March* 9, 1862.

"MY DEAR SIR,—I place a high value on your letter, independently of the source from which it comes, as it is an effort for you to write. I wish I had the time, if I have the ability, to respond by one as good.

"I send Augusta the certificate of the best surgeon here, who is at the head of the Sanitary Committee, relative to my wounded foot, or, perhaps, I might more properly call it a diagnosis. I have pain in my foot; but you will see from the certificate that there is no danger to be apprehended, unless it is to the government from my not being able to give personal attention to my varied duties. Still every moment of my time from seven A.M. till eleven P.M. is occupied with office duties. I am on crutches, and should be happy at the idea of being able to lay them aside.

"I have to work against a good deal of opposition. Not even a Navy officer at home can conceive of the magnitude of my work—navy-yard and fleet duties; and I would not again pass through the mental agony and bodily effort, certainly for all the credit I do or can receive from the public. It is a bitter cup, and I can hardly drink it. It has added ten years to my age, and it is quite enough to break any man down. I do not like the course that has been pursued in regard to me. On the 28th of January I suggested the attack on Fort Henry, and gave my orders two days before the fight for Lieutenant-Commanding Phelps to proceed up the Tennessee, and destroy the rebel gun-boats and their property as far as the river was navigable, and off he went to Mississippi and Alabama without a word from Halleck. Yet he and McClellan got the credit of the thing. The rebels and many of our Army officers say that our desperate fight demoralized the rebels at Fort Donelson, so much so that they could not even cut their way through the lines the next day in their attempt to escape; and if they had not been demoralized, why, a military man would ask, did they not hold on in their intrenchments? Still I fought Fort Donelson four days before I was ready, as I wanted my six mortar-boats; but General Halleck urged me, and I determined to take the only course, by a close action, which could secure us a victory without the mortar-boats. Then I went up and took possession of Clarksville, hoisting our flag and issuing the proclamation, and General Halleck says in his official dispatches it was four days afterward occupied by General Smith, making no allusion to my command. I was then ready to proceed on and take Nashville, and was about starting when I received an order not to do it, which if I had done, the Assistant-Secretary of the Navy says, I would have saved a million dollars' worth of rebel arms and a factory for making percussion-caps. The citizens expected the gun-boats, and General A. S. Johnston advised them to leave and abandon the city, as I was coming—hence the panic; and, after all, Buell could not march in until he got a gun-boat first off the city. Now I am wanted to go, even if not prepared, to the attack of Island No. Ten and New Madrid, and Assistant-Secretary Scott urges me; but I have refused positively to do it, and will wait till Wednesday, when I will have the mortar-boats and the *Benton*, and can, God willing, who gives the victory, do it easily. I have no fears for this week's work.

"Oh, how I long for this war to terminate! I have had enough of it, and I think the South will also have been taught to respect Yankee pluck. I pray that God may soon send us peace and prosperity. As for myself, wonderful to say, excepting my foot, I am in remarkable health.

"Excuse my haste, as I have more than I can possibly attend to in the way of business, and I may have to delay writing to Augusta; if so, please show her this. I hope to return here after going down about sixty miles to attack No. Ten and New Madrid. In the mean time, let Augusta write as usual, and I will write when I get a chance. With love to all. Very truly yours, A. H. FOOTE."

"'BENTON,' CAIRO, *March* 12, 1862.

"MY DEAR WIFE,—Your excellent letter and William's came this morning like sunbeams just as I was writing a letter of sympathy and condolence to our dear friend Commodore Smith on Joe's death.* It was a sad affair; but such things will happen in war. I can not express my horrible pressure of responsibility; and now, honestly, I am almost crazy that no troops have been furnished to accompany me and occupy

* This promising young officer went down in the *Cumberland* at Hampton Roads, March 8th, 1862. Senator Grimes, of Iowa, spoke thus of him in the United States Senate, March 13:

"But while I would thus honor the gallant living, I would bear my tribute of affectionate respect for the memory of the heroic dead who fell in the engagement in Hampton Roads. Let the remembrance of that brave young officer, whose obsequies are now being performed in another part of this city, who, when his vessel was sinking beneath his feet, replied to a summons to surrender that he would never give up the flag intrusted to his keeping, and the next moment met death with composure, be cherished by his countrymen. The name of Smith, already illustrious in the annals of the American Navy, will be added to the bright galaxy of those who have freely laid down their lives at the call of their country."

We can not refrain from adding the father's response to the letter referred to, for its manly pathos.

"*March* 21, 1862.

"MY DEAR FOOTE,—I duly received your kind note of condolence, and now I have to sympathize with you in your bereavement and loss of a darling boy. We must bow our heads and lick the dust, and say, 'Though He slay me, yet will I trust in Him.' I was relieved by receiving the mutilated remains of my son, and I deposited them with those of his mother. We are looking most anxiously for reports of your success at No. Ten. God give you the victory.

"I have just received a letter from my only son, and he inclosed one for you, which I forward herewith. He has a hard time with his gunboat, but I pray he may be spared to me. I fear Farragut has a difficult task to ascend the Mississippi—his vessels draw too much water; but I hope you may meet him at New Orleans.

"Our arms seem to be victorious every where except in the untoward event at Newport News. We have been too indifferent about the monster *Merrimack*. I am glad to know my son performed his duty as well as any man could under the circumstances. I am almost crazy with the cares that rest upon me, which I shall endeavor to dispose of to the best of my ability; but I am old, and my mind is somewhat impaired; yet I shall stick to my post, and do all I can for the cause of the Union and the defense of liberty.

"I am taxed to the utmost of my power. God bless you.

"Yours as always, JOSEPH SMITH.

"Flag-Officer A. H. Foote."

Island No. Ten, if we take it, since, if I leave it unoccupied, the rebels will come back to their batteries and reoccupy it, and keep our supplies from coming to us from here. I do not understand such movements. I would not, my dear, be in the position I am—the vast responsibility of this river, which, if disaster occur to my boats, the rebels could retake Columbus, capture St. Louis, and command the Mississippi River—for all the world can give. The mere fight, my mere life, is nothing in the consideration. An officer said truly this morning that no man in the nation had the dreadful responsibility upon him that I had. Cullum is sick, and gone to St. Louis, and Scott ordered home, and Governor Strong, a citizen volunteer, is in command here. Thus it goes. I am apprehensive of disaster for want of management on the part of the Army. I write, my dear, that if disaster come, you may know the reason, and have my vindication; for I have done all that should be done to avert it. You will know the result by telegram before this reaches you, and you need not caution me against being spoiled by success, as I was never more humbled. I would this moment give all I am worth could I be on the Atlantic a captain of a good steam-frigate, instead of being out here under a pressure which would crush most men; and how I have stood it thus far I can only account for by the fact that 'God has been my helper.' I have not time to answer yours in detail. All is confusion, and I am almost in despair. Oh, my dear, if our affairs, if our 'house were put in order,' and our children older and doing well, what a relief it would be to quietly wait God's time, and joyfully leave this world for the glories of a blessed immortality. That is the bright spot—the sunshine amid the gloom and darkness. Here we must do our duty, and I pray for strength to do mine, and to God let us commend ourselves and our children and all whom we hold dear. He has placed me here, and I hope I may in a proper spirit perform his will. To your parents and cousins my love, and love and kisses to the children. Am glad to hear darling Emily is more free from pain.

"Ever affectionately your dear husband, A. H. Foote.

"Beauregard and General Bragg are here.

"Later.—General Halleck telegraphs 'not to make an attack on No. Ten till further orders, as he wishes to wait till General Pope gets his heavy guns in position to cut off the enemy's retreat.' This may induce the rebels to evacuate it. At all events, we shall go better prepared; so don't give yourself uneasiness about me."

The writer of these letters was not a man who loved war for war's sake. He was ready to use it, and use it with terrible effect, for great ends; but he would have been glad at any moment to retire from its troubled scenes. He was a man, at heart, of peace, of kindly domestic affections, and of humane ideas and desires for the highest happiness of his fellow-men. The war-worn fighter murmured in his heart—

"But we grow old. Ah! when shall all men's good
Be each man's rule, and universal Peace
Lie like a shaft of light across the land,
And like a lane of beams athwart the sea,
Through all the circle of the golden year?"

CHAPTER XXI.

INVESTMENT AND BOMBARDMENT OF ISLAND NUMBER TEN.—DEATH OF SON.—CUTTING CANAL ACROSS PENINSULA.

In order to understand clearly the history of naval operations at Island No. Ten,* the following letters are important:

"Department of the Mississippi, Cairo, *March* 8, 1862.

"Flag-Officer Foote, U. S. N., commanding Flotilla, Western Waters:

"Flag-Officer,—Major-General Halleck desires that a demonstration by gun and mortar boats should be made by Monday morning next upon Island No. Ten, and then upon New Madrid, in order to relieve the command of General Pope, now in front of that place. The forces of General Pope are needed for movement up the Tennessee, and *must* be ordered back without results unless we can bring them by river early next week, after capturing Island No. Ten and New Madrid. To effect these important results, I desire to know whether you can have ready for service by Tuesday night four gun and four mortar boats; if so, I will provide transports for movement by land forces for as many as may be necessary to remove from New Madrid such portion of General Pope's forces as can be safely spared after capturing New Madrid and Island No. Ten.

"Your immediate attention will greatly oblige,

"Yours respectfully, and most obedient servant,

"Geo. W. Cullum, Brig.-Gen., Chief of Staff, and Engineer."

"Cairo, *March* 8, 1862.

"General,—I have repeatedly stated to you, and to Assistant-Secretary Scott, that I shall not be ready with the flotilla, to move on Island No. Ten and New Madrid, until Wednesday, leaving here in the course of that day with gun and mortar boats.

"If I am peremptorily ordered to move before that time by Assistant-Secretary of War Colonel Scott, I shall try to do it, but under a remon-

* For map of Island No. Ten, and its surroundings, see p. 267.

strance that I shall deem it an act involving, in all probability, the most disastrous consequences to the flotilla, and to the service which it was designed to perform.

"The pilot-houses are unsafe, and the vessels are not in a condition which would enable them to make any thing of a stand against such a resistance as the rebels have made in every instance. I can not, therefore, except under this strong remonstrance, be a party to an act which I believe would terminate in the utter demoralization of my command.

"I am, respectfully, your obedient servant, A. H. FOOTE, Flag-Officer.

"Brig.-Gen. Geo. W. Cullum, Chief of Staff and Engineer."

In a letter of the same date to Lieutenant Henry A. Wise (Bureau of Ordnance and Hydrography, Washington) he speaks of his preparations:

"The *Benton* is under way, and barely stems the strong current of the Ohio—five knots per hour—in this rise of water, but I hope by putting her between two iron-clad steamers to-morrow she will stem the current and work comparatively well. On Wednesday I hope to take down seven iron-clads and ten mortar-boats to attack Island No. Ten and New Madrid. A portion of iron plating for pilot-houses and chains got aboard a steamer from Cincinnati, which was prepared to go up the Cumberland, but will be here to-morrow or next day. As the current is in some places in the Mississippi seven miles per hour, the iron-clad boats can hardly return here; therefore we must go well prepared, which detains us longer than even you would imagine necessary from your navy-yard and smooth-water stand-point."

General Pope had just seized New Madrid with his land forces, and planted his batteries so as to command the stream down the river; and when the gun-boats assailed Island No. Ten from above, the place would be thoroughly invested, and the siege—so full of picturesque and wonderful incidents, as it proved to be—would fairly commence.

This order from General Halleck was received March 12th:

"TO FLAG-OFFICER FOOTE:

"You will not make an attack on Island No. Ten till further orders. I wish to wait till General Pope gets his heavy guns in position to cut off the enemy's retreat. H. W. HALLECK, Major-General."

The following letter, of the same date, shows the writer's state of mind in regard to the enterprise:

"'BENTON,' *March* 12, 1862.

"MY DEAR SIR,—I am grateful beyond expression for your kind letter of the 7th, and beg to be excused for this hasty answer, as we leave to-day for No. Ten and New Madrid, and I trust that God will give us the victory. Island No. Ten is very strongly fortified, and we shall have a hard fight. I shall be very cautious, as I appreciate the vast responsibility of keeping our flotilla from falling into the rebels' hands, as it would turn the whole tide of affairs against us.

"I will not show, nor have I shown jealousy against the Army. I am on the best of terms with Generals Grant, Smith, McClernand, and with all the junior officers. I thank you for your valuable friendship, and will strive to retain it. Respects to your family. I can hardly get through my work, so excuse this.

"I have the honor to be your friend, A. H. FOOTE.

"The Hon. Gideon Welles."

On the morning of the 14th Foote moved down the river with his flotilla, consisting of seven iron-clad gun-boats and ten mortar-boats. He was joined at Columbus on the same day by Colonel Buford, in command of some twelve hundred troops, and reached Hickman that evening with the flotilla and transports. The boilers of the *Louisville* were here found to leak badly, and she was sent back to Columbus for repairs. We continue the narrative of events for the next two days in the flag-officer's own words, in his report to the Secretary of the Navy:

"On the 15th instant, at daylight, the flotilla and transports moved down the river, arriving in the vicinity of Island No. Ten at 9 A.M. The rain and dense fog prevented our getting the vessels in position, other than two mortar-boats, for the purpose of ascertaining their range.

"Early on the morning of the 16th instant I placed the mortar-boats in as good a position as the circumstances would admit, when they shelled several regiments out of their encampments, and, at extreme range, reached the batteries on No. Ten, the floating battery, and the five batteries on the Tennessee shore. The mortar-boats are in charge of Cap-

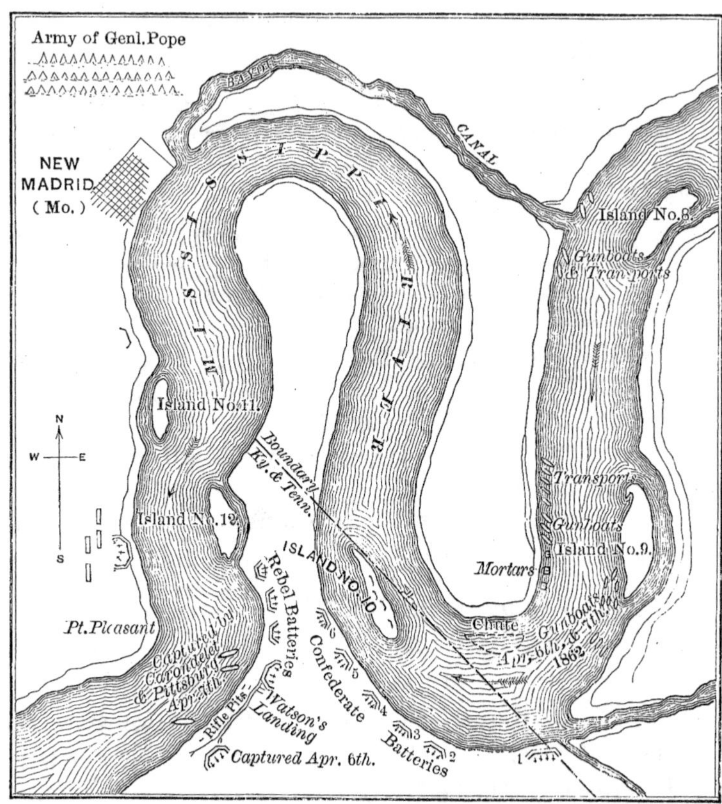

tain Maynard, United States Army, as ordnance officer, assisted by Acting Lieutenant-Commanding J. P. Sandford, United States Navy, who volunteered his services.

"This morning, the 17th instant, soon after daylight, the mortar-boats being in position, I had the *Benton* lashed between two other steamers—the *Cincinnati* and the *St. Louis*—and with the remaining iron-clad steamers made an attack on the forts, at a distance of two thousand yards or more, on account of the rapid current rendering the boats too unmanageable to come within a shorter range, without endangering their being carried under the enemy's guns, and as a nearer approach would expose the bows and quarters of the vessels—their most vulnerable points—to a fire of six other batteries, mounting forty-three guns. We opened fire on the upper fort on the Tennessee shore at meridian, and continued to give and receive quite a brisk fire from this and also four other batteries on the same shore until darkness obscured the forts from view. The ten mortars, in the mean time, shelled the troops out of range, excepting those manning the batteries.

"The upper fort was badly cut up by the *Benton* and the other boats with her. We dismounted one of their guns, and the men, at times, ran from the batteries.

"Colonel Buford has been busily and I trust profitably engaged in making reconnoissances, and is preparing to mount his siege-guns.

"In the attack of to-day this vessel (*Benton*) received four shots, while a rifle-gun burst aboard the *St. Louis*, killing and wounding fifteen, officers and men. I inclose a list of casualties. The *Cincinnati* has had her engines injured, which may render it necessary for me to send her to Cairo for repairs.

"I hope to be able to silence the upper battery to-morrow, after which we can plant the mortars in a position where we expect to be able to shell the rebels out of their batteries. The place is even stronger and better adapted for defense than Columbus has ever been. Each fortification commands the one above it. We can count forty-nine guns in the different batteries, where there are probably double the number, with ten thousand troops.

"From exhaustion, arising from continuous service and want of sleep, you will excuse this incoherent, discursive report.

"Our shells bursting prematurely, we have to drown them before loading the guns. The fuses—many of which, I am informed, were made before the Mexican War—ought to have been condemned."

This was really a spirited and well-fought engagement, although it resulted in nothing definite. The *Benton* was frequently struck. The vessels at one time drew quite near to the batteries, and attacked them in something of the old dashing, desperate style, although this method could not possibly be carried out under the circumstances, since the boats were really not adapted to fighting in the strong and rapid Mississippi; but we must pause a moment in these warlike scenes to take notice of a sorrowful and touching event. On the day (the 14th) when Commodore Foote set forth from Cairo in all the pomp and circumstance of his numerous and powerful command upon his expedition against Island No. Ten, his sec-

Gun-boats *St. Louis*, *Benton*, and *Cincinnati*. Gun-boats *Carondelet* and *Mound City*. Mortars.

BOMBARDMENT OF ISLAND NO. TEN.

ond son, William Leffingwell, died at his father's house in New Haven. He was a manly and promising boy of thirteen years, who had already developed noble traits of character. He had been ill a week, and but a few days before he was the image of health—a handsome, rosy-cheeked lad. He was to his father as the apple of his eye. He received the telegram of his son's death during the thick of the battle. The following was the brief telegram to his wife, sent in response to the sad tidings, and the telegram was received in New Haven on the afternoon of the 17th:

"NEAR ISLAND NO. TEN.

"May God support us. The shock stuns me in midst of fight. Thy will be done to us and ours. A. H. FOOTE."

It was followed by this letter, written a day or two afterward:

"'BENTON,' OFF NO. TEN, *March* 19, 1862.

"MY DEAR WIFE,—I know how you feel; I feel it all myself. I want all the time to be writing to you; still I know that our dear boy has escaped great evil, and no doubt he is far better off than in this life; but Nature mourns. Let us have consolation in our bereavement. I do hope it will be the means of doing us all good, and making us live nearer to God. It is all right, my dear; for God, our kind, heavenly Father, has done it, and, as Sanford said yesterday, 'You ought, flag-officer, to rise above your grief, and not dwell so on it.' Nothing but a death in the family could at this critical moment, when so much is upon me, so draw off my mind from my duties; it shows the power of my grief. It is much on your account I so feel; but we must pray to God that he will enable us to submit with Christian faith, even if he take more of us away.

"We are not making much progress, firing almost beyond the enemy's range. I hope to have General Pope here soon from New Madrid, and attack upon the rear of the enemy. This place is stronger than Columbus in all respects; still, if we can get General Pope here, we will take it. We are throwing mortar-shells into the forts at night, which, showing the burning fuse, makes a beautiful sight, like a shooting star in a parabola; but how little do I enjoy it, or any thing else! I feel that

Willie is better off, and therefore my intense feelings must in a good measure be sympathy for you.

"I am well and have no headache, although I am only five hours in my bed.

"If I can get General Pope's army here in a week, I think we will have a grand victory.

"Love to all, kisses for children, and again tell our dear boy Augustus to love and fear God, and believe me, as always,

"Your devoted husband, A. H. FOOTE.

"P. S.—I do not feel myself in special danger. Still, should I fall, it will be in a holy cause, and I shall die content. So do not mourn on my account. You know my feelings. I have never kept any thing from you, and God will provide for you and yours. While I talk thus, I do not consider myself in any more danger than I have been before. Still we are at war, and I am under fire. Again I commend you all to God and his grace. A. H. F."

Death and Life—how closely are their black and gold threads commingled! At the very time when he received the news of his great bereavement, this joint resolution, expressive of the thanks of Congress, was passed:

(Public Resolution, No. 22.)

"*Resolved by the Senate and House of Representatives of the United States of America in Congress assembled,* That the thanks of Congress and of the American people are due, and are hereby tendered to Captain A. H. Foote, of the United States Navy, and to the officers and men of the Western Flotilla under his command, for the great gallantry exhibited by them in the attacks upon forts Henry and Donelson, for their efficiency in opening the Tennessee, Cumberland, and Mississippi rivers to the pursuits of lawful commerce, and for their unwavering devotion to the cause of the country in the midst of her greatest difficulties and dangers.

"Approved March 19, 1862."

While this resolution was under consideration by the Senate, in Committee of the Whole, Hon. James W. Grimes, Senator from Iowa, made a speech, in which he elaborately reviewed the origin, history, and achievements of the Western

Flotilla, and gave the credit due to the American Navy in the war. He said:

"I am anxious that the people of this entire country may feel that the exploits of the Navy, wherever performed, are their exploits, that its glory is their glory, and that while they are taxing themselves to support it, they are supporting the right arm of the National defense. I desire the citizen of the most remote frontier to feel that he is equally protected and equally honored by the brave deeds of our naval officers with the citizen of the Atlantic coast. I wish the men of Iowa and Minnesota to know that they are as effectually defended in their liberties at home and in their honor abroad, by the achievements of Dupont and Goldsborough and Stringham and Foote on the water, as they can be by any victories won by our armies on the land."

Senator Grimes quoted, with strong approval, a letter furnished him by Senator Wilson, of Massachusetts, written by a gentleman of high military authority at the West, from which this is an extract:

"When Fort Henry surrendered, the gate was opened by which the rebellion will be finally and utterly crushed. In a few days Commodore Foote will open the Mississippi, provided he is not hampered, and also provided he is properly supported by government. He has done a great work for his country—a work which, I am sorry to say, has not been properly appreciated. He has improvised a navy with almost insurmountable obstacles against him. I see it stated in the papers that the gun-boats did but little service at Donelson, which is a monstrous mistake. They silenced nearly all the enemy's guns, and had not the wheel of one boat and the tiller-ropes of another been shot away, in fifteen minutes more the batteries would have been flanked, and the entire rebel army exposed to the broadsides of the fleet. He would have mowed them down like grass. As it was, he made the work of the army in the fight of Saturday much easier than it otherwise would have been. Several of the Mississippi officers (prisoners) informed me that the shells of the gun-boats had a demoralizing effect upon their men. The Memphis *Appeal* says it dispirited them.

"I have had a fair opportunity to observe the operations of both Army and Navy, and I can say with emphasis that there are no more self-denying, patriotic, hard-working, faithful men than the flag-officer and his captains—Stembel, Pennock, Phelps, and others. I make these statements from my own sense of justice and honor, and not from any man's prompting or request."

But neither public praise nor private sorrow were permitted to interfere for one moment with the pressing duties of the hour.

The following reports continue the narrative of naval operations:

"FLAG-STEAMER 'BENTON,' OFF ISLAND NO. TEN,
March 19, 1862.

"SIR,—On the 17th instant I communicated to the Department an account of our leaving Cairo for the purpose of attacking Island No. Ten, and expressing the hope that to-morrow (yesterday) we should be able to capture the upper fort at this point.

"Yesterday we were firing on the upper fort at long range, reaching it occasionally, and dismounted another gun, while the mortars were playing on the lower fortifications, having driven the encampments down the river, just out of range of our shells. As the forts are distinct from each other, and occupy but little space, and have been mostly constructed for four or five months, it is impossible to use the mortars with as much effect as could have been done at Columbus, where the batteries were more compact and exposed, and the troops having less shelter than here. We are, however, keeping up an occasional fire day and night, to prevent the enemy from repairing his damages, gradually approaching his strongest holds, and I trust we will be able, in co-operation with General Pope's army, soon to get possession of the place. This position was selected by the rebels on account of its being inaccessible by land, in a high stage of waters, on the Missouri side, which side General Pope's army occupies at New Madrid; and he has no transports of any kind with which to cross over to the Tennessee side and march in upon the rear of the rebels. I have this morning sent him two tugs, and hope to be able to get two gun-boats also through the same bayou or slough to him. If we can do this, with the gun-boats coming up and attacking the forts from below, with the land attack, I have no doubt but that we shall secure a complete victory. We must proceed here slowly and cautiously, which alone can prove effective, especially bearing in mind the rapid current and certainty of falling into the hands of the enemy in these slow boats if we run as close to the batteries as we might do were the rebels up stream. Colonel Buford, commanding the troops here, amounting to about fifteen hundred, will be ready to perform all service required until the arrival of General Pope in force. We shall not be able to make the grand attack for several days. This will depend upon the arrival of General Pope. Your obedient servant,

"A. H. Foote, Flag-Officer.

"The Hon. Gideon Welles, Secretary of the Navy."

"Flag-Steamer 'Benton,' off Island No. Ten,
March 20, 1862.

"Sir,—Most of the iron-clad steamers, including this vessel, are still lying within long range of the rebel forts, and occasionally, with the mortar-boats, are throwing shells into the enemy's batteries, which have induced them to withdraw all their superfluous men not required for serving their guns. To-day the upper battery opened upon us, but was silenced in half an hour, this ship dismounting a gun. I send, to-night, a boat to sound in a narrow and shallow channel, in hopes the present rise of water in the river will enable me to dispatch a small steamer with light draught to General Pope, near New Madrid, who, as I have already informed the Department, has several times requested that I would send him two or three gun-boats, to enable him to cross over to the Tennessee side, with the view of attacking the rebels in the rear at this point, while we make the attack in front or on the river side. I am apprehensive, however, from our ill-success thus far, that this project may not prove feasible. To-day, for the first time since I have been in command of the flotilla, I called a council of war, with the view of ascertaining the opinions of the officers with reference to sending, or attempting to send, aid to General Pope. The officers, with one exception, were decidedly opposed to running the blockade, believing it would result in the almost certain destruction of the vessels which should attempt to pass the six forts, with fifty guns bearing upon them. I have been seriously disposed to run the blockade myself with this vessel, which is better protected than the other boats, although she is slow, and works sluggishly; but, upon reconsideration, as her loss would be so great if we failed, and my personal services here are considered so important with the fleet and transports, I have, for the present, abandoned the idea.

"This place is admirably chosen for defense by the rebels, as its rear can only be approached, in this stage of water, by the river opposite New Madrid, it being surrounded by bayous or sloughs, while its long line of six forts, commanding one another from the river front, render it almost impregnable from an attacking force. General Pope has no transports, and, without our reaching him by running the blockade, is unable to cross over to the Tennessee side from New Madrid, where he now is in force; and it is impossible for him, from the inundated state of the country, to send or march his troops to this point. Were we to attempt to attack these heavy batteries with the gun-boats, or attempt to run the blockade and fail, as I have already stated in a former communication, the rivers above us—Mississippi, Ohio, and Cumberland—would be greatly exposed, not only frustrating the grand object of the expedition, but exposing our towns and cities bordering those rivers; especially so should General Pope be unable to hold his position at New Madrid. Under these circumstances, and our boats being so ill-adapted to fighting down the river, with two rifle-guns having burst and our shells imperfect, I am induced to act with great caution, and expose the flotilla less than under more favorable circumstances it would be my duty to do, for the great object for which the fleet was created. For the future, in the absence of instructions from higher authority, I shall be governed by circumstances as they may arise. When the object of running the blockade becomes adequate to the risk, I shall not hesitate to do it. The place may be occupied by us in a short time without an assault, as the rebels must be cut off from their necessary supplies. Still, if this do not soon take place, it may become necessary to force the blockade, or adopt some other measures which have not yet suggested themselves. Your obedient servant, A. H. Foote, Flag-Officer.

"The Hon. Gideon Welles, Secretary of the Navy."

Island No. Ten was a hard nut to crack, giving pause to the most experienced military men. It was a characteristic sentence in the last of the above reports, "When the object of running the blockade becomes adequate to the risk, I shall not hesitate to do it." That time—according to the commodore, whether he erred or not in judgment—had not yet arrived; but it could not for a moment be doubted that, whatever the risk, either by himself or by a subordinate commander, the thing, when he thought it ought to be done, would be done.

The mortars used by Foote were formidable ordnance, each carrying a shot weighing 215 pounds, and itself weighing

17,280 pounds. It was a 13-inch mortar—that is, it would receive a bomb-shell thirteen inches in diameter. The boats were firmly moored to the bank, and a derrick was used on shore to drop the immense ball into the mouth of the mortar. Twenty-three pounds of powder were required for a charge, and the concussion was so heavy that the men were forced to take refuge behind the timber works when a mortar was fired; while the distance was so great, and the object aimed at so comparatively small, that the slightest disturbing cause was enough to destroy the accuracy of the aim. Nevertheless, the bombardment was kept up. The roar and hiss of the heavy mortar-shells were heard along the sombre shores of the river night and day. Foote did not come, however, to close encounter with the forts, and kept his boats in good trim, not exposing or weakening his fleet, because he learned that the rebels had a force of thirteen gun-boats, independent of the five below New Madrid, and the much-talked-of *Manassas* at Memphis. They might come up at any moment, and dispute the possession of the Mississippi above Island No. Ten, and he thought it best to be careful of his boats. General Halleck, judging from the following dispatch, seems to have concurred in this opinion:

"HEAD-QUARTERS OF THE DEPARTMENT OF THE MISSISSIPPI,
ST. LOUIS, *March* 21, 1862.

"SIR,—I have just received your report (without date) of your operations against the enemy's batteries in the vicinity of Island No. Ten. While I am certain that you have done every thing that could be done successfully to reduce these works, I am very glad that you have not unnecessarily exposed your gun-boats. If they had been disabled, it would have been a most serious loss to us in the future operations of the campaign; whereas the reduction of these batteries, this week or next, is a matter of very little importance indeed. I think it will turn out in the end that it is much better for us that they are not reduced till we can fully cut off the retreat of their troops.

"Every thing is now progressing well on the Tennessee River toward opening your way down the Mississippi. The reduction of these works is only a question of time, and we are in no hurry on that point. Nothing is lost by a little delay there. I am directing all my attention now to another object, and when that is accomplished the enemy must evacuate or surrender. Very respectfully, your obedient servant,

"H. W. HALLECK, Major-General Commanding.

"Flag-Officer Foote, commanding Naval Forces."

Foote himself came to the conclusion that the only effectual way of taking the island was to send boats and transports to General Pope, in order that he might cross the river from below, and attack the rebel works from the Tennessee shore. But how to get them to him was the question. To pass the forts was generally considered impracticable. Two councils of all the captains of the fleet were called together by Foote, and they voted that the thing was too hazardous. This plan therefore, for the time, was abandoned. The other plan was to send boats around the forts and island, through the swamps on the western side of the Mississippi, bringing them out at New Madrid. He thus reports concerning this:

"U. S. FLAG-SHIP 'BENTON,' ISLAND NO. TEN,
March 26, 1862.

"SIR,—Since my communication of the 20th instant we have been lying off the forts at long range, occasionally giving a rifle-shot, and more frequently throwing mortar-shells upon the island and at the fortifications on the Tennessee shore. The rebels still hold the forts, but the encampments are moved beyond range, with a sufficient number of men to serve their heavy guns, which seem to be well protected from our shells by their breastworks. A communication from General Halleck (a copy of which is inclosed) leads me to hope that we may yet derive support from the Army, irrespective of General Pope's force, which will cross over from New Madrid and attack the enemy in the rear, while we make the attack in front, in case we succeed in getting two steamers and several cutters, which are now working their way toward that point, through the bayous or sloughs. Should this effort be successful, I hope to hear that a land force of some ten thousand men will be in the rebels' rear in the course of five or six days. With the exception of a ridge of higher land on the river bank of the Tennessee side, from directly opposite New Madrid to nearly opposite Island No. Ten, the whole country is inundated, or at least so much so as to prevent troops from other points reaching the rebels' rear, showing how admirably their position has been chosen for defense.

"We now have here six iron-plated gun-boats, one wooden gun-boat, the *Conestoga*, and sixteen mortar-boats; one iron-clad gun-boat being at Nashville, one guarding Columbus and Hickman—the two wooden boats up the Tennessee; while the *Essex*, Commander Porter, is repairing at St. Louis. We have all the mortar-boats we can use to any advantage, and still want two tow-boats for these, of greater force, as we have a strong current, requiring the greatest vigilance to prevent them and the gun-boats from being carried down stream, from the want of steam-power of the latter. Colonel Buford, commanding the troops, has a force of between nineteen hundred and two thousand men; but who, in fact, living, as they necessarily do, aboard the transports—the banks being overflowed, and they surrounded by water—can not accomplish any thing of consequence. Thus we are waiting to open communication with General Pope at New Madrid.

"I forward herewith a copy of a letter sent me by General Strong, commanding at Cairo, from which it will be seen that the rebels have thirteen gun-boats, independent of the five below New Madrid, and the *Manassas*, or ram, at Memphis. I presume that these boats are not equal to ours; still we have no means of ascertaining their character, especially those at New Orleans. I have ordered the rifle-guns as they arrive at Cairo to be sent to us, as our rifles are unsafe, and must be condemned as soon as others can be supplied. The rifle-shells, as well as those of the 8-inch guns and thirty-twos, also burst prematurely, and I have been obliged to drown all fuses for a distance exceeding one thousand yards.

"I shall proceed with caution in our work here, being fully aware of our disadvantages. If, however, any disaster should occur from circumstances beyond my control, I have ordered the two iron-clad gun-boats *Cairo* and *Louisville*, with the wooden boats *Taylor* and *Lexington*, to meet at Cairo, or as far down as Columbus, and even Hickman, to prevent the rebel gun-boats from ascending the river beyond Cairo, which place is now so nearly overflowed as to render it necessary for us to remove all our ammunition. I have the honor to be, etc.,

"A. H. Foote, Flag-Officer.

"The Hon. Gideon Welles."

The opening of the canal, fifty feet wide and twelve miles long, from the bend of the Mississippi near Island No. Eight, across the neck of the swampy peninsula, to the neighborhood of New Madrid, was the joint work of the Army and Navy, and was one of the most energetic and remarkable achievements of the war. It was actually suggested by General Schuyler Hamilton, and was executed in the space of about two weeks, under the command of Colonel Bissel. Three fourths of a mile was through solid earth, and six miles of the way was hewn through a dense growth of heavy timber, which had to be cut off in some places four feet under water.* Advantage was taken of narrow channels connecting bayous, or places with more open water, and near New Madrid a small stream ran down from the swamp, which aided the enterprise; but it was a herculean task, and for nineteen days soldiers and sailors worked and floundered together in water and mud, cutting down and dragging out trees and stumps, with capstans, saws, and axes. Four light steamers and two or three gun-barges aided them in this. It was impracticable to make a passage deep enough for the great gun-boats; but, after incredible labor, the canal was finished, and in the first week of April a small fleet of light steamers and transports, gliding through the depths of a Mississippi forest, reached New Madrid, with the almost wild rejoicings of the troops there. In the mean time, on the 1st of April, a gallant feat was done by a boat expedition manned by seamen of the *Benton* and four other gun-boats, with fifty soldiers, the whole under the command of Colonel George W. Roberts, of the Second Illinois Volunteers. At eleven o'clock at night they started, rowing softly, and hugging the eastern shore in the shadow. They proceeded to the upper (Rucker's) battery, or the first of the seven forts on the Tennessee shore, and as they approached

* Lossing's "Civil War in America," vol. ii., p. 244.

within thirty feet the sentinels perceived them, uttered a cry of surprise, fired, and fled. The alarm was also communicated to the rebel steamer *Grampus;* but the movements of the invaders were rapid; they landed, threw out a detachment of twenty men between the battery and the rebel camp, and proceeded to spike the guns, which they did successfully, and returned without loss to the fleet, although the rebel steamer was already bearing down upon them. This shore-battery, consisting of eleven guns, one of them a 10-inch columbiad, was one of the most formidable batteries of the enemy, and was so situated that for a boat to run by it it must pass within three hundred yards of the fort. The commodore speaks of this expedition in a letter to his wife:

"FLAG-STEAMER 'BENTON,' OFF ISLAND NO. TEN,
April 2, 1862.

"MY DEAR WIFE,—The mail arrived at 9 P.M. last night, but brought me no tidings from you, which leaves me in a feverish state of excitement, as your letter three days ago spoke of your own and the children's illness. The *Conestoga* will soon be down with the mail, and I pray God that the news from you may be good, or more favorable.

"The expedition last night was entirely successful, as you will have heard from my telegram before receiving this. We have spiked all the guns in No. One, or the first fort on the Tennessee shore above No. Ten. The sentinels fired on our boats and ran, while our men jumped from the boats into the fort and spiked their guns, and got safely off. Just as they reached this vessel, a squall of thunder and lightning of the most terrific character struck us, as if it would destroy our fleet; but, thank God, no serious damage has been done except to two steamers, which fouled the *Cincinnati.* The rebels are firing briskly upon us this morning, which we are returning. I suppose they are indignant and demoralized somewhat at the spiking of their guns. No other news. I will write more when the mail comes. In the mean time, rest assured that, next to God, you and the dear children are in my thoughts. I send from a rebel paper a good piece, which you must apply to yourself and children. I know you will. Sanford is in my cabin, and dines with us to-day. He is in tolerable spirits. We all feel a little more encouraged from putting to rest Fort No. One. The men are singing psalm tunes near the cabin, but, I am sorry to say, I hear more oaths than praises among them. Secretary Scott has been to see me this morning. He, as well as Colonel Buford, rather urge me on to a fight, but I resist and am cautious, and they have great confidence in my judgment. Read the rebel slip, and tell me if you do not fully indorse it, come what will. William often expressed Christian sentiments. I will add a word if the mail come before this goes, which is doubtful. Affectionately, A. H. F."

One of the obstacles in the way of sending a gun-boat down the river past the forts was removed, and another formidable obstacle was the next day also done away by the destruction of the enemy's floating battery, moored at the head of the island. The flag-officer thus speaks of it in his dispatch:

"CAIRO, *April* 4, 1862.

"This morning the *Benton*, *Cincinnati*, and *Pittsburg*, with three mortar-boats, opened, and continued more than an hour, a fire on the rebels' heavy floating battery at Island No. Ten, when the latter, having received several shells from the rifles and mortars, cut loose from her moorings and drifted down the river two or three miles. The shells were thrown from the rifles into the different forts of the island, and into the rebel batteries lining the Tennessee shore. The return fire produced no effect on the squadron. No more men than were actually necessary to man the batteries were visible. A. H. FOOTE, Flag-Officer.

"The Hon. Gideon Welles, Secretary of the Navy."

Thus the flag-officer was gradually feeling his way, in his own method and time, toward making the move which should secure the capture of Island No. Ten. It is true that General Pope, waiting unemployed after his struggle and success at New Madrid, began to be extremely impatient; it is true that the country itself began to think that it was time for the downfall of the defiant stronghold—the key of the Mississippi, as it was considered; it is true that our naval Marcellus seemed to have suddenly become a very Fabius in his caution; it is true that Farragut had turned his prow up stream at New Orleans, and had sent word that he would meet Foote coming down the Mississippi; yet it is also true that up to this point Foote (whether he erred or not in judgment) did not think that the time had come to safely try the last experiment, to make the grand throw; and it is also true that what he there did, and at the time he did it, won the long-contested prize, and it dropped like ripened fruit into his waiting hand. It is not impossible that the desired end might more speedily have been attained by the same means that was finally employed—but we defer the account of the completion of this hard contest to another chapter.

CHAPTER XXII.

CAPTURE OF ISLAND NUMBER TEN.

Foote was now waiting for a favorable moment, or, in other words, for a dark night, to carry out the plan, of the necessity of which he had become fully convinced, and which was also earnestly urged by General Pope, to send a gun-boat down past the batteries. He had lessened the difficulties of the feat by silencing the rebels' upper and floating batteries; and he had issued the following general order to Commander Walke, of the *Carondelet*:

"U. S. Flag-Steamer 'Benton,' off Island No. Ten,
March 30, 1862.

"Sir,—You will avail yourself of the first fog or rainy night, and drift your steamer down past the batteries on the Tennessee shore and Island No. Ten until you reach New Madrid.

"I assign you this service, as it is vitally important to the capture of this place that a gun-boat should soon be at New Madrid for the purpose of covering General Pope's army while he crosses at that point to the opposite shore, or to the Tennessee side of the river, that he may move his army up to Island No. Ten, and attack the rebels in rear while we attack them in front.

"Should you succeed in reaching General Pope, you will freely confer with him, and adopt his suggestions, so far as your superior knowledge of what your boat will perform and enable you to do, for the purpose of protecting his force while crossing the river.

"You will also, if you have coal, and the current of the river will permit, steam up the river while the army moves, for the purpose of attacking their fortifications. Still, you will act cautiously here, as your own will be the only boat below.

"You will capture or destroy the rebel steam gun-boat *Grampus* and the transports, if possible, between this place and Island No. Ten, at such time as will not embarrass you in placing yourself in communication with General Pope at the earliest possible time after leaving this place.

"On this delicate and somewhat hazardous service to which I assign you, I must enjoin upon you the importance of keeping your lights secreted in the hold or put out, keeping your officers and men from speaking above a whisper when passing the forts, and then only on duty; and of using every other precaution to prevent the rebels suspecting that you are dropping below their batteries.

"If you successfully perform the duty assigned you, which you so willingly undertake, it will reflect the highest credit upon you and all belonging to your vessel; and I doubt not but that the government will fully appreciate and reward you for a service which, I trust, will enable the army to cross the river and make a successful attack in rear while we storm the batteries in front.

"Commending you and all who compose your command to the care and protection of God, who rules and directs all things, I am, respectfully, your obedient servant, A. H. FOOTE, Flag-Officer.

"Commander H. Walke, commanding *Carondelet*.

"P. S.—Should you meet with disaster, you will, as a last resort, destroy the steam machinery; and, if impossible to escape, set fire to your gun-boat or sink her, and prevent her from falling into the hands of the rebels. A. H. F."

After comparing together many accounts, both official and private, and after personal conversation with Admiral Walke, the chief actor in the scene, we have thought that all the facts and features of this extraordinary passage of the *Carondelet* are so accurately and graphically given in the following narrative that we could not do better than to transfer it *in extenso* into our pages:

"On the morning of the 4th of April preparations were begun for executing the above order,* should the state of the weather permit. The deck was defended somewhat against plunging shot by planks stripped from the wreck of an old barge. All surplus chains were coiled over the most vulnerable parts of the boat—a device employed soon after at New Orleans on a larger scale. A very large hawser (11-inch) was wound

* The order referred to is the one which has just preceded.

around the pilot-house as high as the windows; the hammocks were stowed in the nettings; and, for greater security still, cord-wood was piled up around the boilers on the exposed side; and every other precaution that ingenuity could suggest was used to render the boat safe during her short but perilous voyage. Each changing aspect of the heavens was anxiously studied during the day, for in a bright, clear night the passage would have been nearly as dangerous as at midday; and the moon was at a stage when her light would have revealed the boat as fully, for every purpose of the rebel gunners, as the sun itself.

"Late in the afternoon there was every prospect of a clear, moonlight night, and it was determined to wait until the moon was down, and then to make the attempt, whatever the prospect might be, because, after such extensive preparations had been made, the moral effect of abandoning the scheme would be nearly equal to a failure. At sundown, however, there were signs of an approaching change in the weather. A haze began to spread itself over the more distant scene, and to creep along the river. The wind shifted, and, as evening drew on, dark clouds, indicating a thunder-storm, began to lift themselves above the northwestern horizon. The precautions adopted were very minute, and the orders for observing them were positive and strict. No lights were to be allowed where they could be visible; the guns were all run in, and the ports were closed. The sailors were all heavily armed; pistols, cutlasses, muskets, and boarding-pikes were within reach on all sides or in hand, on the supposition that, if the vessel should be partially disabled, there would be an attempt to capture her by boarding. Hand-grenades were provided, and hose was attached to the boilers for throwing scalding water over any who might attempt to board.

"It was decided to sink the boat rather than burn her, if it should be found impossible to save her, because the loss of life would probably be very great by the explosion of her magazine. At dusk, twenty sharpshooters came on board from the Forty-second Illinois Regiment, under Captain Hollenstein. At eight o'clock the gun-boat went up the river about a mile for a barge containing baled hay, which was to be lashed to the exposed side. One course of bales was laid over the stern casemates, as these would be exposed for a long distance after the batteries had been passed. The barge and the piled hay reached as high as the broadside port-holes; but as the batteries on shore were some twenty feet above water, the protection thus given was not very important.

"At ten o'clock the moon had gone down, and the sky, the earth, and

THE "CARONDELET" PASSING THE BATTERIES.

the river were alike hidden in the black shadow of the thunder-storm, which had now spread itself over all the heavens. The time seemed most opportune for starting: the order was given, the lines cast off, and, with her barge of hay on one side, and another with coal on the starboard side, the gun-boat rounded out heavily and slowly, and laid her course down the river. In order to avoid the puffing sound of the high-pressure engine, the escape-steam was led into the wheel-house, where its harsh voice was muffled—a device which probably led to their discovery by the fire from the chimneys. For half a mile every thing went smoothly and quietly, and all thought they might succeed in passing the batteries unobserved, when suddenly a bright, steady flame rose several feet high from each chimney-top, and for a moment it seemed as if the steamer was carrying aloft two immense torches to light her on her way. Her upper decks and all about her brightened for a moment in the red glare. Strange as it may appear, what was deemed by all a serious accident, which would bring upon them at once the enemy's fire, created no movement in the rebel batteries. When nearly opposite the upper fort the chimneys again took fire, and at once the sentinels there gave the alarm to the fort below by firing their muskets.

"Signal-rockets were sent up both from the mainland and the island, and a cannon-shot came from Fort No. Two. It was evident that the alarm was now thoroughly given. Not a shot, however, came from the upper battery—a fact which showed how thoroughly its dangerous guns had been silenced by the party that had landed and spiked them.* This, and the drifting away of the floating battery, had had very much to do with the safety of the *Carondelet*.

"But one course was now possible for the officers of the gun-boat. The vessel was at once put under full head of steam, and was urged down the river at her utmost speed, for the rebels were now making swift preparations at every gun that could be brought to bear. The storm was then at its height; and its fearful character, which would have been thought dangerous at any other time, was welcomed as increasing the chances of escape. The darkness was so intense as to shut out earth and heaven alike, except as lighted momentarily by the lightning's glare. The gleam and roar of the guns of the batteries could scarcely be dis-

* This is not entirely correct, as it is known that Fort No. One fired shots within twenty-four hours after the spiking, and fired at the boat this night.

tinguished from the flash and the thunder of the cloud. The fires of heaven and earth were mingled, and none could tell whether the deck were shaken by the explosion above or the cannon below. The rain fell in the sweeping torrents of a summer shower. Shot and shell, and rifle and musket balls, sang and shrieked and roared around so as to be heard above the storm. Each flash of lightning revealed the rebels loading, training, and firing their guns as the boat came within range. The steamer also was disclosed for a moment; but as she was moving swiftly with the current, it was nearly impossible to get her range; it was evident that what is called a chance shot would strike her. Most of the balls and shells flew high above her, owing to the fact that the alternations of light and darkness were so rapid as to deceive the enemy's gunners as to the gun-boat's position. She was much nearer to them than they supposed, and they fired at a wrong elevation. The boat was guided as close along the bank as she could safely run—where, indeed, it would have been difficult to depress their guns so as to strike her, even had she been plainly seen. At this point their greatest danger was not from the rebel batteries: the current was not only rapid, but shifted from side to side with the sharp curve of the stream; and bars also ran out from either shore. The intense darkness prevented the pilots from knowing the exact position of the boat; and the pilots learned their position only as they caught glimpses of the shore by the flashes of lightning. On the forecastle the lead was kept going, and the depth of water was constantly reported. It contributed largely to the steamer's safety that she had on board Captain Hoel, first-master of the *Cincinnati,* who had been engaged in navigating the Mississippi for more than twenty years. This gentleman stood on the deck, exposed to the double torrent of rain and bullets; and, watching for each momentary revelation which the lightning made, gave directions for steering the boat. The gleams of lightning, the momentary report of the soundings, and his intimate knowledge of localities, enabled Captain Hoel to judge correctly, in the main, of the gun-boat's position. Once, however, during the passage she was in great danger of being lost. The steamboat and her barges, of course, presented a very large surface to the current, and this gave her occasionally a heavy sheer. In the darkness and the blinding rush of the storm this was not always on the instant noticed. Caught in this manner by the swift stream, she was drifting toward a dangerous bar, where she would have grounded under the guns of the batteries, when a broad flash lit up the river a moment, followed instantly by the sharp, repeated command,

'Hard a-port!' and she obeyed her helm, and regained the current just in season to save her.

"Contrary to expectation, they found no battery at the foot of the island, where it was reported that one of the long-range guns had been planted. The floating battery, which had drifted from its moorings at the head of the island, was three miles below, and this remained to be passed. As the *Carondelet* was not in a fighting trim, she kept close to the Missouri shore, the battery firing only a few harmless shots as she passed; and then the peril of the passage was over, and exulting shouts burst from the crew and the soldiers; and the signal-guns were fired announcing their safety to the fleet above; and soon the gun-boat rounded to at New Madrid, welcomed by bonfires and every possible exhibition of joy. All felt that the fate of Island No. Ten at length was sealed. In rounding to, a slight accident occurred, through a misunderstanding of an order by the engineer, and the boat was run hard aground; but after an hour of effort, by shifting some of the bow guns to the stern and bringing all the men aft, she was safely backed off, and the perilous voyage was over at 1 A.M."*

Foote sent the following dispatch to Pope:

"U. S. FLAG-SHIP 'BENTON,' OFF ISLAND NO. TEN,
April 4, 1862.

"GENERAL, — The gun-boat *Carondelet*, Commander Walke, left her anchorage this evening at ten o'clock, in a heavy thunder-storm, for the purpose of running the fire of the batteries on Island No. Ten and those lining the Tennessee shore, to join your forces at New Madrid. By a previous concerted signal of three minute-guns, twice fired at intervals of five minutes, which have since been heard, as near as the heavy thunder would enable us to ascertain, leads me to hope that the blockade has been run successfully, although the batteries opened upon her with forty-seven guns while passing.

"I am, therefore, so exceedingly anxious to hear the fate of the noble officers and men who were so readily disposed to attempt the hazardous service, that I beg you will immediately inform me by bearer if Commander Walke have arrived with his vessel, and the condition in which you find her and her officers and men. I am, respectfully, your obedient servant,
A. H. FOOTE, Flag-Officer.

"Major-General Pope, commanding Army at New Madrid, Mo."

* Boynton's "Hist. of the Navy during the Rebellion," vol. i., p. 549 seq.

General Pope at once answered this, and accompanied his answer with a strong request that another gun-boat should be sent down to guard the transports in conveying over the troops, which request was complied with by the *Pittsburg's* running the batteries and the fire of seventy-three guns on the night of the 6th, also in a heavy thunder-storm. Commander Walke's dispatch to his flag-officer relative to the *Carondelet's* achievement was as follows:

"U. S. GUN-BOAT 'CARONDELET,' NEW MADRID, *April* 5, 1862.

"SIR,—I have the honor to report my arrival here last night about one o'clock—all well. On our way all of the rebel batteries and a large number of infantry opened fire upon us, which was continued until we were out of range. Providentially, no damage was done to the vessel or the officers and crew, who conducted themselves with admirable courage and fidelity. The terrible storm which prevailed at the time rendered it impossible to make any reliable observation.

"Most respectfully, sir, your obedient servant,

"H. WALKE, Commander U. S. Navy.

"Flag-Officer A. H. Foote, commanding U. S. Naval Forces, Western Waters."

In a letter to his wife at this time, the running of the *Pittsburg* past the batteries is spoken of by Commodore Foote:

"FLAG-STEAMER 'BENTON,' *April* 7, 1862.

"MY DEAR WIFE,—'Anxious night,' as Dr. —— used to say when he charged five dollars for his visit. Commander Thompson, whom you well know, ran the blockade last night in a heavy thunder-storm with the *Pittsburg*, under a fire of seventy-three heavy guns. We don't know yet whether he is hurt vitally or not; but the scene was terrific and grand, as you may imagine. At two A.M. Thompson started, and we could only see him as the lightning flashed. I am anxious to hear from him, though I slept well. A terrible cannonading is going on near New Madrid, caused, no doubt, by Walke and Thompson fighting the rebel batteries where General Pope must land to get here. They will prove too much for the rebels in my opinion. Thus we go ahead slowly, and God grant that we soon may take No. Ten, and all in and around it. The crisis is close at hand, and we are anxious to meet after this long suspense. My foot is *statu quo.* A chronic tenderness and swelling, uncomfortable up to the knee at times. I have no apprehension of a serious result; but it greatly impairs my activity and efficiency, as I can not inspect the steamers or make alterations. Still, we must submit to all that God sends us.

"I have a great deal of writing to do, and much in the way of granting interviews and giving orders, which, as I trust nobody else to do, you will excuse my short and hurried letters. I will add, if any thing come up before mail. I write you, and have done so for ten or twenty days, every day. Do you get all my letters? I send some of Prentice's criticisms in the Louisville *Journal.*

"Mail ready. Very affectionately, with kisses and love to all,

"A. H. Foote."

On the 7th, in the morning, the two gun-boats that had run the batteries went down the river and attacked and silenced the enemy's field-guns that had been stationed to prevent the crossing of the land forces. Thereupon the transports with the troops immediately prepared to cross the river; but before this was accomplished, the rebels saw that their works were rendered defenseless, and they commenced abandoning the batteries along the Tennessee and Kentucky shores that Foote was on the point of attacking with a grand assault in co-operation with the Army. Equal consternation prevailed at Island No. Ten; and at twenty-five minutes past three on the morning of the 7th of April a flag of truce came to Commodore Foote, surrendering to him the island. The surrender was made even before the news had arrived at the island of the silencing of the field-guns below, and the crossing of General Pope's army to the Tennessee side. Pope's forces, as soon as they were landed, were marched toward Tiptonville, to intercept the rebels retreating from the batteries and from Island No. Ten. They were successful in this, and drove the fleeing enemy into the swamps, and on the 8th made them prisoners in large numbers, but few escaping. Thus, although the Army and Navy were co-operative in the capture of this important stronghold, and both were essential to this end, Island No. Ten was at the last actually surrendered to the gun-boats. The following are Flag-Officer Foote's official reports of the event:

"FLAG-STEAMER 'BENTON,' OFF ISLAND NO. TEN,
April 8—1 A.M.

"My telegram, three hours since, informed the Department that Island No. Ten had surrendered to the gun-boats. Captain Phelps has this instant returned, after having had an interview with the late commandant. I have requested General Buford, commanding the troops, to proceed immediately, in company with two of the gun-boats, and take possession of the island. The batteries on the Tennessee shore have been hastily evacuated, where we shall find, no doubt, in the morning, large quantities of munitions of war.

"I communicate with General Pope, who has, under cover of the two gun-boats which gallantly ran the blockade, crossed the river in force, and was ready, as well as the gun and mortar boats, with General Buford and his troops, to make a simultaneous attack upon the rebels, had they not so hastily evacuated the Tennessee shore and surrendered Island No. Ten. A full report will be made as soon as we can obtain possession of the land-batteries, and I am able to communicate with General Pope.

"A. H. FOOTE, Flag-Officer.

"The Hon. Gideon Welles, Secretary of the Navy."

"FLAG-SHIP 'BENTON,' ISLAND NO. TEN,
April 8, 1862 (via Cairo).

"I have the honor to inform the Department that since I sent the telegram last night announcing the surrender to me of Island No. Ten, possession has been taken of both the island and the works upon the Tennessee shore by the gun-boats and the troops under command of General Buford. Seventeen officers and three hundred and sixty-eight privates, besides one hundred of their sick and one hundred men employed on board the transports, are in our hands, unconditional prisoners of war.

"I have caused a hasty examination to be made of the forts, batteries, and munitions of war captured. There are eleven earthworks, with seventy heavy cannon, varying in calibre from 32 to 100 pounders, rifled. The magazines are well supplied with powder, and there are large quantities of shot, shells, and other munitions of war, and also great quantities of provisions. Four steamers afloat have fallen into our hands, and two others, with the rebel gun-boat *Grampus*, are sunk, but will be easily raised. The floating battery of sixteen heavy guns, turned adrift by the rebels, is said to be lying on the Missouri shore below New Madrid. Two wharf-boats, loaded with provisions, are also in our possession.

"The enemy upon the mainland appears to have fled with great precipitation after dark last night, leaving, in many cases, half-prepared meals in their quarters; and there seems to have been no concert of action between the rebels upon the island and those occupying the shore; but the latter fled, leaving the former to their fate. These works, erected with the highest engineering skill, are of great strength, and, with their natural advantages, would have been impregnable if defended by men fighting in a better cause.

"A combined attack of the naval and land forces would have taken place this afternoon or to-morrow morning had not the rebels abandoned this stronghold. To mature these plans of attack, absolutely required the last twenty-three days of preparation. General Pope is momentarily expected to arrive with his army at this point, he having successfully crossed the river yesterday under a heavy fire, which, no doubt, led to the hasty abandonment of the works last night. I am unofficially informed that the two gun-boats which so gallantly ran the fire of the rebel batteries a few nights since, yesterday attacked and reduced a fort of the enemy opposite, mounting eight heavy guns.

"I am, sir, respectfully, etc.,

"A. H. Foote,

"Flag-Officer, commanding Naval Forces, Western Waters.

"The Hon. Gideon Welles, Secretary of the Navy."

In regard to the operations below the island of the two gun-boats, the *Carondelet* and the *Pittsburg*, that were so effective in the final result, this is the commodore's report:

"U. S. Flag-Steamer 'Benton,' off Island No. Ten,
April 11, 1862.

"Sir,—I have the honor to inclose a report from Commander Walke, of the gun-boat *Carondelet*, detailing the services rendered by him and the *Pittsburg*, Lieutenant-Commanding Thompson, in the vicinity of New Madrid, from which it will be seen that the boats opened upon and effectually silenced and captured several heavy batteries on the Tennessee side of the river, on the 6th and 7th instant, without which destruction it would have been impossible for General Pope to have crossed the river for the purpose of attacking the rebels in the rear at Island No. Ten, while the gun and mortar boats would make the attack in front.

"There has been an effective and harmonious co-operation between the land and naval forces, which has, under Providence, led to the glorious result of the fall of this stronghold, Island No. Ten, with the garrison and munitions of war; and I regret to see in the dispatches of Major-General Halleck, from St. Louis, no reference is made to the capture of forts, and the continuous shelling of gun and mortar boats, and the Navy's receiving the surrender of Island No. Ten, when, in reality, it should be recorded as an historical fact that both services equally contributed to the victory—a bloodless victory—more creditable to humanity than if thousands had been slain.

"I also inclose reports from Lieutenants-Commanding Gwin and Shirk, of the gun-boats *Taylor* and *Lexington*, on the Tennessee, giving a graphic account of that great battle, and the assistance rendered by these boats near Pittsburg; stating that 'when the left wing of our army was being driven into the river, at short range, they opened fire upon the enemy, silencing them, and, as I hear from many army officers who were on the field, totally demoralizing their forces, and driving them from their position in a perfect rout in the space of ten minutes.'

"These officers and men, as well as those of the *Carondelet* and *Pittsburg*, behaved with a degree of gallantry highly creditable to themselves and the Navy.

"I proceed to-day, with the entire flotilla, to New Madrid, and leave to-morrow for Fort Pillow, or the next point down the river which may attempt to resist the raising of the blockade.

"I have the honor to be, very respectfully, your obedient servant,

"A. H. Foote, Flag-Officer.

"The Hon. Gideon Welles, Secretary of the Navy, Washington, D. C."

Foote was extremely jealous of the reputation of his little fleet, and we can not blame the pertinacity with which he insists upon justice being rendered to the brave men who did so much to clear Kentucky and Tennessee and the Mississippi River of all the obstacles that the enemy, with their utmost effort and skill, could rear. The capture of Island No. Ten—

concerning which the enemy is reported to have said, "Thus far shalt thou go and no farther"—was a great event; and coming simultaneously with the hard-won battle of Pittsburg Landing on the 6th and 7th, in which the gun-boats so efficiently participated, it produced a profound impression North and South; and once more the Southern line of defense was broken, and the hopes of a northern advance of the rebel arms at the West totally and forever frustrated.

The taking of Island No. Ten was a triumph of the most decisive character. "The number of prisoners taken by Pope and Foote together was seven thousand two hundred and seventy-three, including three generals and two hundred and seventy-three field and company officers. The spoils of victory were nearly twenty batteries, with one hundred and twenty-three cannon and mortars, the former varying from 32 to 100 pounders; seven thousand small-arms; an immense amount of ammunition on the island and in magazines at points along the Kentucky and Tennessee shores; many hundred horses and mules with wagons, and four steamers afloat."*

This most valuable victory, shared by the Army and Navy, the result of patience, mingled with timely action, and not even marred by the sorrow of sanguinary slaughter—a bloodless victory—was a fitting end to the active military career of him who was not a man of blood, though a man of the sword. But a few days more of honorable responsibility, anxiety, and suffering, and the longed-for rest came.

* Lossing's "Civil War in America," vol. ii., p. 247.

CHAPTER XXIII.

OPERATIONS OF FLEET AT FORT PILLOW.—ILL-HEALTH, AND GIVING UP OF ACTIVE COMMAND.

The reception of the news of the fall of Island No. Ten by the government and country, although waited for long and with much impatience, was most enthusiastic. The following letter of congratulation was telegraphed to the commodore on the 9th of April:

"Flag-Officer A. H. Foote, commanding Gun-boats, Western Waters:

"Sir,—A nation's thanks are due to you and the brave officers and men of the flotilla on the Mississippi, whose labors and gallantry at Island No. Ten, which surrendered to you, have for weeks been watched with intense interest. Your triumph is not the less appreciated because it was protracted, and finally bloodless.

"To that Being who has protected you through so many perils, and carried you onward through successive victories, be the praise for his continued goodness to our country, and especially for this last great success of our arms.

"Let the congratulations to yourself and your command be also extended to the officers and soldiers who co-operated with you.

"Gideon Welles, Secretary of the Navy."

So greatly was confidence in the Union cause restored by these victories at the West that government securities, which were two and a half and three per cent. below par, immediately commanded a premium. Panic prevailed among the Confederates on the Mississippi, even to New Orleans. Martial law was proclaimed in Memphis, and the specie in the banks was removed to places of supposed safety.*

---

* Lossing's "Civil War in America," vol. ii., p. 249.

Foote and Pope did not rest upon their victory, but on the 13th of April an army of twenty thousand men was convoyed by the gun-boats down the river, and landed in the vicinity of Fort Pillow, just above Memphis, and the combined naval and land forces prepared to attack that fortification. Five rebel gun-boats of Hollins's fleet that came out to oppose them before they reached Fort Pillow were engaged, and were chased in under the protection of the guns of the fort.

This engagement took place on Sunday morning, and when the hour for reading the service came, the commodore suggested that the firing should cease, and the crew be mustered for a brief space. He himself read the service; and, after a short extemporaneous prayer, he set forth in clear and concise terms to the men that duty to one's country often called them to do, as they were doing, something entirely opposed to the usual proper manner of observing the sacred day, and the reasons for this. The men listened attentively, as they always did, to his remarks, and then they were piped down to their work at the batteries. Several shells burst over the ship during this remarkable service.

The plan marked out in these operations by Foote and Pope was that the mortar-boats, protected by the gun-boats, were to be placed on the Arkansas shore within range of the enemy's batteries, while General Pope was to strive to get into the rear of the fort, the boats attacking in front.

During these active preparations for assault the following telegram reached the flag-officer, showing how useful and indispensable were his gun-boats in another quarter:

"U. S. GUN-BOAT 'TAYLOR,' PITTSBURG, TENNESSEE,
April 14, 1862.

"I have the honor to inform you that the *Taylor* and *Lexington* convoyed two transports, containing two thousand troops, infantry and cavalry, under the command of General Sherman, to Chickasaw, Alabama, where they disembarked, and proceeded rapidly to Bear Creek Bridge, the crossing of the Memphis and Charleston Railroad, for the purpose of destroying it, and as much of the trestle-work as they could find.

"I am happy to state that the expedition was entirely successful. The bridge, consisting of two spans, one hundred and ten feet each, was completely destroyed (*i. e.*, the superstructure), together with some five hundred feet of trestle-work, and half a mile of telegraph line.

"The rebels made a feeble resistance to our cavalry, one hundred and twenty in number; but soon made a hasty retreat, losing four killed; our loss, none.

"I regret to state that, in firing a salute on the 12th, John D. Seymour, boatswain's mate, was so much injured by the premature discharge of a gun as to cause his death yesterday morning.

"Allow me to congratulate you, and those under your command, on your great success at Island No. Ten. Inclosed I send you Lieutenant-Commanding Shirk's report. Very respectfully, etc.,

"William Gwin, Lieutenant,
"Com. Division of Gun-boats on Tennessee River.

"Flag-Officer A. H. Foote, com. Naval Forces, Western Waters."

It was necessary to destroy the lines of railway communication southward from Tennessee and Virginia, and thus to prevent the rapid reforming of the broken lines of rebel defense; and the value of the gun-boats in this work, both in conveying troops and in affording protection to transports, was great. These gun-boats—the *Taylor* and the *Lexington*—we have seen, were an important means of saving our army from destruction at the terrible battle of Shiloh. If this almost equal battle had been decisively won by the Confederates, the gun-boats on the Tennessee, Cumberland, and Mississippi rivers would have been forced to play a prominent part in defending conquered territory, and in holding back the furious rebel advance; hence the cautiousness of Commodore Foote in not rashly exposing his vessels at Island No. Ten seemed to be far-sighted and wise. These vessels were also destined to perform much valuable additional service on the Mississippi; and the names of the *Benton*, *Cincinnati*, *Carondelet*, *Louis-*

ville, figure in many hard-fought battles and sieges after their old flag-officer had been compelled to retire from their command. As the Trojan fleet become almost like living personages to the reader of Virgil, so these black gun-boats of our American "*pius Æneas*," with their varied qualities and fortunes, grow vividly familiar in the memory of one who studies the history of this little flotilla.

In regard to the operations in front of Fort Pillow, which were actually the last that Commodore Foote was permitted to take an active personal share in, we give his own accounts of them, for we have already discovered that much of the published history of the military operations at the West during the period when Foote was a prominent actor therein, is really nothing more than an embodiment of his letters and reports; for he was the pen as well as the sword of many of the scenes in which he was engaged. These are also interesting as being the last of his official papers:

"FLAG-STEAMER 'BENTON,' OFF FORT PILLOW,
April 14, 1862.

"SIR,—I have the honor to report that on the 11th instant I proceeded with our flotilla from Island No. Ten to New Madrid, and left that place with all our force on the 12th instant, and anchored the same evening near and just below the Arkansas line, fifty miles distant from New Madrid.

"Early in the morning, General Pope, with transports conveying his army of twenty thousand men, arrived from New Madrid. At eight o'clock five rebel gun-boats rounded the point below us, when the gun-boats, the *Benton* in advance, immediately got under way and proceeded in pursuit; and when within long range opened upon the rebels, followed by the *Carondelet*, *Cincinnati*, and other boats. After an exchange of some twenty shots, the rebel boats rapidly steamed down the river, and kept beyond our range until they reached the batteries of Fort Pillow—a distance of more than thirty miles. We followed them to within a mile of Fort Pillow, within easy range of their batteries, for the purpose of making a good reconnoissance, at considerable expense, however; but it was not till we had rounded to and ran some distance up the stream that the enemy opened upon us, and then with no effect, their shot, most of them, going beyond us. Having accomplished our object, I tied the flotilla up to the banks of the Tennessee side, out of range of the forts, for the night.

"General Pope, with Assistant-Secretary Scott, came aboard at 3 P. M., when it was arranged that the mortar-boats should be placed in the morning on the Arkansas shore, within range of the forts, to be protected by the gun-boats; and General Pope, with most of his force, should land five miles above, with the view of getting his army, if possible, to the rear of the fortifications, and make the attack in rear, while we should, with gun and mortar boats, attack them in front.

"This place has a long line of fortifications, with guns of heavy calibre; their number and the number of their men I have not yet been able to ascertain. The secession feeling here, as I learn from several persons coming on board, is very strong; and they express the opinion that the resistance will be very determined.

"*Three P. M.*—General Pope has returned with his transports, and informs me that he is unable to reach the rear of the rebels from any point of the river above, and proposes to cut a canal on the Arkansas side, which will enable us to get three or four of the gun-boats below, and thus enable him to cross the river below the upper forts, and thus cut off the batteries. We shall thus have three iron-clads above and four below, which, I presume, will be all that will be required in case the six gun-boats of the rebels make an attack upon either division, as three of our gun-boats ought successfully to cope with six of theirs.

"The mortars are now firing, and have driven the rebel gun-boats out of range down the river.

"I shall continue to keep the Department advised of our movements.

"The effects of my wound have quite a dispiriting effect upon me, from the increased inflammation and swelling of my foot and leg, which have induced a febrile action, depriving me of a good deal of sleep and energy. I can not give the wound that attention and rest it absolutely requires until this place is captured.

"I have the honor to be your obedient servant,

"A. H. Foote, Flag-Officer.

"The Hon. Gideon Welles, Secretary of the Navy."

We here insert a private letter, of which and similar letters Secretary Welles says: "I send herewith half a dozen letters written by Admiral Foote in the spring of 1862, when, suffering from wounds and domestic afflictions, with a load of care and responsibility upon him, he displayed the fortitude, heroism, and resignation of the soldier and the Christian in these unofficial communications. They were written, I apprehend, in the most interesting and critical period of his life. They exhibit his devotion to his country under great trials and severe personal suffering. In them the character and qualities of the man and officer are displayed."

"STEAMER 'BENTON,' OFF FORT PILLOW, *April* 17, 1862.

"MY DEAR SIR,—I am grateful to you beyond expression for your kind and sympathizing letter of the 9th instant. I feel it the more from our early intimate friendship, and especially at this time of affliction and bodily suffering, increased by our peculiar position to-day through the unexpected withdrawal of the army before this stronghold. I was quite hopeful last evening that in four days we should have this place, and be in Memphis in two more; but General Pope's departure has really left us in quite a forlorn condition, comparatively speaking. The two regiments left are not of the right kind, and have no tools to work with. I will do all I can, but have little hope of doing much in the face of such forts. It is the most trying position that a man can be placed in, as we can not reinforce, while the enemy is receiving troops and gun-boats.

"I did not foresee all this when I so truthfully stated my case to you, and left it with the Department to decide whether to keep me here or relieve me in view of the public interest, for I am ready to die for my country; but I do hope that if disaster come you will vindicate my memory, as I have been and am doing all that a man could do, although now I am suffering so much I can not well attend to my duties, and am unable to move except in case of great necessity—or, rather, to go on deck on crutches with my foot raised causes increased inflammation.

"I am sorry to respond to your kind letter in such a dolorous strain; but really I am weak, and have more to do than my strength enables me to perform properly.

"We have seven iron-clads and one wooden gun-boat here, two wooden ones up the Tennessee River, and one iron-clad at Hickman, near Columbus. Please excuse this poor note.

"With high esteem, yours truly, A. H. FOOTE.

"The Hon. Gideon Welles."

"U. S. Flag-Steamer 'Benton,' off Fort Pillow,
April 17, 1862.

"Sir,—I have the honor to inform the Department that yesterday and the day preceding I had, with General Pope, made such arrangements, by combining my own with the forces of the army, that our possession of this stronghold seemed to be inevitable in less than six days. I had stronger hopes of this desirable result than I even entertained at Island No. Ten, till the actual surrender was tendered. Our object then, after leaving a force to garrison the place, was to proceed to Memphis immediately, where, I have good authority for stating, we would have been received without opposition. But the sudden withdrawal of the entire army of General Pope this morning, under orders to proceed directly up the Tennessee River to join General Halleck's command at Pittsburg, has frustrated the best-matured and most hopeful plans and expectations thus far formed in this expedition. Two volunteer regiments, under command of Colonel Fitch, were left here by General Pope to co-operate with the flotilla. While I deeply regret the withdrawal of General Pope's command, I am not at all questioning the propriety, and even the necessity, of its presence at Pittsburg; and I shall use every exertion with the force remaining to accomplish good results.

"It is a very great object to obtain early possession of this place and Memphis, as ten of the rebel gun-boats are now at Fort Pillow, and ten others are reported as *en route* to Memphis, and daily expected at that place. It is reported that Commodore Hollins left Fort Pillow on Sunday to bring up the heavy gun-boat *Louisiana*, now about completed at New Orleans. With the exception of this vessel, however, we have little to apprehend from the other rebel gun-boats, according to the representations of the four or six deserters lately coming to us from the gun-boats at Fort Pillow. At all events, the Department may rest assured of every exertion being made on our part to accomplish the great work intrusted to this expedition. I have the honor to be your obedient servant,

"A. H. Foote, Flag-Officer.

"The Hon. Gideon Welles, Secretary of the Navy, Washington, D. C."

"U. S. Flag-Steamer 'Benton,' off Fort Pillow,
April 19, 1862.

"Sir,—I have the honor to inform the Department that since my last communication of the 17th instant we have been occasionally throwing shells into the rebel fortifications from the mortar-boats, which have been returned from their rifled guns, without producing any effect. Ours have compelled one encampment to remove its quarters; and from several deserters we learn that they have otherwise disturbed them.

"One or two examinations made by Colonel Fitch, commanding the two regiments left to co-operate with the flotilla by General Pope on withdrawing his army, have been unsuccessful thus far in finding a bayou for our boats, and a position below Fort Pillow where a battery can be placed to command the river below. I shall again render him assistance by sending over small boats, in hopes that at a distance farther up the river we may be able to discover a bayou leading into a lake, in which water sufficient may be found for our gun-boats, with a view of erecting a battery under their protection, which will blockade the river below, and enable his force, although not exceeding fifteen hundred men, to come upon the rebels in the rear, while, with the remaining gun-boats here, we attack them in front.

"I am greatly exercised about our position here on account of the withdrawal of the army of twenty thousand men, so important an element to the capture of the place. Fort Pillow has for its defense at least forty heavy guns in position, and nine gun-boats—six of them, however, being wooden boats, but armed with heavy guns—with a force of six thousand troops. Our force consists of seven iron-clads and one wooden gun-boat; sixteen mortar-boats, only available in throwing shell to a distance, and even worse than useless for defense; and a land force of two regiments, not exceeding fifteen hundred troops. Under these circumstances, an attack on our part, unless we can at first establish a battery below the fort under the protection of the gun-boats, and to co-operate with it after its completion, would be extremely hazardous, although its attempt might prove successful, and even be good policy under the circumstances; but it can hardly be now so regarded, as a disaster would place all that we have gained on this and other rivers at the mercy of the rebel fleet, unless the batteries designed to command the river from below are completed at No. Ten, or at Columbus, which I very much doubt. I therefore hesitate about a direct attack upon this place now, more than I should were the river above properly protected, although by it and loss of time the rebels may succeed in getting up to Fort Pillow their entire fleet of gun-boats. As I stated in my last communication, had not General Pope's army been withdrawn, we have every reason for believing that a plan we had adopted would have insured the fall of Fort Pillow in four days, and enabled us to have moved on Memphis in two days afterward. It has always been my expectation that a large army would co-operate with the gun-boats; and now the fall of Corinth and movements of our troops on to Memphis seem to be essential to our holding this place, and reaching Memphis with the flotilla. * * *

"I have the honor to be, very respectfully, your obedient servant,

"A. H. FOOTE, Flag-Officer.

"The Hon. Gideon Welles, Secretary of the Navy, Washington, D. C."

"U. S. FLAG-STEAMER 'BENTON,' OFF FORT PILLOW,
April 23, 1862.

"SIR,—I have the honor to inform the Department that since my last communication, with the exception of a day or two, when the heavy rains caused the mortars to recoil dangerously on the wet platform, we have been shelling the rebel batteries at Fort Pillow, and most of the time kept their gun-boats beyond our range. Colonel Fitch, in command of the twelve hundred infantry left here by General Pope, has been examining bayous and creeks, with a view of getting guns to blockade the river, and prevent the new gun-boats from coming up from New Orleans and Memphis; but, as the rebels are in great force, and no tools or conveniences for cutting through the swamps were left by General Pope when his army, so unfortunately for us, was withdrawn, he has made as yet no satisfactory progress.

"I am doing all in my power toward devising ways and means preparatory to a successful attack on the forts, and shall continue to do so; but as the capture of this place was predicated upon a large land force co-operating with the flotilla, or its being turned by the army marching upon Memphis, and considering the difficulties of fighting the flotilla down stream with our slow boats compared with up-stream work, the Department will not be surprised at our delay, and at our having made no further progress toward the capture of this stronghold. I shall, however, do all in my power to be successful here, and exert myself, even beyond my impaired health and strength, toward the accomplishment of this great object.

"The rebels are strongly fortified on land, and have eleven gun-boats lying near, or rather below their fortifications. A resident of the place informs me this morning that thirteen gun-boats are now here, seven of which, however, are mere river steamers, with boilers and machinery sunk into their holds, and otherwise protected; but they carry from four to six or eight guns of heavy calibre, some of which are rifled. The other boats are iron-plated or filled in with cotton. The large steamer, of sixteen or twenty guns, being plated, and named the *Louisiana*, has not arrived; but is daily expected from New Orleans.

"I have thus given the Department the best information I can obtain from the most reliable sources—from resident Union men, and the twelve deserters from the enemy; whose accounts, however, are conflicting, many of them giving fabulous numbers of men, guns, and gun-boats. We have not force enough to hold the place if we take it.

"I have the honor to be, very respectfully, your obedient servant,

"A. H. FOOTE, Flag-Officer.

"The Hon. Gideon Welles, Secretary of the Navy, Washington, D. C.

"P. S.—In a picket skirmish yesterday the rebels lost one killed and one or two wounded. No loss on our side. A. H. F."

This private note followed these official communications:

"STEAMER 'BENTON,' OFF FORT PILLOW,
April 24, 1862.

"MY DEAR SIR,—I have given you, in my official letters, the state of things here as correctly and fully as my state of health would enable me to do. I am very much prostrated by the continuous draft on my physique from my inflamed foot, which appears to be slowly but steadily growing worse, till I am confined mostly to my cabin with a swollen, painful leg, affecting my whole system, and rendering it impossible for me to give that attention to my duties which circumstances require. I have, however, substantially stated all this, indorsed by the surgeons; and it is for the Department to decide whether I shall remain under these circumstances. If I am to do so, I trust that I shall not be held responsible for matters, as if I had health to perform my duties. I wanted to see this expedition reach New Orleans; but still I deemed it my duty to represent my case as it is to the government, and let it judge how to dispose of it.

"*Entre nous*, Colonel Fitch, who is a celebrated surgeon, and commands the small force left here by General Pope, examined my case yesterday, and said that a suppuration might take place in my foot, which would probably permanently injure or destroy it. I feel discouraged about it, and it has taken most of the energy out of me. Excuse this incoherent note. With high respect, your obliged friend, A. H. FOOTE.

"The Hon. Gideon Welles.

"P. S.—We are shelling the forts with mortars, and the rebels are replying with gun for shell. When I sent the surgeon's opinion, General Pope was here, and I confidently expected that yesterday we should be in Memphis, and no serious obstacle would intervene from thence to New Orleans; but General Pope left the next evening, and all my plans were frustrated; and although my foot goes from bad to worse, I stood up against it to the very last. A. H. F."

While thus condemned to keep watch and ward of Fort Pillow, without the possibility (deprived as he was of the army's assistance) of taking it, he received many pleasant and cheering letters, of which the following from one of his officers is a good specimen:

"CAIRO, *April* 22, 1862.

"MY DEAR FLAG-OFFICER,—I deeply regret to learn that your foot troubles you so much, and that your general health is affected by it. Do give yourself a little more rest. You need it, and should take it, not only for your own sake, but also for that of your country. A great deal depends upon you. It would be a calamity if you were obliged to give up your command, and it would create confusion and disorganization in the flotilla. I hope to hear that you are better, and are taking good care of yourself.

"The weather here has been exceedingly disagreeable, but it has not kept us from working. I was greatly relieved when our Cairo magazines were emptied.

"I sent you by the *De Soto* the articles you desired; call upon me always, for it gives me great pleasure to attend to your wants.

"I am snugly domesticated on board the wharf-boat. I have two rooms nicely fitted up—thanks to friend Wise, who is never so happy as when he is contributing to the comfort of others. Mrs. Wise, Mrs. Stembel, and Mrs. Pennock enjoy their new home. We are decidedly more comfortable than we were at the hotel. If the river continue high, we may have to take to salt grub, but no one will mind that.

"We commenced to-day getting on board Porter's 9-inch guns preparatory to shipping them to St. Louis; dragging them through mud and water is no easy task. If the Department do not give us official information with regard to the rams now building at Pittsburg and Cincinnati, and there is delay on that account, we must not be blamed for it. It will take time to select suitable pilots and masters for them. I have telegraphed to Wise that if you were expected to officer the rams, timely notice should be given. If I can secure good masters and pilots for the *Eastport*,* had I not better do so? If Captain Porter have no need of the services of Lieutenant McGunngle, had he not better be ordered here? I do not hear of any rams being built at St. Louis. Remember me kindly to Phelps. Sincerely your friend, A. M. PENNOCK."

Paymaster-Captain Wise writes also from Cairo:

"There is considerable apprehension that the levee will give way, as at our landing the water is only a foot or two from the top. From my room I can look down upon Cairo; and sociable visiting is carried on in boats, while first floors are used as bath-rooms and fish-ponds. The St. Charles Hotel will probably for once be cleansed, as the river is expected to make a new channel through it. There is much alarm among the boarders, and Mrs. Stembel and Mrs. Pennock have both taken refuge on board our ark."

We can well imagine the grim jokes and fun among those sea-dogs at thus being cooped up and nearly drowned like rats in these fresh-water towns.

The following letter of the commodore's is in a more hopeful and cheerful vein, evidently from the fact that something positive had been decided upon by the government:

"'BENTON,' OFF FORT PILLOW, *April* 27, 1862.

"MY DEAR SIR,—I have but a moment of time to respond to your exceedingly kind note of the 21st instant, referring to Captain Davis and my services, as the mail leaves for Cairo in a few minutes.

"I am greatly relieved by your letter and the manner in which you have disposed of my case. I considered it to be my duty to take the step I did, and then leave the issue with the Department. I shall strive to do my duty to the last; and in the mean time will take the best possible care of my wound, and hope in Him who has hitherto been my Helper for wisdom to guide me in my duty.

"Like all great men, I see that you have your detractors. I have even myself been asked why the Navy Department did not render me more aid. But I have invariably said that as this flotilla was a hybrid concern,

* The captured rebel steamer that Foote had been authorized by the President to put in fighting trim.

it has been and of course should be neglected, as neither the Army nor the Navy Department could feel that interest in it, or responsibility for it, as if it had been exclusively under Navy or Army control; that it was true we had been neglected, but I could not find fault, as the neglect naturally followed upon the very character of its organization. I have always spoken of the wonderful energy of the Navy Department in improving the force we have, contrasting it with the few vessels we had, mostly on foreign stations, when you assumed the office of Secretary. Toward you and Assistant-Secretary Fox I have expressed those sentiments repeatedly, and am ready to express them publicly. It is true we are badly fitted out, and it is only a wonder to us all that with the means at hand we could have brought out any thing like effective gun-boats. We are much weaker as gun-boats than the rebels or our people suppose, therefore I dare not run great risks. I made a bold dash at Fort Henry to inspire terror, and it succeeded. We then fought up stream. At Donelson I wanted to wait three days and get four mortar-boats, and fight at a longer range; but General Halleck was in a hurry, and we went in at close range against my judgment. But still the rebel officers said that our fire had so demoralized their troops that they could not afterward be brought up to their work; and the commander of the fort actually went down to Captain Dove on the *Louisville*, and offered to surrender the fort to him as my representative. I will do the best I can; but do not expect, as the country does, too much of us, for really our means are not adequate to the work assigned us. I also want to impress upon you that when I sent the surgeon's certificate to you General Pope and two thousand men were here; and we had a plan which, with God's blessing, was sure to enable us to take Fort Pillow in three days; and I expected to be in Memphis by the time Davis could reach here, and that no obstruction to our advance to New Orleans would be at all formidable. I had thought of this matter at No. Ten, and intended to have made my plan known to you, but we pushed on so soon that I had no time. I am really a great sufferer from my wound; still feel that you have taken the best course. Excuse my haste. Respectfully yours, A. H. FOOTE.

"The Hon. Gideon Welles, Secretary of the Navy, Washington, D. C."

The following telegram was sent April 27th:

"TO FLAG-OFFICER FOOTE:

"Farragut has passed the forts below New Orleans, and appeared off the city at 1 P. M. of the 24th instant. His orders from the Department are to push up the river until he meets you. G. V. FOX, As't.-Sec."

While one star, which had so steadily shone, giving hope to fainting hearts, was now in the wane, another star was rising. Thus a man's place who has done well in a good cause is at once filled by another, and the good work itself goes on.

From what is hinted in the above reports, the wound of the flag-officer was becoming, from want of care and rest, quite serious in its character, and his whole system was prostrated by it; in fact, he had been now for several months a physically shattered man; and in the following private letter to Secretary Welles, we see that Foote himself was already meditating a temporary retirement, or at least the giving up of the main responsibility of the flotilla:

"STEAMER 'BENTON,' OFF FORT PILLOW, *April* 28, 1862.

"MY DEAR SIR,—I replied to your kind note in reference to Captain Davis's coming out to the flotilla for a short time to render me such aid as might be necessary. I shall probably want him to visit St. Louis, where Commander William D. Porter is still at work on the *Essex*, and one or two other vessels, under some authority from Washington, of which I know but little, situated as I have been with the flotilla, and for seventy days suffering from my wound. I could not possibly give my attention to matters in St. Louis. I have sent Commander Porter's last letter, wanting money, to Quartermaster-General Meigs. The second in command of so large a flotilla has a right, from his position, to act a good deal for the chief in the absence of the latter; and I have therefore directed Commander Porter to act under the directions of General Halleck and the War Department, with whom he is and long has been, I believe, in communication. I am greatly disappointed, however, in not having the *Essex*, as she is greatly needed now; but Commander Porter says that want of funds alone has prevented him from being ready.

"Until I was wounded at Fort Donelson, I changed my flag from gun-boat to gun-boat, as the *Benton* was not ready. Since then I have been permanently on board this vessel. In the former case, when in robust health, I could, unaided, attend to all the duties depending upon me; but under present circumstances I have received great assistance from Lieutenant-Commanding Phelps, who opened the Tennessee to Florence—who previously had cruised with such good results in the Tennessee and Cumberland rivers—who had been in two well-fought actions—and whose skill and bravery, and even diplomatic ability, have been productive of the best results to our interests here; and may I respectfully, in view of this officer's services, ask for him promotion to the grade of commander, as I know of no one in the Navy whose services could have been greater to the government. If, therefore, any promotions for gallantry and general merit are made, I trust that he will be among the first thus honored.

"A report came to me last evening that the steam-ram *Louisiana*, of sixteen guns, had arrived at Memphis; and that in ten days she would be up here and clear the river to a certainty. We shall make as good a fight as we can with the means we have. I saw Colonel Fitch in consultation to-day in reference to this report, which may be exaggerated. I forward a letter found at Island No. Ten; but so much time has elapsed that we have concluded that this report of the readiness of the vessel to come up here has been greatly overdrawn. By telegraphing in cipher to Commander Pennock at Cairo, he will send a steamer to me in twenty hours after its receipt.

"In haste, truly and respectfully yours, A. H. FOOTE."

"The Hon. Gideon Welles."

Commodore Smith also refers to the reported sending of Davis to Foote's assistance:

"*April* 28, 1862.

"MY DEAR FOOTE,—I have yours of the 16th instant, with its addendum of the 17th. I regret exceedingly that you have been disappointed in losing the services of General Pope; but the impending battle at Corinth, I presume, is the cause.

"I have talked to the Secretary about your health. He has ordered Davis to help you, as he seems to be the man you select, and I trust and hope he may meet your expectations of him. When he arrives, if I were in your place, I would not remain, if you are to sacrifice your life by it. You have done your share. But, God willing, I trust you will meet the Atlantic squadron at New Orleans or higher up the river, where, after the taking of New Orleans, the force of Farragut is ordered to proceed. I regret the Army does not work more kindly with you, or at least that General Halleck seems to pass over your services, and to notify those under him that they are not under your orders. Certainly, then, you are not under his orders. The Navy will work its way anyhow. We are expecting in a few days the great battle at Yorktown to come off. God grant us victory. If we are successful, I think the war will come to a close. I have been so pressed with work that I have no time to think of any private affairs. The Secretary puts a heavy load upon us, which I will try to bear to the best of my ability. You are considered by the community the man of the war. Nothing can wipe that out. The glorious news from New Orleans through Secesh source is refreshing. I have been at work getting up iron-clad boats for the rivers—don't know their requirements, but I know it is impossible to shield them properly with iron and have light draft of water; so we must do the best we can.

"Yours very truly as always. In haste,

"JOSEPH SMITH."

A letter of sympathy was also received at this time from his former pastor at Brooklyn, Rev. Dr. Budington, from which we extract the following:

"I have wished to express to you my sympathy on the occasion of the death of your dear Willie, an event which was announced to me on Sabbath morning upon entering the pulpit, and which led me to ask the prayers of the congregation on your behalf. Be assured you have them, and that the hearts of our people have followed your late series of successes. You know that you are surrounded by the thanks and admiration of your countrymen, and it can not fail to be a solace and satisfaction to you, in the discharge of your high trust, at this solemn crisis of our country's history; yet outward glory, as it can not shield the heart from the shafts of affliction, so it can not prevent an aching heart nor eradicate a pang. I rejoice to know that for this you can go to One who is able, and will do for you what the world with its best wishes can not. May you find Him unspeakably near and precious to you in the endurance of this great and unlooked-for bereavement; and while God is filling your largest ambition for service to your country, may the benefits of a sanctified affliction defend you from the temptations of wordly applause, and keep undisturbed the equipoise of a soul truly consecrated to God, and holding earthly distinctions in their true relations to eternal issues. At the same time you were bereaved, General Casey, of the Army of the Potomac, a member of our church, lost his wife in Washington, and public prayers were offered for both of you at the same time. Amid the deep and widespread sorrows of our country in this war, it seems to be God's will that our leaders, who are leading us out of it so triumphantly, should themselves be partakers of tribulation."

The matter of being relieved of his active duties by Captain Davis was at this time the uppermost question, and he wishes to have the exact grounds of that action (unselfish in its motives on his part) clearly understood, as will be seen in the following private communication to the Secretary:

"FLAG-STEAMER 'BENTON,' OFF FORT PILLOW,
April 29, 1862.

"MY DEAR SIR,—Your unofficial note of the 23d, referring to Captain Davis being ordered to report to me, but on no account to relieve me in command, has been received. As you will perceive from my letter of yesterday, I have had no idea of leaving the squadron at any time, unless the Department should consider me, with my wound and its effects, less efficient than some other officer who might be chosen to relieve me. I placed my remaining or leaving solely on public considerations—what would best promote the cause of the Union—not on private grounds; for in former letters I stated that I should remain, and give my life to the vindication of the flag.

"I am pained to see myself represented in the papers as having applied to be detached on account of my wound, implying that I want to leave the command on personal grounds. This is doing me great injustice; and may I beg of you to have this impression removed, by its denial, as publicly as the misrepresentation has been made? for I would far rather die in the harness from sickness or a shot, than to leave my post in face of the enemy on personal grounds. This would be so unofficer-like, if not even pusillanimous, that I can not quietly rest under the imputation.

"I have no idea of leaving now to go up to Cairo or St. Louis; still I am happy to learn that Captain Davis is coming out, as I am really unable to cope, in my ill-health, with the heavy duties of flag-officer, organized and conducted as this service is, involving far more work and care than a regular squadron elsewhere.

"Several deserters came to us yesterday, and informed me that thirteen rebel gun-boats below were to attack us at 3 o'clock this morning, six or seven of which were rams. We made some further preparations by tying four gun-boats stern up stream to the banks, so as to bring the head down stream ready for a fight; the *Benton* being farthest down toward the forts, and where the gun-boats and rams would approach. We were on our arms all night, ready for a hard fight, but the rebels did not make their appearance. This morning three more deserters came, and report that the

A Columbiad. Water-Battery. Fort Pillow.

FORT PILLOW.

rebels were ready to make the attack, when a council of war was held, and it was voted to be impracticable to make the attack. Still we are as well prepared, night and day, as our means will allow us to be, and our officers and men are in good heart.

"The deserters paid me the compliment to say that my name was as much among them as Beauregard's—but we know deserters are not to be depended upon in their statements. I only report this in a private letter, as you kindly alluded to the prestige of my name; but I am now but a comparatively weak officer. I am not what I have been even; still I know that I possess the confidence of the flotilla. You will excuse my egotism.

"I seriously thought of running the blockade last night, and attacking the rebels' gun-boats and rams; but now it is well we did not. A disaster would have exposed the upper rivers. Our means render our position very embarrassing; but I look to Him who reigns in all worlds for wisdom and strength to do my duty. Excuse my hasty letter.

"With great respect and esteem, your obliged friend and servant,

"A. H. FOOTE.

"The Hon. Gideon Welles."

"Fort Pillow, afterward Fort Wright, was on the first Chickasaw bluff, about eighty miles above Memphis, and was in command of General Villepique, a creole of New Orleans, who was educated at West Point as an engineer, and was regarded as second only to Beauregard. The fort was a very strong one, and the entire works occupied a line of seven miles in circumference. Jeff. Thompson was there with about three thousand troops, and Hollins had collected there a considerable flotilla of gun-boats."* Such was the problem, after he had driven the boastful Hollins under the guns of the fort, that Foote was left, alone and unaided, to solve. But he was not to have that satisfaction, for the problem solved itself, after the flight of Beauregard from Corinth, when the garrison, on the night of the 4th of June, evacuated this strong position. In the mean time, on the 22d of April, Captain C. H. Davis, who

* Lossing's "Civil War in America," vol. ii., p. 296.

had done good service with Dupont at Port Royal, was, at Foote's own request, appointed to assist him. Although Foote retained the command of the flotilla until June 17—so that Fort Pillow was actually captured while he was still in command—he left the fleet in Davis's hands as early as the 9th of May. His letter to Davis was as follows:

"FLAG-SHIP 'BENTON,' OFF FORT PILLOW,
May 9, 1862.

"SIR,—In consequence of the state of my health, the Secretary of the Navy has directed you to report to me for the purpose of performing such duties as the circumstances of the flotilla require.

"By authority of the Secretary of the Navy, and the advice of a board of surgeons, I leave the flotilla this day temporarily, for the purpose of recruiting my health at Cleveland, Ohio; and you will be pleased, during my absence, to perform all the duties of the flag-officer; and as such, and being hereby invested with flag-officer's authority, all officers and others attached to and connected with this flotilla will obey your orders and act under your instructions.

"I am, respectfully, your obedient servant,

"(Signed) A. H. FOOTE, Flag-Officer.

"Commodore Charles H. Davis, U. S. N., commanding pro tem.
U. S. Naval Forces, Western Waters."

Soon after this date, Hollins's flotilla came out to challenge combat, and after a brilliant fight, in which Commodore Davis showed great skill as a commander, the rebel boats were signally defeated with heavy loss, although on our side the brave Captain Stembel, of the *Cincinnati*, was severely wounded, and his vessel sunk. For three weeks more the two fleets lay watching each other at Fort Pillow, momentarily awaiting an encounter, when suddenly the fort was abandoned and the rebel gun-boats left. Reinforced by Ellet's "ram fleet," the National vessels followed down the river, and Memphis was attacked by them on the 6th of June, and another desperate engagement with the enemy took place, in which the powerful *Benton* distinguished herself, giving the finishing blow to the fight. In this purely naval combat the rebel fleet was badly cut up, there being but one sole survivor, the *Van Dorn*, which escaped; and Memphis, at the demand of Davis, was forced to surrender to the gun-boats. This battle brought to an end the naval power of the rebels on the Mississippi. We now return to him who, in feebleness and pain, had been compelled to forego these triumphs, which his foresight and patient skill had prepared, and which, as far as human prescience went, he had fully anticipated for himself. Notwithstanding all he had done, the disproportion between his aspirations and his achievements, to so generously ambitious a nature, could not but be a source of keen disappointment. But he was a thoroughly Christian man, and no loss of this kind could trouble him overmuch.

CHAPTER XXIV.

CORRESPONDENCE AT CLEVELAND. — DETACHED FROM THE COMMAND OF THE WESTERN FLOTILLA.

When Commodore Foote left the scene of action on the Mississippi, he went at once to Cleveland, Ohio, the home of his brother, Hon. John A. Foote, where he was joined by his wife, and where he would have quiet and rest, but at the same time could exercise a general supervision over the fleet, and receive the reports of his officers. The citizens of Cleveland welcomed him among them with great delight, tendering him a public reception and the hospitalities of the city. In his reply to their communication, he said:

"Sympathizing as you do with my physical condition and impaired health, and sharing with me, as you so feelingly express, my desire to rejoin my command at the earliest possible moment, I know you will permit me to decline these distinguished honors.

"I should be as able to renew the fight with my flotilla as to be the recipient of your favors; and I know too well the intelligent citizens of Cleveland to doubt for a moment that they would esteem this my duty.

"If I were in better health, and had completed the mission with which I am charged, nothing would give me greater pleasure. We are, however, in the midst of our work, and my brave comrades may this day be engaged in deadly strife for the vindication of our flag; therefore I could not, consistently with my views of duty, accept your kind invitation."

Commodore Foote's relations to the flotilla now became a matter of earnest thought to him, and many letters passed between him and Secretary Welles. Mr. Welles was willing to grant him a temporary release, but not willing that he should be wholly detached from the command. He says in one of his letters, dated April 21:

"Your life and services are too valuable to be put in jeopardy, even if great events are dependent on your continued active duty. I do not think it necessary or expedient, however, to detach you from the command of the flotilla: you must have a respite.

"I propose, therefore, to send Captain Davis to you, agreeably to your request, to relieve you from active physical and mental exertion. He can take temporary charge while you are off duty, and with the aid of the skill and experience of Lieutenant-Commanding Phelps, and your general direction and advice, I trust matters will go forward efficiently and well. Unless it is absolutely indispensable, I should be reluctant to have you leave a position where you have earned such just renown, and where the whole country desires you to remain. No other man can inspire the people with equal confidence in the position you occupy; and it is no disparagement to others to say no one has the experience and right comprehension that you have of the required service. I can not express to you how much I have been gratified with your labors and efforts. They have given heart to the whole country, and I, personally, have been sustained and encouraged by them."

Again he says (April 23):

"I mentioned that Captain Davis would be ordered to report to you, but on no account do I wish to detach you from the position you occupy. If you deem it necessary to go to Cairo or St. Louis, you will still remain flag-officer in command, and Captain Davis will be next in command under you. Your name and prestige I deem important, and therefore do not wish the rebels to know that you are disabled even. Let the enemy know that they have you to combat them."

When Foote reached Cleveland, letters from the Secretary followed him, full of friendly expression, and yet earnest that he should recover his health entirely and thoroughly, in order to resume his command. Knowing his spirited and excitable temperament, he warns him against allowing the deeds of Farragut to destroy his rest, and to incite him to a rash and hasty resumption of active duty; but urges him to get well, to fight the enemy again in his gun-boats.

On the other hand, his good old friend Commodore Smith counsels him to give up at once. His letter is characteristic for its blunt sincerity:

"*May* 30, 1862.

"MY DEAR FOOTE,—I have yours of the 27th inst. You ask for my advice; I give it cheerfully. Take care of yourself. You have done enough. Your duty is to your country, and to yourself and family. As the summer will bear hard upon you, even if you recruit, I would not run any risk of the climate in your present state of health. You require repose and retirement; therefore I would retire and go home, and leave Davis—who was your choice, not mine—as your successor. Every body knows that you encountered every kind of obstacle, and surmounted them all. While ——— was here for months preparing his squadron and expedition, and had the choice of ships and the pick of the Navy List, you were sent off without notice or much consultation, and officers sent to you not of your selection; funds and men were not furnished; you were thwarted in many of your plans by others; and yet you overcame all with your tact and talent, and won a glorious victory. After all this, it will be an unthankful task for you to return to the flotilla, and contend with a summer climate on the river, in your state of body and mind. Therefore relinquish it, and let others take a hand and do what you have left undone—which is not much, I apprehend, in the way of fighting.

"You are not bound to 'die in harness.' Nobody would thank you for doing so in your present condition, and, as I said before, the country may require you another day.* We are in perilous times, great events are in embryo. God only knows what is to be the end. We hope for a peace, but it does not appear to me to be at hand to-day or to-morrow. I have just seen the Secretary. He says you had better remain where you are for the present; that you can come East or go where you please, but prefers to have your name cover the flotilla, and so I suppose you must keep to your tethers. My kind regards to Mrs. Foote.

"Yours, as always, in haste, JOSEPH W. SMITH."

There is an interesting series of letters from Lieutenant-Commanding S. L. Phelps to Commodore Foote while the

* Referring to war with England, which the writer strongly anticipated.

latter was in Cleveland, reporting the movements of the gun-boats, some of which we give in full, as they contain much of the history of the fleet with which Foote was so vitally connected. The first letter recounts the naval fight at Fort Pillow:

"U. S. GUN-BOAT 'BENTON,' OFF FORT PILLOW,
May 11, 1862.

"FLAG-OFFICER FOOTE, U. S. N., Cleveland, Ohio:

"MY DEAR SIR,—You will have heard of the fight yesterday morning. Eight rebel gun-boats came up to the point, and four or five of them proceeded at once toward the *Cincinnati*, then covering the mortar-boat, one of the rebel boats, with masts, being considerably in advance. Captain Stembel in the most gallant manner steamed up, rounded to, and, opening fire, stood down for the rebel. As he approached, the fire was withheld, the ram striking Stembel's vessel in the quarter, and swinging broadside to, when, the muzzles absolutely against the rebel boat, a broadside was poured into her, making a terrible crashing in her timbers. The rebel, swinging clear, made down stream, with a parting salute of other guns, in a helpless condition. By this time the *Benton*, *Mound City*, and *Carondelet* were far enough down, half-way at least, to Stembel's assistance, to open an effective fire. The *Pittsburg*, not yet clear of the bank, and the *Cairo* just sending a boat out to cast off her hawsers. The *St. Louis* came down pretty well. Two rams were making for the *Cincinnati*, and once again hit her in the stern, receiving the fire of the stern guns. That boat struck Stembel twice, doing little damage, but using sharpshooters to such effect as to dangerously wound Stembel, and the fourth master, Mr. Reynolds, and one man in the leg. By this time we were in their midst, and I had the satisfaction to blow up the boilers of the ram that last hit the *Cincinnati* by a shot from our port bow 42-pound rifle. I fired it deliberately with that view, and when the ram was trying to make another hit. Another ram had now hit the *Mound City* in the bow, and had received the fire of every gun of that vessel in the swinging that followed the contact. We interposed between another and the *Mound City*, and the fellow, afraid to hit us, backed off, where he also blew up from a shot hitting a steam-pipe or a cylinder. All the rams drifted off disabled, and the first one that blew up could not have had a soul remaining alive on board, for the explosion was terrific. We could have secured two or three of them had we had steam-power to do so; but, as it was, we saw them drift down helpless under the fort, and one is said to have sunk in deep water. The mortar-boat men acted with great gallantry, firing away to the end. The rebels fired two 32-pound shots through the mortar-boat, and two volleys of musketry into her, without hurting a man.

"The *Mound City* had her bow pretty much wrenched off, and was run into the shoal opposite where we had been lying. The *Cincinnati* ran to the bank below where we lay when you left, and sank in eleven feet of water. The *Champion* steamer fortunately arrived, having on board a 20-inch steam-pump, and the *Mound City* is now afloat, but greatly damaged. The *Cincinnati* will be raised in twenty-four hours. My plan of suspending logs is immediately to be tried. The wounded of the squadron are five; killed, none. Stembel we hope will recover. He did splendidly. The loss of the rebels must be very heavy. Their vessels were literally torn to pieces, and some had holes in their sides through which a man could walk. Those that blew up—it makes me shudder to think of them. I have written very hastily, knowing that you would find excuses for my style in remembering by what busy circumstances we are surrounded just now; and I am nervous from an unwonted amount of exertion. I count off the days, anxious for them to roll round, when you will return with the *Eastport* with some (steam) power. Come to the squadron with your flag flying.

"All hands went into the fight with a will. We have no news from below. Colonel Fitch will land his force in the morning.

"This, I believe, is the first purely naval fight of the war. May heaven bless you, and restore you to us in health very soon.

"Respectfully and very truly yours, S. L. Phelps."

"U. S. Gun-boat 'Benton,' off Fort Pillow,
May 17, 1862.

"My dear Sir,—Since my hurried letter after the fight the other morning, I have been absolutely unable to write. The *Cincinnati* was only raised night before last, and got off for Cairo.

"The bell boat had no crew, and we had trouble about the machine. Mr. Hoel was left alone. One master killed, and two sick. We ran the *Benton* to the stern of the *Cincinnati*, and remained there till she left, and I assisted Mr. Hoel, besides getting logs, chains, railroad iron, etc., with which to secure the boats against rams. We are putting railroad iron about the stern of this boat, which is her weak part. General Quimby is coming down with some artillery, cavalry, and infantry, and a combined attack is to be made on the fort in about three days' time. Every thing has been quiet about the fort and where the gun-boats lie below. Two of their rams are missing. Deserters say that one hundred and eight were buried from their vessels after the fight. A good many deserters and refugees are coming in and passing up to Cairo—some thirty to fifty per day.

"We are now anchored across the river a little below where we lay when you left. Captain Dove is here with the *Louisville.* Now we have the *Cairo*, *Pittsburg*, and *Louisville* to count among the six vessels of the fleet. Kilty did handsomely in the fight. Neither the *Pittsburg* nor *Cairo* got into it, and the *St. Louis* can hardly be said to have done so. Commodore Davis has got the run of matters very well. The plan of attack proposed is the old one—land on the bluff, open heavy mortar fire, and follow up with attack by gun-boats. What the rebel boats can do remains to be seen. The great craft building in Memphis has been taken up the Yazoo to be finished, and a mechanic from there says it will be fifteen days before she will be ready. We must catch her, then, before she can be fitted out. I have not time this morning, being so much interrupted, to write about all the little matters of the fleet, of which I know you would like to be informed. Suffice it to say that things go on much as before. I miss you a great deal; though, of course, with such a gentleman as Captain Davis, there could be nothing but the most agreeable relations. Captain Pennock writes that the *Eastport* will be ready in thirty days. I trust then you may be entirely recovered, and come to realize a little pleasant cruising in what will be the dashing vessel of the fleet. Thirty days make but a little count, and will soon pass. I am respectfully and very truly yours, S. L. PHELPS."

"U. S. GUN-BOAT 'BENTON,' NEAR FORT PILLOW,
May 21, 1862.

"MY DEAR SIR,—I had the pleasure to receive your kind letter written from Cleveland several days since. I am exceedingly gratified with its contents, and reciprocate with a warm heart the friendship it evinces. How great has been the error of all naval commanders who have relied upon power rather than upon generous consideration and sympathy to develop and arouse the energies and active co-operation of subordinates upon which the superior's success so much depends.

"I have been really unfortunate in my efforts in writing to you. This is my third note—the two first written in great haste, at times when I really had my hands full. Now I write with a sore and heavy head. Day before yesterday, while on board the *De Soto*, looking to their way of getting guns on board, a spar broke, the pieces falling some fifteen feet. I found myself knocked over and my head badly cut. I have suffered with headache and nausea a good deal since, but these are becoming less. I am thankful to have escaped so easily, and, for me, I have been very patient.

"Some four of the so-called 'rams' are here, and one or two more are expected to arrive soon. General Quimby came down yesterday with a battery of artillery and some infantry and cavalry. I think now the plan adopted in the proposed attack will be what you and General Pope had agreed to undertake. There is a flag of truce here this morning, making bitter complaint that two of the two hundred and two exchanged prisoners sent down by the Army for the commodore to deliver at Fort Pillow were sick of the small-pox. Nothing, of course, was known of the condition of the men by the commodore. They were sent down in the boat in which they came from Cairo. Lieutenant McGunngle now has the *St. Louis*. Mr. Erben is adrift again. Lieutenant Hall, who went to New York by summons of the Retiring Board, has returned to Cairo. Captain ——— came down to the fleet, arriving just in time to witness the fight, and applied to be sent to Cairo to superintend work on the *Eastport*, or to St. Louis to perform similar duty, and thither he has gone. This looks as if pressure of public opinion in Boston sent him out. There is a good deal of sickness. I shall have to stop, as I am increasing my headache. There are many inquiries for the news from you. You carry with you the earnest wishes of the entire flotilla for your speedy recovery and quick return. While I, who must needs feel your absence more than all others, desire greatly to see you return to finish the work that is of right yours to do, I am exceedingly anxious that you should not return too soon. The climate is a trying one, and you should feel quite sure that you are entirely recovered before you come.

"Respectfully and most sincerely your friend, S. L. PHELPS."

"U. S. GUN-BOAT 'BENTON,' NEAR FORT PILLOW,
May 22, 1862.

"MY DEAR SIR,—This morning I had the pleasure to receive your most welcome letter of the 19th inst., and avail myself now of a quiet moment, before going to bed, to give you what little gossip I can recall relating to the fleet, that may serve to interest you, and to thank you for your letter. I am feeling very comfortable for the time, the doctor having just bathed my sore head, and put me in good-humor for the nonce. I have been about a good deal to-day, and by to-morrow I shall be myself again, ready for any thing but long exposure to the sun.

"The *Mound City* is now here, ready for service again, and the *Cincinnati* will be ready in about one week. It is strange how that inevitable month in the case of the *Eastport* drags its slow length along; never beginning—always one day in advance of present time. To-day's mail informs us that she will be ready in one month—so did the mail on the 22d of April last. General Quimby examined the river bank opposite Fulton to-day, and the guns have arrived to put in battery there, so that by the day after to-morrow we may hope to have something doing. The commodore sent Captain McGunngle down with the party reconnoitring. Seven gun-boats are reported at Fulton. Driving those and the rams away with a battery, so as not to be in our way while under the fort, is, of course, leaving us free for the main work. Some of the boats are secured to a considerable extent about the bow and stern, and all have logs suspended along the sides where there is no plating. We are putting railroad iron on the stern and quarters of this vessel. The rebels have dismounted nearly every gun on their vessels, depending on small-arms and rams. Jeff. Thompson, the nightmare of every port commander on the Mississippi, is the commodore of the rebel fleet just below us. Yet the commandant at New Madrid this night lies in an unquiet bed, assured that the immortal Jeff. is after him with those naked and starved swamp-rats. The *Taylor** and *Lexington* are forced out of the Tennessee by low water, and will join the fleet here, being much needed. Will you believe it, application was made for them to remain at Cairo to protect that place, there being considerable apprehension? The *Conestoga* is to look after Hickman and Columbus, and will be within call of Cairo. Affairs go on much as usual with the squadron. Some few changes among the lower officers caused by sickness. Mr. Parker has gone as fourth master to the *Louisville.* Mr. Reed has applied for a master-mateship on board the *Great Western.* I suggest sending Mr. Wilkins there, and keeping Mr. Reed here as the best of the two for our purposes. Cap-

* This was the original name of the boat, which was called after General and President Taylor; but toward the close of the war she began to be called the *Tyler*, which makes some confusion even in official reports. We have chosen to call her uniformly by her original title.

tain Walke I have not seen for several days. Little Thompson is very busy getting his vessel secured so that when the rebels 'come around the Point' again he can 'pitch into them.' Of the *Cairo* nothing is known, except that she was heard of to-day as wanting coal, being about out of that commodity, and pretty much ashore for provisions. The *St. Louis* I am satisfied will now be found up to time every where. That hospital-boat has not yet come down. It takes so long to do any thing! There are a good many sick—in this vessel more than one in ten.

"Sanford is not here, having gone to look after the ordnance at Cairo and St. Louis, and now is gone to the latter place. I can not, therefore, deliver your messages. I, too, wish an exception could be made in his case without a dangerous and ruinous precedent. I received notice from Mr. Grimes, through Mr. Whittlesey, of the action of the Naval Committee on the nominations before it was published. I should most certainly let ———'s vanity have full swing. It will yet hang him. He only follows his master in attacks on the flotilla. We can afford to let both go unnoticed. If familiar with Sancho's 'saws,' you will remember one applicable to his case.

"*May* 23.—There is nothing new this morning. Mrs. Phelps will probably have the pleasure of seeing you in Cleveland, as she is about leaving Paducah to go to my father's in Ohio. I trust you are improving as rapidly and surely as the universal desire of the flotilla would have you. You could wish no more.

"Very respectfully and truly yours, S. L. PHELPS."

"U. S. FLAG-SHIP 'BENTON,' OFF FORT PILLOW,
May 28, 1862.

"MY DEAR SIR,—I was a good deal disappointed this morning not to have heard from you either directly or through Commodore Davis. I, however, have seen a paragraph taken from the Cleveland papers stating that you are improving in health since causes of excitement have been removed.

"I am like the host twice made glad—glad because the people manifest an appreciation of your character and services, and glad because the same people have concluded to let you get well and in a fit condition to return to us. All the gun-boats are being secured as far as possible against rams, by putting railroad iron about the bows and sterns, and slinging logs about the sides. This vessel is being secured extensively. I have had three bars of railroad iron secured between and along the fan-tails, so as to prevent cutting there, and also heavy frames inclosing rudders, and ironed. Along the casemate, where the iron is light, I have had ½-inch plate flanged and firmly bolted, to increase the strength of the angle at that vulnerable point. If we have time to secure the bows with ¾-inch plates already here, we will be able to split any boat that hits us there.

"Colonel Ellet is here now with some half-dozen rams. I am exceedingly glad that no naval officers were asked to take these same rams. They serve to count as it is; and if we can get among the rebel fleet, and by our fire prevent the use of their guns, these rams ought to be of service in sinking the rebel craft, which, on account of their being so stuffed with cotton, is a difficult thing to accomplish with shot alone. I have written this amid great confusion and many interruptions. I have been thinking how much I had reason to be thankful for in the fortune that has befallen me in this war. The success with the crazy *Conestoga*, the transfer to this fine command, with you as commander-in-chief, and now, in your temporary absence, with Commodore Davis in your place, is a series of good luck that I am fully sensible of, and, I trust, duly grateful for. Few, if any, have been so favored.

"Respectfully and very truly yours, S. L. PHELPS."

Ellet's rams, according to the writer's testimony, did effective work a few days after this at the great fight at Memphis; but the following extract from a letter, dated June 4th, is very amusing:

"Our Ram Colonel is as crazy as our friend Sturges. He has been writing absurd things to the commodore, quoting his instructions from the War Department to prove that he is not under orders of the naval officer commanding; and he proposed running the fire of the fort and attacking the rebel fleet below. In his letters to the War Department, he styles his mode of warfare as *peculiar*, and not likely to be approved of by naval officers; and that, therefore, it is not possible that he should be restrained by their authority. The War Department is cautious in replying; but, upon the whole, desires that the naval commander should not interfere, unless the operations of the Ram Colonel would greatly interfere with the regular naval operations, or imperil public interests, or to that effect. The Ram Colonel wrote that he proposed immediately to proceed against the rebel fleet, passing the fire of Fort Pillow. The commodore replied that while he did not approve of the enterprise, he would offer no opposition, and wished him all luck. Two or three days after, sure enough, the Ram Colonel got under way in a rain-squall, and started down around Craighead Point, followed by the junior rams. Head ram had not passed from our view before a fire was opened from the fort, and ram's head came around double quick, and all the rams paddled back, followed by a sharp fire from the fort, though we could not in the rain judge of how the shot fell. A few minutes after our rams had come up, two rebel rams appeared round the Point, and, as plainly as rams ever talked, said, 'Come on, Yankee rams; we are here on neutral ground ready to butt our difficulties out;' but Yankee rams said not a word. The conclusion is, we shall hear no more from our Ram Colonel about running batteries."

Paymaster Wise writes, May 25th:

"As long as you remain in Cleveland, we feel that you are yet our dear flag-officer, only away for a short time; but if you go to New York, we fear they won't let you come back."

Quartermaster-General Meigs says at the close of a business letter:

"I regret that your wound should have compelled you to leave the flotilla, built up by your exertions, and led to victory, before its work was all completed by a junction with the fleet from below; but congratulate you upon the successes you were allowed to obtain, and upon the love and admiration which you have secured from all true Americans."

Although sick and weak, he seems during his stay at Cleveland to have written much, especially in favor of the claims of certain naval officers, to obtain for them positions and commands which he thought were deserved for past faithful services. He did not forget his friends; he followed up their claims with great persistency until he had secured the prize. They knew they could depend upon his practical support in the struggle for honorable advancement, and this knit him to them with hooks of steel. One of them says:

"It is no fault of yours that I am not to be confirmed—indeed, you have labored hard for it; and if it should be so decided that we do not meet again in the flotilla, accept my thanks for past kindnesses, with the assurance that I shall always entertain the strongest possible friendship and esteem for you."

At the May session of the Connecticut Legislature, the following vote of thanks was passed:

"STATE OF CONNECTICUT GENERAL ASSEMBLY,
May Session, A.D. 1862.

"*Resolved*, That the State of Connecticut has abundant reason to be proud of her heroes in the Army and Navy of this nation; and that while history can not fail to do justice to our fallen martyrs, we, without invidious motives, do now accord to Commodore Andrew H. Foote, of the Navy, our earnest and unqualified praise for the great energy, perseverance, and patience which he has exhibited while in command of the Federal flotilla on the Western rivers; and especially for the great bravery and skill with which he has fought and won his successive battles. And most cordially do we sympathize with him while suffering from wounds received in battling for the right.

"*Resolved*, That as a testimonial of our kind regard for him, the clerks of this General Assembly be directed to prepare and transmit to him a copy of these resolutions."

The main features of the naval battle of Memphis have already been briefly mentioned; but the particulars of this combat are given in a letter of Phelps to Foote in a way that one could not give who had not been himself an actor:

"U. S. FLAG-STEAMER 'BENTON,' MEMPHIS,
June 9, 1862.

"FLAG-OFFICER A. H. FOOTE, U. S. N., commanding Flotilla, Western Waters, Cleveland, O.:

"MY DEAR SIR,—I have been most anxious to write to you since our battle on the 6th instant, but must in justice to myself confess that I have hardly known whether I have been on my head or heels since that date. I had two days and nights of hard work and anxiety before the fight took place; have had prizes—war vessels and transports—to save, send off, repair, and provide with people, to say nothing of a thousand wants of the people of Memphis to look after.

"I sent you yesterday a copy of the *Memphis Appeal*, containing a really fair statement of the fight, which was witnessed by thousands on the bluff. The rebel boats insisted on remaining before the city, notwithstanding that we were an hour under way half a mile above, giving a fair opportunity for them to come up to the attack if they intended fighting away from the city, or to drop below where we could follow and attack them. The rebels forced us to fire on them without regard to the consequences to Memphis by opening upon us. We exchanged a number of shots, when Colonel Ellet, with the *Ocean Queen* and *Monarch*, dashed down at the enemy, we at the time turning one 'slow length' around for the same purpose. The rebels were evidently disconcerted by this move; and the *Ocean Queen* failing to hit the *Beauregard*, made a pass at the *General Lovell*, cutting her through; and that vessel sunk in a few minutes, many of her crew going down with her; and she is entirely out of sight. This is all the rams did, except the confusion created by them gave us better chances at the rebel craft. The *Monarch* missed the *General Price*, and the *Beauregard*, missing the *Monarch*, cut away entirely the port-wheel and wheel-house of the *General Price*. This ended the rams' doings, as rams, on either side. The *Beauregard*, in backing out from the *General Price*, gave me a broadside shot, at close range, with a 42-pounder, and I sent a shot into her boiler, blowing her up. Some fourteen of the scalded people are on our hands. How many were killed we do not know. The vessel soon sank, and has since gone to pieces. The *Benton* then, as throughout the action, was considerably in advance of the other vessels, seemingly the most speedy of them all, and pursued the now retreating rebels with an accuracy of fire and an execution really terrible. The *Jeff. Thompson* was disabled and set on fire by shells, and was destroyed in a splendid explosion. The *Sumter* was soon disabled, and then the *Bragg*—which vessel had been fired by one of our rifled shot bursting in her cotton protection. The *Little Rebel* received a shot in the boiler about the same time the *Beauregard* did, and her fate was sealed. Mr. Bishop has command of the *General Bragg*, Mr. Erben of the *Sumter*, and Mr. Hoel will have the *Little Rebel*. The *General Van Dorn* escaped, but was badly injured. If the rams had done their duty, she would have been captured also; but after the first dash we saw no more of them. Colonel Ellet was wounded by a pistol-shot in the leg, and his vessel was disabled. His dash was bold and well executed. There was some firing of small-arms from the woods, and at the same time cheers from the banks. This is a destruction of their fleet which there is no dodging. Fifteen thousand people witnessed it. I carried the demand for the surrender of the city to the mayor, and was saluted by a number of ladies; and passed through the immense crowd without molestation, or evidence of an exasperated or bitterly hating people, and saw no scowling women. The city is quiet, and things go on smoothly. I have been much distressed to hear of your continued ill-health. I had hoped that by this time you would have been entirely recovered and ready to return to your fleet; but I fear this is as remote in prospect as at any time heretofore. I have not heard from you since about the 27th ultimo. Do let me hear as frequently as you can. You must know that my anxiety to hear of your condition is very great, being bound to you alike by personal attachment and a grateful sense of continued kindness and assistance. S. L. PHELPS."

When we think that the *Benton*, so powerful in fight, had been prepared by Commodore Foote especially for his own flag-steamer, we can not but imagine that these letters, recounting her force and success, must have gone home to the heart of the sick man laid aside almost hopelessly; while at the same time he rejoiced at his fleet's efficiency, thus making its way conqueringly down the river.

A letter from Captain Paymaster Wise brings into view another side of the flotilla—its needful but quiet hospital work:

"OFFICE OF THE NAVAL DÉPÔT, CAIRO, *June* 12, 1862.

"MY DEAR COMMODORE,—Your letter of May 30, and your note, by Mr. Henriques, of the 5th of June, I duly received. We all regret that you do not improve more rapidly, and think that a little mountain air would help you.

"Mr. Henriques is here, and Paymaster Dunn and myself will do all we can to effect a speedy and proper settlement of his affairs. Mr. Henriques is improving in health. I will see that his pay accords with your wishes.

"I wish that you could see our hospital-boat, the *Red Rover*, with all her comforts for the sick and disabled seamen. She is decided to be the most complete thing of the kind that ever floated, and is every way a success. The Western Sanitary Association gave us in cost of articles $3500. The ice-box of the steamer holds three hundred tons; she has bath-rooms, laundry, elevator for the sick from the lower to the upper deck, amputating-room, nine different water arrangements, gauze blinds to the windows to keep the cinders and smoke from annoying the sick, two separate kitchens, for sick and well, and a regular corps of nurses.

"We think that the gun-boats have nearly finished their work, and that a different kind will be required for the future. The old boats will be used as floating-batteries, to be stationed at New Orleans, Vicksburg, Memphis, and Island No. Ten. Fast boats, with light, powerful armaments, will act as river police and keep the river open. I see the Act transferring the flotilla to the Navy has passed the House of Representatives, and will no doubt pass the Senate. This change will be for the better.

"Captain Pennock is as busy as usual. Winslow has gone down the river to take command of the *Cincinnati*. Sanford is now in Cairo. Porter is getting the *Essex* ready, and if she do not draw too much water, she will be a very efficient vessel. I send you Porter's official seal.

"Hoping soon to hear good accounts of you, and again to see you and thank you for all your kindness to me,

"I am respectfully and truly yours, GEORGE D. WISE."

Commodore Foote did not continue to grow stronger; on the contrary, he became so reduced that, in the language of another, "he was but a shadow of himself," and much of the time he was forced to keep his bed. His physicians urged the entire giving up of care in order to save his life; and at length, after submitting to the examination of a surgical board, he sent the following letter to the Secretary of the Navy:

"CLEVELAND, *June* 13, 1862.

"SIR,—It becomes my unpleasant duty to inform the Department that my health, in the estimation of the best medical advice of this city, is such as would imperil my efficiency were I to resume my duties on the Mississippi River for two or three months to come.

"Under these circumstances, I submit to the decision of the Department whether I shall return immediately to my duty in the flotilla, or receive a three-months' leave of absence, or even be detached altogether from my command, for the purpose of trying the effects of salt air, as recommended, with the hope of an early restoration to health.

"I am aware that, while there seems to be little or no prospect of further fighting on the Western rivers, which may now be said to be cleared of their powerful rebel batteries and gun-boats, the reorganizing, arranging, and distributing of the flotilla to protect the peaceful commerce of the rivers against a guerrilla warfare, superadded to the great difficulties incident to the settling of accounts, require an officer of experience; yet may I not, without detriment to the service or to my professional standing, be permitted to have the necessary time to recuperate my exhausted health?

"If it will not be considered premature, I wish further to remark that when this rebellion is crushed, and a squadron is fitted out to enforce the new treaty for the suppression of the African slave-trade, I should be pleased to have command; but so long as the rebellion continues, it will be my highest ambition to be actively employed in aiding its suppression.

"Inclosed is the certificate of my attending physicians.

"I have the honor to be, very respectfully, your obedient servant,

"A. H. FOOTE, Flag-Officer.

"The Hon. Gideon Welles."

The report of the physicians referred to in the above was as follows:

"The undersigned, having been in professional attendance on Commodore A. H. Foote during his visit to this city, deem it due to him to say that, in our opinion, he will not be able to return to active service for some three or four months without seriously jeoparding his health. The inflammation following his wound, his inability to take exercise except on crutches, and the debilitating effects of a diarrhœa and fever, have reduced his strength and flesh to a great degree. The wound evidently was the predisposing cause, superinducing the attack of diarrhœa and hemorrhoids—sequents of an enlarged liver and malarious influences.

"Although in some respects his symptoms are more favorable, he still continues much emaciated, having left his bed but a few times for the past fortnight. We therefore unite in the opinion that a change of position to the sea-coast would materially expedite his recovery.

"(Signed) THOMAS L. RODMAN, M.D.
E. CUSHING, M.D.

"Cleveland, O., *June*, 1862."

Flag-Officer Foote was, therefore, at his own request, detached from his command of the Western flotilla on the 17th of June, 1862. The following note, from the Secretary of the Navy, came soon after:

"WASHINGTON, *June* 17, 1862.

"MY DEAR SIR,—I can not be satisfied with a mere formal official letter detaching you from the flotilla, where you have rendered such great service to the Department and the country, without expressing in a more earnest and friendly manner my appreciation of your labors and achievements. The country feels and acknowledges its indebtedness to you; but few know, as I do, the difficulties you have been compelled to encounter and overcome, in first creating the flotilla, and then carrying it into a series of successful actions, which have contributed so largely to the suppression of the rebellion throughout the Southwest.

"It was with some reluctance that I gave the orders which carried you to the field where you have acquired so great and just renown; for, aware of some of the embarrassments by which you would be tried, I saw also that the Army failed to estimate the necessity and value of the naval branch of operations on the Western rivers. Some of these matters we talked over before you left; but I did not express to you all the discouragements that appeared to me then, and which you have so well surmounted. The history of these matters is yet to be written, for only the results are now patent to the country.

"I have watched and participated in every movement that has been made, uninfluenced, I believe, by censure or complaint or denunciation from the thoughtless and the designing, which has been inflicted on the Department from the commencement of hostilities; and every victory obtained and advance made cheered my heart scarcely less than your own.

"Most sincerely do I regret the necessity which compels you to seek rest, and ask to be detached from that command which you have so much honored; but I am consoled with the belief that you will be able in a brief period, with vigor and renewed health, to again elevate your flag and render additional service.

"I shall bear in mind your request; and, remembering our associations in boyhood, be happy, as a friend and an officer, to exhibit at all times my confidence and abiding friendship.

"Please make my respects to your brother; and wishing you speedy restoration to health and to active duty,

"I remain very truly and sincerely your friend,

"GIDEON WELLES.

"Flag-Officer A. H. Foote, Cleveland."

CHAPTER XXV.

CORRESPONDENCE.—RETURN TO THE EAST.—VOTE OF THANKS BY CONGRESS.

Commodore Foote remained until the 23d of June in Cleveland, when he left that place with his wife for the East, and arrived at their home in New Haven on the 25th. Their quiet departure from Cleveland and their arrival in New Haven, as well as their rapid transit, though meant to escape popular notice, were accompanied by every mark of public respect. While still in Cleveland, he is thus spoken of by a visitor who saw him:

"The commodore was on his crutches, but he hastened across the hall and gave us a cordial greeting. His fine, manly countenance and bright black eyes are lighted up with genius and intelligence; his soul glows with patriotic ardor, and he longs to return to his command. He thinks he will be able soon to do so, but he must go on his crutches. The quietness of his manner while telling us how he was wounded at Fort Donelson I can not convey; but his story was something like this: 'The shells were flying about pretty thick, and I stepped into the pilot-house to see that the boat was kept in position. Just then a shell came in and killed one of the men at the wheel; the other man seemed to lose his presence of mind, and I seized the wheel to keep her right; but it was not till some time after that I discovered that I was seriously hurt."

Since Admiral Foote's personal appearance is alluded to in the above, and as the photograph from which the frontispiece was drawn was taken about this time, this seems a good place to speak a word concerning it. His countenance was indeed a fine one: his forehead was broad and full, and his large, bright black eyes, restless and piercing, took in all things at a glance; his firm-shut mouth had a grip and strength that showed the invincible will of the man. His stature was of medium size, but square-built and compact. He was always very neatly dressed, carrying his professional notions in this respect to a nicety. He had a sailor-like alertness of step, and his motions were quick and nervous; yet his address was exceedingly suave and gentle. He gave the impression of a man of active brain and of great energy, though held well in restraint. At one time he had a hobby that he had weak eyes, and he wore large green goggles, giving his naval friends much amusement. He was, in fact, quite apt to ride hobbies; and these "charming foibles," as one of his friends calls them, made him a most fascinating man to all who knew him and loved him.

His correspondence with his subordinate officers, especially with Lieutenant-Commander Phelps, continued to be frequent and of much general interest, as containing details of military matters not found in historical works. We select a few letters:

"U. S. FLAG-STEAMER 'BENTON,' MEMPHIS, *June* 17, 1862.

"FLAG-OFFICER FOOTE, U. S. N.:

"MY DEAR SIR,—It has occurred to me that you would be interested in knowing what we found Fort Pillow to be on close examination. It would be much more proper to say that this examination was simply a hurried glance at the main features. The commodore directed me to report on 'an hour's examination.' We were there but a short time. I will copy my report from the files of the Department: 'The outer line of intrenchments, flanking upon Coal Creek at the point some six hundred yards above the upper river battery, ascends the bluff in an irregular zigzag to a prominent and narrow ridge, lying between the River Hatchie and the Mississippi, whence the lines trend away, at a sharp angle, along the ridge in the direction of Fulton, and flank upon the bluffs on the Mississippi above that landing, making a circuit of from four to five miles. These lines consist of a heavy embankment, planked upon the inner face, with a dry ditch of an average of about eight feet depth and width.

Considerable numbers of pieces of artillery had once been mounted along this extended line. An abatis of fallen timber, of six hundred yards in width, is cut throughout the entire length. There is an inner line of works of similar construction, though not of one unbroken circuit, as in the case of the outer line; and it is estimated that the total length of the intrenchments is ten miles. The entire land embraced within the circuit of these works is exceedingly rough and broken—sharp ridges, deep gorges and valleys, with small springs and rivers that traverse it in all directions; while a greater part of the surface is covered with a heavy forest growth. There are prominent batteries along the inner line of defense, from which artillery swept the outer works; while intrenchments and rifle-pits were disposed to enfilade and command the approaches offered by the broken surface. Two crescent batteries are also erected near the summit of the river bluffs to assist in the landward defenses.

"'The water-batteries are constructed at the base of the bluff, in the face of it, and in the gorges by which it is broken. The water-battery proper consisted of ten guns, but was much injured by the late flood. A heavy columbiad was mounted on a casemated work, constructed in a ravine above the level of the ten-gun battery. This work was destroyed by fire. To the left and higher up is a sunken battery of six heavy guns. Still higher up, occupying another ravine, is a 10-inch columbiad, sweeping over a great arc. Below the water-battery on the river, and constructed by heavy excavations from the bluff at some elevation, is a bastioned work of six heavy guns in front, and several flanking. In this is a 13-inch mortar, bursted. Still higher up the bluffs are other columbiads, mounted mostly in works across ravines, and in batteries of one and two guns. Single guns (32-pounders) are also placed in position along the bluff as far as Fulton, three miles below the fort.

"'These works are constructed and disposed with great skill and with vast labor; but a fatal mistake had been made in the depression that could be given the guns in all save the water-battery, since in a moderate stage of the river our boats could have hugged the shore and passed under their fire.

"'I will here mention that Colonel Fitch, commanding the Forty-sixth Indiana Regiment, had constructed a road through swamps on the upper side of Coal Creek, where no such attempt seems to have been anticipated; and had made preparations for crossing the creek, and entering the works within the lines while the fleet should open fire in front. From thence he could easily have captured, by a rear attack, the crescent battery on the bluff above; after which the different river batteries would have been entirely exposed to his riflemen firing from above and in rear. The movement was made in accordance with this plan, adopted and prepared several days in advance; but the rebels had fled from the works during the night, burning every thing in their power.'

"You will acknowledge that this is evidently the result of a very imperfect examination. When I went on shore I did not understand that I was expected to make any report whatever. The work is of immense strength, and a place from which gun-boats would find it difficult to dislodge troops.

"Captain Kilty you know has gone to White River with the *Mound City*, *St. Louis*, *Lexington*, and *Conestoga.* Yesterday he sent up a splendid steamer as a prize. The rebels are filling the river with rafts, trees, etc., to obstruct navigation.

"To-day we have reports that the rebel ram and gun-boat *Arkansas*, of which we heard so much, sailed down the Yazoo on Sunday last, and is expected to destroy the entire Yankee fleet. The rebels boast that she is another *Merrimack.* We hear nothing from the fleet below Vicksburg.

"I suspect they find trouble in the navigation, and no doubt will be obliged to proceed down to that point. When will these craft get back? the distance is now four hundred miles!

"I have been very busy with prizes, and the like. We now have the *De Soto*, *Kentucky*, and *Victoria* for mail-boats. The *Hill* is a spare boat. We hear that a prize agent is to be sent out. I am encouraged to think that we may still see you out here again by the accounts given us by two gentlemen from Cincinnati who saw you very recently in Cleveland. As much as we like Commodore Davis, we all look to you as the natural and rightful head. It would give so much pleasure to see you back in the health you were enjoying at Fort Henry! Captain Walke desired me this evening to remember him to you very warmly; and the commodore charges me to give 'his love' to you.

"Yours respectfully and most truly, S. L. PHELPS."

"CAIRO, *June* 21, 1862.

"MY DEAR FLAG-OFFICER AND FRIEND,—Your kind letter of the 15th was received, and ought to have been replied to immediately, but I had not the energy to undertake letter-writing. I have not been at all well for over two months—the 'Mississippi River disease' having clung to me with great fondness. As usual, I devote all the energy I possess in my particular duties. I hear that you do not contemplate returning to take command again of the 'Foote Flotilla'—is this so? The news comes in a questionable shape, through some indefatigable newspaper reporter or other. I regret that you were not at the taking of Memphis; it would have been your province to be there; but you have done enough to let the balance go to some one else. I hope we may see you again among us, if it be for never so brief a period. I was not satisfied with your leave-taking of the fleet. Would you not come back and do it, at any rate, more formally and distinctly—presuming, of course, that you purpose giving up the command? Very sad news reached us last night. The *Mound City* received a shot through her steam-drum, up the White River, on the 16th, and lost about one hundred and twenty men and officers. Dear old Kilty was badly scalded about the face and hands. All the engineers were killed; and the only officers saved were Kilty, Dominy, and a purser's steward, Brown. Master-mate Brown's and Paymaster Gunn's bodies were brought up last night—the last now lies near me at the ordnance store-room door. The rebels shot our poor boys when in the water; and fired a large shot at a boat of the *Conestoga* that was filled with the scalded, picked up. Several were killed. This was an inhuman act, not to be forgotten by any man in the fleet. The men on board the gun-boats swore vengeance. Colonel Fitch took the batteries that exploded the steam-drum of the *Mound City* at the point of the bayonet, killing about a hundred and twenty out of a hundred and fifty rebels. Fry—formerly of the Navy—who commanded the rebels, was wounded and made prisoner. He, it is said, gave orders to shoot the men in the water. When he was being carried down to the *Conestoga's* boat, he said, 'I don't wish to be touched by a private.' No sooner said than a soldier drew out his revolver, aimed and fired; his arm was struck up just in time to save Fry's life. He is now on board the *Conestoga*. The people of Memphis are becoming reconciled to things as they are. There are not so many nostrils offended by the presence of the Yankees as there were. Coffee, tea, and edibles are coming into use there. This seems to have a pleasant effect. Pennock is quite sick, but nothing serious. Mrs. Wise and Mrs. Pennock left for New York last Monday morning. We miss their faces at our table. We keep you, my dear commodore, always in our remembrance.

"Yours, sincerely and cordially, J. P. SANFORD."

Z

"U. S. Flag-Steamer 'Benton,' Memphis, *June* 23, 1862.

"Flag-Officer A. H. Foote, U. S. N.:

"My dear Sir,—I have been influenced to-day with varied feelings by the arrival of an appointment as flag-officer for Commodore Davis. I had foreseen that the Department would relieve you upon the certificate of 'necessity,' because you would give yourself no rest, but let an uneasy mind and an anxious heart prey upon your feeble strength. Once free of all care or thought of responsibility, and with no hope deferred as to when you would return to the command, we may hope that you will mend apace. I have feared this hope might not be realized, yet now I look forward with confidence. There can be no contradiction in saying that, while I esteem it great good fortune to be associated as I am with so superior an officer as the commodore, and one too whom I so much like, I yet feel a disappointment, that there is no shaking off, in the breaking up of relations formed in a fullness of purpose and cemented by kindness. We all probably indulge the imagination in pictures of what is to come, and mark out a future associated with the friends about us. I have done this in this war with an intensity the greater because of its stern realities, and the entire manner in which the sense of duty had taken possession of my mind. When you induced me to withdraw that application, I did it designing to return to my duty in these waters with still greater earnestness of purpose; but the whole future was to be inseparably connected with you. Whatever I might hope the flotilla would accomplish, it was with you as leader. All we have passed through since you left us has not sufficed to turn my thoughts from the plans and wishes for the future confidently built upon months since. It does not yet seem natural that some one else should appear as chief actor in the scene. I have more reason than all others combined to feel your absence, and I have more acts of benefit and kindness to remember and cherish than they; and I too have more reason to feel grateful for the foresight and solicitude that so soon led you to apply for and secure Commodore Davis for your relief. I have fallen upon a strange strain, terribly egotistic, in which I shall fail to make myself understood. A few words would have told all better.

"The hospital-boat was dispatched from here last evening to get the poor sufferers from the *Mound City* to more comfortable quarters. That has been the most terrible event known in these waters. No imagination can picture to itself the condition of those burned, scalded, and wounded who still live. It is the most piteous spectacle human suffering could present. Poor Kilty was, they said, doing well; but he suffers terribly. His heart is as tender as a woman's. Scarcely any of them are recognizable. Dr. Jones is more prostrate than Captain Kilty, and less likely to survive. Mr. Dominy, first master, happened to be on deck, and escaped. One engineer, the carpenter, and one other officer are still alive, but most sadly burned. One hundred and twelve have died thus far. The Sisters of Charity, who came down at once, advised all being sent to the Mound City Hospital, which they represent now as very perfect for its purposes. The *Cincinnati* is in White River with the *St. Louis* and *Lexington*. A crew is here for the *Mound City*, and will be sent down to-morrow. The White River has fallen so much that our vessels are obliged to leave it. I presume we will move down the river soon, as this place may be considered safe. General Grant arrived here last evening, and takes command. Our troops are not very strong here, but will soon be increased. Colonel Webster is military commandant at Memphis (local). The place has rapidly improved since our arrival. There is one thing very evident—that it was unfortunate for the rebel cause that the gun-boats should have chosen this spot for their fighting ground. There were too many witnesses. Captain Dove flourishes here. Walke is a perfect ship-keeper. There is a prospect that the *Eastport* will be ready in 'one month.' I flatter myself that I have arranged our quarters on board of her so as to promise the greatest amount of comfort. The *Bragg* has been fitted up with extra accommodations for the flag-officer in case of need. The *Price* will be repaired—is now in Cairo—so that we shall have to thank the rebels for three rams, to say nothing of the *Little Rebel*. I will now arrange with Commodore Davis about the mess affairs, and will have the ration matters settled, so as to send to you the proper amount. Your kind proposition, so far as regards myself—my share—is so like you that I recognize the same spirit of increasing kindness. The mortars I will send to New Haven by express. Is there any thing else here? I do trust this will find you greatly improved.

"Respectfully and very truly yours, S. L. PHELPS."

"WASHINGTON, *June* 24, 1862.

"MY DEAR SIR,—I regret that through any inadvertence or informality you should have suffered a moment's uneasiness. On receiving your letter proposing to relinquish your command, I gave the matter full consideration; and while I deeply regretted the necessity, I came to the conclusion that you had acted wisely, and that it was due to you and to the service that you should be relieved from all care until your system had recovered its vigor. When this decision was reached, the mere routine letters were prepared and sent; but when I reached home that evening, and had a moment to myself, I felt it right to express my feelings and opinions in a free and less formal manner in regard to the great service you had rendered. This I followed up with an additional line the next morning.

"I might, perhaps, have embodied some of the views and thoughts that naturally presented themselves in my official letter, but I think it better as it is. The history of events that have occurred during your active command on the Mississippi and its tributaries is yet to be written; and if my life and health are spared to a season of greater leisure, I hope I may be able to do yourself and others justice. Should it not survive, the hasty notes I have addressed to you will be testimony from one who, better than any one else perhaps, knows of the difficulties and embarrassments which beset you; and there were some connected with the anomalous organization of the flotilla that (even) you can hardly be aware of. Every step I have watched with inexpressible solicitude; for I was, of course, held accountable for your success. Had you made a false step, or been unfortunate, the censorious would have held me responsible for your acts. I was willing to assume that responsibility, and have not been disappointed.

"I believe the public justly appreciate your labors and sufferings, and will be ready to manifest it. They should; for all honor to the men who peril their lives for their country. Those of us who labor in another sphere must be content to witness the applause bestowed on those whom we have had the good fortune or sagacity to select, for it reflects credit on ourselves. I have been very proud of your achievements in every respect.

"*27th.*—I was interrupted the other evening, and meeting your brother the following morning, I had discarded my letter; but finding it on my table this evening, I conclude to send it.

"I was extremely glad to meet your brother, and to hear from him that you are so rapidly improving. We shall, I trust, have the pleasure of seeing you here before a great while, but first take care of your health; get that fully re-established and your wound well. There is a good deal yet to be done, I apprehend, before this causeless and wicked rebellion is suppressed. Certainly our Navy has great labor in future, and its best men will be required to give it efficiency and character. It is evident from what has transpired on our Western waters, that the Navy, as a means of national unity and strength, has an importance that few had anticipated before these domestic troubles developed its capabilities. We all know its value and necessity for exterior purposes, but were not aware of its internal strength in sustaining the government. Our armies in the West would have been comparatively powerless without the gun-boats, and no future conspiracy can make such formidable headway, if, availing ourselves of the wisdom derived from experience, we shall be prepared with a proper naval armament on the interior waters.

"I trust it will benefit you to get home and visit old scenes, breathe the natal air, and meet early friends. You will have more leisure than myself, and must write me freely and without reserve, making such suggestions and giving such advice as your experience and observation authorize, and as you believe will be valuable.

"Hoping we may see you before a great while, and glad to learn that your health continues to improve, I am very truly and sincerely yours,

"GIDEON WELLES."

"WASHINGTON, *July* 4, 1862.

"MY DEAR SIR,—Congress has just passed a bill for reorganizing the Navy Department. You will have seen it perhaps; but if not, you will, from your familiarity with the service, understand its general provisions. I am desirous of gathering here as our Board of Admiralty the very best men that we have. The Chiefs of Bureaus must constitute the advisory and suggestive counselors of the Department. Our country is to be one of the great maritime powers of the world, and must have a Navy commensurate with its strength and position as a nation. This domestic war and attending events are creating a revolution in many respects in our Navy, and it becomes important that we take a new departure. The bill alluded to is a pioneer measure, and if we can get the Department properly officered and manned, we shall make a successful beginning.

"I doubt if you would render more valuable service to the country elsewhere than in Washington at this juncture, or perhaps at any period. The Bureau of Equipment and Recruiting is one requiring administrative ability, and must necessarily be one of the most important, if not the most important, pillars of the Department and the service.

"Are you disposed to take this position, and give us your talents and experience in the creation and government of a Navy that shall be worthy of the country? Take the matter into consideration, and write me as soon as you conveniently can on the subject.

"The hard fighting at Richmond has not given us all we wished. The loss on both sides has been very severe.

"Hoping to hear from you soon, I am very truly your friend,

"GIDEON WELLES.

"Commodore Foote, New Haven, Conn."

"WASHINGTON, *July* 5, 1862.

"MY DEAR FOOTE,—I have yours of the 2d instant. I have no time to write. I am sad at our reverse at Richmond. The gun-boat came to the rescue, after all. I fear if we do not capture Richmond in twenty days, we shall have more trouble than we bargained for or expected.

"The Secretary has invited you to the Bureau of Equipment. I hope you will take it—but you can have any thing you want. How Congress cut at the Navy pay, while nothing is said of the respect the Army receives over the Navy. I am getting old and useless, besides am troubled with vertigo. Regards to madam.

"Yours as always, in haste, JOSEPH SMITH."

"U. S. STEAMER 'BENTON,' NEAR VICKSBURG,
July 6, 1862.

"FLAG-OFFICER A. H. FOOTE, U. S. N., New Haven, Conn.:

"MY DEAR SIR,—Now that the 'Line Bill' has passed at least one of the Houses of Congress, I may hope soon to escape the annoyance of writing so awkward a title before your name.

"I have missed you so much in this meeting of the two fleets, an event so strange in all its historical bearings. Though not here, your works are here to represent you. The *Benton*, *Cincinnati*, *Louisville*, and *Carondelet*, with the provision and ordnance boats and six mortar-boats, left Memphis on the 29th, arriving here on the 1st inst. The *Conestoga* has since come down from White River. This is our force. At this point, some five or six miles above Vicksburg, we found Flag-Officer Farragut's fleet, which had run the blockade some three days before—or, rather, eight vessels of his fleet—his flag flying on board the *Hartford*. You may suppose there was great cheering at the 'meeting.' The lower fleet has vessels of the class of the *Richmond*, *Iroquois*, and *Winona*, all beautiful specimens of their class. How great the contrast of the two forces! We found the officers discouraged about the place they had passed, and all of the opinion that nothing could be done except with the aid of a land force. The batteries are on bluffs, much scattered, and covered by a large army. These bluffs do not rise abruptly, but with a slope such that the batteries, placed at some distance from the river, sweep the slope and river shores. The fleet had suffered considerable loss, and had inflicted little or no injury; and the question is asked, 'For what purpose did the fleet come above the batteries?' The flotilla already controlled the river above. I shall surprise you very much by telling you that the 'New Orleans fleet' is 'at sixes and sevens.' Farragut's system seems to be embraced in the order to Captain Preble: 'Follow the *Kennebec*, and fire at any thing you see.' His vessels can not attack down stream any better than ours, and can not fire ahead; they must, therefore, again run the gauntlet, and, turning below, attack again batteries made stronger than when the fleet came up. There is a great deal of gossip among the officers. Captain Craven has differed with the flag-officer, and, after failing to get by the batteries the other day, has demanded leave, and has actually gone home. There are criminations and recriminations. I am happy to inform you that our flotilla manifests its lessons under your hands, and has no outside gossip in return for the abundance offered by the lower fleet. It is presumed that the fleet will not linger here, but will run back to below the batteries very soon. One thousand negroes are working hard upon a canal across the point here (one and a quarter miles long), which, if successful, will leave Vicksburg some four or five miles from the river. Commodore Porter is shelling the batteries and town from below, and Maynadier from above. We are soon to go up the Yazoo to destroy the *Arkansas* and clear the river out. It is expected that a large land force will reach here from above. The *Lexington* is in White River. Colonel Fitch has some 3000 or 4000 men, but will have to retire, the river being too low for navigation. Nothing of the *Essex* yet. The *Eastport* will be ready *in time*—if enough be given. The *Sumter* is on the way down, and the *Bragg* leaves Cairo to-day. The *St. Louis* and *Mound City* are at Memphis, and the *Cairo* at Fort Pillow. The *Pittsburg* is at Cairo for repairs. Commodore Davis desires me to give you his best love, and to say that he gladly accepts your proposition about the mess. I have some ration-money belonging to you; as soon as it is settled with Henriques, I will forward it to you. I have written at length, but I hope not to tire you. I am most anxious to hear from you, and learn how the change has effected you, and how your recovery progresses, as are all in the flotilla.

"Respectfully and most sincerely yours,

"S. L. Phelps."

We see by this letter that there can be anger in celestial minds, and that our naval heroes, like those of the Homeric fleet, had their little bickerings and rivalries among themselves; but these letters from Foote's officers, and those that follow, prove how deep a hold their late commander had of their affections. They show how kind-hearted and great-hearted was the man who could call forth such expressions. He still led them in spirit; they still looked to him for encouragement and inspiration. There is a genuine ring of the heart in these letters; they are not servile flatteries of one who no longer controlled them, or from whom they expected to gain any thing. They came from real esteem and love, and from the grateful memory of long-continued kindness and friendship. It is not often that a military leader has such a profound *personal* relationship to those under him, which shows something more than a confidence in his ability or an admiration of his courage—it shows the possession in him of high moral qualities. We will give at this time but one other brief extract from the letters of his officers—from the brave Captain Gwin, who soon after was killed in a naval combat on the Mississippi:

"You may rest assured that the laurels won by the flotilla under your command will never be tarnished."

Those who saw Commodore Foote when he first returned from the West were struck by the excessive pallor of his face, the unnatural brilliancy of his eyes, and the sternness of his expression. It seemed as if he had passed through a fiery ordeal, and had not yet escaped the sense of its tremendous pressure. He had come home with a work unfulfilled. He had come with a prophet's burden on him to arouse the country to greater exertions for its salvation. While cheerful and gentle, and courteous far beyond his strength in seeing and entertaining his friends, it was evident that his mind was preoccupied with a great purpose; and this, combined with his ill-health and constant suffering from his wound, produced a high-strung state of mind and body, which both awed and saddened those who knew and loved him best.

Public invitations, honors, and ovations began to pour in upon him, some of which will be noticed in the following chapter; but he declined most of them, or those of them which did not have a direct bearing upon popular sentiment, and the stirring up of the public mind to more devoted love of the Union and to greater sacrifices in carrying on the war.

In the beginning of July the President sent to the Senate and House of Representatives the following recommendation:

"I most cordially recommend that Captain Andrew H. Foote, of the U. S. Navy, receive a vote of thanks of Congress for his eminent services in organizing the flotilla on the Western waters, and for his gallantry at Fort Henry, Fort Donelson, Island No. Ten, and at various other places, while in command of the naval forces, embracing a period of nearly ten months. ABRAHAM LINCOLN.

"Washington, July 1, 1862."

This was acted upon in the following resolution:

"*Resolved by the Senate and House of Representatives of the United States of America, in Congress assembled,* That the thanks of Congress be, and the same are hereby tendered to Captain Andrew H. Foote, of the United States Navy, for his eminent services and gallantry at Fort Henry, Fort Donelson, and Island No. Ten, while in command of the naval forces of the United States.

"SEC. 2. *And be it further resolved,* That the President of the United States be, and he is hereby requested to transmit a certified copy of the foregoing resolution to Captain Foote.

"Approved July 16, 1862."

CHAPTER XXVI.

APPOINTED CHIEF OF BUREAU OF EQUIPMENT AND RECRUITING.—SPEECHES AND LETTERS AT ENLISTMENT MEETINGS.—CORRESPONDENCE.—ALUMNI MEETING AT YALE COLLEGE.—APPOINTED REAR-ADMIRAL.

On the 22d of July Commodore Foote was made Chief of the "Bureau of Equipment and Recruiting;" but he did not go at once to his post in Washington. His physical system was in a totally unstrung and wretched state, and he hoped by good nursing at home to be brought into a better condition for public service. The government, as will be seen by the following letter, was, under the circumstances, willing to wait for him:

"Washington, *July* 24, 1862.

"My dear Sir,—I have yours of the 22d, and am glad to learn that you are so rapidly improving. Under the circumstances, I should advise that you should remain until the time specified by you—the 6th of August. We should be glad to have you here, but there is no sufficient reason to jeopard or retard your permanent cure. Until you come, the Construction Bureau will discharge the duties of Equipment as heretofore, and we will attend to Recruiting in the Department proper; so that you can remain satisfied and undisturbed. I shall be glad to have your counsel and advice on many matters, for concentrated wisdom and the results of many good minds strengthen measures and insure good action.

"How effective light-draft boats, which can not carry heavy armament, may be on the Western rivers, in low stages of the water and the banks high, is a question. They can do some service doubtless; but more, I apprehend, would be expected than they could perform. Instead of being incidental to land operations, the Navy is, from events, considered primary and indispensable to Army operations. They tell us the Navy took New Orleans; why can it not take Richmond? It overcame obstructions on the Mississippi; why can it not overcome them on James River? Having done more than was expected, it is now expected we will do impossibilities.

"But to revert to the object of this letter. It is best that you should take your own time to come on. I know you will do it at such time as you are satisfied it will be best for yourself and the service.

"Very respectfully, GIDEON WELLES."

But our wearied veteran was not suffered to enjoy perfect rest even at home. It was a time of uncommon excitement, uncertainty, and despondency in war matters. The cry was "On to Richmond;" but the Union armies seemed to advance no nearer to Richmond than they had done months before. Vast preparations and expectations had been bitterly foiled. Great numbers of troops were needed to fill up the voids made by sickness and battles in our hosts. Immense war-meetings were organized in all our large cities, and every means was taken to arouse popular enthusiasm and to swell enlistment. At one of these great enlistment meetings, called on the evening of the 8th of July, in New Haven, Commodore Foote presided. In the newspaper account of this meeting the presiding officer is thus spoken of:

"The meeting in Music Hall last evening, called by a number of prominent citizens, to take into consideration the subject of raising the Connecticut quota of the troops called for by the President, was fully attended and very enthusiastic. Commodore A. H. Foote, as before announced, presided. His entrance upon the stage was the signal for prolonged and vociferous cheering. The meeting was called to order by N. D. Sperry, who proposed three cheers for the gallant commodore of the Western waters, which were given with a will.

"Commodore Foote briefly addressed the audience. He was pleased to see so many ladies present. It was an encouraging sign. He felt diffident in attempting to preside at so large an assembly. His life had been mostly upon the water, and his speaking had been confined to giving a few peremptory orders. He spoke in complimentary terms of Governor Buckingham, who sat near him. He spoke in terms of highest praise of Secretary Welles. Connecticut was honored by such a son. He referred to Commodore Gregory, who regretted that he could not be here to-night — his duty in superintending some monitors, that will give the English, French, and every body else who may have the temerity to interfere with us, a warm reception, calling him away from the city. The commodore concluded his remarks with an expression of his belief in the justice of the cause of the Union, and his firm reliance upon divine Providence for ultimate success."

Earnest and patriotic speeches were made by Governor Buckingham and others, and at the close the following resolution was passed:

"*Resolved*, That the thanks of this meeting are due, and are hereby most heartily tendered to our presiding officer, Commodore Foote—not only for his dignified and courteous demeanor this evening, but also for the invaluable services which he has rendered to our country."

In a day or two after, a similar war-meeting was held in Hartford, during which the president of the evening read, amid great applause, this letter:

"New Haven, *July* 9, 1862.

"My dear Sir,—Your kind and complimentary note of invitation, in behalf of the committee, to attend a meeting in the city of Hartford to-morrow evening for the purpose of encouraging enlistments, has been received.

"In view of the condition of the country, requiring immediate reinforcements to the Army of the Potomac to secure the possession of Richmond, the great stronghold of the rebels, I would, under other circumstances, most joyfully be with you, and add my mite toward forwarding the grand object of your meeting; but having been forced away from my command on the Mississippi, on the eve of consummating its grand object—of clearing the Western rivers of all rebel obstructions—in consequence of a wound received at Fort Donelson; and suffering to-day from the effects of presiding at the large, enthusiastic meeting here last evening, render it my duty to decline your kind invitation. But, although necessarily absent, I shall be with you in sympathy; and in another field I hope soon, in action, to do my part, as I hope and beg that every citizen will also do his, either in person or by finding a substitute, toward speedily and forever crushing this wicked, causeless rebellion.

Let the ladies urge the young men to the field by their persuasive influence; or, if necessary to secure the quota assigned our state, let them decline the attentions of young gentlemen until they shall go and return from the field of battle—having vindicated the honor of our flag, and contributed their part toward transmitting to posterity the rich legacy of that free government which our fathers have bequeathed to us at the sacrifice of much of their best blood and treasure.

"We ask nothing for the Navy, which, under the efficient administration of Secretary Welles, of whom Hartford, the State of Connecticut, and the nation may justly be proud, is ready to do its part in the future, as it has done it in the past, toward vindicating our flag and sustaining the supremacy of the laws. And shall we now, after so many glorious victories, suffer an ignominious defeat for want of a timely reinforcement to the Army? No! we spurn the thought. We will furnish the gallant McClellan with men; and, patriots of Connecticut, let us rush to the rescue, and the God of Battles will continue to crown our arms with victory—enabling us to sustain our proud position, against enemies internal and external, as one of the most powerful nations of the earth.

"I am respectfully and very truly yours, A. H. Foote.

"Hon. William J. Hamersley, Mayor of Hartford."

We will not mention other meetings, which were characteristic of the times, and in which the letters of the fighting commodore—whatever may be thought of them in other respects—were "weighty"—were full of spirit and fire, and stirred the country like the blast of a trumpet.

In the mean time letters from the West, detailing in full the operations of the flotilla, continued to come, as if distance and separation made no difference in the feeling of unity between him and his "old command." We have space but for extracts from one of these:

"U. S. Flag-Steamer 'Benton,' Mississippi River,
July 29, 1862.

"Flag-Officer A. H. Foote, U. S. N., New Haven, Conn.:

"My dear Sir,—I had the great pleasure to receive your letter of the 19th instant this morning, and I am most grateful to you for it. I am attempting to answer it under difficulties, having a felon upon the forefinger of my right hand. I am very glad, indeed, to hear of your improved health, and that the foot is mending. Count the months since you were wounded; does it not seem an age? and all so different now from what we hoped for after the fall of Donelson. . . . I wrote to you a short time since, which letter, I believe, shared the fate of the *Sallie Wood*, fired into and burned on her way up to Memphis. Should I be in error, you will know why I go back over most of our stay at Vicksburg.

"Before we went down, a plan had been made by Flag-Officer Davis for an expedition up the Yazoo River, intending to destroy the enemy's vessels there, and especially the *Arkansas*. . . . Refugees brought very contradictory reports about the *Arkansas;* but Commodore Davis, seeing that the lower fleet remained quietly above, resolved upon a move up the Yazoo, and first dispatched a reconnoitring force to ascertain the strength of the batteries covering the obstructions, and to learn generally what force to send up. The *Taylor* and ram *Queen of the West* were to go on this reconnoissance, while the *Carondelet* should go up to the mouth of the 'old' river, and remain till the return of the first two. The boats left here at 4 A.M., and before 6 A.M. began firing, as we supposed, on guerrillas, bushwhackers, or the like. We, however, soon ordered steam up. It appears that the boats met the *Arkansas* very soon; that she had a few minutes' fight with the *Carondelet* at close quarters, in which she (the *Arkansas*) seems to have got holes below the water-line, as they were seen pumping and bailing; and that, after shoving the *Carondelet* on shore, she pushed on, now using her two bow guns with effect on the old *Taylor's* square stern at some two hundred yards' distance. Gwin made a good fight. The ram *Queen* ran away on the beginning of the firing. They were soon down upon us. Not one of the lower fleet had fires kindled. The old *Benton* smoked vigorously; still there was not steam to move her huge hulk; and other vessels had so crowded about us that we could not slip and drop down with the current till such time as steam was ready, and by the time we began to move the rebel was a mile below. He had received the fire of Farragut's fleet, scarcely one doing him harm except the *Richmond*, Captain Alden, whose broadside made the iron fly splendidly—whole bars going up twenty feet in the air. It was hard times with the rebel evidently. None of his shot hurt any one on board the vessels at anchor, or did damage worth mentioning. One cut away a stanchion for us, and left its traces on the back of my sack-coat—so much for the favors of my friend Brown. We followed the *Arkansas* down till fired upon by the batteries. She had escaped. . . . It was settled that we at six o'clock should engage the upper batteries while the lower fleet was passing, which would leave ample daylight for them to see the rebel gun-boat, which is painted an earth color, not distinguishable at night. Anchors were suspended from main-yards, and grapplings from the cross-jack yards; in short, most elaborate preparations were made for the advantage of the rebel intruder, and none could doubt of its immediate destruction. One grand ram, the *Sumter*, was loaned for the occasion. At six o'clock we were under way; and, while the sun still blazed in his glory, were again in hot exchange of compliments with the enemy's battery of six rifled guns. No vessels of the other fleet moved yet, and for three quarters of an hour we were still watching to see them come. At last, as the twilight began, they started, and we could scarcely tell when the foremost vessel passed the upper battery, and saw nothing of the hindmost ones. The thing was a failure. We had no need of reports from below to tell us that. . . . The next night came and passed undisturbed by one sullen sound. The day after there were still threats of destruction to the horned enemy; and this went on till, finally, the *Essex* and ram *Queen of the West* made their attempt. This was against Commodore Davis's judgment. Flag-Officer Farragut himself came up, spent most of the day with Commodore Davis, and matured a plan of attack, which was this: The *Essex* and ram *Queen of the West* were to go down and attack the *Arkansas* at daylight next morning, we covering them at the upper batteries, while the lower fleet should attack the lower batteries, and prevent them firing with effect on the attacking boats. The *Sumter* was also to go up to assist. . . . Morning came; we engaged the upper batteries; the *Essex* and ram *Queen* in due time passed down. No guns from the lower fleet could be heard; we continued to listen in vain, and our hearts grew heavy. Our two vessels, unsustained, could not endure the fire of both batteries and rebel gun-boat. The rebel fire was very heavy. Presently the *Queen* came up badly shattered. She had struck the rebel, but not effectively; and in the terrible fire upon her could not renew the attempt. The *Essex* had poured her fire into the enemy, but in the swift current could not be managed well enough to lay by the fellow, enduring the while the terrible raking fire of those lower batteries as well as of the others. The lower fleet was at anchor; the *Sumter* not to be seen. It is a fact worthy of notice that when the *Queen* struck the *Arkansas*, half the crew jumped overboard. The *Essex's* shot made big holes in her sides, and cries were heard on board. No explanation was made of the failure of the lower fleet to do its part in the attack. The *Sumter's* orders required her to wait till that fleet should open upon the lower batteries, which was to have been simultaneous with our fire upon the upper works, when she was to push up to the attack. Erben waited vainly for the concerted signal. I am told that Commodore Davis's letter was construed as a request to make no attack on the lower batteries. Knowing the plan, as I have described it to you, however imperfectly, is it possible to render it in that manner? It was no part of the plan to pass those batteries, but to attack them at twelve hundred or fifteen hundred yards from below. The whole thing was a fizzle. My growl is done. The lower fleet left, and not a vessel was sunk in the attempt to take the *Arkansas*. The land force also left. Of three thousand two hundred men, only eight hundred remained on duty. It now became proper to consider the state of the flotilla, and what it could effect. Five of the thirteen vessels were undergoing repairs; two of them had got below Vicksburg, uselessly on the failure of the lower fleet, and of course could not get back. Of the six remaining vessels, one is at Fort Pillow, another at Memphis, and four with us. Evidently we could do nothing with Vicksburg without a land force. Forty per cent. of our people were already sick with the fever. General Curtis had been forced from the interior of Arkansas back upon the Mississippi, at Helena, and evidently is pressed by superior numbers. Our vessels on the river were being fired into at various points by field batteries. We had no gun-boats with which to convoy, or even to keep open communications. No good could arise from remaining where we were; but co-operation with General Curtis offered a field, and the climate at the same time would no doubt be beneficial to our numerous sick. Evidently our vessels were soon to be entirely disabled by sickness if we should remain where we were. For these reasons we are now on our way to Helena, Arkansas.

"However much this long letter may bore you, I trust you will give me credit for persistence, at least, for writing it has been a painful undertaking. I feel keenly what reflects upon the flotilla. The escape of the *Arkansas* is very annoying. It should, however, be remembered that it was impossible to keep steam up to 120 or 130 lbs., while the lower fleet put out fires.

"I have read with interest your speech at New Haven and your published letters. You have planted yourself firmly in the hearts of the people, and I have no doubt you will always be foremost there. When will you go to Washington? Do not forget the flotilla when you have the cares of the Bureau upon you. I am ever mindful of the debts I owe your friendship, and trust I shall not prove unworthy to retain my place in your esteem.

"Respectfully and most truly yours, S. L. PHELPS."

The foregoing is an inside view, written evidently with a sore mind, of the unsuccessful attempts of the gun-boats, single-handed, to do any thing toward the capture of Vicksburg —it remained for General Grant to throw the weight of his sword into the scale. The *Arkansas* fairly caught the vessels napping, and, coming upon them so unexpectedly, was able to drive her furious, and, as it actually proved, destructive way through the fleets. The first attempt of Farragut to destroy her was unsuccessful, doubtless owing to the darkness; and the second attempt by Davis was not followed up by a general attack of the lower fleet, owing, it would seem, to a misunderstanding; however, this letter of an able officer and honest man, written though it may be from a partisan stand-point, is one of the data upon which reliable history must be formed. His strictures are not to be carelessly disregarded or contemned.

This friendly letter from Commodore Paulding is a sample of the hearty and brotherly style of correspondence and intercourse that, for some reason or other, prevails in the Navy, in which, if we mistake not, there is more of real *esprit de corps* than even in the Army; the heart speaks right out, and there is an almost womanish tenderness among men who have seen danger and toil in their sternest aspects:

"NAVY YARD, NEW YORK, *July* 27, 1862.

"MY DEAR FLAG-OFFICER,—I was charmed to get your letter yesterday, which I scarcely deserved for having so long omitted to tender you my congratulations on your safe return to your home, family, and friends. For one, I long felt great solicitude about you, and feared there were many chances against a partial recovery even of your limbs; and when you told me of swelling, fever, and loss of appetite, I feared greatly for the gallant friend whose deeds have swelled my heart with pride and pleasure.

"I am glad they have paid you the compliment of placing you at the head of a Bureau, and am sure that any place you may assume will be well filled; and yet for your health, and for the service that we want you to perform, might well question the propriety of your doing any thing just now to irritate your lameness or hazard your permanent cure at an early day. To go from your home in Washington, wherever it may be, to the Department, in the condition your foot is in, may do this; and, with all my interest in what may concern your present pride and dignity, I could have wished they had let you alone until you had time to get well. You could well help on at the West when there was so much to be done—fighting and working on crutches while there was any thing left of you; but now, in a different position in public life, they should let you alone, or give you the nominal supervision of your Bureau.

"I have tried to write every day since your letter came, but my interruptions are so continual that I am eye and head weary.

"I had a letter from ——— yesterday from Mosquito Inlet, where he is commander-in-chief, and so desperately in love with his wife that nothing but a fight, I should think, would take the homesickness out of him.

"I read to Leonard what you said of him. He made no reply, but is always full of admiration of your naval skill and cool, determined valor.

"The only picture I have in my house is yours. Come and see it, if you can, when you pass on. I will give you good quarters and hearty welcome. Your friend Captain Boggs, of the tug, has just stepped in. He says there is nobody like you. I write in some haste. My kind congratulations and all my good wishes to Mrs. Foote, *Petite*, and the boy.

"Your friend, H. PAULDING."

During these years of the war, and especially the eventful year 1862, when the country was passing through its profoundest crisis, every convocation of the people—political, religious, or educational—partook of the warlike and patriotic character of the times. The country's safety was the uppermost topic. The toga then yielded to arms. The men of action went before the men of thought. The churches were assemblies of those who prayed for the success of the Union arms or sought strength to make great sacrifices. The colleges and schools of learning were filled with this patriotic and martial spirit. The Commencement Day of Yale College in New Haven this year occurred on the 30th of July. There was a large gathering of the alumni of the college; and although the usual business of the meeting was duly dispatched, evidently the great controlling object of the assembly was that of the country's condition. This was the gravitating current of every address and the intense thought of every heart. Those present will not forget the impressive scene when, advancing slowly through the crowd of scholars and civilians, Commodore Foote made his way on crutches and took his seat upon the platform. For a moment there was a hush of silence, and then a burst of enthusiastic greeting. He was dressed in full uniform. His head, carried erect and proud, his full, black eye, his earnest brow, his pale face, his form bearing the marks of wounds and sufferings, contributed to make a picture both noble and pathetic.

After a resolution in relation to the public exigency had been introduced and spoken upon by Hon. W. W. Ellsworth, Prof. Thacher rose and quoted the Latin phrase, "*Ex pede Herculem*," which the audience translated by loud cries of "Foote!"

He thereupon arose and spoke briefly. He referred to the advantages of a college education in every department and business of life, and paid a tribute to Yale as not forgetting the claims of a practical nature upon every true man, and the good of the country and of humanity, in her method of education. He spoke also of the Western campaign, gave high praise to General Halleck, and urged on educated young men the necessity of engaging at this critical hour in the service of the country. He concluded by an allusion to his old friend President Roberts, of Liberia, who was seated near him,

On that day, 30th of July—although the appointment dated back to the 16th—he officially received the appointment of Rear-Admiral on the Active List.

He had thus risen to the highest rank belonging to his profession, and risen, not by a sudden leap, but by regular steps, by filling every subordinate position, by hard labor and toil, by actual worth and noble deeds.

CHAPTER XXVII.

CONGRATULATIONS AND CORRESPONDENCE.—SWORD PRESENTATION AT BROOKLYN.

CONGRATULATORY letters from old friends in great numbers followed upon his new appointment, of which we subjoin two or three:

"WASHINGTON, *August* 2, 1862.

"MY DEAR ADMIRAL,—It was my intention to have sent my congratulations on your promotion with the commission, but my time is not within my control. You know that my congratulations and regard are none the less sincere than if earlier tendered. Long may you live to bear the title and wear the honors you have so gallantly earned.

"I trust your health and wounds continue to improve. It has occurred to me that, under the circumstances of your debility, it might be imprudent for you to come from the North, at this early period, to such an unhealthy place as Washington is at this season. Should such be the case, and you would prefer to delay your entrance upon your Bureau duties, I do not think any particular inconvenience would result therefrom for the present. I mention this in order that you may take your own time to come here, for affairs can go on as heretofore for a few weeks without serious injury.

"I am in hopes I shall be able to leave Washington the latter part of the month for a week or two. Respectfully, GIDEON WELLES."

"'SABINE,' NEW LONDON, *August* 1, 1862.

"MY DEAR ADMIRAL,—It is a source of deep regret that I could not make you a visit. A dispatch from the Secretary yesterday, directing me to send 'every available man on board to Cairo, Ill., immediately,' gave me, as you may suppose, occupation, and necessitated my foregoing the pleasure of visiting you.

"My good ship has really created an excitement in New London; and, touching the facilities of the harbor for naval purposes, it promises great advantages. I wish you could have seen my ship. To have had her inspected by you, and to have given you your first salute as an admiral, believe me when I say it, would have been to me most gratifying. Resting as the *Sabine* does in the waters of your own state, there appears to me something peculiarly appropriate in this, and I lament that your departure will prevent me having the pleasure of extending the hand to you. Allow me to ask the favor to be very kindly presented to Mrs. Foote, and I wish you to know how pleased I am to address you as Admiral. Very truly your friend, C. RINGGOLD."

"FORTRESS MONROE, VA., *August* 4, 1862.

"ADMIRAL FOOTE, U. S. N., New Haven, Conn.:

"MY DEAR SIR,—It is with great joy I hasten to congratulate my old and esteemed commander—and the service and country as well—on his well-merited promotion to the high grade of Admiral. I felt when I read the news as if I myself had been honored; and I think I will hold on to the notion, since I declared when you were put in command at the West that you were the right man for the place, and I accordingly invested in you my entire stock of confidence. Success is almost certain where professional skill, heroism, and Christian faith are combined. I am sure you will be greatly encouraged to go on in setting us all a high example of what constitutes the true officer.

"I am paymaster in charge of stores for the squadron, with my stores and clerks on board of store-schooners scattered over all this now extensive station. I wish you could come here as admiral of the squadron. I learn that Admiral Goldsborough has applied to be relieved. I have been hoping you might come.

"Very truly and respectfully yours, THOMAS H. TOOKER.

"P. S.—I trust your wounds are healing rapidly."

"ALBANY, *August* 12, 1862.

"REAR-ADMIRAL FOOTE,—Is not that a good title? And how heartily I congratulate you on it, you very well know.

"I wrote you a few days ago at New Haven, and hope you received the precious document. I leave here on Monday next for Cairo. I go with heavy heart, in view of the acting-lieutenancy that I still hold; nevertheless, I go with mind brimful of patriotism.

"The last pay-bill gives to acting-lieutenants $1875, and a ration when at sea. Is there no way that I can be regarded as on sea-service? I think

I ought to be placed on the sea-list, as all my stores are afloat. I shall be the only sea-officer in the Western flotilla who receives shore pay. You know how responsible my duties are, and how constant they are, and that I deserve the increased pay. I have hope that the next Congress will do me justice.

"If you get the command of a fleet, recollect that I must go with you. I expect to hear of your having the Hampton Roads fleet any day. I have had such quiet and domestic happiness in my visit hence, that it is hard to leave my family. When leisure and inclination prompt, let me hear from you. Sincerely yours,

"J. P. SANFORD, Ordnance-Officer of Flotilla."

The following is a letter of more sombre hue; and, as a son pleading the cause of a father, it is so noble that we insert it here:

"MISSISSIPPI FLOTILLA, CAIRO, ILL., *August* 28, 1862.

"MY DEAR ADMIRAL,—I have just learned, what you have probably known before, that my father has been considered by the late Advisory Board unfit for promotion to the rank of Commodore—in other words, has been overslaughed.

"I have taken the liberty to address you, for I know you are one of my father's fast friends. By the Retiring Board of 1854, which scrutinized the merits of officers far more strictly than the present Board could have had time to do, nothing was alleged against him. From that time until the breaking out of the present war he was not on duty, notwithstanding repeated applications, because his position in the list obliged him to wait, as you well know, until others above him had been served in turn.

"At the breaking out of the war father was assigned to the *Mississippi*. He continued in command for some nine months, when he was suddenly relieved by Captain Melancthon Smith, and ordered home. Upon reaching Washington, he was informed by the Department that he had been relieved 'upon vague and indefinite rumors' in relation to the ram *Manasses*.

"The facts in this instance were, that when the *Mississippi* was blockading off Pass à l'Outre, the *Manasses* remained in sight of the *Mississippi* two days, but all the while inside of the bar. Some newspaper correspondent reflected severely upon father for not attacking her. There were seventeen feet of water on the bar; the *Mississippi* drew twenty-one feet. At the time of the attack upon New Orleans, with every thing out of her, it required all her power and that of two other steamers to force her over. Admiral Farragut never made any report in the case, and the whole rests upon the bare statement of an ignorant newspaper correspondent.

"My father was terribly mortified and chagrined. He told Secretary Welles, and I believe he meant it, that he would rather have been shot than ordered home.

"You have all the facts as far as I believe that any thing rests against him.

"No officer in the Navy loves his profession better, or has sought to do his duty more strictly than my father—I feel you will agree with me. By accident I happened to see him on his return from the Gulf, and the deep depression of spirits and mortification, which he could not seem to throw off, make me fear that this last blow will be almost too much for him to bear. But there is a good God who rules all things, and it is my prayer that He will not try him without giving to father divine strength to meet this undeserved disgrace with resignation.

"I would make a personal request of you, my dear sir—that you would see the Secretary, and obtain decided information whether father will now be retained in command of the *San Francisco* for three years or not. It was mother's intention to have joined him in California, with some of the family, the coming October. It will save her much expense, and a long and arduous journey, if you can obtain this information and let her know, directing to the care of J. I. Soley, Esq., Boston.

"I trust you will excuse this long letter from me. I feel deeply—very deeply—this blow at father's reputation, because I know it is so entirely undeserved. Father's professional path has in the later years of his life been strewn with thorns; and to one to whom professional reputation has been so great an object, this last injustice, I know, will bring him in sorrow to the grave.

"With renewed hopes that you may soon recover that health whose loss you have suffered in the service of our beloved country,

"I have the honor to be most sincerely your obedient servant,

"Thomas O. Selfridge, Jr.,

"Lieutenant-Commanding U. S. N."

Such a letter as the foregoing could never have been addressed to one who had not the power of drawing out the confidence of others—who had not great simplicity and sympathy. It could not have been written to a mere official, who looked at things in a routine way, and who had lost the true feelings of a man in a merely quarter-deck view of authority.

In regard to the flotilla, the correspondence during the summer and autumn of 1862, more fitful and far between, is still kept up between Foote and his former associates at the West. In point of discipline, efficiency, and fighting power, the fleet rather degenerated after the battle of Memphis, chiefly on account of the changes among and loss of old officers. The *Benton* still remained formidable; the *Cairo* and *Pittsburg* were of little use, and the *Louisville* hardly better; the *Cincinnati* leaked badly after coming off the stocks; the *Carondelet* had been badly cut up by the *Arkansas*, while the *Mound City* remained without a crew, until Captain Gwin took her and made her an efficient vessel. The *Benton* and the *Eastport* were really the only effective iron-clads left on the river. We would anticipate a few months, and give a letter of David D. Porter, who succeeded Davis in the command of the Mississippi squadron, and then we must dismiss the fortunes of that flotilla which has necessarily occupied so much of our attention:

"U. S. Mississippi Squadron, Yazoo River,
January 3, 1863.

"My dear Admiral,—I have not had time to answer your letter in relation to ——— ———. I appointed him a master-mate, and he got drunk the first night he went on shore, and broke his liberty; so says the report of his commander, who recommended him for promotion. I could not overlook the offense, and keep up my character for consistency. We have had lively times up the Yazoo—imagine the Yazoo becoming the theatre of war. We waded through sixteen miles of torpedoes to get at the forts (seven in number); but when we got thus far, the fire on the boats from the riflemen, in pits dug for miles along the river, and from the batteries, became very annoying; and that gallant fellow Gwin thought he could check them, which he did until he was knocked over with the most fearful wound I ever saw. He could not advance, the torpedoes popping up ahead as thick as mushrooms, and we have had pretty good evidence of their power for mischief. I never saw more daring displayed than by the brave fellows who did the work. The forts are powerful works, out of the reach of ships, and on high hills, plunging their shot through the upper deck, and the river is so narrow that only one vessel could engage them until the torpedoes could all be removed. The old war-horse (*Benton*) retained her ancient renown, and, though much cut up, is ready for any thing. Gwin there is little hope for: no man could live with such a wound. He is a noble, gallant fellow. I have him in my cabin, and do all I can for him; his sufferings are terrible.

"The same day the army made an assault on the forts back of Vicksburg; it was a fearful place they went through, with double their number opposed to them. They drove the rebels like sheep, who fired into their own fugitives, and knocked them over like nine-pins. That helped our party some; but our reserve (a new regiment) fired into our own troops while they were going to the batteries, and the supporting brigade did not come up to the scratch. The men on the batteries were cut off by the rebels when they saw them unsupported, and were cut to pieces. We lost fifteen hundred men in about ten minutes. Vicksburg was at one time ours, but we had not men enough to repeat the experiment. The result has been, in two days Vicksburg has been reinforced by twenty thousand men from Grenada, and ten thousand from Jackson, and we can do nothing until reinforced. In front, Vicksburg is unassailable, as it is fortified in every direction with the best of guns. I don't know what the army will do now.

"McClernand has just arrived, and will take command. Our plan was for Sherman to arrive here on the 25th, while Grant pushed on to Canton with fifty thousand men, to come in on the rear of Vicksburg. Grant has not been heard from, and it was deemed necessary to attack Vicksburg before it could be reinforced; now it will take a large army to capture it. The rivers are all too low for the Navy to operate with any thing but light-draft boats, but in a month we will begin to have water. The old iron-clads are all breaking down; but in two months I expect to get some of the new ones, which are pretty good vessels. I have to send away four vessels to-morrow, in consequence of fears entertained by some generals about invasion. Don't be astonished at the list of darkies I send you. I could get no white men, so I work them in. They do first-rate, and behave far better than their masters. Give my kindest regards to Mrs. F., and believe me very sincerely yours, DAVID D. PORTER.

"Rear-Admiral Andrew H. Foote, U. S. N., Chief of Bureau of Equipment and Recruits, Washington, D. C."

In the month of May, 1862, Commodore Foote received a note from a number of gentlemen in Brooklyn, N.Y., signifying their desire to present him a sword as a token of personal esteem and of admiration for his public services, and requested him to name a time for the presentation. About the middle of the following September the presentation took place in the Brooklyn Athenæum, in the presence of many distinguished naval officers and of a brilliant assembly of citizens. The sword was ornamented with devices having reference to the exploits of our hero in various parts of the world.* In

* The sword was an elegant one, having cost $3500. It is thus described: "The pummel represents a golden hemisphere, studded with stars, on which rest branches of olive and oak, beneath a group of trophies. The guard, which is part of the chief feature of the whole, contains a basso-relievo of Neptune returning triumphant on his car. The figure of Neptune, bold and spirited, stands in his car, leaning upon his trident; at his feet are the spoils of victory. Two vigorous horses draw the car of the god, attended by sea-nymphs and tritons blowing trumpets. This basso-relievo is encircled by open scroll-work, forming a rich and harmonious arrangement of lines, the effect of which is exceedingly pleasing. At the bottom of the guard is a boldly modeled head of a dolphin. On the scabbard are a series of relievos, illustrating some of the prominent exploits of the bold sailor to whom this was given. First is exhibited Foote's bombardment of Chinese forts, with appropriate ornamental emblems and scenery. The second exhibits skillful and daring operations in the bombardment of Island No. Ten, wherein the uncouth mortar-boats are wrought out in great perfection—the slanting sides, smoke-stacks, port-holes, etc., of the bomb-ketches being set forth with great accuracy. There are also various incidents of operations on the Cumberland and Tennessee rivers. Lower down are emblematic allusions to Foote's experience on the African coast. The following inscription is cut on the scabbard in beautiful characters: 'Presented by the citizens of Brooklyn to Flag-Officer Andrew H. Foote, as a testimonial of their high personal regard, of their appreciation of his eminent professional character, distinguished public services, and moral influence in a long career of active duty; and especially of his efficiency in the suppression of the slave-trade on the coast of Africa; his gallant conduct in the destruction of the Barrier Forts in China; his masterly skill and energy in the creation of a flotilla, and of his brilliant and intrepid bombardment therewith of the rebel fortifications of the Tennessee, the Cumberland, and the Mississippi.' The sword-blade is richly covered with artistic designs, and

his reply to the address which was made to him he made reference to those scenes represented upon the sword, saying, among other things, that "the difficulties of creating the flotilla—the days and nights of mental agony in its preparation—rendered the subsequent fighting, speaking comparatively, a pleasant episode;" and he closed his speech with these words, which were received with great applause:

"Again, then, I thank you for this beautiful sword, which I shall ever regard as a personal gift of friends who have elevated and ennobled the walks of civil life. I shall carefully preserve it. I shall endeavor to be worthy of it. And I shall hope to transmit it to my latest posterity as an evidence of your friendship and appreciation, and as an inducement to them to be faithful in vindicating our glorious Union, and the supremacy of the Constitution and the laws—at home and abroad—against internal and external enemies. I will wield it for the whole country against any state—aye, even the State of New York or Connecticut—should either prove recreant in attempting to withdraw their star—the emblem of their state—from the blue union of our glorious old flag.

"To this end I pray that I may be enabled to act as faithfully in the future as I humbly hope I have done in the past—when meeting our enemies in the East, as in my efforts toward crushing this atrocious rebellion in the South. I say this atrocious rebellion; and is it not an atrocious rebellion, when the South is presenting the mournful spectacle to the civilized world of having voluntarily gone into the election of the Presidency as prescribed by the Constitution, and, finding itself in the minority, attempts to rule or ruin the government it had, in common with the North, fought to establish?

"The occasion and circumstances have led me to revert to past scenes and personal services. Having done this, permit me, in this solemn crisis, to add that a glorious future is assuredly open to us and to our country, under Providence, on the condition that the entire loyal North immediately arises in its might, laying aside all other considerations, and concentrates its power to the work of crushing this monster rebellion finally and forever."

---

near the hilt, surrounded with graceful scroll-work, is the motto—'*Ducit amor patriæ.*'"

One of the papers of the day, in its account of this affair, says:

"As soon as the noble sailor made his appearance, the audience arose and gave cheer upon cheer, waving their hats and handkerchiefs with a patriotic enthusiasm seldom witnessed. Admiral Foote is not only a good fighter, but an eloquent impromptu speaker, with a full, rich voice, and a ready command of language. In person, he is of ordinary stature, well built, with plump limbs and square shoulders. He has dark brown hair, not silvered enough to be noticed; but his whiskers are well frosted. His head is finely developed, and when he speaks his eyes flash with electric fire. When he raised the beautiful sword and wielded it, saying, 'I will draw this sword in defense of the Union and the Constitution and the country,' the spell-bound audience broke forth in demonstrations of applause."

CHAPTER XXVIII.

LOSS OF CHILDREN. — CORRESPONDENCE AT WASHINGTON. — APPOINTMENT TO COMMAND OF SOUTH ATLANTIC SQUADRON.—LAST DAYS AND DEATH.

Public honors were quickly followed by a deep family affliction, the death of the admiral's two youngest daughters, Emily Frederica and Maria Eudocia, within ten days of each other. The first of these was a little blind girl, whom her father regarded with a peculiar tenderness, always asking when he came into the house, before he spoke with any one else, "Where is my little Emily?" The second was a lovely child of seven years of age; and thus, within six months, three children were taken from him. The letters of sympathy which came from men overwhelmed with great public cares do honor to their writers' hearts. Admiral Joseph Smith, before little Maria had died, prays that "*Petite*" may be spared to her father; and as the following letter has relation also to the movements and plans of the subject of this memoir, we here give it in full:

"Washington, *October* 15, 1862.

"My dear Sir,—Admiral Smith submitted to me your note to him announcing your affliction, and has doubtless written you my desire that you would, under this dispensation, take your own time and your own way to resume your duties.

"Believe me, my dear sir, I most deeply sympathize with you as a friend and parent, for I also have been bereaved, having five times followed to the grave those who, in the course of nature, I had anticipated would have done me that sad office.

"The sufferings and death of our children are hard to endure, and our consolation is not of this world when such sorrows are upon us. To Him who gave and who has taken to himself the gifts that are so precious we must look, and in Him put our trust.

"Give yourself no thought or care of the duties now. They shall be attended to.

"With kindest regard and sincerest sympathy to Mrs. Foote and yourself, believe me, very truly yours, GIDEON WELLES."

Although Admiral Foote could not enter as yet entirely upon his duties as Chief of Bureau of Equipment and Recruiting, he still was in consultation with the government in regard to its affairs, as this extract from a letter dated September 20, 1862, emanating from his office, will indicate:

"I have carefully considered the proposition and views of Mr. de la Montagnie, consul of the United States at Nantes, with reference to obtaining sailors for the Navy.

"I consider the plan objectionable, especially that part of it inducing the Norwegian sailors in Nantes to leave their vessels in England, as it would involve a responsibility of employing an agent or agents in different ports of England for the transportation of them to the United States; besides, the number of Norwegian sailors thus obtained would be but comparatively few to the amount of expense and risk of implication.

"While Norway possesses the largest merchant marine of any country in Europe except England and France, yet comparatively few Norwegian sailors enter our service, and the reason is, they seldom desert their vessels in foreign ports, and are strongly attached to their homes.

"As emigration is increasing, and our mode of warfare at sea of late has been modified by the iron-clads, we require a less number of sailors. Landsmen are quickly trained in the exercise of guns, etc. I am induced to believe the better plan would be to employ some agent or agents to publish in different parts of Germany and in the North of Europe the high wages, etc., that the United States Government pays to seamen, landsmen, and boys who are entering our Navy; this might have the effect of inducing young men, especially in the North of Europe, to emigrate for the purpose of entering the service.

"In the free port of Hamburg, more sailors could be procured than in any port in Europe; and should any effort be made to secure foreign seamen, this free port would afford us the greatest number without implicating our government.

"Hamburg is, as you know, a free port, and sailors from all nations are there largely represented."

We are glad to insert here one letter from that noble sea-paladin, Farragut, albeit it is of an entirely business character:

"NEW ORLEANS, *March* 7, 1863.

"DEAR ADMIRAL,—I have received yours of the 16th ult., in which you give me the pleasing intelligence that you have sent me one hundred recruits by the *Circassian.* If they had been twenty days sooner, they would have been invaluable to me; as it is, they are very valuable. I will take the men I want from the *Pensacola*, and let Commodore Morris supply himself temporarily from the recruits.

"I am dreadfully in want of both officers and men. I do not wish to place the vessels of war in the hands of inexperienced men, and yet I do not know how to avoid it. Very truly yours,

"D. G. FARRAGUT, Rear-Admiral.

"Rear-Admiral A. H. Foote, Chief of Bureau of Equipment and Recruiting, Washington, D. C."

At the end of the year 1862, and the beginning of 1863, we find the admiral settled with his family in Washington, busy with the duties of his new office, apparently throwing himself into them with the same ardor that he did into active service; and we hear little in regard to his health, although it was in no sense reassured, but continued growing perhaps gradually worse. Much of his time and attention seems to have been taken up with the matter of furnishing naval vessels at all occupied stations on our extended coast with coal, and fighting with contractors, public carriers, and owners of freight-vessels and chartered vessels in regard to their exorbitant war-prices. It was his habit to carry through his measures at any cost, but the old Connecticut blood in him prompted him to the greatest economy practicable. He was strict and scrutinizing in business matters, and was ever in favor of retrenchment. He never gave way to the feeling of irresponsibility in the lavish expenditure of the public funds even in times of great public demoralization and peril, but kept a shrewd eye to the main chance.

In the midst of these busy scenes at the heart of the war-activity of the country, he still found time for a large correspondence both of a public and private nature. He forgot no one, and interested himself, though unsuccessfully, to procure a situation in his Department commanding a good salary for his colored friend, John H. Brooks, whom he soon afterward employed as a personal attendant to go with him to Charleston. He gave advice in regard to the management of naval academies; he was active in his duties as President of the Connecticut Soldiers' Aid Society; he pressed his matters of naval reform and temperance, and the better observance of the Lord's day, with his usual persistency; he found time and heart to write in a playful strain to his few old friends and his relatives who thoroughly knew him; but his mind was, for the most part, borne down with sorrow and care, though always hopeful for the country. A strictly private letter speaks somewhat of his feelings:

"BUREAU OF EQUIPMENT AND RECRUITING,
WASHINGTON, *January* 17, 1863.

"MY DEAR SIR,—It has been my intention to snatch a few minutes from the heavy pressure of my public duties for the purpose of writing to you. Thus, as the will has been always ready, I know that your high-toned patriotism will not only excuse my silence, but even approve and applaud it.

"The governor and his good wife are with us, and are doing good, as they always do wherever they are. The governor is sharply looking out for the comfort of the soldiers of your noble and gallant state, which, as my friend General Buford remarked to him, is 'the banner state in this war.'

"My duties are laborious in organizing my new Bureau, but I hope in this Department of which I have charge to render the Navy more efficient. I want as soon as possible to be afloat again, and there remain till we, under God, crush this atrocious rebellion, which I have the strongest faith God will enable us to do in his good time.

"I send an interesting discussion which the governor heard, also Senator Hales's attack on my old friend Commodore Smith.

"I am led to make my grateful acknowledgments to you for the kind and encouraging manner in which you have sustained me in my efforts thus far in helping to crush the rebellion. A kind Providence has certainly favored my humble efforts, and to God I would give all the glory.

"We all send love to the family. Please excuse my haste, as I have no time for private correspondence.

"Very respectfully your friend and servant, A. H. FOOTE.

"Benjamin Hoppin, Esq., Providence, R. I."

A note of the admiral's to the United States Christian Commission, in reply to a letter inviting him to be present at a meeting of that body in Philadelphia, was as follows:

"BUREAU OF EQUIPMENT AND RECRUITING,
WASHINGTON, D. C., *Jan.* 28, 1863.

"MY DEAR SIR,—It is with extreme regret that I am compelled, from a heavy pressure of public business, to decline your kind invitation to be present and participate in the exercises at the meeting of the Christian Commission on Thursday evening.

"The object and importance of your commission can not be overestimated. It will supply a want long existing in the Army and Navy, and must enlist the sympathies and prayers of all true Christian patriots.

"To supply the spiritual wants of the public service on the battle-field and upon the ocean, and to lead our warriors to go forward valiantly in the fight, acknowledging God as our ruler, and looking to him for success, will, I have no doubt, soon cause this wicked rebellion to culminate in the restoration of our Union.

"I am, very respectfully, A. H. FOOTE.

"George H. Stuart, Esq., Chairman Christian Commission, etc., Philadelphia."

One of the many letters of his friend Captain Simpson, of the Newport Naval Academy, brings up the names of old ships that are familiar to the readers of this book:

"U. S. ACADEMY, NEWPORT, R. I., *November* 18, 1862.

"MY DEAR ADMIRAL,—I have received your kind note showing how willingly you undertook to labor for my advancement; I am very much obliged to you both for your successful and unsuccessful efforts. As to copies of my book, I suppose that Captain Dahlgren will order them from the publisher.

"I have written a letter to the Superintendent, calling his attention to the want of a ship with two decks for a practice-ship; the crew of the *John Adams* were very much crowded last summer, owing to the amount of the berth-deck that was appropriated to the midshipmen, of whom I carried only eighty. The *Plymouth* was our old practice-ship, but the rebellion destroyed her. The *Portsmouth* is the ship that I want as a substitute for the *John Adams;* but, to make her perfect for practice purposes, she must have a light deck put on her. It is this that I have applied for in my letter to the Superintendent, and he has promised to send a copy of my letter to the Department. I fear that he will not take much trouble to recommend it, and, as I know the need, I feel the importance of it. If I have the *Portsmouth* next summer, I can carry at least fifty-five more midshipmen, make my men comfortable, and have many other advantages; but if nothing is done soon about it, I shall have to go in the old *John* again, which is a very good old ship, but is not so well adapted for the purpose.

"It would be necessary to order the *Portsmouth* home at once from the West Gulf squadron, where I doubt if her loss will be felt. If it is to be done at all, it had better be done at once; and I will be much obliged to you if you will endeavor to put the old ship, which you commanded with so much credit and distinction, to a useful purpose—the most useful, perhaps, that a sailing-vessel can be applied to at present.

"Very respectfully and truly yours,

"E. SIMPSON, Commandant of Midshipmen."

How changed the times in respect to naval matters since the *Portsmouth* pushed up her wooden walls to the side of stone forts in the Canton river! Iron and earth had taken the place of wood and stone. Dashing boldness in storming and assault was now yielding to more exact science and calculation as to the resisting quality of iron, and the smashing and dislodging power of shot. Admiral Foote, as has been said before, belonged both to the old and the new periods. His audacious boldness in attack has been compared with that of Paul Jones and Decatur; but he gladly availed himself of the invention of iron-clads, and he looked forward to the time when, in his *Benton* or *Eastport*, or some still more formidable floating battery, he could compete with the highest military engineering on shore, and the most scientific form of heavy ordnance afloat. His Mississippi gun-boats for the time, and in an aggressive sense, were even better than Ericsson's "monitors" for their purpose, though they were not invulnerable, as, in fact, in the progress of science, nothing is or can be.

To turn to another subject, a naval friend from the Boston Navy Yard brings out amusingly in his letter a prominent trait of the admiral's character. He says:

"Do you remember when you called at my quarters with a flattering invitation to accompany you to Chelsea to deliver a lecture on China? You had a cold and a sore throat, and wanted me in case you broke down to take your place with my 'Jerusalem' lecture. Mrs. M—— wished to know how it went. 'Did Mr. Foote or you lecture?'—'Why, Mr. Foote, of course. He didn't break down, nor did he mean to do so. Do you think he intended that I should take the wind out of his sails?'—So when you were before Island No. Ten, and all was excitement and anxiety, I said (remembering old times), 'Foote will have No. Ten. He never gives up a job or an argument to any body.' When Island No. Ten was ours, all was rejoicing and exultant, and a great burden of apprehension was removed from the public mind; but with me it was a foregone conclusion, and I took it very philosophically."

This self-reliance and persistency of character which led him to do things for himself, and take the lead in all that fell to his hand, though brought out jestingly in the foregoing extract, had by this time made itself pretty generally known both to the government and the people. The war had witnessed some lamentable failures in its leaders and great men; and although most important successes had crowned the Northern arms, yet the first months and the spring of the year 1863 did not open brightly for the cause of the republic. At the close of 1862, the battle of Murfreesboro, while ending in victory, crippled the victors almost as much as the vanquished; and although the new year began auspiciously with the Emancipation Act, which sent fresh hope through the land, and although there were seven hundred thousand loyal men in the field, the actual successes in a military point of view were few and far between. The Army of the Potomac was discouraged and disappointed; the dreadful battle of Chancellorsville, fought under Hooker in the spring, ended in signal defeat and rout; and Lee, great general, though in a bad cause, was gathering together his legions, and already meditating that bold invasion of the North which was carried out some months later. Richmond seemed as far off as ever, while the interference of foreign powers was, in the view of the least timid, inevitable. At the South and West, Banks was operating in Louisiana and its neighborhood with more enterprise than success; the Mississippi was still closed up between Fort Hudson and Vicksburg; and Vicksburg, proud and defiant, baffled the most strenuous efforts of our land and naval forces. Above all, Charleston, the fount and heart of the great rebellion, lay safe behind her ring of mighty bulwarks, with Sumter grimly guarding the harbor's mouth. Dupont in the early part of April had tried his strength against the Charleston defenses, and after a most intrepid fight with his monitors and ironsides, had drawn off completely cut up, and bitterly declaring that the thing, at least in that way of doing it, was impossible. The government and the people, however, whether Dupont were right or wrong, did not agree with him: nothing was impossible to Northern hearts; and the cry went forth, Who will come to the rescue?—who will lead the forlorn hope of the land? The right man was all that was asked for. The true instinct of the government and country pointed to but one man, and that man was—Andrew Hull Foote.

His indomitable character was then called to mind, and in spite of his physical feebleness and unfit condition, both of body and mind, he must go. It seemed, and thousands will bear us out in this statement, that at that moment the fate of the whole republic hung upon him. He, too, wished to go. As early as April he sent his family home to New Haven, coming himself with them as far as New York, and then returning to Washington. As he wrote in a private letter which has been quoted, "I want as soon as possible to be afloat again, and there remain till we, under God, crush this atrocious rebellion."

On the 4th of June, 1863, he was detached from his position as Chief of the Bureau of Equipment and Recruiting, and appointed to take Admiral Dupont's place as commander of the South Atlantic blockading squadron.

One of the leading newspapers, commenting upon this appointment, said:

> "Admiral Foote is a progressive man. He has inventive capacity sufficient at once to estimate the value of new and untried appliances. He is therefore eminently qualified for the position of commander of the South Atlantic blockading squadron, and we trust he will put his formidable fleet of monitors to some immediate and practical use."

Another journal remarked:

> "He is believed to be the very man to show the full capabilities of the monitors and iron-clads in opposition to fortifications."

Admiral Gregory wrote to him:

> "I shall be one of the first to hail your return; your daring will be the best prudence; and I shall ever be proud of the recollection that forty years ago the little boy first dipped his paddle into the great sea under my care."

After making his final preparations in Washington, he came to New Haven to take leave of his family before repairing to his new post. He evidently did not believe that he should see his family again in this life. Captain Simpson, one of his dearest friends, who knew him best, declared that "he would take Fort Sumter or go to the bottom." He expected either to die in battle or from the effects of coast malaria acting upon his enfeebled frame. It had been a common saying with him, "I can't join in the prayer, Deliver us from sudden death;" and he made the sacrifice cheerfully. The brief time he was in New Haven he was in good spirits and full of hope, though so weak that the signing of his name for autographs for a Ladies' Fair for sick soldiers almost overcame him. He was once, in fact, near falling in the street from a sudden turn of nervous prostration, and was only rallied by strong restoratives. He would sometimes sink into his chair with an air of complete lassitude, and exclaim, with his hands pressed to his head, "Rest—oh, for rest!" It seems now, in looking back upon it, extraordinary that the government, or at least his own friends, should not have seen how very ill a man he was, and that such a burden laid upon so exhausted a frame would be fatal. But it was his spirit that deceived his friends and led them to a delusive hope. His unconquerable mind made all others and himself believe that all things were possible. The following letter, which came to him in New Haven, indicates somewhat of the plans that were discussed between the government and himself in regard to the Southern coast:

"WASHINGTON, D. C., *June* 12, 1863.

"DEAR ADMIRAL,—I have your note of the 10th inst. The matter of an attack upon Wilmington has been up for the last six months, and Lee has been in constant communication with the Department, sometimes personally, upon the subject. The monitors can not get into Wilmington, and the army can not co-operate at present. Fort Caswell is surrounded by a glacis, instead of being exposed to fire like Sumter. Lee has full information about that fort and the defenses, and has discussed the matter with General Totten. If three or four monitors could have effected any thing alone, we should have been in long ago. It must be a joint affair, and there is no army now except at Port Royal. The *Tuscarora* sailed yesterday for New York. Truly yours, G. V. Fox."

Port Royal was Foote's objective point, where he was to join the squadron and co-operate with the land forces upon Charleston. While waiting in New Haven for orders, he received a sudden summons to embark at once in the *Tuscarora* from New York. He left New Haven quite early in the morning, his family—some of them—seeing him then for the last time in life, as he turned in the carriage and made them his parting adieux. When he arrived in New York, he found that the *Tuscarora*, by some emergency, with a number of other vessels, had been ordered off a few hours before. He went at once to the Astor House, and telegraphed to his family that his sailing was delayed for two or three days. In company with Admiral Gregory, he inspected monitors that were being constructed; and when at the hotel attended to numerous visitors. After incessant occupation all day, he started at night for Washington, transacted business in that place all the following day, and returned to New York the same night. The next day he was kept in a round of excitement, and that night was taken with the first painful symptoms of his disease. In the morning he felt better, but a return of pain made it necessary to depart from simple remedies and to send for physicians. Shortly after, there was a consultation of physicians, and it was decided that the case was one of Bright's disease of the kidneys, which had been aggravated by his harassed life at the West, his wound, and especially his exertions and anxieties for the last few days. Upon the 16th came the following:

"Navy Yard, New York, *June* 16, 1863.

"Admiral,—I am authorized by the Department to charter a steamer to take you and your suite to Port Royal. The *Union* will sail for that destination on the 18th, and I think you might find her preferable to a chartered steamer.

"Be pleased to inform me which you prefer. I shall be most happy to second your wishes in any manner you shall name. My constant occupation here has prevented my calling to see you. Should you determine to go in the *Union*, it is desirable that the captain should be informed as to what number of officers you take, and what preparation you wish made.

"I am, very respectfully, your obedient servant,

"H. PAULDING, Commandant."

But by this time he was too ill for such matters. On the 18th and 19th he had rallied somewhat, awakening some hopes of his restoration; but he soon fell back, and he himself deliberately gave up all expectation of recovery. His wife, his daughter, his brother Augustus, with other members of his family and some of his naval friends, had now joined him, and with them he talked freely, and told them—as if the order to "cast off moorings" had been sent to him from a higher authority—"My disease is fatal; but I am prepared to meet death in this way, if God has so ordered it." Indeed, as his pastor, Dr. Budington, who was also present, writes: "It seemed as if the admiral, as usual, was the chief actor, discharging some difficult duty, and keeping all about him employed under his direction; but the work he had now in hand was to die, and this he went about as patiently and earnestly as he had ever cleared the decks for action. His life, the mainspring of which was a constant activity in the service of God and country, was closing in the energetic performance of his last commission—to die."

He said to his brother, when he first came into the room, "I'm glad to have one of my brothers with me;" and then, his face brightening up with almost a gleam of humor, he added, "I always told you I should go before you and John, and you see now I was right." His brother replied, "That is not so certain by any means." He rejoined, "You are certainly mistaken—I know I am right, and you will see." His brother remarked, pleasantly, "You are the same that you always were, and you never will yield your point." The admiral then went on to say: "I wanted to go to Charleston and help the government all I could, but it is just as well. It is only a question of killing more men. I am perfectly resigned to the will of God."

He was extremely anxious that the government should know the cause of his delay; and when he understood that an officer had returned from Washington with kind messages from the Secretary of the Navy, he seemed much relieved. He was also anxious that Admiral Dupont should be informed that it was no effort or intrigue on his part that had effected the change in the command of the squadron. After he was satisfied on these points, he quieted himself like a child, and appeared in a great measure to put away from his mind worldly things. He suffered severe pain from the rapid progress of his disease, which was a complicated affection of the liver and kidneys, that had been aggravated by his wound and his constant burden of mental anxiety; but he endured his pains with such unmurmuring patience as to draw praise from his attendants. He said once, "If 'twas God's will, I should like to have a little quiet and sleep."

The simple affectionateness and loving qualities of his warm sailor nature came out in all his words and looks. He greeted those who approached his bedside with a smile; and when his daughter, Mrs. Reese, was announced, he called her his dear child, and put his arms around her neck and kissed her.

He gave his last directions concerning his family and his affairs with entire clearness, and as apparently free from all excitement as if he were going upon a short journey.

Captain Sanford, his old ordnance-officer in the Western flotilla, and Captain Simpson were with him constantly, and from them and other brother-officers of the Navy, he received the most tender and unwearied attention. Captain Simpson writes: "His sufferings were so great that there were but few opportunities permitted him of saying words that could be stored up by his friends. His door was besieged by callers, but all were denied except a few family relatives. I told him of the frequent callers, but he said he could not see them—it was too much effort to speak. One day I told him that an officer, who had fought gallantly under him at the West, had asked to see him. He thought for a minute, and then said, 'Who knows what a dying man's word may do—I will see him.' The officer came to his bed, and Foote spoke to him. I know not what he said, but I saw the man's frame convulsed with emotion, and as he laid down Foote's hand he burst into tears. At one time I was doing something for him, when he looked at me and said, 'Well, and what will you do?' I replied, 'I will try and follow you.' He put his arm around my neck and kissed me. I shall never forget that kiss. I spoke to him of his work on board the old *Portsmouth*, and he rejoined that it was little he had done. He dwelt on the worthlessness of worldly reputation, and said that such deeds as the world gave him credit for he valued now as nothing; and charged me that nothing would give peace at last but the consciousness of having resisted evil. All thought of worldly vanity, praise of men, and renown had disappeared from his mind."

He at length became more disturbed, and his speech at times grew incoherent; but he was rational at intervals. In one of these calm moments he said, "I thank God for all his goodness to me—for all his loving kindness to me." He also said to a relative in the earlier stages of his illness, "God is dealing gently with me. He may bring dark hours; but thus far it grows brighter and brighter with me." He continued in this way, wavering between life and death—now growing stronger, and then sinking away again, like the ebb and flow of the tide—for some days.

His faithful colored man, Brooks, toward whom he had ever

manifested great esteem and kindness, testifies to his saying, with much earnestness, on the night of June 20, "We will have them, North and South"—repeating this several times. Brooks asked him what he meant by this. He replied, "The colored people. Yes, we will have them;" and he then added, "We must have charity—charity—charity."

For thirty-six hours immediately previous to his death he was probably wholly unconscious, and he gently expired at a quarter past ten o'clock on Friday night, the 26th day of June, 1863, at the comparatively early age of fifty-six.

Surgeon Bache, of the Navy, observed with emphasis to Admiral Foote's brother, as they were standing together in the chamber of death, "Your brother has literally worn himself out in the public service. He is as truly a victim of this war as if he had perished on the battle-field."

But now no more of wearing toil, anxiety, and care, of the uproar and confusion of battle, of the terrible mission of war and blood—he had at last found rest. The God whom he loved and served so well—who is the God of peace as well as the God of battles—had given his beloved sleep.

CHAPTER XXIX.

HONORS TO THE MEMORY OF ADMIRAL FOOTE. — FUNERAL OBSEQUIES.

THROUGHOUT the land the illness of the generous, self-sacrificing sailor in New York, arrested as he was by a higher hand while on the point of throwing himself into a new and desperate service, excited unbounded sympathy. His death was a shock to the nation. In fact, his death at that time was the death of the greatest man who had yet fallen. The newspapers—even in that hurried period when important events were taking place and nothing held the public mind long—were filled with elaborate notices and eulogies of the departed hero. This official order of the Naval Department was published on the day succeeding his death:

"WASHINGTON, *June* 27.

"GENERAL ORDER NO. 16.

"A gallant and distinguished naval officer is lost to the country. The hero of Fort Henry and Fort Donelson, the indomitable spirit that created and led to successive victories the Mississippi flotilla—the hero and Christian sailor who, in the China seas and on the coast of Africa, as well as the great interior rivers of our country, sustained with unfaltering fidelity and devotion the honor of our flag and the cause of the Union, Rear-Admiral Andrew Hull Foote, is no more. On his way to take command of the South Atlantic Blockading Squadron—a position to which he had been recently assigned, and the duties of which were commanding the earnest energies and vigorous resources of a mind of no ordinary character—he was suddenly prostrated by disease, and breathed his last at the Astor House in New York on the 26th instant.

"Among the noble and honored dead whose names have added lustre to our naval renown, and must ever adorn our national annals, few will stand more pre-eminent than that of the gallant and self-sacrificing Christian sailor and gentleman whose loss we now deplore. Appreciating his virtues and his services, a grateful country has rendered him while living its willing honors, and will mourn his death.

"As a mark of respect, it is hereby ordered that the flags at the several navy yards, naval stations, and on the flag-ships of squadrons, be hoisted at half-mast; and that thirteen guns be fired at meridian on the day after the receipt of this order. GIDEON WELLES, Secretary of the Navy."

To show how events marched on in that time, and how sternly in earnest was the government, it should here be mentioned, and also as completing the official naval biography of Rear-Admiral Foote, that on the day before his death, the 25th, he was detached on account of sickness from his command of the South Atlantic squadron, and Rear-Admiral Dahlgren was appointed to fill his place.

On Saturday afternoon, the day succeeding the death, the vestibule and parlors of the Astor House were thronged by a concourse of people, among whom were many distinguished men of the nation and intimate friends of the deceased. Visitors poured into the room of death for two hours, and passed out with thoughtful and saddened faces. As the hour approached for the transportation of the remains to New Haven, a large crowd assembled in front of the hotel to witness the scene. Two companies of marines, detached from the receiving-ship *North Carolina*, arrived from the Navy Yard, and a great many citizens also joined the escort. Just before the body was removed, a lady stepped forward and laid a cross of white flowers and immortelles upon the coffin-lid. With dirge-like music the train moved on, the bearers who accompanied the body to the boat being Admiral Storer, Admiral Stringham, Captain Sands, Captain Drayton, Captain Mead, Captain Leslie, Captain Eagle, and Dr. Truslow. On the same day civic honors were paid by the city of New York, and resolutions were passed by the municipal government to the memory of the departed hero.

In New Haven the remains of Admiral Foote lay at his home until Tuesday, the day of the funeral, when they were deposited for a while in the rotunda of the State House. There they were viewed by thousands, and it was remarked that the face, while it was more worn and thin than in life, had a natural look, though with a singular expression of majesty.

Rarely has there been in this land a more impressive funeral scene than was witnessed on Tuesday, June 30th, in the beautiful city of New Haven. The day was a calm and bright June day; the stately elms of the city were in their first luxuriance of foliage; flags drooped from all the public buildings and many of the private residences; business was suspended; and the entire city and the neighboring towns, and it might be said the whole state, flowed in toward the place where the last honors and religious rites were paid to him whom all mourned. Although all felt his loss profoundly at this critical hour of the country's history, yet his life had been so pure and his task so well done—nothing to human eye imperfect or wanting in that life of obedience to duty and of loyal self-sacrifice—that it was impossible to grieve or to be sorrowful overmuch; therefore a sober cheerfulness pervaded the scene, and men's burdened hearts were purified by this grand example of a true life brought before them, and were lifted above their personal sadness into a kind of calm joy. The human soul, even the most selfish, is so formed that it takes pleasure in goodness, and pays unconscious tribute to true worth—that worth, above all, which has in it the elements of love and sacrifice for others. At the religious services in the Center Church, an address was made by Dr. Leonard Bacon, which, after recounting the incidents of the good admiral's career, closed thus:

"Where or how he was to die he had cared but little; he had thought much of the privilege of dying among his friends, though he had expected to meet his end in the din of battle. Around his bedside, strong and warlike men, who had been and soon will be again in the crash of battle, were assembled in tenderness and sympathy. His last words were but few. Once he said: 'God is dealing kindly with me; he has brought me through dark hours, but thus far it grows brighter.' Again he expressed a wish that his life might be blessed to the conversion of many in the Navy; 'but not only in the Navy,' he added, 'but to all.' To an officer who said to him, 'You must not leave us; your place can not be supplied,' he replied: 'God will supply a better one.' His last words were: 'I thank God for all his goodness to me—for all his loving kindness to me; he has been very good to me; I thank him for his kindness.' We are all here as mourners; yet this is only a representation of the Government and Navy, which together mourn the loss of our naval Hercules. The nation is the chief mourner of all. Shall we not, in its name, bless God for such an example—such a stimulus to thousands of hearts yet to be—in the love of country, man, and God?"

The procession which followed the body to its last resting-place was a host for multitude, and was composed of large bodies of state military, of two companies of marines, and a detachment of midshipmen from Brooklyn, of the civil authorities of the principal cities of Connecticut, of the faculty and students of the University, and a great number of citizens. Four admirals acted as pall-bearers—Gregory, Smith, Storer, and Davis — accompanied by Captain Glynn, Commander Simpson, Lieutenant Marven, and Ensign McGregor. Admirals Smith and Davis—both his life-long and tried friends, and the last his trusted successor in the command of the Western flotilla—were specially deputed by the government to attend the funeral; and the officer under whom he made his first voyage, and who now went with him on his last brief journey—Admiral Gregory—was there. The bowed heads and sorrowful faces of these war-worn veterans showed that they felt his loss deeply. His faithful colored man, Brooks, walked behind the hearse carrying his sword.

Under the shadows of the overarching elms and through the calm sunshine, silently, except when the stillness was broken at intervals by the firing of artillery and the tolling of bells, the long procession moved slowly on to the old cemetery; and, after the brief and solemn Episcopal service had been read at the grave, the body was laid down in the ground where slept the dust of many great and good men, and some of more recent fame, who were the first martyrs of the war for the Union, among whom was the brilliant young Theodore Winthrop—but none nobler and truer than he who had now come to ask a place to rest beside them.

CHAPTER XXX.

CONCLUDING WORDS AND LETTERS OF FRIENDS.

IT would seem superfluous to add aught to the simple record that has gone before—certainly not in the way of bestowing praise; for it has been a constant embarrassment to repress the uniform flow of eulogistic remark that has permeated these pages, because it has pervaded almost every letter, document, and public notice that has fallen into our hands. We are conscious, too, of the American fault of exaggeration; and it must be confessed that were the subject Washington himself, hardly nothing more could be said in the way of encomium than has been said by this one and that one of the subject of this memoir. Much doubtless has been said indiscriminately, and of the nature of mere rhetoric; but yet, when all this is deducted, there remains a residuum of pure gold.

Admiral Foote, if not a great man when judged by the highest intellectual standards—and how few there are that are truly great in every sense of that word!—surpassed common men in some things. He surpassed them in moral force. The central element of his character was this—an immutable resolution, under a religious sense of duty, to pursue the right. The principles he had deliberately chosen he carried to sea with him and into public life, and into his intercourse with men every where and under all circumstances. He was an ardent believer in the Christian faith and a believer in prayer—these had been wrought into his spirit in his youth, and he sailed under that flag to the day of his death. He wrote to his wife after the capture of Fort Henry that "he had agonized in prayer for victory." Another man might have won the battle, and not have prayed for it; but he did, and he recognized the hand of God in the victory that was gained. Some may doubt whether this had any thing to do with his military efficiency; but none can doubt that he acted on those principles, and that they formed the deepest spring of his vigor.

He may be thought to have been too radical in his ideas of reform. Some of his naval friends held this opinion, and did not scruple to tell him so. Indeed, in his early professional career, he often endured contempt and persecution on this account; but all who knew him learned to respect him, because he was in earnest. He was one of the instances in history of "the saints who are in Cæsar's household," or men true to their convictions of duty in circumstances of peculiar difficulty and temptation. He believed in total abstinence as the sheet-anchor of sailor character; therefore at the East and West he fought out his temperance principles, till at last —by his speeches, letters, and, above all, personal example— he carried through the temperance reform in the Navy, and abolished spirit-rations. His own crews were noted for their sobriety and good conduct, not only on shipboard, but when they were ashore, at home or in foreign ports. So it was with the observance of Sunday, the prohibition of profanity, and many other things that he had made up his mind about as being right—and because he believed them to be right, without much consultation with others, as far as his authority extended, he put them in practice. If reasoning would not do, he did it by command. He held to a principle to the last breath. Some of the latest acts of his life, during the short period that he was at the head of the Bureau of Equipment and Recruiting, had reference to the question of temperance reform on board government vessels. The venerable Admiral Smith writes: "Rear-Admiral Foote's character is well known in the Navy. One of the strongest traits of his character was great persistence in any thing he undertook. He was a man who could neither be shaken off nor choked off from what he attempted to carry out. He was truly a pious man, severely an honest man, and a philanthropist of the first order. He was one of our foremost Navy officers—none before him."* There are hosts of good men; but of those who stand by their colors as an enthusiasm and a life, and who advance them into the enemy's line, who make conquests in the realm of evil—of such there are few. Admiral Foote was, as his old friend said of him, a true philanthropist. His wish seemed to be—his wisdom may not always have been commensurate with his zeal—but his earnest desire seemed to be to raise the character and condition of men about him, of sailors, of his fellow-officers, of all with whom he had any influence. His mental traits, if not extraordinary, were not commonplace. He had a strong, clear head. His mind was practical; but it had some finer grains that showed him capable of a highly scientific and even literary culture, had his career been one of books, and not of arms. He derived his ideas from men rather than books, and if he did not think profoundly, he was by no means wanting in sound ideas. His perceptive faculties were uncommonly acute, and his powers of invention and organization were by no means contemptible. If he did not possess genius, he had that vivific or energic quality of mind that, having clearly seized a point, drove toward it with power, and carried it by immense strength of will.

He was not a dry-hearted egotist, either as a Christian or an officer. He was open, cordial, and confiding. He was extraordinarily social in temperament. When he was in good health and spirits, wherever he was, there was hearty life and hilariousness. He was not, perhaps, a man of real humor,

* Private letter to author, dated August 13, 1872.

but he was noted for telling a good story, appreciating a good jest, and enjoying a good laugh; and, until borne down by the burden of care, he was the best company in the world, and to the day of his death his boyish and fun-loving spirit flashed out. A genial temper, thoroughly kind, though not without a sprinkle of the salt of rough ocean, made this hero of iron-clads a delightful man in society. The little that he was permitted to have of this kind of life on shore he was thoroughly happy in; and when with his own family and in the circle of his friends, both young and old, then he was seen at the best, and his frank, loving, cheerful nature came out to great advantage. Like many men whose professions doom them to the constant companionship of men, he enjoyed all the more the few opportunities he had of mingling in the society of the gentler sex, and he was every whit a sailor in this respect. His intercourse with the world, and with those of the highest position in all parts of the globe, had given his manners great ease and polish.

He was not, too, without the faults that belong to warm and lively natures. He was sometimes surprised into anger under the sense of wrong, but was very placable, and could not rest, in opposing the will of others, until he had justified himself, if possible, in their minds. Although he possessed great natural hopefulness, yet he was sometimes sadly jangled and out of tune. In times of inglorious inactivity he grew dispirited, but cleared up again like a generous flame at the call of action. He was nervously anxious about results when only thinking of them or imagining them, and therefore over-cautious in preparation; but when the moment came to do, his natural courage drove away all these mists of anxiety and apprehension. He never was so happy as when he was driven most. He loved praise and distinction. He had in this respect the military temperament, which, for some reason, is even more intense in the Navy than in the Army. He was extremely sensitive about his professional reputation. When he did a praiseworthy deed, he wished to have the credit of it, and was jealous of those who he thought would rob him of his just fame. This weakness, if it be such, it can not be denied that he had; yet, after all, it did not go deep, and was a weakness rather than a fault. It might have sprung from his strong sense of right. He did not pull down others to build up his own reputation. He was always ready to praise and help those who might in some sense be considered his rivals. As an instance of this, his hearty commendation of General Grant had a great effect in putting a stop to much newspaper abuse which that commander received in the early part of his career. He never suffered this love of distinction to override duty, and more than once in his life, for what he thought was right, he put himself squarely across the path of his own interests, and brought down upon himself the peril of unpopularity, and even of official disgrace and ruin.

A somewhat mercurial vein of conversation, or small talk, which, as a social man, he fell into, and which did not represent his real mind, joined to the exhibition at times of an innocent personal vanity, masked his character to some, and they did not perceive the fundamental truth, solidity, and greatness of his nature. But he had no overweening estimate of himself, and he was deeply modest as to his own abilities; yet he was simple, open-hearted, and pleased with the sound of glory; yet few, if any, of the leaders of the war were more entirely unselfish in their devotion to country, and, like Mr. Lincoln, he was a type of the American democracy of the true kind, on which the hope of the republic rests, and that, sooner or later, will leaven the whole mass. There was not a purer patriot among them all. His life and all he had belonged to his country.

Like other men of strong character, he was, as has been often said, positive in his opinions almost to obstinacy. He not only "believed he was right," but "he went ahead." He loved argument for argument's sake. Some vessels are freight-carriers, and some are batteries and rams; some men are the rich accumulators of knowledge, others the sturdy opposers of wrong. Let not the men of ideas or of words despise the men of action; the last war showed who occupied then the front rank and who had to take the second place. Each should respect the other.

As a military man, Admiral Foote was not reticent, nor was he swift of decision. He liked and sought counsel, not to be ruled by it, but to be supplied with the materials of a good judgment, which he arrived at himself independently of all outside influences. It was impossible to know beforehand how he would act in any given case, except that old Polonius's advice was pretty sure to be followed:

> "But, being in,
> Bear't, that the opposed may beware of thee."

His personal courage can not be doubted. He has been called "the Stonewall Jackson of the American Navy." Though quiet and almost like a clergyman in his appearance at ordinary times in society, when he was in battle he became a changed man—his eye flashed fire, and then the sailors knew what was coming, and prepared for close quarters. It was highly in character when, with a linen umbrella hoisted over his head, he toiled through rice-fields and ditches at the head of his crew in the hot sun, and was among the first to enter the breached Chinese fort. His men would follow him any where, and that is a sure test of bravery. He said of his sailors at the West, "I have such confidence in my men and they in me, that if I say, Go there, I know they will go if it can be accomplished by flesh and blood." But upon this point, as well as upon others, this letter, coming from such a source, must be regarded as most valuable:

"WASHINGTON, D. C., *September* 23, 1873.

"MY DEAR SIR,—Your letter of September 21st is received, and I am extremely pleased to hear that you have ready for the press a work in commemoration of the late Admiral Andrew H. Foote, U. S. Navy.

"The admiral was in command of the Mississippi flotilla during the operations up the Tennessee and Cumberland rivers, and down the Mississippi during that most important campaign of the winter of 1861–2. At that time I was acting in a sphere too subordinate to enable me to form a judgment of his capacity and power; but in February, 1862, I had occasion several times to see him at Cairo and Paducah, at which latter place I was in command. He was personally very active, and could be seen at all times, either at his office in a wharf-boat at Cairo, or on one of the iron-clad boats of that day, superintending the equipment and armament of his flotilla. He had all the frankness and heartiness of the Old Navy, and was as full of enthusiasm and adventure as a young man. His personal courage at Forts Henry and Donelson (where he was wounded by a cannon-ball while in the pilot-house) was the subject of universal praise, especially by the army that saw and appreciated the gallantry of his conduct, and its important bearing on the campaign. According to my memory, it was the wound he received at Donelson that disabled him, and forced him to obtain relief from a command for which he was so eminently qualified; and in his departure we all felt we had sustained a loss almost irreparable. To me he resembled Farragut, in the simplicity of his mode of life, his intense love of country and profession, and the extraordinary personal courage that made him an example to all the commanders of vessels in his squadron; who in boats of strange form were subjected to danger from shore batteries and guerrillas firing from behind trees and logs—so different from that to which they had been bred on the high seas. As one who recognizes the most valuable services of the Navy on our Western rivers, and is willing to concede to them a large share in our common victories in that quarter, I again express myself gratified that you have in hand the biography of so pure a patriot, so brave an officer, and so kind a gentleman as was the late Admiral Foote, the pioneer of the Navy on the Western waters.

"With great respect, your friend and servant,

"W. T. SHERMAN, General.

"Professor Hoppin, Yale College."

Upon the reasons that led to his appointment to the command of the South Atlantic squadron, and upon other points in his military career, and in the estimation with which he was held by the government as an officer, as well as in the expression of personal friendship and intimate insight into his qualities as a man, the following communication from one who knew him best will be read with great interest:

"HARTFORD, *October* 8, 1873.

"DEAR SIR,—I have your letter of the 4th inst., and am gratified to know that you are engaged in writing the life of my friend, the late Rear-Admiral Foote. Whether I can contribute any facts or incidents to give interest to your work, in addition to those you have already collected, is uncertain. 'We were boys together' at Cheshire Academy more than half a century ago, and the friendship then commenced continued to his death. He was three or four years my junior, but some of our studies were the same. After leaving the academy, we corresponded for a time; but his profession and absence from the country, with the lapse of years, caused it to be interrupted. Occasionally, after long intervals, we met and kept alive the remembrance of schoolboy days, but we were seldom brought in contact until I was called to administer the Navy Department in 1861. He was at that time the executive officer of the Brooklyn Navy Yard, and in that position, at that critical period of our affairs, his services, though not as demonstrative and as generally known, were scarcely less important and valuable to the country than those rendered soon after on our Western waters in the cause of the Union. His labors and efficiency were felt and acknowledged in aiding the Navy Department to create and call into existence that impromptu Navy which, within a few months, to the surprise of our country and the world, established an effective blockade of three thousand five hundred miles—a fact which, when the blockade was ordered, eminent foreign statesmen pronounced a material impossibility, but which the same distinguished authorities within one year admitted to be conclusive, and that in no previous war had the ports of an enemy's country been so effectually closed by a naval force.

"At the very commencement of our difficulties, when the expedition to Sumter was ordered, and there was a deficiency of vessels in commission for the service, he by direction of the Navy Department prepared the steam-frigate *Powhatan* for sea in one week, an unparalleled performance when the condition of that vessel is understood, she having returned but a few days previously from a three years' cruise. Thenceforward, until ordered in September to other duties, he labored with an assiduity and zeal which, being quiet and unheralded, the country never realized or fully appreciated. Headly, not always reliable, in his biography of Admiral Porter, represents that officer as sitting for 'six days and nights in Commodore (Commander) Foote's office, directing the different operations and urging on the work' of fitting out the *Powhatan*—'shoved the President's orders at Foote so hard, and insisted so pertinaciously on a compliance with them, that the latter had finally to give in, and went to work.' Foote was not a man who needed to be 'shoved' at any time, nor would he be likely to have a junior officer in his office directing his operations. He was not one who ever hesitated to obey legitimate orders. The statement of Headly does Foote great injustice.

The organization and employment of a naval flotilla on the rivers of the West was a question much controverted and discussed in the early days of the rebellion. Military officers had at that time little faith in the utility and power of gun-boats on the inland waters. It was asserted that shore batteries would riddle and destroy vessels faster than they could be brought into service, unless protected by the Army. Boats, it was admitted, would be serviceable as transports, but of little account for fighting purposes. But under the persistent and strenuous urging of Western gentlemen, particularly the Attorney-General, Mr. Bates, and the celebrated engineer, James B. Eads, of St. Louis, the administration decided that a co-operating naval force would be essential, if not indispensable to Army movements on the Mississippi and its tributaries. When this decision was reached, it was claimed that the river service would not be strictly naval, and that any flotilla which might be ordered should be an appendage to the Army, and subject to military control—that the War Department would make the expenditures, purchase the boats, and furnish the force to man them. This was readily acceded to by the Secretary of the Navy, who had at that period as much as he could do to create a Navy and establish squadrons on our maritime frontier. It was soon ascertained, however, that while the War Department would purchase and build boats, naval officers and naval gunners were required to fit out, command, sail, and fight the vessels and discipline the crews. The Secretary of the Navy, therefore, on application, detailed Commander John Rodgers with assistants for that duty. But time was necessary to procure suitable boats, and to prepare and properly arm and equip them, and there were soon discontent and murmurs at the delay. This had its influence, and General Fremont, on assuming command of the Western Department, asked for another and different naval commander. It would be difficult, however, at any time, to find a more bold and resolute officer than John Rodgers for any service. Besides, the duty was novel, and at that time not popular with the Navy. The officers naturally preferred sea duty, and were reluctant to come under Army control. Moreover, the service actually required a peculiar and high order of talent, for a Navy was to be created without a navy yard and its appliances, and to be manned without sailors. Foote appeared to possess the requisite qualities, and to have the experience wanted beyond any other officer to build up a Navy—was prompt, full of resources, fired with patriotic zeal, and, in active service afloat, had wonderful command and influence over his men in reconciling them to any duty. His labors had been unwearied and unceasing from the beginning of the rebellion. His fidelity to the government was as marked in the purchase, construction, and repair of vessels in the navy yards as in the line of his profession afloat. Prudence, economy, vigilance, and an anxious desire, not only to obey orders, but to serve the country, identify himself with the government, and, if possible, anticipate its requirements, were marked traits of his character, and these were precisely the qualities which were wanted in the anomalous service of the naval commander on the rivers of the West. It was with great reluctance that the Department detached him from the Navy Yard at Brooklyn, where his services had been so useful; but he seemed to be, and results proved that he was in every respect, the man to be intrusted with the responsible duty of calling into existence and commanding the Mississippi flotilla, which soon became so formidable, rendered such invaluable service, inspired so much confidence in the Union cause, and was the terror of the rebels wherever any of his gun-boats appeared. His battles gave him renown, but his patient and herculean labors in procuring and organizing the flotilla with which those battles were fought were less known but almost incredible.

"It is not my purpose in this hasty letter to attempt any description of the achievements which distinguished his brief career while in command of the flotilla. Those, as related by himself and his officers in their official dispatches, are published with the Navy Reports of the period, and belong more properly to his biography than to this letter. Instead of being protected by the army, his gun-boats were soon in demand for the defense of the military. It shortly became evident that the two branches of the service would be more effective were they independent, but co-operating and acting jointly. Congress at an early day ordered a transfer of the flotilla from the Army to the Navy, but it was not until after Foote had been relieved. With the officers of the Army he maintained a good and friendly understanding; though the restrictions which General Halleck, the successor of Fremont, put upon his movements he always felt to be not only a grievance to himself, but an injustice to the country; and he never hesitated to say that little progress would be made toward capturing Vicksburg, opening the Mississippi, or subduing the insurrection while Halleck was in active command of the Western Department.

"Wounded at Donelson, he still continued on active duty, unwilling to relinquish his command until I felt compelled, by reason of his debility, to relieve him. While on leave, and suffering from his wound, he was in July promoted to the office of Rear-Admiral; and Congress having directed a reorganization of the Navy Department, with three additional Bureaus, he was simultaneously with his promotion, and while disabled from service afloat, appointed Chief of the newly authorized Bureau of Equipment and Recruiting. Some delay attended his assumption of Bureau duty in consequence of the serious nature of his wound, which was long in healing. As soon as his health permitted, he entered upon this work with all the assiduity and zeal he had displayed in the Navy Yard or on the Mississippi. A few months, however, sufficed to show that Bureau duty was not congenial, and that his health suffered from clerical confinement. He signified to me that service afloat, whenever the Department could give him an appropriate command, would conduce to his health and public usefulness. His wife, though sympathizing with her husband, regretted that he could not remain contented in his position, and expressed her repugnance to his again and so soon leaving his family, which had recently experienced severe affliction; but she at length called on me without his knowledge, and said she was convinced the admiral was suffering in health from confinement to clerical and shore duty. Frequently and freely, in friendly conversation, she had expressed her wish that he would not again take active command during the war; but she now felt it necessary to withdraw all objections, and to entreat that, should he be assigned to active duty, it might be to sea and not river service, where the risks were great, disease prevalent, and the labors too exacting. When the admiral learned that she had called on me, he was very much annoyed. He was particularly disturbed that she had made any exception to river employment, for he considered it a duty to obey orders of any and every kind—to go wherever the Department directed or thought he could be most useful, for it could best judge as to the wants of the service.

"The hesitancy and reluctance of Admiral Dupont, during the winter of 1863, to attack Sumter, the failure of the assault when made in April, followed by his total want of confidence in further effort, and an express desire and intention to withdraw the vessels from Charleston harbor, with the injurious effect of his dispiriting influence upon his subordinates, were matters of deep concern to the Navy Department and the administration. Foote participated in the general disappointment over the result at Charleston; his friendship for Dupont, however, prevented him from giving utterance to any opinion adverse to that officer. But personal feeling was not permitted to interfere with public duty. It was finally determined, as a matter of necessity, to relieve Dupont; but there was some difficulty in regard to the selection of a successor. Among three or four names that were canvassed, Foote's was prominent; but so sensitive were his feelings toward Dupont, and the delicacy of his position in connection with the Department, that he frankly expressed a wish that he might not be called upon to supersede his friend. But after a thorough examination of all the circumstances, and with a full knowledge of his views in regard to operations, freely expressed before the failure of Dupont and when success was considered certain, it was decided to give him command of the South Atlantic squadron. To relieve Dupont, who had court friends and admirers, would be likely to cause commotion, though he had indirectly invited it. Foote had shown his ability for the position, and possessed in an eminent degree, beyond any other officer suggested except Farragut, the confidence of the country. Farragut could not be withdrawn from his important command in the Gulf and on the Lower Mississippi. I therefore, on the 29th of May, invited Foote to an interview, and after a frank and free interchange of opinion in regard to the duties expected and required of the commander of the South Atlantic squadron—the rigid enforcement of the blockade of the entire coast, and particularly of operations against Charleston, and the absolute sealing up of its harbor—informed him that he was designated for that command. On the same day I introduced him to General Gilmore, who had been selected by the War Department to take the place of General Hunter, and was with the military forces expected to co-operate with him and the Navy in joint movements in Charleston harbor. That conference, though interesting, was never in its details consummated by Foote. It was arranged that Rear-Admiral Dahlgren, distinguished for his proficiency in ordnance, between whom and Foote there was close intimacy and friendship, should be associated with him as second in command for special duty in the anticipated operations against Charleston.

"The question being settled, and Foote having received his orders, he entered with alacrity upon his new duties. The necessary details were at once commenced, and on Sunday, the 31st, I met him at the door of the church as I was leaving after the morning service, and we spent some time together on the subject of his command. He proposed to leave that evening for New York with Commander Simpson, whom he had selected as his confidential executive officer. Although noted for his strict religious sentiments, he would not permit the sanctity of the Sabbath to interrupt him in the necessary discharge of his duty. That week he was engaged in active preparation for his departure; but there was unexpected delay on the part of one habitually and proverbially prompt in his movements in leaving, or in specifying the day on which he would leave for his command. I had a letter from him on Monday, the 8th of June, and its unusually desponding tone, complaining of disability and bad health, alarmed me; but on the following day (Tuesday, the 9th) he made a flying visit to Washington, when his earnest manner and evident and expressed satisfaction with his new command, dissipated and put at rest any apprehension I might have entertained from his letter. He also explained the cause of his depressed feelings, and the reason why his departure had been delayed. It might also, he said, lead to a further detention of two or three days, unless the necessities of the service demanded his immediate departure. Dupont he was aware had been advised that he would be relieved, and it was important that the change of commanders should take place as speedily as possible; but on reaching home, preparatory to his departure, the appearance of Mrs. Foote, whose delicate and failing health was evidently giving way, alarmed him. On conversing with the attending physicians, he was frankly told her case was hopeless—that her days on earth were numbered, and she could not long survive. It became necessary, therefore, for him to make arrangements for his family wholly different from what he had expected. When he should leave for his station, it would be with the melancholy knowledge on his part that it was a final earthly separation—that they would never again meet in this life. Nevertheless he had so far completed his arrangements that he intended to leave on the *Tuscarora* on Monday, the 15th, for his station. He took his leave of me that evening to return to New York, expecting to embark on the succeeding Monday. We never met again. On the morning of Thursday, the 18th, I received information that he was lying dangerously ill at the Astor House, in New York, having arrived there on his way to his command. The tidings on that and the succeeding day were alarming, and on Saturday Dr. Wheelan, Chief of the Bureau of Medicine, an old friend and admirer, in whom Foote had great faith, left Washington to attend him. Admiral Dahlgren, who was associated with Foote, and had been in New York expecting to accompany him to Port Royal, returned to Washington, and called on me on Sunday. He said Foote's case was hopeless—that he had an interview with him on Saturday, when the admiral told him all was over, that it was 'the last of this world, and he was prepared for the event.' He lingered until the 26th, when he died. His devoted and loving wife, for whom he felt so much solicitude, and from whom he expected an earlier and final earthly separation, attended him in his last illness, and survived him several months. Next to Farragut, Foote was, unquestionably, at the time of his death the most popular officer in the Navy, and had more fully the confidence, not only of the Navy, but of the government and country. He was proud of his profession, and did much, by his example and precept, to elevate the tone and character of the Navy. No man had greater influence over his men. His earnest sincerity inspired confidence which was felt in battle, and led his command to do or die; in peaceful times it had improved their habits and elevated their character and self-respect. The unexpected death of this gentleman and truly Christian sailor was deplored by those who knew him, and was an irreparable loss to the government and country.

"Very respectfully, GIDEON WELLES.

"Professor James M. Hoppin."

As to what Admiral Foote really accomplished in the last war, nothing need be added to what has been said. The simple facts are the best witnesses; but it is a singular thing in regard to the kind of service that he rendered, that he who passionately loved the sea, and who coveted the fame of the older sea-captains, who fought their ships in blue water, should have been above all a fort-batterer, a fort-taker, and that his principal exploits should have been in this line against earthworks and stone-works, such as the Chinese Barrier Forts,

Fort Henry, Fort Donelson, Columbus, Island No. Ten. He had no opportunity to lead a squadron or a single ship to the encounter amid the winds and waves of the open ocean, where seamanship and skill are almost of as much account as valor; but we may imagine that the same qualities of mingled caution and daring would have characterized his operations, and that, once tackled to an enemy, he never would have released his hold. He was, we would say in this connection, as a seaman, thorough but prudent, and from being overcautious when first in command, he is said by those competent to judge to have grown extremely bold in his seamanship, and ready to do any thing that the circumstances dictated.*

He is to be judged by the quality of what he did in the war, rather than the quantity—he was in active service considerable less than a year. During that time the blows he struck were telling blows—there were none more so. He had the sagacity to perceive the right point of attack where the blow would be felt. Before he was thought of as one to take command at the West, and before naval operations in that quarter were decided upon by the government, he advanced the opinion that there would be need of gun-boats on the Western waters; and when he really took hold of the matter, he saw at once the value of the idea, and threw himself into it with all his force, until it grew to be a mighty fact under his hand; so that, in the words of another, whereas "not a gun belonging to the Navy was to be found on the Mississippi or its tributaries at the beginning of the war, before the close of the war there were a hundred steamers armed with new American guns." Not that Foote accomplished all this, but he was a main factor in its accomplishment. When once the instrument was

* I am indebted to Surgeon S. Henriques of the Bureau of Equipment and Recruiting, one of Admiral Foote's oldest friends, who sailed with him in the *Portsmouth*, and who was with him at the West, for much information on professional points.

shaped to his hand he used it with great skill. He brought it to bear with tremendous effect.

He seized with the intuition of genius upon the strategic importance of Fort Henry as a key of the enemy's position in Northern Tennessee, and the impulse as well as the plan to capture that stronghold went from him. That was the beginning of the end of the Southern power in the Southwest. The permanent hold of the loyal arms upon the South was then established, which was never afterward essentially weakened, and which slowly but surely from that moment advanced in strength. We quote the following words as including in a comprehensive form a fair statement of the military services that Admiral Foote rendered to his country during the War of the Rebellion: "By these brilliant operations of the Army and Navy, the rebel line of defense was broken at the centre, and this made it a necessity for them to abandon the two wings of this line—Bowling Green on their right, and Columbus on the Mississippi. It was one of the great hinge-points of the war, the first great blow which the rebellion received. A forced lodgment in the heart of Tennessee involved, almost of necessity, the final overthrow of the rebel cause. The naval battles which had been fought on the Atlantic coast were perhaps more brilliant; but none, unless it were that between the *Monitor* and the *Merrimack*, were followed by more important results."

As a friend of the sailor, Admiral Foote will be long and warmly remembered. He saw the rough diamond in Jack's nature. He knew his wants and temptations. The seaman recognized him instinctively as his friend, and went to him for help in his troubles; and one of the most touching tributes paid to the admiral's memory was in some resolutions passed immediately after his death by the New York Port Society, in which it was said: "He led the men of his command in battle and inspired them by his valor—he led them likewise in the way of Christian truth. His care for the men was marked not alone in the line of his official duty, but he sought to promote their temporal good, and above all to make them followers of the Captain of salvation. He was wont to proclaim the Gospel to them in public and private. Admiral Foote evinced an earnest interest in behalf of the men of the sea. While we deeply deplore his loss, we confidently believe that our departed friend has now gained the welcome approval of his Lord."

We now gladly give an interesting letter from one who had rare opportunities to know Admiral Foote in the most familiar relations—who sailed with him, and yet who was not a sailor nor a man of war, but a man of peaceful pursuits, and at an age, too, when persons are the most critical—just when youth is turning into manhood. The captain's private secretary, if at all a shrewd observer, must have had pretty good opportunities on a long voyage of seeing his commander just as he was —in his weakness as well as strength:

"PARSONAGE, ORANGE VALLEY, NEW JERSEY,
October 1, 1873.

"MY DEAR SIR,—My acquaintance with the late Admiral Foote began when he was a lieutenant-commanding, and had just returned from that cruise on the coast of Africa concerning which he has himself written. Coming back to New Haven on furlough, I used to see him in the Sunday-school, where I was a scholar and he a teacher, and in frequent visits at my father's house. Soon afterward, when my impaired health made it necessary for me to abandon my studies for a while, he kindly promised me that I should go with him on his next cruise as captain's clerk.

"The next cruise turned out to be an eventful one. He was given the command of the *Portsmouth* sloop-of-war, which at that time (1856) was considered one of the very best among our sailing-vessels. The *Portsmouth* was fitted out at Norfolk with great care, and carried a battery of 8-inch guns, in the working of which Foote and his friend Dahlgren felt the deepest interest. It was the first time, I believe, that a ship of the *Portsmouth's* class had been fitted with a battery of such heavy ordnance. And the service which she was called to render in the reduction of the Barrier Forts in the Canton river proved to have great value as showing the efficacy of the heavy metal which a sloop-of-war of her size could carry. The results of that bombardment were made the subject of a special report to the Ordnance Department and of private letters to Dahlgren, whose scientific reputation was as highly valued by Foote as if it had been his own. It was an eminently wise choice which, years afterward, in the war of our rebellion, put these two men together in that important service in Charleston harbor to which Foote was ordered when his death occurred. They would have worked together as hardly any other two men in the service could have worked—each of them helping out the other's characteristics with his own peculiar qualities. It is idle, of course, to conjecture what might have happened if Foote had been spared to carry out the plans which the Department had marked out for him. But to those of us who knew him best it seemed that he was standing on the threshold of an opportunity which would have given to him and to the flag for which he fought a renown even more illustrious than his career had yet furnished.

"The only time I ever saw him engaged in active hostilities was when the *Portsmouth* was occupied in the reduction of the Barrier Forts. At this distance of time, when almost all the actors in it have passed away, there is no harm in saying that that fight was Foote's from the beginning to the end of it. There were three of our ships engaged in it; but it was his determination and energy which gave to the action its prompt and vigorous success. I need not repeat the story of the engagement; but I shall never forget the impression of vehemence and concentration of purpose which the admiral's conduct produced, not only on me, but I think I may fairly say upon the whole squadron. He was a splendid fighter, with just that combination of audacity and caution, of impetuosity and persistence, of natural combativeness and scientific skill, which makes the very best kind of military or naval leadership. In the fight at the Barrier Forts he exposed himself to the greatest danger; while he was bringing his ship to anchor at close range, two round shot passed within a foot or two of his head; and he led in person the landing-party which assaulted the forts at the close of the bombardment. He gave me, I remember, sealed letters to his family, written at the latest moment before starting for the shore, with instructions to forward them if he should not return. And in all his behavior he showed that highest kind of courage which recognizes to the full the peril of the hour, and, recognizing it, is no way disquieted or hindered by it. Moreover, there was that kind of natural and professional fondness for a fight, for the fight's sake, which I suspect a mere civilian can not fully comprehend nor appreciate.

"I am not very competent to estimate his seamanship; but I know that the skillful handling of the *Portsmouth* was matter of general remark and admiration at the various ports of our cruising-ground. And I remember one officer, not personally friendly to Foote, who nevertheless acknowledged that he was the best sailor he ever saw. His vigilant and intelligent oversight of the smallest details in the management of the ship was something which I could not help seeing. He could never put off responsibility on his subordinates. Even when he was prostrated with the sick-headaches which used to torment him at frequent intervals and drive him almost crazy with suffering, he would insist on knowing what was going on. I would hear him groaning with distress in his room one moment, and the next he would be on deck directing the management of the vessel. Nothing would excuse him from the personal oversight of all the ship's affairs. His command was never a sinecure. If there were not work enough to keep him busy, and to keep the ship's company busy also, then he would make work. And, somehow or other, his cruises were almost always famous and eventful.

"It seems to me that the admiral never appeared to the best advantage except when he had upon him the pressure of the very gravest and most responsible duty. So long as his work was easy and commonplace, the superficial defects of his character were evident. He might appear to be a fussy, fidgety man, of inordinate self-consciousness, and with a love of approbation which could easily pass for vanity with those who chose to call it so. But let him have a burden of work and responsibility put upon him which would have crushed an ordinary man, and it straightway appeared how far he was from being an ordinary man. The superficial defects of his character disappeared. His love of approbation was only a wholesome stimulus to duty. His self-consciousness only gave him the more complete self-mastery. And his restless nervousness became an intense and wary vigilance which was an almost certain assurance of success. What would break down most men only served to steady him, and put him in the best trim and attitude for achievement.

"There was no mistake about the religious character of the man. It was genuine and admirable. He was in earnest to do good, and eager to have his influence felt where it would tell for righteousness. On board the *Portsmouth* he repeated the experiment which was so successful on board the brig *Perry* on his previous cruise—the experiment of persuading the crew to a surrender of their grog-ration. Most of the ship's company agreed to it, after listening to the lively and well-put speech in which Foote stated the case to them just before we sailed from Norfolk. During the voyage out to China, I think no spirit-rations were served. But presently the discontent of a few broke up the plan, and before the cruise was finished the total abstinence had generally come to an end. The good effect of their captain's influence, however, was not lost upon the men. There was no mistaking the kindness and Christian faithfulness of his interest in their welfare, even if this special endeavor in behalf of temperance was partially defeated.

"So, too, with the religious services on shipboard. It was the captain's custom to conduct these in person in the absence of a chaplain—reading a part of the service from the Prayer-book of the Episcopal Church, and sometimes a printed sermon. Besides this, he would sometimes hold a more informal prayer-meeting on the berth-deck, at which the attendance was not compulsory; or he would gather the apprentice boys in a Sunday-school class, and attempt some simple instruction of them in religious truth. Always when in port he took pains to have his religious profession and endeavor understood. Knowing how often the influence of officers and men is not especially manifest on the side of Christian faith and charity, he went out of his way to show that his influence was not to be of that sort; so that the arrival of the *Portsmouth* was always as welcome, to say the least, to the missionary families of any port as to the mercantile or diplomatic community. He believed in showing his colors. When the Second King of Siam came down from Bangkok to visit the *Portsmouth*, he expressed some courteous surprise when Foote asked a blessing at the table as they sat down to dinner. He had supposed, his majesty intimated, that only missionary folk did that sort of thing. And he received some new light in regard to religious life in Christian lands when the admiral seized the opportunity to class himself among the missionary folk, and to identify their faith and their endeavors as his own. And so always and in all company, rather than have any thing doubtful or equivocal about his own position, he would make an opportunity to declare it. He never forgot his loyalty to Christ and to his Cross. And he was anxious, if it were possible, to be not only a Christian man, but a Christian officer—bringing his flag with him in his religious service, and making the nation which he represented to be known as not in name only, but in fact, a Christian nation. How successful he was, on one or two notable occasions, in accomplishing this endeavor, the story of his life, as you have written it, will, I doubt not, abundantly show.

"It was partly his broad religious spirit which saved him from becoming a merely technical, routine officer, knowing his profession and knowing nothing else. It was as far as possible from such narrowness. His interest in letters, in science, in politics, was generous and intelligent. His interest in men was kind and thoughtful. In many ways, in little ways as well as in those more important, I was personally indebted to his thoughtfulness and care for me. The two years that I spent with him—the first as his clerk in intimate confidential relationship, the second as his purser—gave me the opportunity to know him thoroughly. The wider reputation which he acquired in the War of the Rebellion did not at all surprise me. I am sure that he would have proved equal to any opportunity which a longer life had brought to him. And his example seems to me one most worthy to be studied and to be followed. Brave, skillful, true—a good sailor, a good fighter, a good citizen, a good man—Christian in word and deed and life—the nation, for which he lived and died, needs only to know him better in order to love him more, and to honor his memory as among its choicest treasures.

"Most truly yours, GEORGE B. BACON."

Toward the last of May, 1874, the writer of this biography met, by good fortune, Commodore Rodgers, Chief of Bureau of Docks and Yards, at the room of Secretary Robeson in Washington, D. C. The conversation turned upon Admiral Foote. "Foote," said Commodore Rodgers, "had more of the bull-dog than any man I ever knew. He did not, like some men, plan gallant deeds on his bed, and when the pinch came discover he was no hero; but when the fighting came, then he was in his element—he liked it. He had some charming foibles, which only endeared him the more to those who knew him; and among these he thought he was an orator, which he certainly was not. He was a man of acute nervous organization, which accounted for some of his impulsive acts. He was a man of deep religious principle, and was one in whom the government entirely confided, and on whom events turned. He was a splendid naval officer. He was a typical man."

Why need we add more words of friends or of our own? Our grateful task is finished. We have striven to give a plain and straightforward story, without exaggeration, without covering up flaws, and without keeping back hearty praise of noble qualities and great actions. Farragut, Foote, Dupont, Goldsborough, Dahlgren, the two Porters, Winslow, Worden—are not these worthy to take their place with the sea-captains of the earlier days of the republic—yes, with those ancient English worthies who, in their nimble little vessels, grappled with invincible tenacity the many-towered ships of the Spanish Armada, and saved England to freedom and the Protestant faith? In them all burned

> "The unconquerable mind, and Freedom's holy flame."

In one of them, we know, burned a still purer and holier flame. No man, says Coleridge, can be in the highest sense a hero who is not a man of faith. It is the overpowering sense of God, of the greatness of the thought of him, of loyalty to his service, that dissipates littleness and selfish fear, raises the mind above material elements, and makes it truly heroic. The faith of a sailor is often one of peculiar power and depth. Where life itself is the price of constant watchfulness, of scrupulous order, of patient endurance, of unflinching obedience to one governing will, the grand law of duty is apt to be well learned in the school of old ocean. Where, too, the ship is alone on the sea, suspended over a mysterious abyss that stretches like a dim eternity before the eye, the thought of God, and dependence upon him, and final accountability to him, fills the religious mind; so that the man who spends much of his life at sea is often a man of strong faith.

And this same ocean, whose storms shake the world, also binds the world closely together. Through its waters pass those lines of national intercommunication which, though they vanish after the track of the ship's keel, are nevertheless the viewless lines which knit the race of man into one brotherhood; and thus the ocean becomes the means of educating and increasing the love of man.

Duty to God—love to man—these were the words written on the colors which he sailed under, the simple and unadorned narrative of whose life has been given in these pages—and he never pulled down his flag.

INDEX.

J.

K.

L.

M.

N.

O.

P.

W.

Y.

THE END.

VALUABLE & INTERESTING WORKS

FOR PUBLIC AND PRIVATE LIBRARIES,

PUBLISHED BY HARPER & BROTHERS, NEW YORK.

☞ *For a full List of Books suitable for Libraries, see* HARPER & BROTHERS' TRADE-LIST *and* CATALOGUE, *which may be had gratuitously on application to the Publishers personally, or by letter enclosing Ten Cents.*

☞ HARPER & BROTHERS *will send any of the following works by mail, postage prepaid, to any part of the United States, on receipt of the price.*

SCHWEINFURTH'S HEART OF AFRICA. The Heart of Africa: or, Three Years' Travels and Adventures in the Unexplored Regions of the Centre of Africa. From 1868 to 1871. By Dr. GEORG SCHWEINFURTH. Translated by ELLEN E. FREWER. With an Introduction by WINWOOD READE. Illustrated by about 130 Woodcuts from Drawings made by the Author, and with Two Maps. 2 vols., 8vo, Cloth, $8 00.

FLAMMARION'S ATMOSPHERE. The Atmosphere. Translated from the French of CAMILLE FLAMMARION. Edited by JAMES GLAISHER, F.R.S., Superintendent of the Magnetical and Meteorological Department of the Royal Observatory at Greenwich. With 10 Chromo-Lithographs and 86 Woodcuts. 8vo, Cloth, $6 00.

HUDSON'S HISTORY OF JOURNALISM. Journalism in the United States, from 1690 to 1872. By FREDERICK HUDSON. Crown 8vo, Cloth, $5 00.

PIKE'S SUB-TROPICAL RAMBLES. Sub-Tropical Rambles in the Land of the Aphanapteryx. By NICOLAS PIKE, U. S. Consul, Port Louis, Mauritius. Profusely Illustrated from the Author's own Sketches; containing also Maps and Valuable Meteorological Charts. Crown 8vo, Cloth, $3 50.

HERVEY'S CHRISTIAN RHETORIC. A System of Christian Rhetoric, for the Use of Preachers and Other Speakers. By GEORGE WINFRED HERVEY, M.A., Author of "Rhetoric of Conversation," &c. 8vo, Cloth, $3 50.

PRIME'S I GO A-FISHING. I Go a-Fishing. By W. C. PRIME. Crown 8vo, Cloth, $2 50.

ANNUAL RECORD OF SCIENCE AND INDUSTRY FOR 1873. Edited by Prof. SPENCER F. BAIRD, of the Smithsonian Institution, with the Assistance of Eminent Men of Science. 12mo, over 800 pp., Cloth, $2 00. (Uniform with the *Annual Records of Science and Industry for* 1871 *and* 1872. 12mo, Cloth, $2 00.)

EVANGELICAL ALLIANCE CONFERENCE, 1873. History, Essays, Orations, and Other Documents of the Sixth General Conference of the Evangelical Alliance, held in New York, Oct. 2–12, 1873. Edited by Rev. PHILIP SCHAFF, D.D., and Rev. S. IRENÆUS PRIME, D.D. With Portraits of Rev. Messrs. Pronier, Carrasco, and Cook, recently deceased. 8vo, Cloth, nearly 800 pages, $6 00.

VINCENT'S LAND OF THE WHITE ELEPHANT. The Land of the White Elephant: Sights and Scenes in Southeastern Asia. A Personal Narrative of Travel and Adventure in Farther India, embracing the Countries of Burma, Siam, Cambodia, and Cochin-China (1871–2). By FRANK VINCENT, Jr. Magnificently illustrated with Map, Plans, and numerous Woodcuts. Crown 8vo, Cloth, $3 50.

TRISTRAM'S THE LAND OF MOAB. The Result of Travels and Discoveries on the East Side of the Dead Sea and the Jordan. By H. B. TRISTRAM, M.A., LL.D., F.R.S., Master of the Greatham Hospital, and Hon. Canon of Durham. With a Chapter on the Persian Palace of Mashita, by JAS. FERGUSON, F.R.S. With Map and Illustrations. Crown 8vo, Cloth, $2 50.

SANTO DOMINGO, Past and Present; with a Glance at Hayti. By SAMUEL HAZARD. Maps and Illustrations. Crown 8vo, Cloth, $3 50.

SMILES'S HUGUENOTS AFTER THE REVOCATION. The Huguenots in France after the Revocation of the Edict of Nantes: with a Visit to the Country of the Vaudois. By SAMUEL SMILES. Crown 8vo, Cloth, $2 00.

POETS OF THE NINETEENTH CENTURY. The Poets of the Nineteenth Century. Selected and Edited by the Rev. ROBERT ARIS WILLMOTT. With English and American Additions, arranged by EVERT A. DUYCKINCK, Editor of "Cyclopædia of American Literature." Comprising Selections from the Greatest Authors of the Age. Superbly Illustrated with 141 Engravings from Designs by the most Eminent Artists. In elegant small 4to form, printed on Superfine Tinted Paper, richly bound in extra Cloth, Beveled, Gilt Edges, $5 00; Half Calf, $5 50; Full Turkey Morocco, $9 00.

THE REVISION OF THE ENGLISH VERSION OF THE NEW TESTAMENT. With an Introduction by the Rev. P. SCHAFF, D.D. 618 pp., Crown 8vo, Cloth, $3 00.

This work embraces in one volume:

I. ON A FRESH REVISION OF THE ENGLISH NEW TESTAMENT. By J. B. LIGHTFOOT, D.D., Canon of St. Paul's, and Hulsean Professor of Divinity, Cambridge. Second Edition, Revised. 196 pp.

II. ON THE AUTHORIZED VERSION OF THE NEW TESTAMENT in Connection with some Recent Proposals for its Revision. By RICHARD CHENEVIX TRENCH, D.D., Archbishop of Dublin. 194 pp.

III. CONSIDERATIONS ON THE REVISION OF THE ENGLISH VERSION OF THE NEW TESTAMENT. By J. C. ELLICOTT, D.D., Bishop of Gloucester and Bristol. 178 pp.

NORDHOFF'S CALIFORNIA. California: For Health, Pleasure, and Residence. A Book for Travelers and Settlers. Illustrated. 8vo, Paper, $2 00; Cloth, $2 50.

MOTLEY'S DUTCH REPUBLIC. The Rise of the Dutch Republic. By JOHN LOTHROP MOTLEY, LL.D., D.C.L. With a Portrait of William of Orange. 3 vols., 8vo, Cloth, $10 50.

MOTLEY'S UNITED NETHERLAND'S. History of the United Netherlands: from the Death of William the Silent to the Twelve Years' Truce—1609. With a full View of the English-Dutch Struggle against Spain, and of the Origin and Destruction of the Spanish Armada. By JOHN LOTHROP MOTLEY, LL.D., D.C.L. Portraits. 4 vols., 8vo, Cloth, $14 00.

MOTLEY'S LIFE AND DEATH OF JOHN OF BARNEVELD. Life and Death of John of Barneveld, Advocate of Holland. With a View of the Primary Causes and Movements of "The Thirty Years' War." By JOHN LOTHROP MOTLEY, D.C.L. With Illustrations. In Two Volumes. 8vo, Cloth, $7 00.

HAYDN'S DICTIONARY OF DATES, relating to all Ages and Nations. For Universal Reference. Edited by BENJAMIN VINCENT, Assistant Secretary and Keeper of the Library of the Royal Institution of Great Britain; and Revised for the Use of American Readers. 8vo, Cloth, $5 00; Sheep, $6 00.

MACGREGOR'S ROB ROY ON THE JORDAN. The Rob Roy on the Jordan, Nile, Red Sea, and Gennesareth, &c. A Canoe Cruise in Palestine and Egypt, and the Waters of Damascus. By J. MACGREGOR, M.A. With Maps and Illustrations. Crown 8vo, Cloth, $2 50.

WALLACE'S MALAY ARCHIPELAGO. The Malay Archipelago: the Land of the Orang-Utan and the Bird of Paradise. A Narrative of Travel, 1854-1862. With Studies of Man and Nature. By ALFRED RUSSEL WALLACE. With Ten Maps and Fifty-one Elegant Illustrations. Crown 8vo, Cloth, $2 50.

WHYMPER'S ALASKA. Travel and Adventure in the Territory of Alaska, formerly Russian America—now Ceded to the United States—and in various other parts of the North Pacific. By FREDERICK WHYMPER. With Map and Illustrations. Crown 8vo, Cloth, $2 50.

ORTON'S ANDES AND THE AMAZON. The Andes and the Amazon; or, Across the Continent of South America. By JAMES ORTON, M.A., Professor of Natural History in Vassar College, Poughkeepsie, N. Y., and Corresponding Member of the Academy of Natural Sciences, Philadelphia. With a New Map of Equatorial America and numerous Illustrations. Crown 8vo, Cloth, $2 00.

WINCHELL'S SKETCHES OF CREATION. Sketches of Creation: a Popular View of some of the Grand Conclusions of the Sciences in reference to the History of Matter and of Life. Together with a Statement of the Intimations of Science respecting the Primordial Condition and the Ultimate Destiny of the Earth and the Solar System. By ALEXANDER WINCHELL, LL.D., Professor of Geology, Zoology, and Botany in the University of Michigan, and Director of the State Geological Survey. With Illustrations. 12mo, Cloth, $2 00.

WHITE'S MASSACRE OF ST. BARTHOLOMEW. The Massacre of St. Bartholomew: Preceded by a History of the Religious Wars in the Reign of Charles IX. By HENRY WHITE, M.A. With Illustrations. 8vo, Cloth, $1 75.

LOSSING'S FIELD-BOOK OF THE REVOLUTION. Pictorial Field-Book of the Revolution; or, Illustrations, by Pen and Pencil, of the History, Biography, Scenery, Relics, and Traditions of the War for Independence. By BENSON J. LOSSING. 2 vols., 8vo, Cloth, $14 00; Sheep, $15 00; Half Calf, $18 00; Full Turkey Morocco, $22 00.

LOSSING'S FIELD-BOOK OF THE WAR OF 1812. Pictorial Field-Book of the War of 1812; or, Illustrations, by Pen and Pencil, of the History, Biography, Scenery, Relics, and Traditions of the Last War for American Independence. By BENSON J. LOSSING. With several hundred Engravings on Wood, by Lossing and Barritt, chiefly from Original Sketches by the Author. 1088 pages, 8vo, Cloth, $7 00; Sheep, $8 50; Half Calf, $10 00.

ALFORD'S GREEK TESTAMENT. The Greek Testament: with a critically revised Text; a Digest of Various Readings; Marginal References to Verbal and Idiomatic Usage; Prolegomena; and a Critical and Exegetical Commentary. For the Use of Theological Students and Ministers. By HENRY ALFORD, D.D., Dean of Canterbury. Vol. I., containing the Four Gospels. 944 pages, 8vo, Cloth, $6 00; Sheep, $6 50.

ABBOTT'S FREDERICK THE GREAT. The History of Frederick the Second, called Frederick the Great. By JOHN S. C. ABBOTT. Elegantly Illustrated. 8vo, Cloth, $5 00.

ABBOTT'S HISTORY OF THE FRENCH REVOLUTION. The French Revolution of 1789, as viewed in the Light of Republican Institutions. By JOHN S. C. ABBOTT. With 100 Engravings. 8vo, Cloth, $5 00.

ABBOTT'S NAPOLEON BONAPARTE. The History of Napoleon Bonaparte. By JOHN S. C. ABBOTT. With Maps, Woodcuts, and Portraits on Steel. 2 vols., 8vo, Cloth, $10 00.

ABBOTT'S NAPOLEON AT ST. HELENA; or, Interesting Anecdotes and Remarkable Conversations of the Emperor during the Five and a Half Years of his Captivity. Collected from the Memorials of Las Casas, O'Meara, Montholon, Antommarchi, and others. By JOHN S. C. ABBOTT. With Illustrations. 8vo, Cloth, $5 00.

ADDISON'S COMPLETE WORKS. The Works of Joseph Addison, embracing the whole of the "Spectator." Complete in 3 vols., 8vo, Cloth, $6 00.

ALCOCK'S JAPAN. The Capital of the Tycoon: a Narrative of a Three Years' Residence in Japan. By Sir RUTHERFORD ALCOCK, K.C.B., Her Majesty's Envoy Extraordinary and Minister Plenipotentiary in Japan. With Maps and Engravings. 2 vols., 12mo, Cloth, $3 50.

ALISON'S HISTORY OF EUROPE. FIRST SERIES: From the Commencement of the French Revolution, in 1789, to the Restoration of the Bourbons, in 1815. [In addition to the Notes on Chapter LXXVI., which correct the errors of the original work concerning the United States, a copious Analytical Index has been appended to this American edition.] SECOND SERIES: From the Fall of Napoleon, in 1815, to the Accession of Louis Napoleon, in 1852. 8 vols., 8vo, Cloth, $16 00.

BALDWIN'S PRE-HISTORIC NATIONS. Pre-Historic Nations; or, Inquiries concerning some of the Great Peoples and Civilizations of Antiquity, and their Probable Relation to a still Older Civilization of the Ethiopians or Cushites of Arabia. By JOHN D. BALDWIN, Member of the American Oriental Society. 12mo, Cloth, $1 75.

BARTH'S NORTH AND CENTRAL AFRICA. Travels and Discoveries in North and Central Africa: being a Journal of an Expedition undertaken under the Auspices of H. B. M.'s Government, in the Years 1849–1855. By HENRY BARTH, Ph.D., D.C.L. Illustrated. 3 vols., 8vo, Cloth, $12 00.

HENRY WARD BEECHER'S SERMONS. Sermons by HENRY WARD BEECHER, Plymouth Church, Brooklyn. Selected from Published and Unpublished Discourses, and Revised by their Author. With Steel Portrait. Complete in 2 vols., 8vo, Cloth, $5 00.

LYMAN BEECHER'S AUTOBIOGRAPHY, &c. Autobiography, Correspondence, &c., of Lyman Beecher, D.D. Edited by his Son, CHARLES BEECHER. With Three Steel Portraits, and Engravings on Wood. In 2 vols., 12mo, Cloth, $5 00.

BOSWELL'S JOHNSON. The Life of Samuel Johnson, LL.D. Including a Journey to the Hebrides. By JAMES BOSWELL, Esq. A New Edition, with numerous Additions and Notes. By JOHN WILSON CROKER, LL.D., F.R.S. Portrait of Boswell. 2 vols., 8vo, Cloth, $4 00.

DRAPER'S CIVIL WAR. History of the American Civil War. By JOHN W. DRAPER, M.D., LL.D., Professor of Chemistry and Physiology in the University of New York. In Three Vols. 8vo, Cloth, $3 50 per vol.

DRAPER'S INTELLECTUAL DEVELOPMENT OF EUROPE. A History of the Intellectual Development of Europe. By JOHN W. DRAPER, M.D., LL.D., Professor of Chemistry and Physiology in the University of New York. 8vo, Cloth, $5 00.

DRAPER'S AMERICAN CIVIL POLICY. Thoughts on the Future Civil Policy of America. By JOHN W. DRAPER, M.D., LL.D., Professor of Chemistry and Physiology in the University of New York. Crown 8vo, Cloth, $2 50.

DU CHAILLU'S AFRICA. Explorations and Adventures in Equatorial Africa with Accounts of the Manners and Customs of the People, and of the Chase of the Gorilla, the Crocodile, Leopard, Elephant, Hippopotamus, and other Animals. By PAUL B. DU CHAILLU. Numerous Illustrations. 8vo, Cloth, $5 00.

BELLOWS'S OLD WORLD. The Old World in its New Face: Impressions of Europe in 1867-1868. By HENRY W. BELLOWS. 2 vols., 12mo, Cloth, $3 50.

BRODHEAD'S HISTORY OF NEW YORK. History of the State of New York. By JOHN ROMEYN BRODHEAD. 1609-1691. 2 vols. 8vo, Cloth, $3 00 per vol.

BROUGHAM'S AUTOBIOGRAPHY. Life and Times of HENRY, LORD BROUGHAM. Written by Himself. In Three Volumes. 12mo, Cloth, $2 00 per vol.

BULWER'S PROSE WORKS. Miscellaneous Prose Works of Edward Bulwer. Lord Lytton. 2 vols., 12mo, Cloth, $3 50.

BULWER'S HORACE. The Odes and Epodes of Horace. A Metrical Translation into English. With Introduction and Commentaries. By LORD LYTTON. With Latin Text from the Editions of Orelli, Macleane, and Yonge. 12mo, Cloth, $1 75.

BULWER'S KING ARTHUR. A Poem. By EARL LYTTON. New Edition. 12mo, Cloth, $1 75.

BURNS'S LIFE AND WORKS. The Life and Works of Robert Burns. Edited by ROBERT CHAMBERS. 4 vols., 12mo, Cloth, $6 00.

REINDEER, DOGS, AND SNOW-SHOES. A Journal of Siberian Travel and Explorations made in the Years 1865-'67. By RICHARD J. BUSH, late of the Russo-American Telegraph Expedition. Illustrated. Crown 8vo, Cloth, $3 00.

CARLYLE'S FREDERICK THE GREAT. History of Friedrich II., called Frederick the Great. By THOMAS CARLYLE. Portraits, Maps, Plans, &c. 6 vols., 12mo, Cloth, $12 00.

CARLYLE'S FRENCH REVOLUTION. History of the French Revolution. Newly Revised by the Author, with Index, &c. 2 vols., 12mo, Cloth, $3 50.

CARLYLE'S OLIVER CROMWELL. Letters and Speeches of Oliver Cromwell. With Elucidations and Connecting Narrative. 2 vols., 12mo, Cloth, $3 50.

CHALMERS'S POSTHUMOUS WORKS. The Posthumous Works of Dr. Chalmers. Edited by his Son-in-Law, Rev. WILLIAM HANNA, LL.D. Complete in 9 vols., 12mo, Cloth, $13 50.

COLERIDGE'S COMPLETE WORKS. The Complete Works of Samuel Taylor Coleridge. With an Introductory Essay upon his Philosophical and Theological Opinions. Edited by Professor SHEDD. Complete in Seven Vols. With a fine Portrait. Small 8vo, Cloth, $10 50.

DOOLITTLE'S CHINA. Social Life of the Chinese: with some Account of their Religious, Governmental, Educational, and Business Customs and Opinions. With special but not exclusive Reference to Fuhchau. By Rev. JUSTUS DOOLITTLE, Fourteen Years Member of the Fuhchau Mission of the American Board. Illustrated with more than 150 characteristic Engravings on Wood. 2 vols., 12mo, Cloth, $5 00.

GIBBON'S ROME. History of the Decline and Fall of the Roman Empire. By EDWARD GIBBON. With Notes by Rev. H. H. MILMAN and M. GUIZOT. A new cheap Edition. To which is added a complete Index of the whole Work, and a Portrait of the Author. 6 vols., 12mo, Cloth, $9 00.

HAZEN'S SCHOOL AND ARMY IN GERMANY AND FRANCE. The School and the Army in Germany and France, with a Diary of Siege Life at Versailles. By Brevet Major-General W. B. HAZEN, U.S.A., Colonel Sixth Infantry. Crown 8vo, Cloth, $2 50.

HARPER'S NEW CLASSICAL LIBRARY. Literal Translations.
The following Volumes are now ready. Portraits. 12mo, Cloth, $1 50 each.
CÆSAR. —VIRGIL. — SALLUST. — HORACE.— CICERO'S ORATIONS.—CICERO'S OFFICES, &c.—CICERO ON ORATORY AND ORATORS.—TACITUS (2 vols.). — TERENCE. — SOPHOCLES.—JUVENAL.—XENOPHON.— HOMER'S ILIAD.—HOMER'S ODYSSEY.— HERODOTUS.—DEMOSTHENES.—THUCYDIDES.—ÆSCHYLUS.—EURIPIDES (2 vols.). —LIVY (2 vols.).

DAVIS'S CARTHAGE. Carthage and her Remains: being an Account of the Excavations and Researches on the Site of the Phœnician Metropolis in Africa and other adjacent Places. Conducted under the Auspices of Her Majesty's Government. By Dr. DAVIS, F.R.G.S. Profusely Illustrated with Maps, Woodcuts, Chromo-Lithographs, &c. 8vo, Cloth, $4 00.

EDGEWORTH'S (MISS) NOVELS. With Engravings. 10 vols., 12mo, Cloth, $15 00.

GROTE'S HISTORY OF GREECE. 12 vols., 12mo, Cloth, $18 00.

HELPS'S SPANISH CONQUEST. The Spanish Conquest in America, and its Relation to the History of Slavery and to the Government of Colonies. By ARTHUR HELPS. 4 vols., 12mo, Cloth, $6 00.

HALE'S (MRS.) WOMAN'S RECORD. Woman's Record; or, Biographical Sketches of all Distinguished Women, from the Creation to the Present Time. Arranged in Four Eras, with Selections from Female Writers of each Era. By Mrs. SARAH JOSEPHA HALE. Illustrated with more than 200 Portraits. 8vo, Cloth, $5 00.

HALL'S ARCTIC RESEARCHES. Arctic Researches and Life among the Esquimaux: being the Narrative of an Expedition in Search of Sir John Franklin, in the Years 1860, 1861, and 1862. By CHARLES FRANCIS HALL. With Maps and 100 Illustrations. The Illustrations are from Original Drawings by Charles Parsons, Henry L. Stephens, Solomon Eytinge, W. S. L. Jewett, and Granville Perkins, after Sketches by Captain Hall. 8vo, Cloth, $5 00.

HALLAM'S CONSTITUTIONAL HISTORY OF ENGLAND, from the Accession of Henry VII. to the Death of George II. 8vo, Cloth, $2 00.

HALLAM'S LITERATURE. Introduction to the Literature of Europe during the Fifteenth, Sixteenth, and Seventeenth Centuries. By HENRY HALLAM. 2 vols., 8vo, Cloth, $4 00.

HALLAM'S MIDDLE AGES. State of Europe during the Middle Ages. By HENRY HALLAM. 8vo, Cloth, $2 00.

HILDRETH'S HISTORY OF THE UNITED STATES. FIRST SERIES: From the First Settlement of the Country to the Adoption of the Federal Constitution. SECOND SERIES: From the Adoption of the Federal Constitution to the End of the Sixteenth Congress. 6 vols., 8vo, Cloth, $18 00.

HUME'S HISTORY OF ENGLAND. History of England, from the Invasion of Julius Cæsar to the Abdication of James II., 1688. By DAVID HUME. A new Edition, with the Author's last Corrections and Improvements. To which is Prefixed a short Account of his Life, written by Himself. With a Portrait of the Author. 6 vols., 12mo, Cloth, $9 00.

JAY'S WORKS. Complete Works of Rev. William Jay: comprising his Sermons, Family Discourses, Morning and Evening Exercises for every Day in the Year, Family Prayers, &c. Author's enlarged Edition, revised. 3 vols., 8vo, Cloth, $6 00.

JEFFERSON'S DOMESTIC LIFE. The Domestic Life of Thomas Jefferson: compiled from Family Letters and Reminiscences by his Great-Granddaughter, SARAH N. RANDOLPH. With Illustrations. Crown 8vo, Illuminated Cloth, Beveled Edges, $2 50.

JOHNSON'S COMPLETE WORKS. The Works of Samuel Johnson, LL.D. With an Essay on his Life and Genius, by ARTHUR MURPHY, Esq. Portrait of Johnson. 2 vols., 8vo, Cloth, $4 00.

KINGLAKE'S CRIMEAN WAR. The Invasion of the Crimea, and an Account of its Progress down to the Death of Lord Raglan. By ALEXANDER WILLIAM KINGLAKE. With Maps and Plans. Two Vols. ready. 12mo, Cloth, $2 00 per vol.

KINGSLEY'S WEST INDIES. At Last: A Christmas in the West Indies. By CHARLES KINGSLEY. Illustrated. 12mo, Cloth, $1 50.

KRUMMACHER'S DAVID, KING OF ISRAEL. David, the King of Israel: a Portrait drawn from Bible History and the Book of Psalms. By FREDERICK WILLIAM KRUMMACHER, D.D., Author of "Elijah the Tishbite," &c. Translated under the express Sanction of the Author by the Rev. M. G. EASTON, M.A. With a Letter from Dr. Krummacher to his American Readers, and a Portrait. 12mo, Cloth, $1 75.

LAMB'S COMPLETE WORKS. The Works of Charles Lamb. Comprising his Letters, Poems, Essays of Elia, Essays upon Shakspeare, Hogarth, &c., and a Sketch of his Life, with the Final Memorials, by T. NOON TALFOURD. Portrait. 2 vols., 12mo, Cloth, $3 00.

LIVINGSTONE'S SOUTH AFRICA. Missionary Travels and Researches in South Africa; including a Sketch of Sixteen Years' Residence in the Interior of Africa, and a Journey from the Cape of Good Hope to Loando on the West Coast; thence across the Continent, down the River Zambesi, to the Eastern Ocean. By DAVID LIVINGSTONE, LL.D., D.C.L. With Portrait, Maps by Arrowsmith, and numerous Illustrations. 8vo, Cloth, $4 50.

LIVINGSTONES' ZAMBESI. Narrative of an Expedition to the Zambesi and its Tributaries, and of the Discovery of the Lakes Shirwa and Nyassa. 1858-1864. By DAVID and CHARLES LIVINGSTONE. With Map and Illustrations. 8vo, Cloth, $5 00.

M'CLINTOCK & STRONG'S CYCLOPÆDIA. Cyclopædia of Biblical, Theological, and Ecclesiastical Literature. Prepared by the Rev. JOHN M'CLINTOCK, D.D., and JAMES STRONG, S.T.D. *5 vols. now ready.* Royal 8vo. Price per vol., Cloth, $5 00; Sheep, $6 00; Half Morocco, $8 00.

MARCY'S ARMY LIFE ON THE BORDER. Thirty Years of Army Life on the Border. Comprising Descriptions of the Indian Nomads of the Plains; Explorations of New Territory; a Trip across the Rocky Mountains in the Winter; Descriptions of the Habits of Different Animals found in the West, and the Methods of Hunting them; with Incidents in the Life of Different Frontier Men, &c., &c. By Brevet Brigadier-General R. B. MARCY, U.S.A., Author of "The Prairie Traveller." With numerous Illustrations. 8vo, Cloth, Beveled Edges, $3 00.

MACAULAY'S HISTORY OF ENGLAND. The History of England from the Accession of James II. By THOMAS BABINGTON MACAULAY. With an Original Portrait of the Author. 5 vols., 8vo, Cloth, $10 00; 12mo, Cloth, $7 50.

MOSHEIM'S ECCLESIASTICAL HISTORY, Ancient and Modern; in which the Rise, Progress, and Variation of Church Power are considered in their Connection with the State of Learning and Philosophy, and the Political History of Europe during that Period. Translated, with Notes, &c., by A. MACLAINE, D.D. A new Edition, continued to 1826, by C. COOTE, LL.D. 2 vols., 8vo, Cloth, $4 00.

NEVIUS'S CHINA. China and the Chinese: a General Description of the Country and its Inhabitants; its Civilization and Form of Government; its Religious and Social Institutions; its Intercourse with other Nations; and its Present Condition and Prospects. By the Rev. JOHN L. NEVIUS, Ten Years a Missionary in China. With a Map and Illustrations. 12mo, Cloth, $1 75.

THE DESERT OF THE EXODUS. Journeys on Foot in the Wilderness of the Forty Years' Wanderings; undertaken in connection with the Ordnance Survey of Sinai and the Palestine Exploration Fund. By E. H. PALMER, M.A., Lord Almoner's Professor of Arabic, and Fellow of St. John's College, Cambridge. With Maps and numerous Illustrations from Photographs and Drawings taken on the spot by the Sinai Survey Expedition and C. F. Tyrwhitt Drake. Crown 8vo, Cloth, $3 00.

OLIPHANT'S CHINA AND JAPAN. Narrative of the Earl of Elgin's Mission to China and Japan, in the Years 1857, '58, '59. By LAURENCE OLIPHANT, Private Secretary to Lord Elgin. Illustrations. 8vo, Cloth, $3 50.

OLIPHANT'S (MRS.) LIFE OF EDWARD IRVING. The Life of Edward Irving, Minister of the National Scotch Church, London. Illustrated by his Journals and Correspondence. By Mrs. OLIPHANT. Portrait. 8vo, Cloth, $3 50.

RAWLINSON'S MANUAL OF ANCIENT HISTORY. A Manual of Ancient History, from the Earliest Times to the Fall of the Western Empire. Comprising the History of Chaldæa, Assyria, Media, Babylonia, Lydia, Phœnicia, Syria, Judæa, Egypt, Carthage, Persia, Greece, Macedonia, Parthia, and Rome. By GEORGE RAWLINSON, M.A., Camden Professor of Ancient History in the University of Oxford. 12mo, Cloth, $2 50.

RECLUS'S THE EARTH. The Earth: a Descriptive History of the Phenomena and Life of the Globe. By Élisée Reclus. Translated by the late B. B. Woodward, and Edited by Henry Woodward. With 234 Maps and Illustrations, and 23 Page Maps printed in Colors. 8vo, Cloth, $5 00.

RECLUS'S OCEAN. The Ocean, Atmosphere, and Life. Being the Second Series of a Descriptive History of the Life of the Globe. By Élisée Reclus. Profusely Illustrated with 250 Maps or Figures, and 27 Maps printed in Colors. 8vo, Cloth, $6 00.

SHAKSPEARE. The Dramatic Works of William Shakspeare, with the Corrections and Illustrations of Dr. Johnson G. Steevens, and others. Revised by Isaac Reed. Engravings. 6 vols., Royal 12mo, Cloth, $9 00.

SMILES'S LIFE OF THE STEPHENSONS. The Life of George Stephenson, and of his Son, Robert Stephenson; comprising, also, a History of the Invention and Introduction of the Railway Locomotive. By Samuel Smiles. With Steel Portraits and numerous Illustrations. 8vo, Cloth, $3 00.

SMILES'S HISTORY OF THE HUGUENOTS. The Huguenots: their Settlements, Churches, and Industries in England and Ireland. By Samuel Smiles. With an Appendix relating to the Huguenots in America. Crown 8vo, Cloth, $2 00.

SPEKE'S AFRICA. Journal of the Discovery of the Source of the Nile. By Captain John Hanning Speke. With Maps and Portraits and numerous Illustrations, chiefly from Drawings by Captain Grant. 8vo, Cloth, uniform with Livingstone, Barth, Burton, &c., $4 00.

STRICKLAND'S (Miss) QUEENS OF SCOTLAND. Lives of the Queens of Scotland and English Princesses connected with the Regal Succession of Great Britain. By Agnes Strickland. 8 vols., 12mo, Cloth, $12 00.

THE STUDENT'S SERIES.

France. Engravings. 12mo, Cloth, $2 00.
Gibbon. Engravings. 12mo, Cloth, $2 00.
Greece. Engravings. 12mo, Cloth, $2 00.
Hume. Engravings. 12mo, Cloth, $2 00.
Rome. By Liddell. Engravings. 12mo, Cloth, $2 00.
Old Testament History. Engravings. 12mo, Cloth, $2 00.
New Testament History. Engravings. 12mo, Cloth, $2 00.
Strickland's Queens of England. Abridged. Engravings. 12mo, Cloth, $2 00.
Ancient History of the East. 12mo, Cloth, $2 00.
Hallam's Middle Ages. 12mo, Cloth, $2 00.
Hallam's Constitutional History of England. 12mo, Cloth, $2 00.
Lyell's Elements of Geology. 12mo, Cloth, $2 00.

TENNYSON'S COMPLETE POEMS. The Complete Poems of Alfred Tennyson, Poet Laureate. With numerous Illustrations by Eminent Artists, and Three Characteristic Portraits. 8vo, Paper, 75 cents; Cloth, $1 25.

THOMSON'S LAND AND THE BOOK. The Land and the Book; or, Biblical Illustrations drawn from the Manners and Customs, the Scenes and the Scenery of the Holy Land. By W. M. Thomson, D.D., Twenty-five Years a Missionary of the A. B. C. F. M. in Syria and Palestine. With two elaborate Maps of Palestine, an accurate Plan of Jerusalem, and several hundred Engravings, representing the Scenery, Topography, and Productions of the Holy Land, and the Costumes, Manners, and Habits of the People. 2 large 12mo vols., Cloth, $5 00.

TYERMAN'S WESLEY. The Life and Times of the Rev. John Wesley, M.A., Founder of the Methodists. By the Rev. Luke Tyerman. Portraits. 3 vols., Crown 8vo, Cloth, $7 50.

TYERMAN'S OXFORD METHODISTS. The Oxford Methodists: Memoirs of the Rev. Messrs. Clayton, Ingham, Gambold, Hervey, and Broughton, with Biographical Notices of others. By the Rev. L. Tyerman. Crown 8vo, Cloth, $2 50.

VÁMBÉRY'S CENTRAL ASIA. Travels in Central Asia. Being the Account of a Journey from Teheran across the Turkoman Desert, on the Eastern Shore of the Caspian, to Khiva, Bokhara, and Samarcand, performed in the Year 1863. By Arminius Vámbéry, Member of the Hungarian Academy of Pesth, by whom he was sent on this Scientific Mission. With Map and Woodcuts. 8vo, Cloth, $4 50.

WOOD'S HOMES WITHOUT HANDS. Homes Without Hands: being a Description of the Habitations of Animals, classed according to their Principle of Construction. By J. G. Wood, M.A., F.L.S. With about 140 Illustrations. 8vo, Cloth, Beveled Edges, $4 50.

www.ingramcontent.com/pod-product-compliance
Lightning Source LLC
LaVergne TN
LVHW021134110826
845150LV00005B/1024

9781425549244